CASE CLOSED™

VOLUME 1

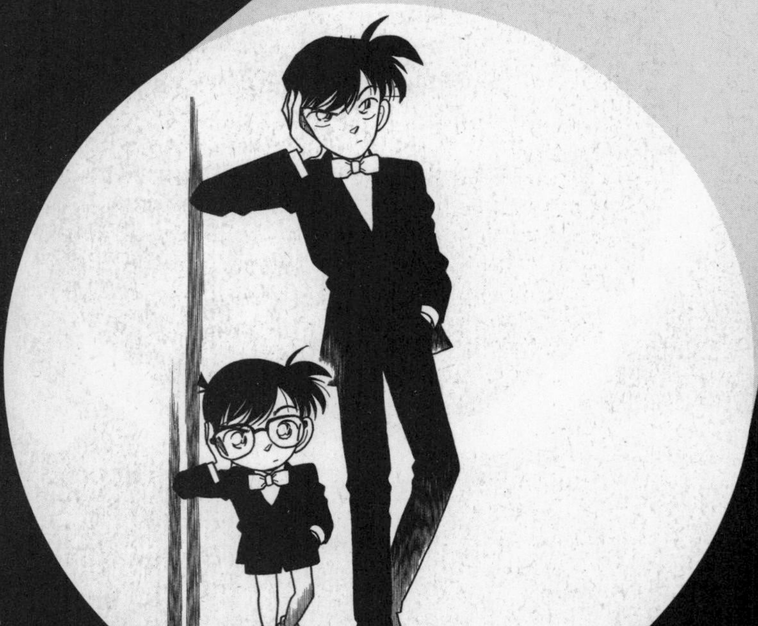

Gosho Aoyama

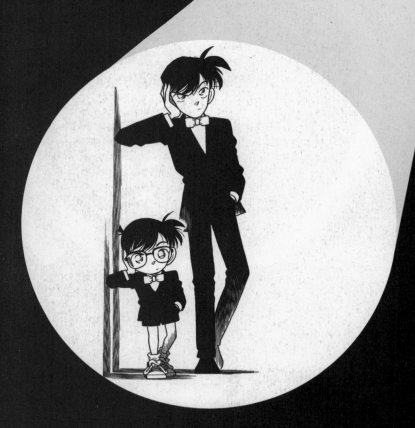

Table of Contents

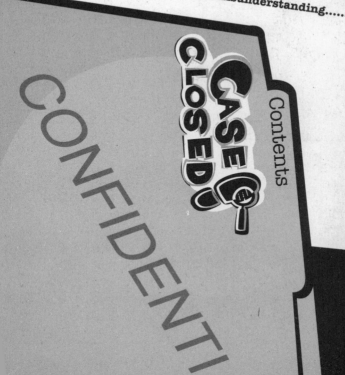

CASE CLOSED

Contents

CONFIDENTIAL

FILE 1: A MODERN-DAY SHERLOCK HOLMES

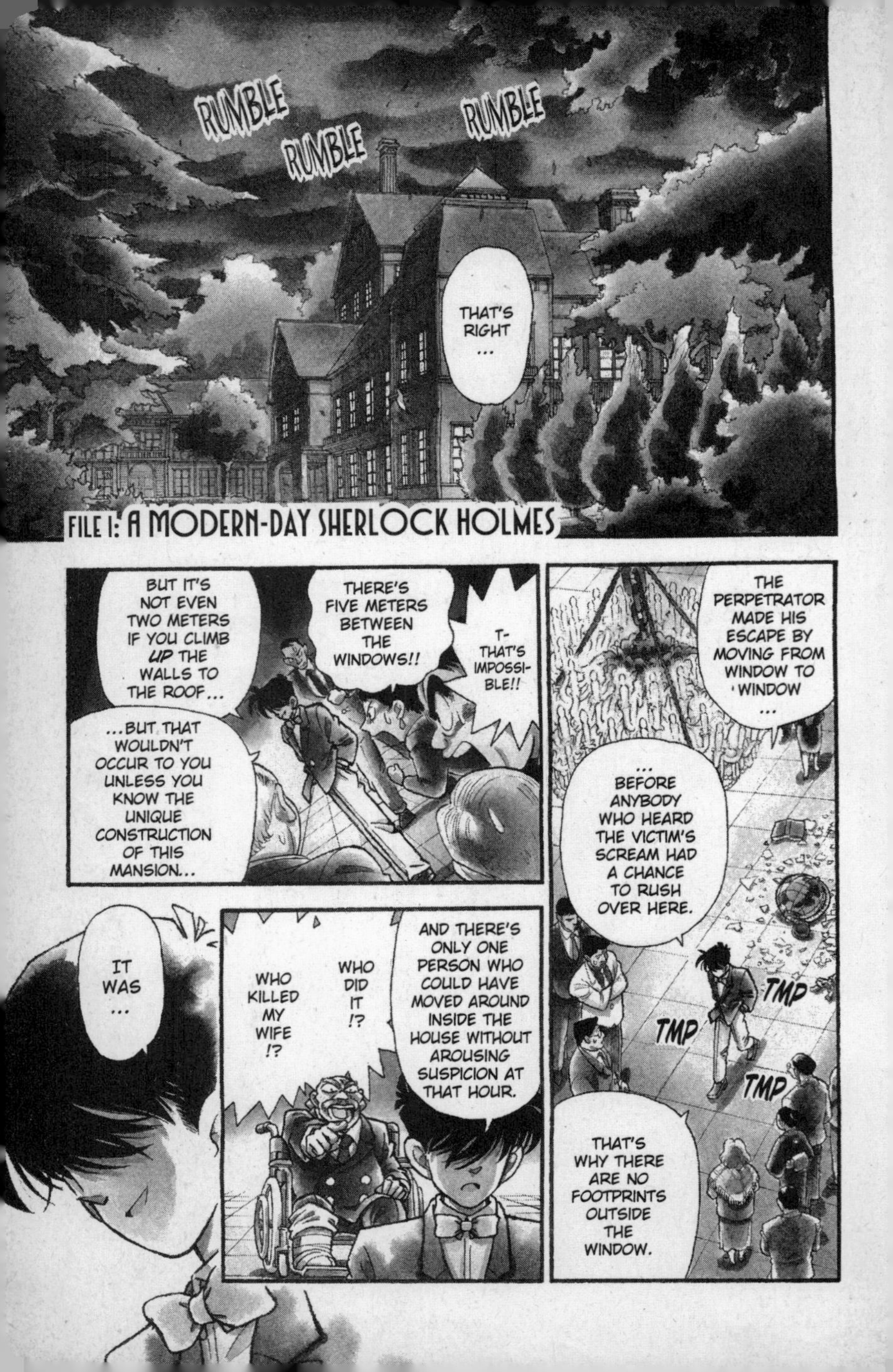
RUMBLE
RUMBLE
RUMBLE
THAT'S RIGHT ...
THE PERPETRATOR MADE HIS ESCAPE BY MOVING FROM WINDOW TO WINDOW ...
... BEFORE ANYBODY WHO HEARD THE VICTIM'S SCREAM HAD A CHANCE TO RUSH OVER HERE.
TMP
TMP
TMP
THAT'S WHY THERE ARE NO FOOTPRINTS OUTSIDE THE WINDOW.
T-THAT'S IMPOSSIBLE!!
THERE'S FIVE METERS BETWEEN THE WINDOWS!!
BUT IT'S NOT EVEN TWO METERS IF YOU CLIMB *UP* THE WALLS TO THE ROOF...
...BUT THAT WOULDN'T OCCUR TO YOU UNLESS YOU KNOW THE UNIQUE CONSTRUCTION OF THIS MANSION...
AND THERE'S ONLY ONE PERSON WHO COULD HAVE MOVED AROUND INSIDE THE HOUSE WITHOUT AROUSING SUSPICION AT THAT HOUR.
WHO DID IT !?
WHO KILLED MY WIFE !?
IT WAS ...

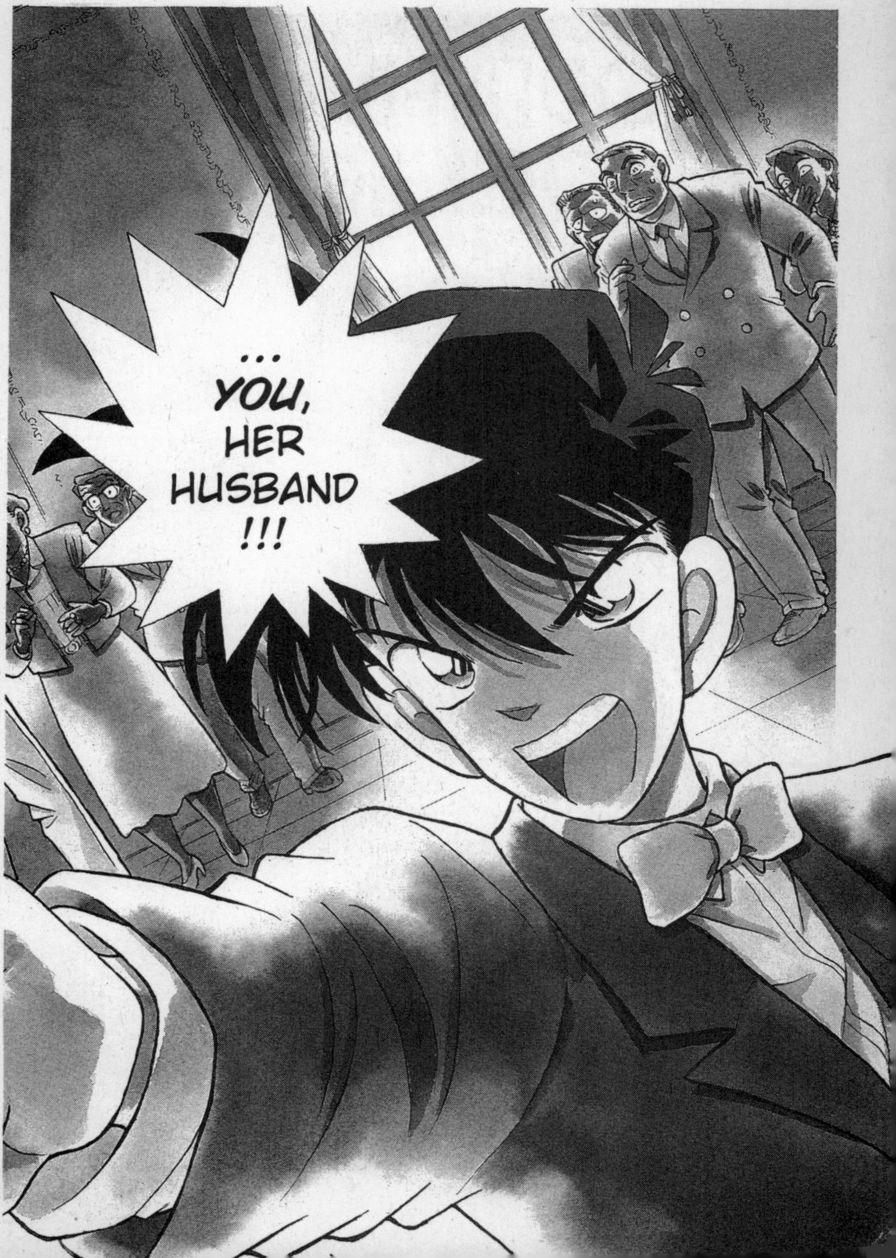
... YOU, HER HUSBAND !!!

FILE 1: A MODERN-DAY SHERLOCK HOLMES

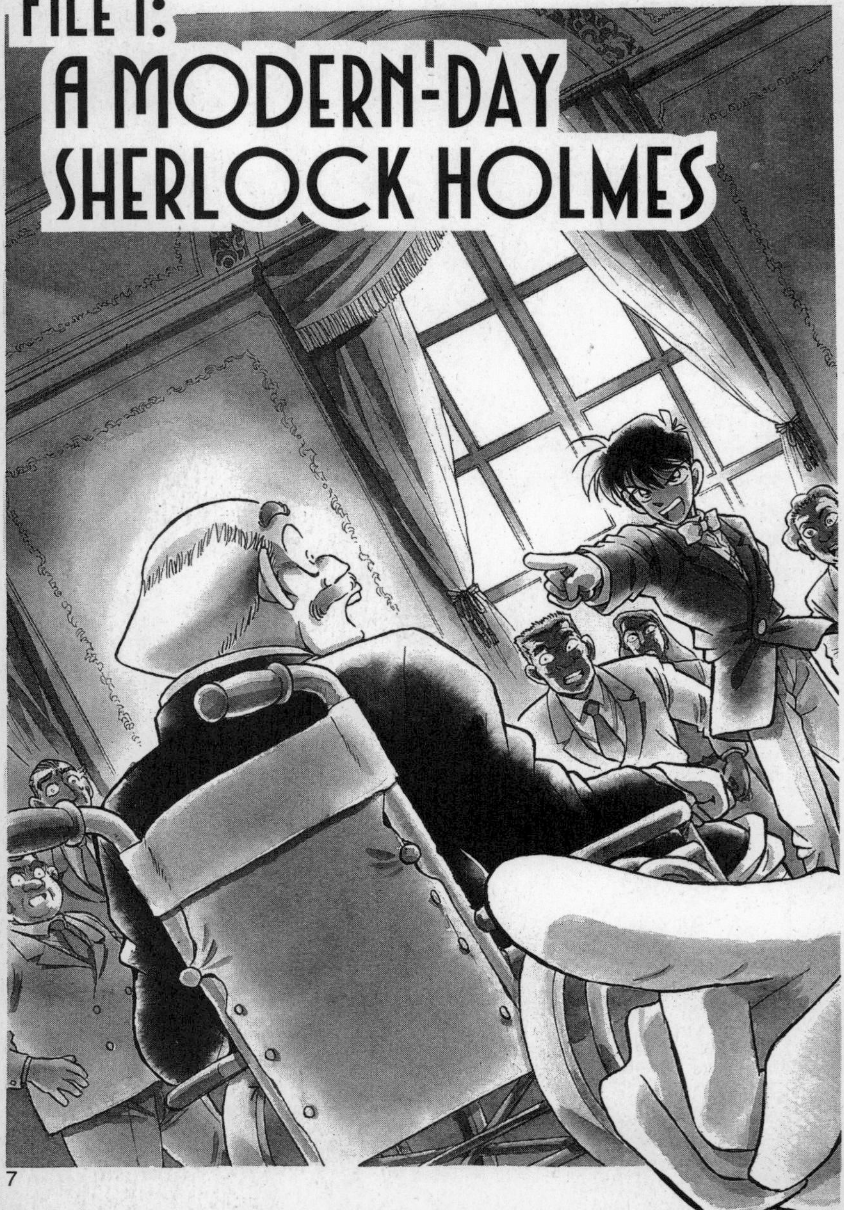

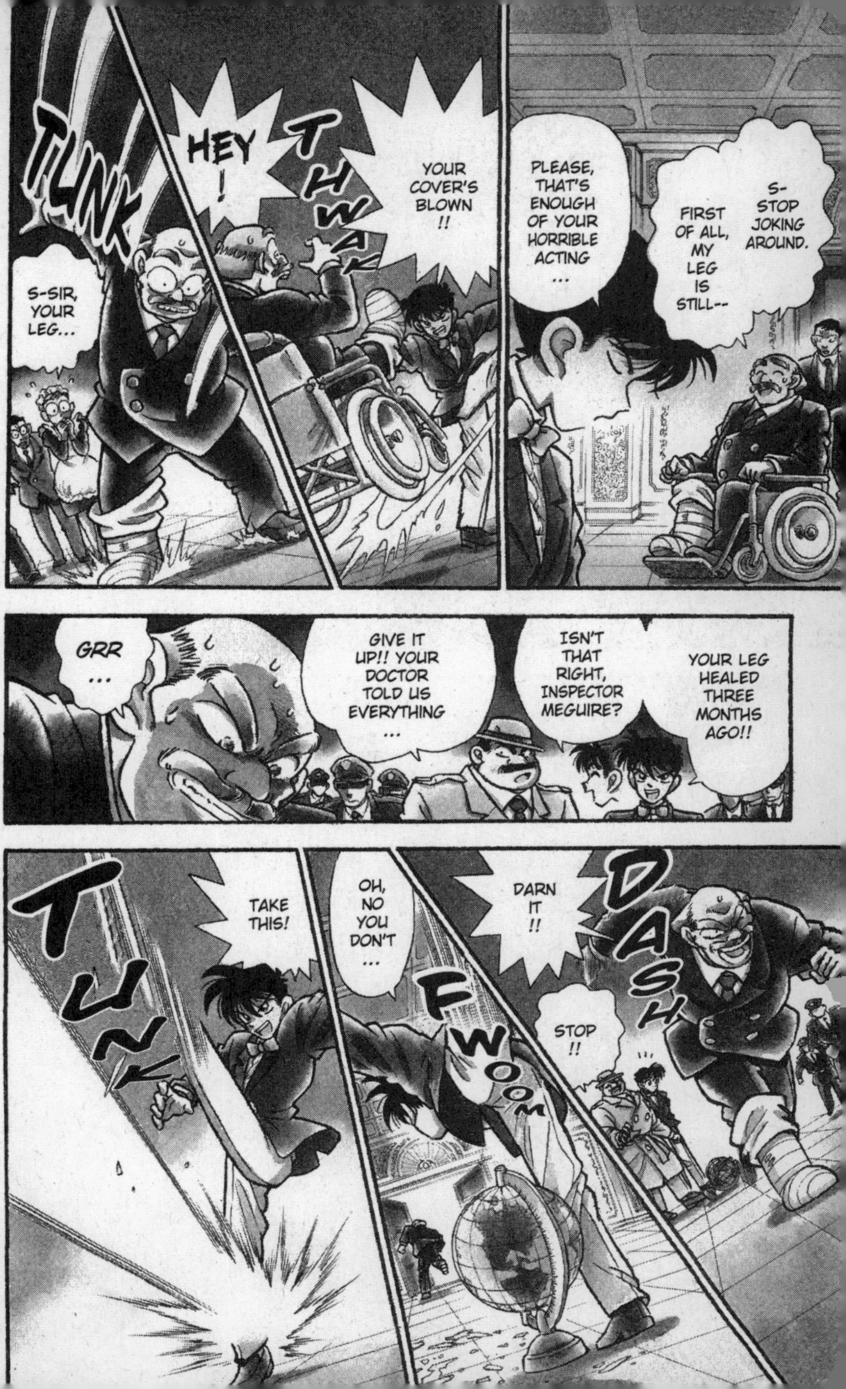
S-STOP JOKING AROUND.
FIRST OF ALL, MY LEG IS STILL--
PLEASE, THAT'S ENOUGH OF YOUR HORRIBLE ACTING ...
YOUR COVER'S BLOWN !!
THWAK
HEY !
TUNK
S-SIR, YOUR LEG...
YOUR LEG HEALED THREE MONTHS AGO!!
ISN'T THAT RIGHT, INSPECTOR MEGUIRE?
GIVE IT UP!! YOUR DOCTOR TOLD US EVERYTHING ...
GRR ...
DASH
DARN IT !!
STOP !!
!!
FWOOM
OH, NO YOU DON'T ...
TAKE THIS!
TUNK

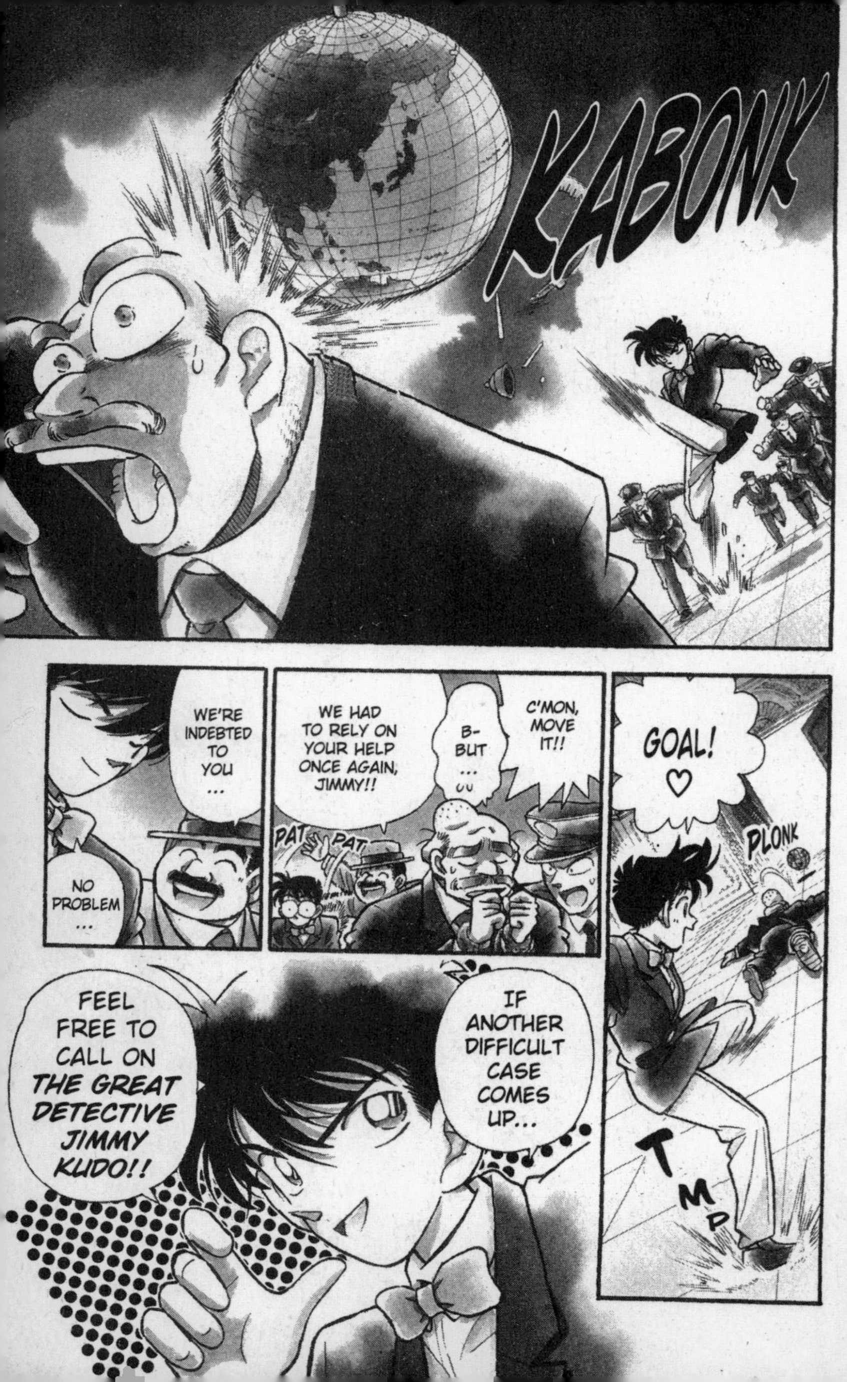
KABONK
GOAL! ♡
PLONK
TMP
C'MON, MOVE IT!!
B-BUT ...
WE HAD TO RELY ON YOUR HELP ONCE AGAIN, JIMMY!!
PAT PAT
WE'RE INDEBTED TO YOU ...
NO PROBLEM ...
IF ANOTHER DIFFICULT CASE COMES UP...
FEEL FREE TO CALL ON THE GREAT DETECTIVE JIMMY KUDO!!

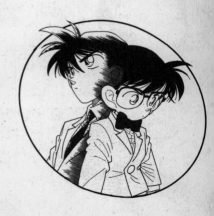

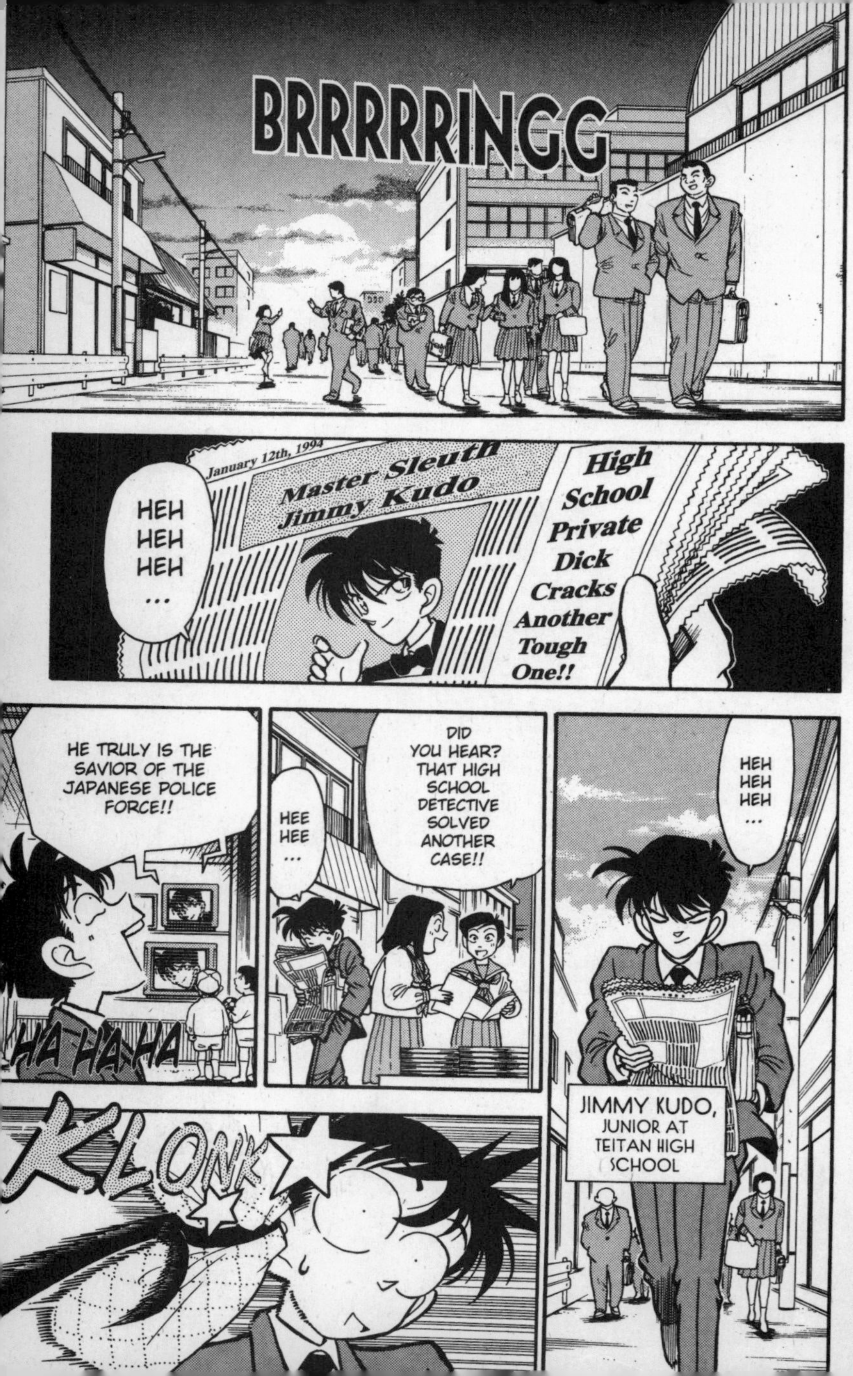
BRRRRRINGG
High School Private Dick Cracks Another Tough One!!
January 12th, 1994
Master Sleuth Jimmy Kudo
HEH HEH HEH ...
HEH HEH HEH ...
JIMMY KUDO, JUNIOR AT TEITAN HIGH SCHOOL
DID YOU HEAR? THAT HIGH SCHOOL DETECTIVE SOLVED ANOTHER CASE!!
HEE HEE ...
HE TRULY IS THE SAVIOR OF THE JAPANESE POLICE FORCE!!
HA HA HA
KLONK

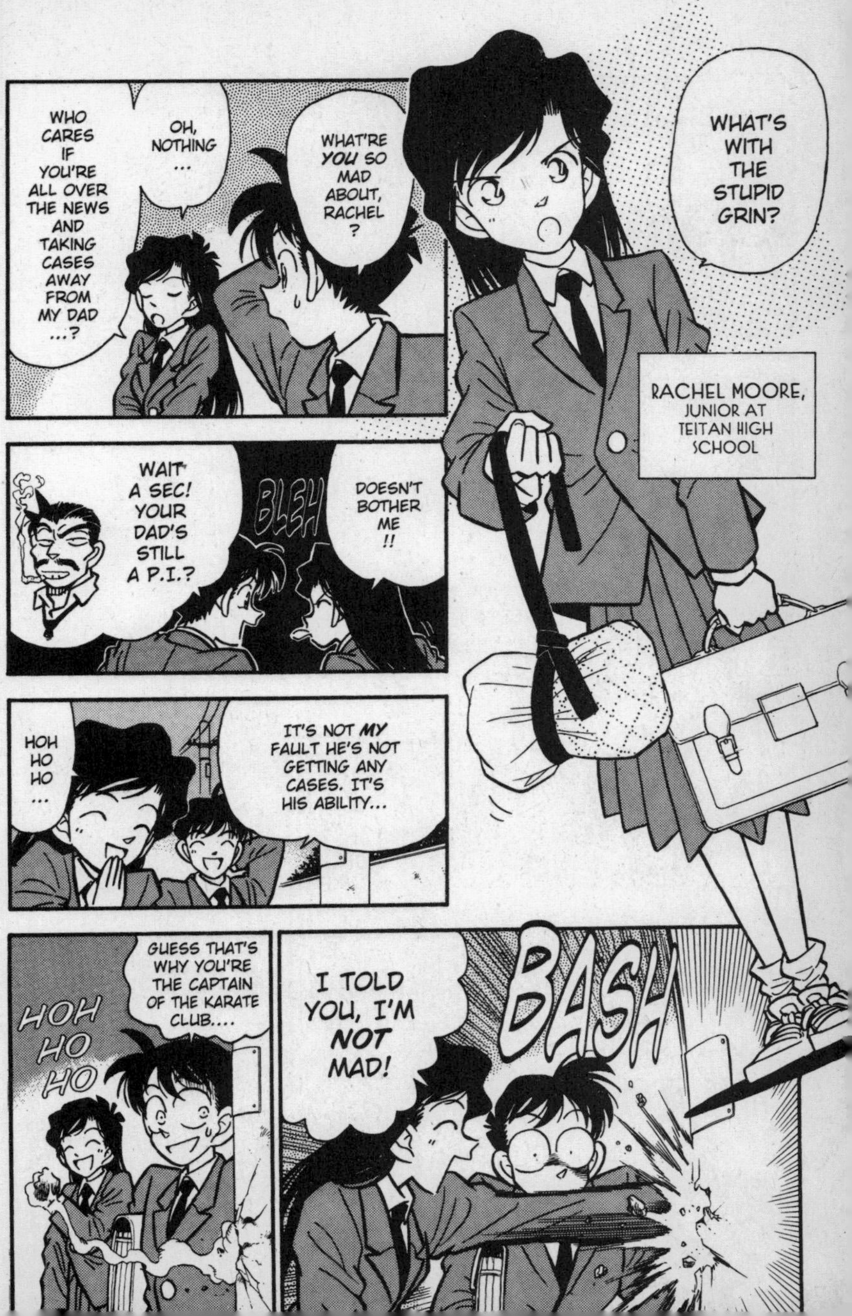
WHAT'S WITH THE STUPID GRIN?
RACHEL MOORE, JUNIOR AT TEITAN HIGH SCHOOL
WHAT'RE *YOU* SO MAD ABOUT, RACHEL?
OH, NOTHING...
WHO CARES IF YOU'RE ALL OVER THE NEWS AND TAKING CASES AWAY FROM MY DAD...?
DOESN'T BOTHER ME!!
BLEH
WAIT A SEC! YOUR DAD'S STILL A P.I.?
IT'S NOT *MY* FAULT HE'S NOT GETTING ANY CASES. IT'S HIS ABILITY...
HOH HO HO...
BASH
I TOLD YOU, I'M *NOT* MAD!
GUESS THAT'S WHY YOU'RE THE CAPTAIN OF THE KARATE CLUB....
HOH HO HO

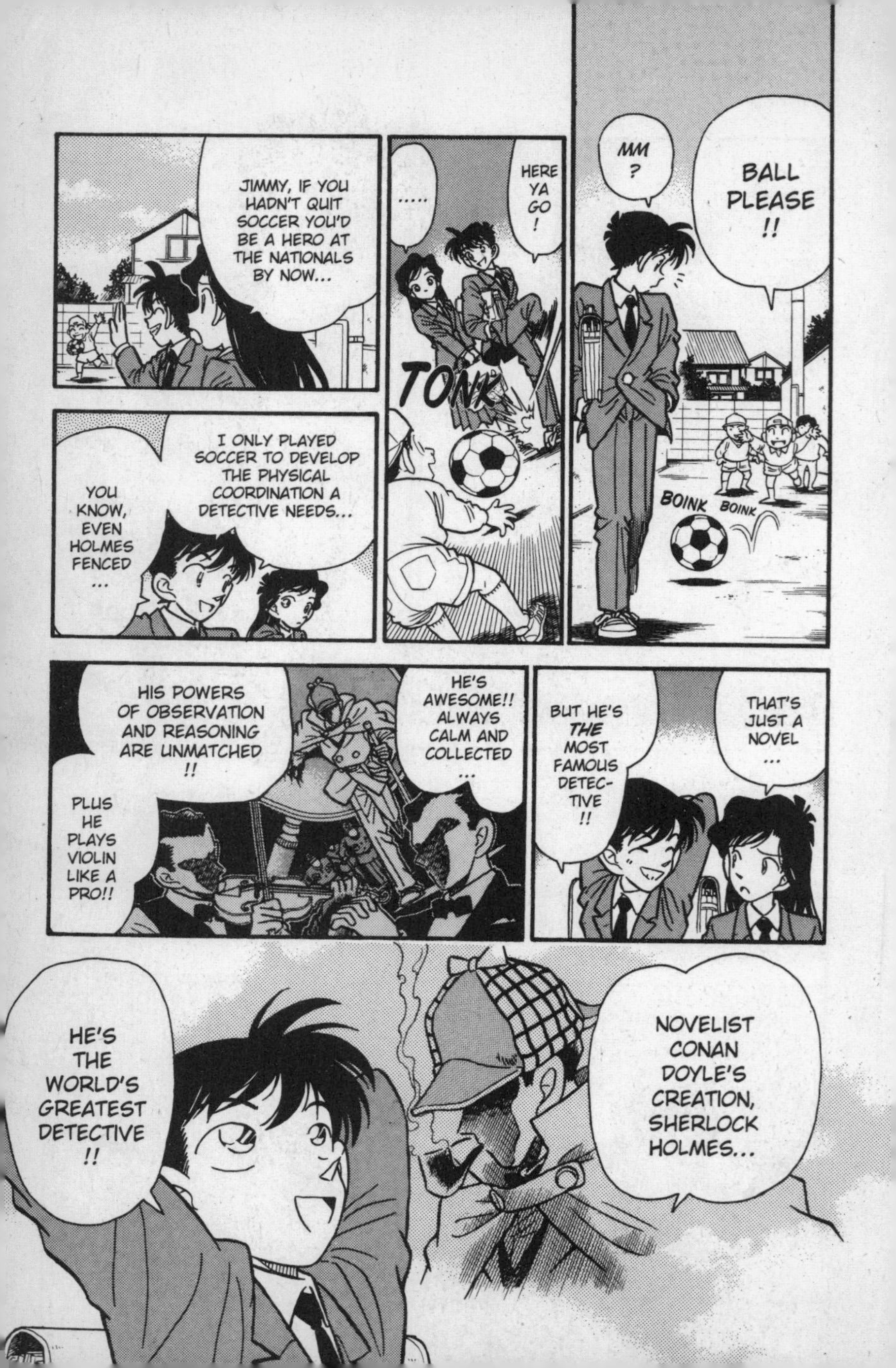
BALL PLEASE !!
MM ?
BOINK BOINK
HERE YA GO !
.....
TONK
JIMMY, IF YOU HADN'T QUIT SOCCER YOU'D BE A HERO AT THE NATIONALS BY NOW...
I ONLY PLAYED SOCCER TO DEVELOP THE PHYSICAL COORDINATION A DETECTIVE NEEDS...
YOU KNOW, EVEN HOLMES FENCED ...
THAT'S JUST A NOVEL ...
BUT HE'S *THE* MOST FAMOUS DETECTIVE !!
HE'S AWESOME!! ALWAYS CALM AND COLLECTED ...
HIS POWERS OF OBSERVATION AND REASONING ARE UNMATCHED !!
PLUS HE PLAYS VIOLIN LIKE A PRO!!
NOVELIST CONAN DOYLE'S CREATION, SHERLOCK HOLMES...
HE'S THE WORLD'S GREATEST DETECTIVE !!

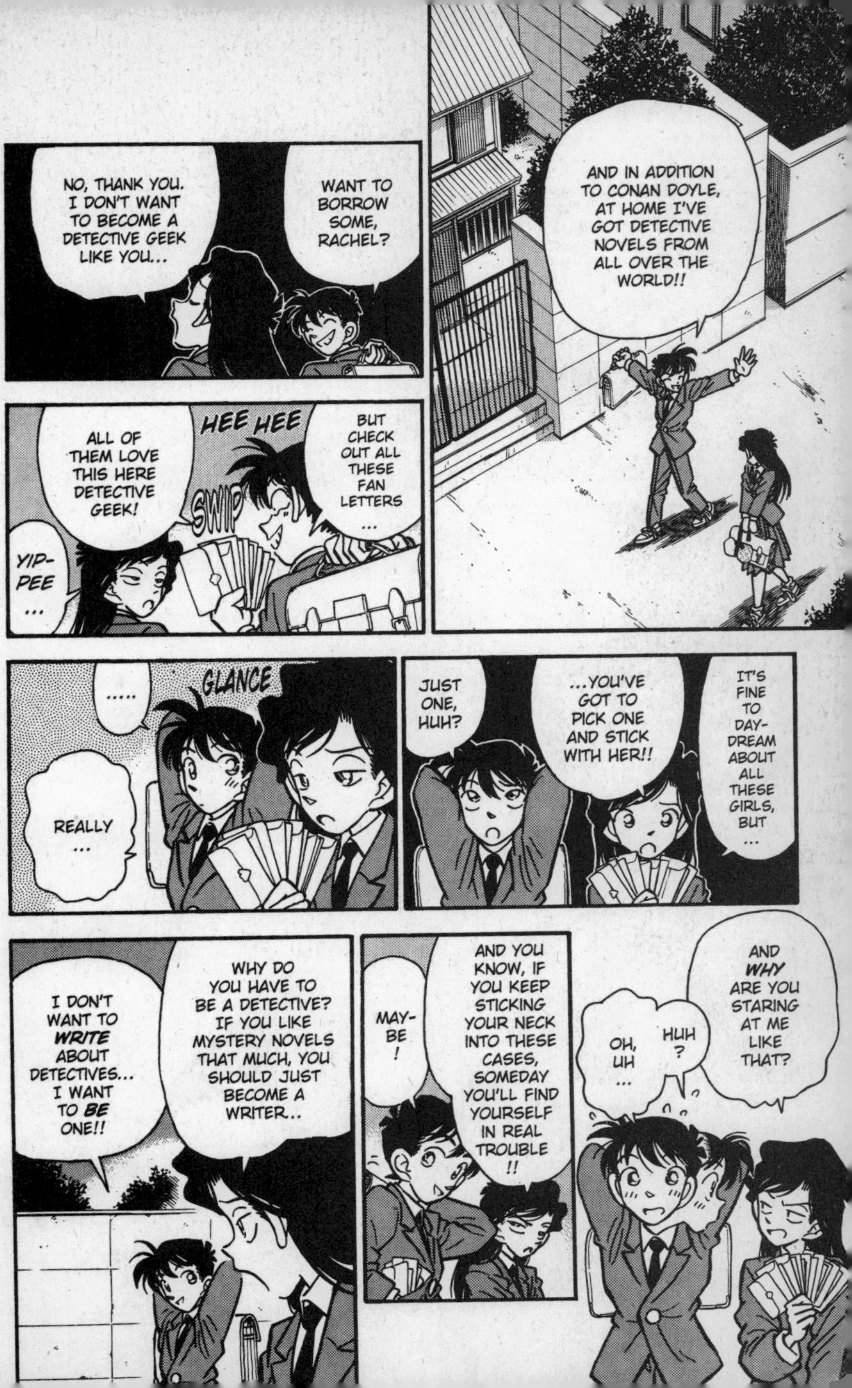
AND IN ADDITION TO CONAN DOYLE, AT HOME I'VE GOT DETECTIVE NOVELS FROM ALL OVER THE WORLD!!
WANT TO BORROW SOME, RACHEL?
NO, THANK YOU. I DON'T WANT TO BECOME A DETECTIVE GEEK LIKE YOU...
BUT CHECK OUT ALL THESE FAN LETTERS ...
HEE HEE
SWIP
ALL OF THEM LOVE THIS HERE DETECTIVE GEEK!
YIP-PEE ...
IT'S FINE TO DAY-DREAM ABOUT ALL THESE GIRLS, BUT ...
...YOU'VE GOT TO PICK ONE AND STICK WITH HER!!
JUST ONE, HUH?
GLANCE
......
REALLY ...
AND WHY ARE YOU STARING AT ME LIKE THAT?
HUH ?
OH, UH ...
AND YOU KNOW, IF YOU KEEP STICKING YOUR NECK INTO THESE CASES, SOMEDAY YOU'LL FIND YOURSELF IN REAL TROUBLE !!
MAY-BE !
WHY DO YOU HAVE TO BE A DETECTIVE? IF YOU LIKE MYSTERY NOVELS THAT MUCH, YOU SHOULD JUST BECOME A WRITER...
I DON'T WANT TO WRITE ABOUT DETECTIVES... I WANT TO BE ONE!!

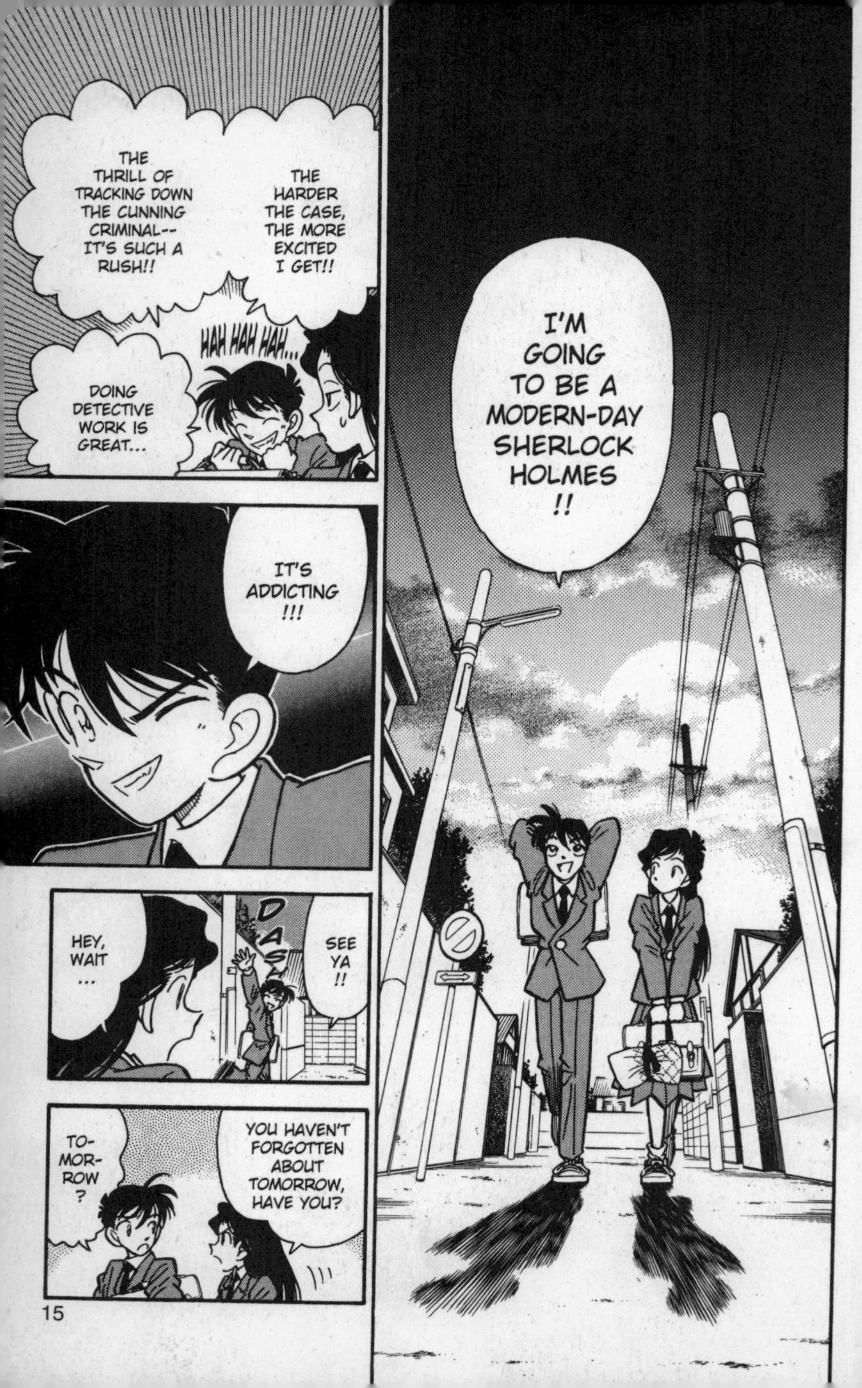
I'M GOING TO BE A MODERN-DAY SHERLOCK HOLMES !!
THE HARDER THE CASE, THE MORE EXCITED I GET!!
THE THRILL OF TRACKING DOWN THE CUNNING CRIMINAL-- IT'S SUCH A RUSH!!
HAH HAH HAH...
DOING DETECTIVE WORK IS GREAT...
IT'S ADDICTING !!!
DASH
SEE YA !!
HEY, WAIT ...
YOU HAVEN'T FORGOTTEN ABOUT TOMORROW, HAVE YOU?
TO-MOR-ROW ?

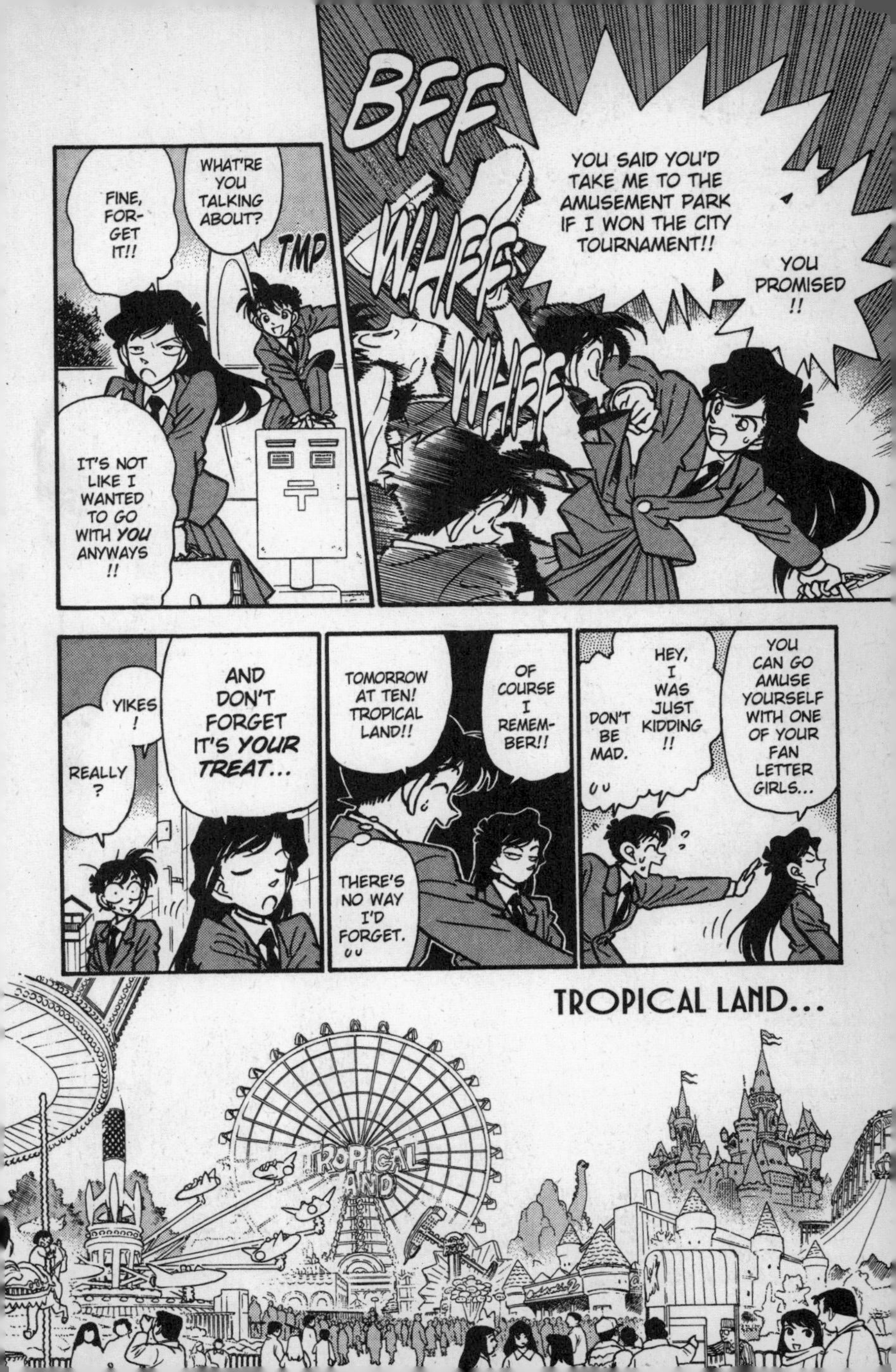
BFF
YOU SAID YOU'D TAKE ME TO THE AMUSEMENT PARK IF I WON THE CITY TOURNAMENT!!
YOU PROMISED !!
WHIFF
WHIFF
WHAT'RE YOU TALKING ABOUT?
TMP
FINE, FOR-GET IT!!
IT'S NOT LIKE I WANTED TO GO WITH YOU ANYWAYS !!
YOU CAN GO AMUSE YOURSELF WITH ONE OF YOUR FAN LETTER GIRLS...
HEY, I WAS JUST KIDDING !!
DON'T BE MAD.
OF COURSE I REMEM-BER!!
TOMORROW AT TEN! TROPICAL LAND!!
THERE'S NO WAY I'D FORGET.
AND DON'T FORGET IT'S YOUR TREAT...
YIKES !
REALLY ?
TROPICAL LAND...
TROPICAL LAND

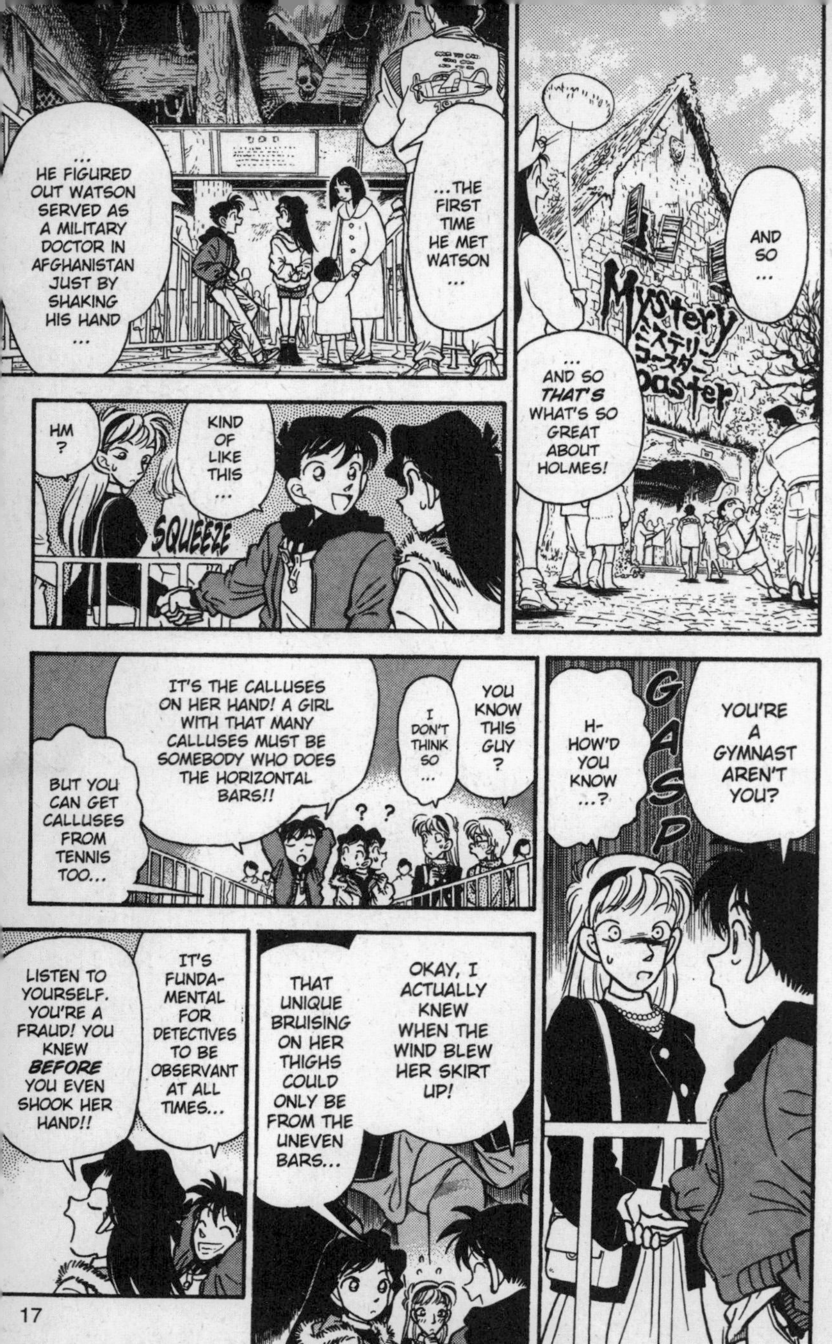
AND SO ...
... AND SO THAT'S WHAT'S SO GREAT ABOUT HOLMES!
Mystery ミステリーコースター Coaster
...THE FIRST TIME HE MET WATSON ...
... HE FIGURED OUT WATSON SERVED AS A MILITARY DOCTOR IN AFGHANISTAN JUST BY SHAKING HIS HAND ...
KIND OF LIKE THIS ...
SQUEEZE
HM ?
YOU'RE A GYMNAST AREN'T YOU?
GASP
H-HOW'D YOU KNOW ...?
YOU KNOW THIS GUY ?
I DON'T THINK SO ...
IT'S THE CALLUSES ON HER HAND! A GIRL WITH THAT MANY CALLUSES MUST BE SOMEBODY WHO DOES THE HORIZONTAL BARS!!
? ?
BUT YOU CAN GET CALLUSES FROM TENNIS TOO...
OKAY, I ACTUALLY KNEW WHEN THE WIND BLEW HER SKIRT UP!
THAT UNIQUE BRUISING ON HER THIGHS COULD ONLY BE FROM THE UNEVEN BARS...
IT'S FUNDAMENTAL FOR DETECTIVES TO BE OBSERVANT AT ALL TIMES...
LISTEN TO YOURSELF. YOU'RE A FRAUD! YOU KNEW BEFORE YOU EVEN SHOOK HER HAND!!

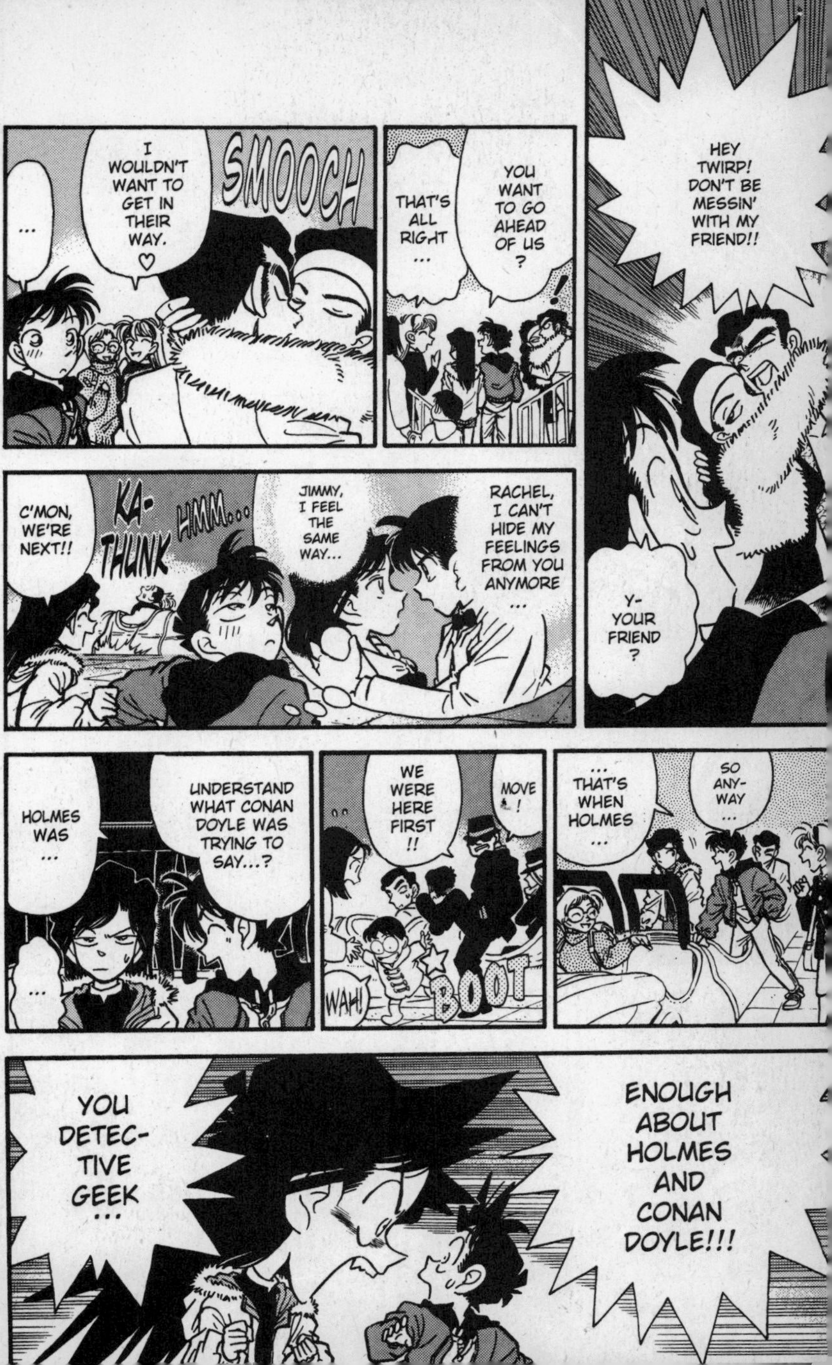
HEY TWIRP! DON'T BE MESSIN' WITH MY FRIEND!!
Y-YOUR FRIEND?
YOU WANT TO GO AHEAD OF US?
THAT'S ALL RIGHT...
!
I WOULDN'T WANT TO GET IN THEIR WAY. ♡
SMOOCH
...
RACHEL, I CAN'T HIDE MY FEELINGS FROM YOU ANYMORE...
JIMMY, I FEEL THE SAME WAY...
HMM...
KA-THUNK
C'MON, WE'RE NEXT!!
SO ANYWAY...
...THAT'S WHEN HOLMES...
MOVE!
WE WERE HERE FIRST!!
BOOT
WAH!
UNDERSTAND WHAT CONAN DOYLE WAS TRYING TO SAY...?
HOLMES WAS...
...
ENOUGH ABOUT HOLMES AND CONAN DOYLE!!!
YOU DETECTIVE-TIVE GEEK...

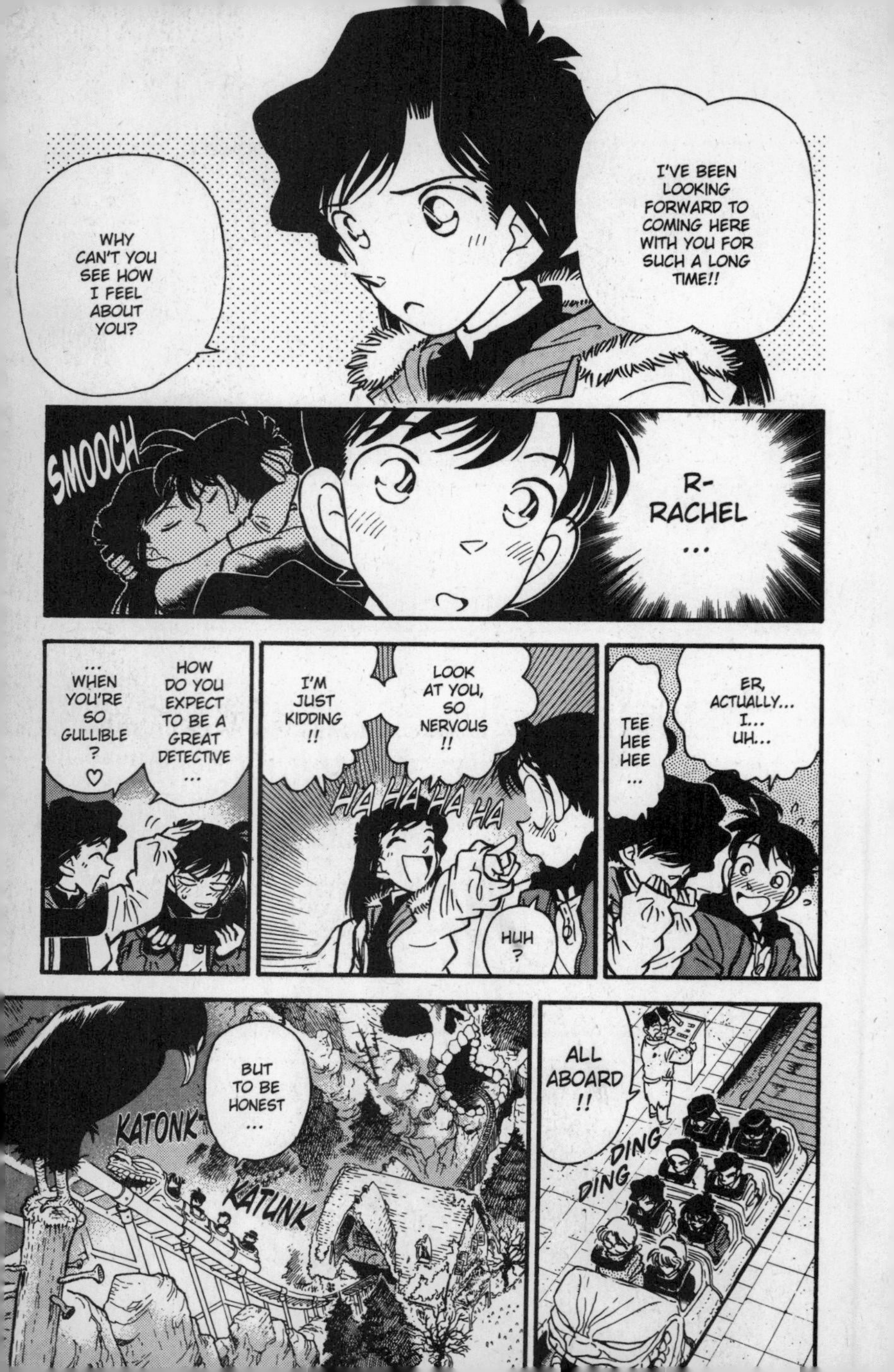
I'VE BEEN LOOKING FORWARD TO COMING HERE WITH YOU FOR SUCH A LONG TIME!!
WHY CAN'T YOU SEE HOW I FEEL ABOUT YOU?
R-RACHEL ...
SMOOCH
ER, ACTUALLY... I... UH...
TEE HEE HEE ...
LOOK AT YOU, SO NERVOUS !!
I'M JUST KIDDING !!
HA HA HA HA
HUH ?
HOW DO YOU EXPECT TO BE A GREAT DETECTIVE ...
... WHEN YOU'RE SO GULLIBLE ? ♡
ALL ABOARD !!
DING DING
BUT TO BE HONEST ...
KATONK
KATUNK

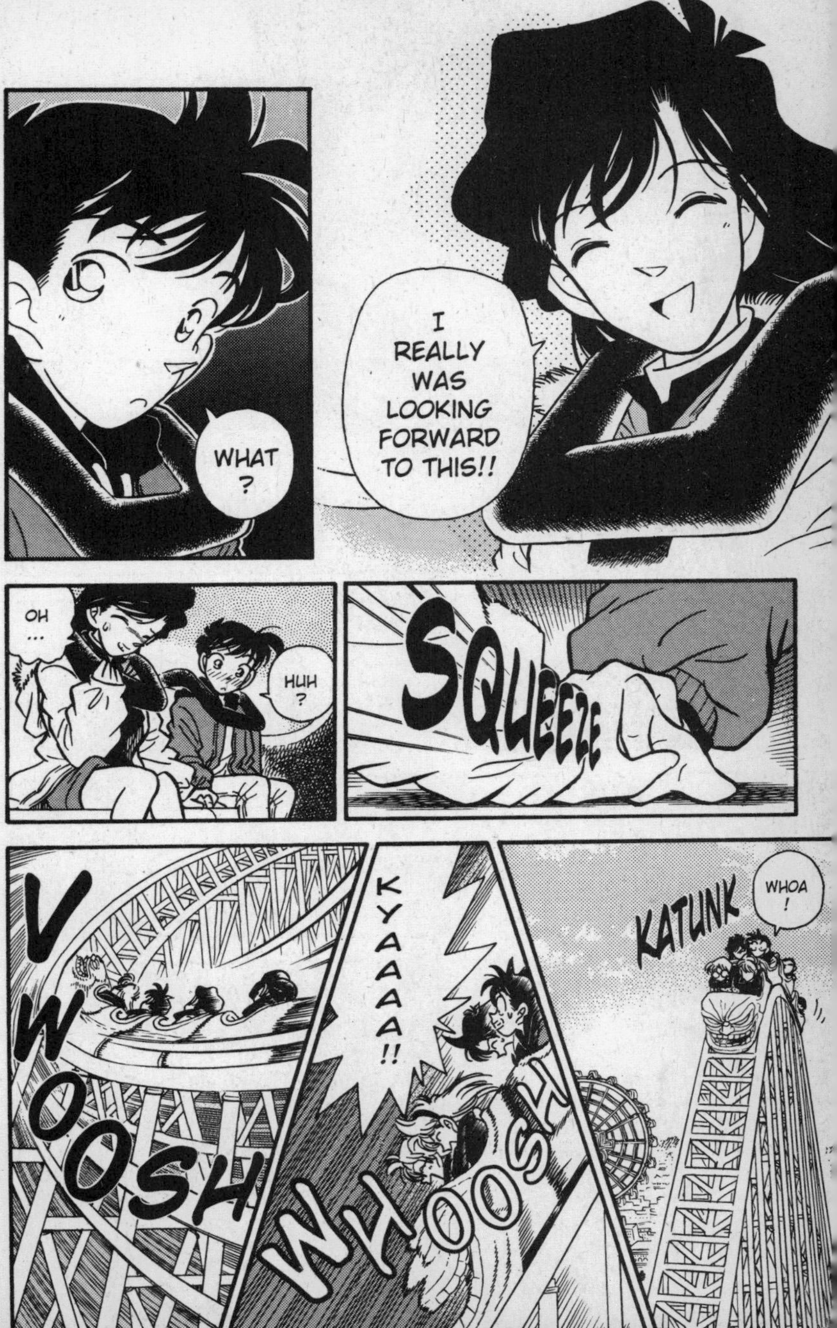
I REALLY WAS LOOKING FORWARD TO THIS!!
WHAT?
SQUEEZE
OH ...
HUH?
WHOA!
KATUNK
KYAAAAA!!
WHOOSH
VWOOSH

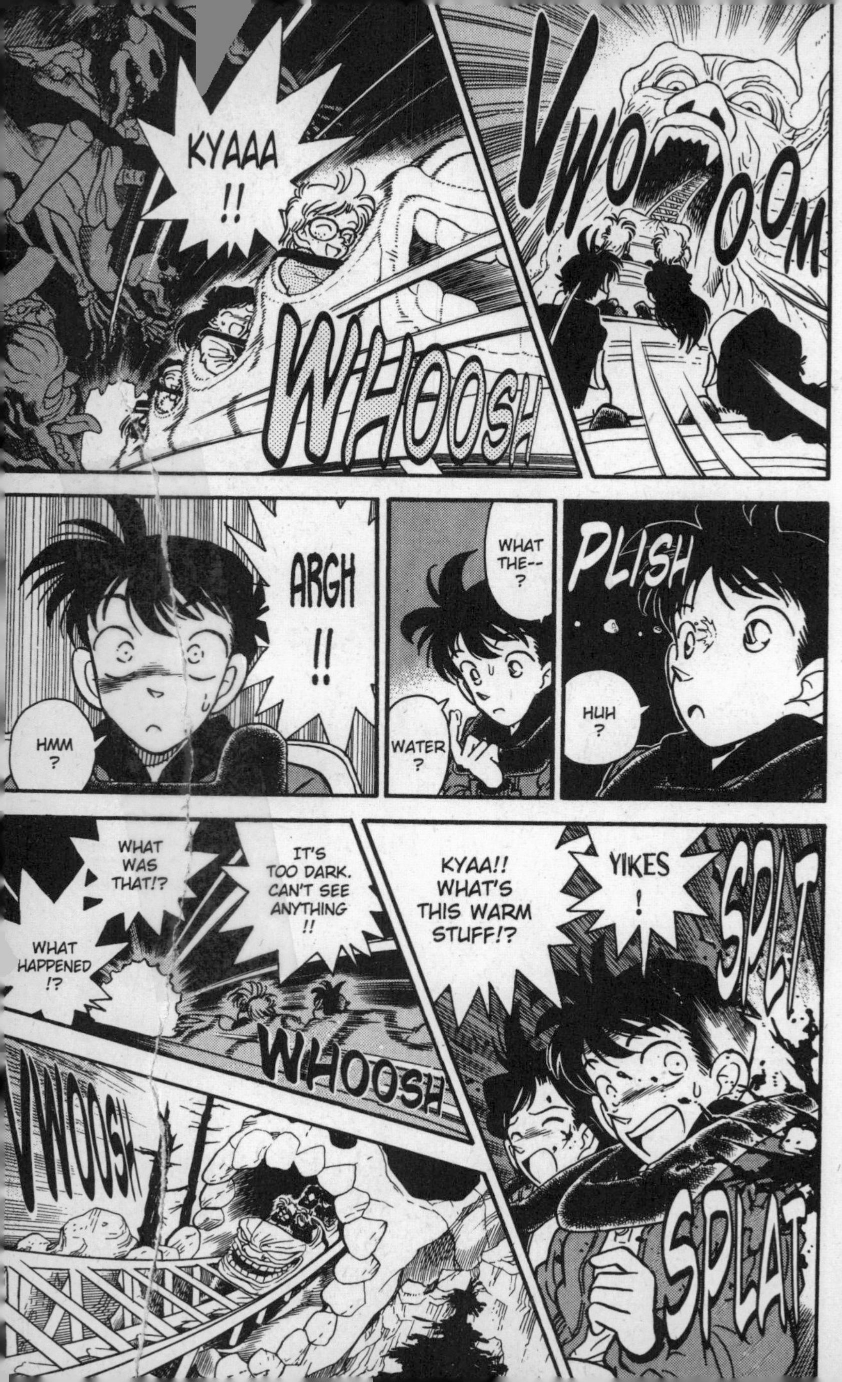
VWOOOOM
KYAAA!!
WHOOSH
PLISH
HUH?
WHAT THE--?
WATER?
ARGH!!
HMM?
YIKES!
KYAA!! WHAT'S THIS WARM STUFF!?
SPLT
SPLAT
IT'S TOO DARK. CAN'T SEE ANYTHING!!
WHAT WAS THAT!?
WHAT HAPPENED!?
WHOOSH
VWOOSH

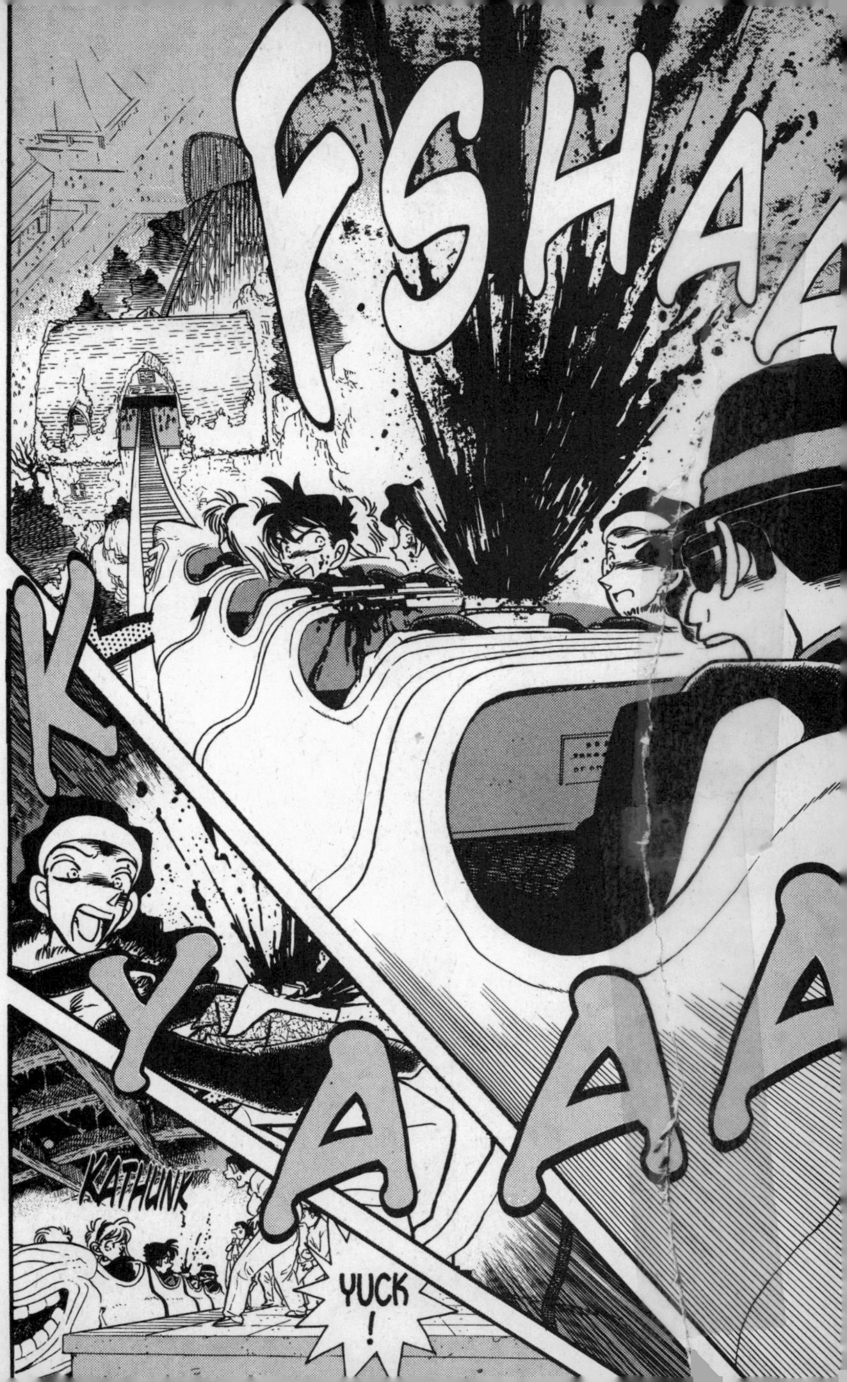
FSHAA
KYAAAA
KATHUNK
YUCK !

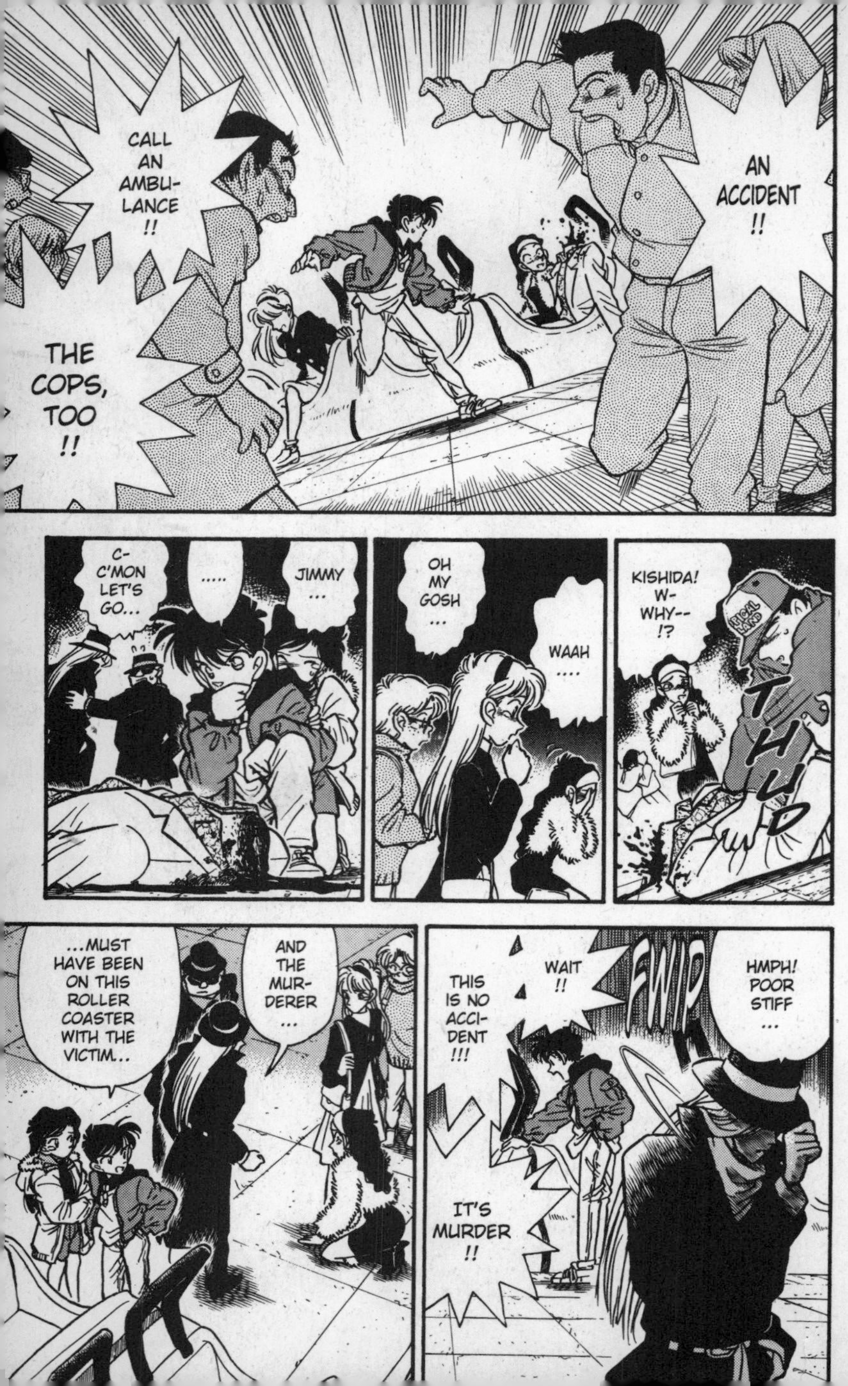
AN ACCIDENT !!
CALL AN AMBULANCE !!
THE COPS, TOO !!
KISHIDA! W-WHY--!?
THUD
OH MY GOSH ...
WAAH ....
JIMMY ...
.....
C-C'MON LET'S GO...
HMPH! POOR STIFF ...
FWIP
WAIT !!
THIS IS NO ACCIDENT !!!
IT'S MURDER !!
AND THE MURDERER ...
...MUST HAVE BEEN ON THIS ROLLER COASTER WITH THE VICTIM...

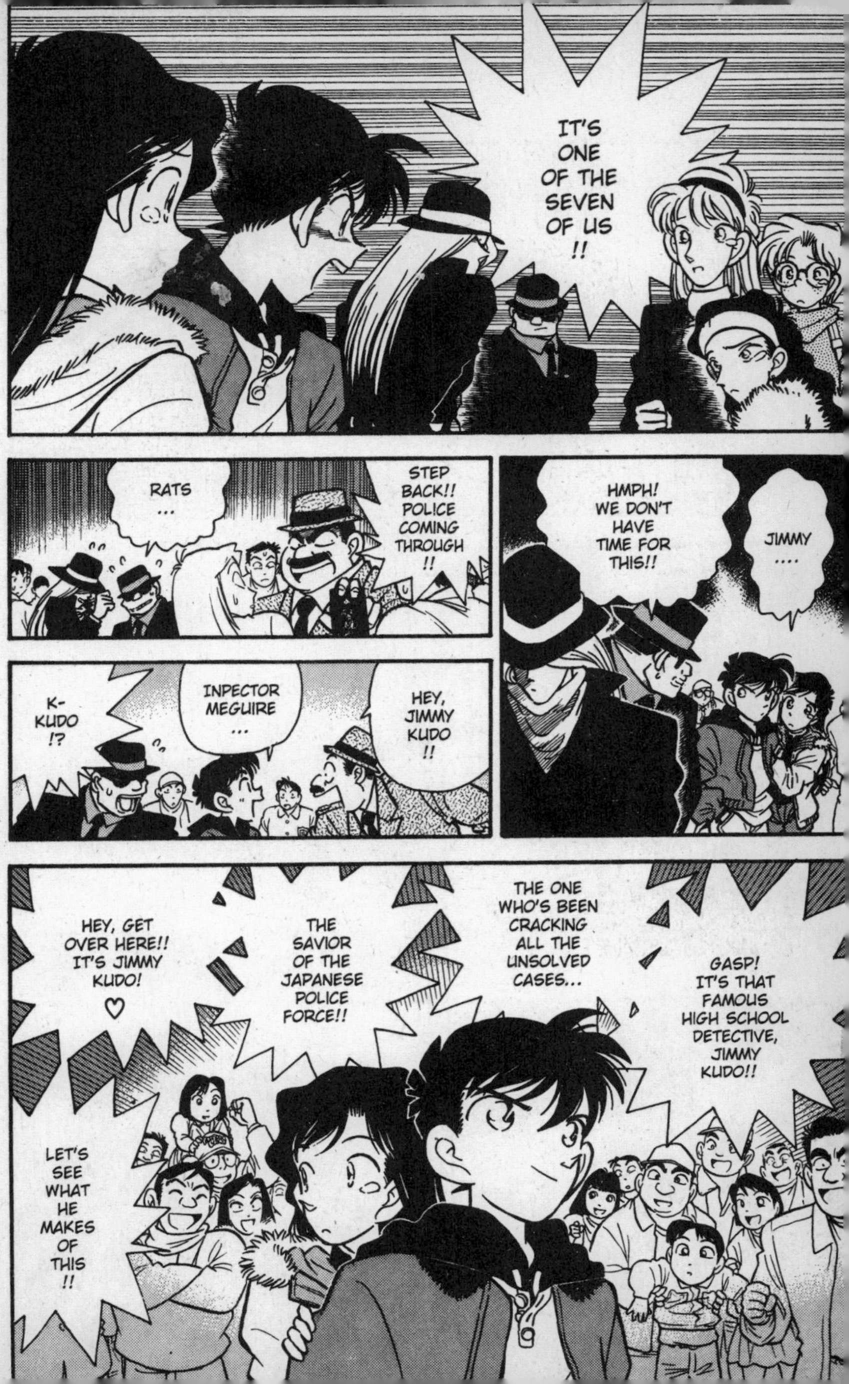
IT'S ONE OF THE SEVEN OF US !!
JIMMY ....
HMPH! WE DON'T HAVE TIME FOR THIS!!
STEP BACK!! POLICE COMING THROUGH !!
RATS ...
HEY, JIMMY KUDO !!
INPECTOR MEGUIRE ...
K-KUDO !?
GASP! IT'S THAT FAMOUS HIGH SCHOOL DETECTIVE, JIMMY KUDO!!
THE ONE WHO'S BEEN CRACKING ALL THE UNSOLVED CASES...
THE SAVIOR OF THE JAPANESE POLICE FORCE!!
HEY, GET OVER HERE!! IT'S JIMMY KUDO! ♡
LET'S SEE WHAT HE MAKES OF THIS !!

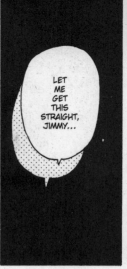

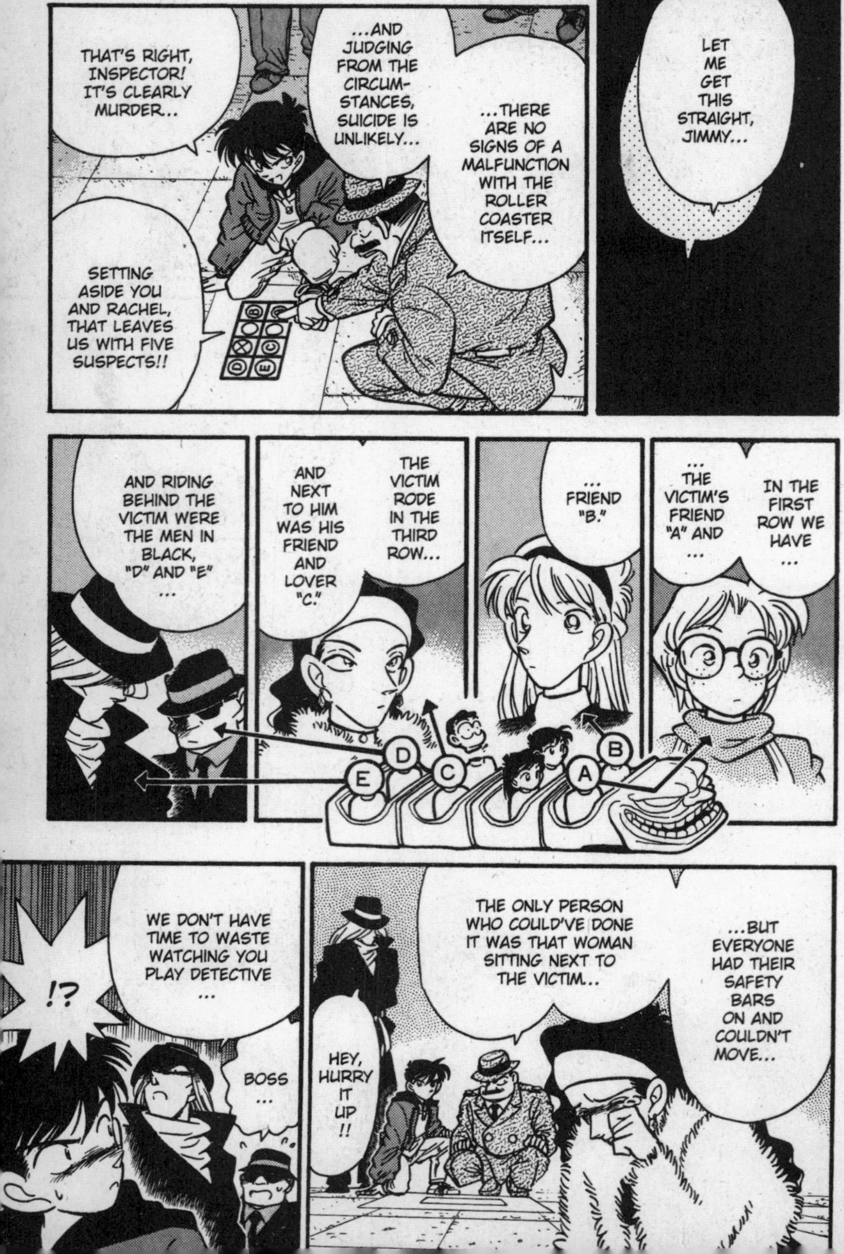
LET ME GET THIS STRAIGHT, JIMMY...
...THERE ARE NO SIGNS OF A MALFUNCTION WITH THE ROLLER COASTER ITSELF...
...AND JUDGING FROM THE CIRCUMSTANCES, SUICIDE IS UNLIKELY...
THAT'S RIGHT, INSPECTOR! IT'S CLEARLY MURDER...
SETTING ASIDE YOU AND RACHEL, THAT LEAVES US WITH FIVE SUSPECTS!!
IN THE FIRST ROW WE HAVE ...
... THE VICTIM'S FRIEND "A" AND ...
... FRIEND "B."
THE VICTIM RODE IN THE THIRD ROW...
AND NEXT TO HIM WAS HIS FRIEND AND LOVER "C."
AND RIDING BEHIND THE VICTIM WERE THE MEN IN BLACK, "D" AND "E" ...
B
A
C
D
E
THE ONLY PERSON WHO COULD'VE DONE IT WAS THAT WOMAN SITTING NEXT TO THE VICTIM..
...BUT EVERYONE HAD THEIR SAFETY BARS ON AND COULDN'T MOVE...
HEY, HURRY IT UP!!
WE DON'T HAVE TIME TO WASTE WATCHING YOU PLAY DETECTIVE ...
!?
BOSS ...

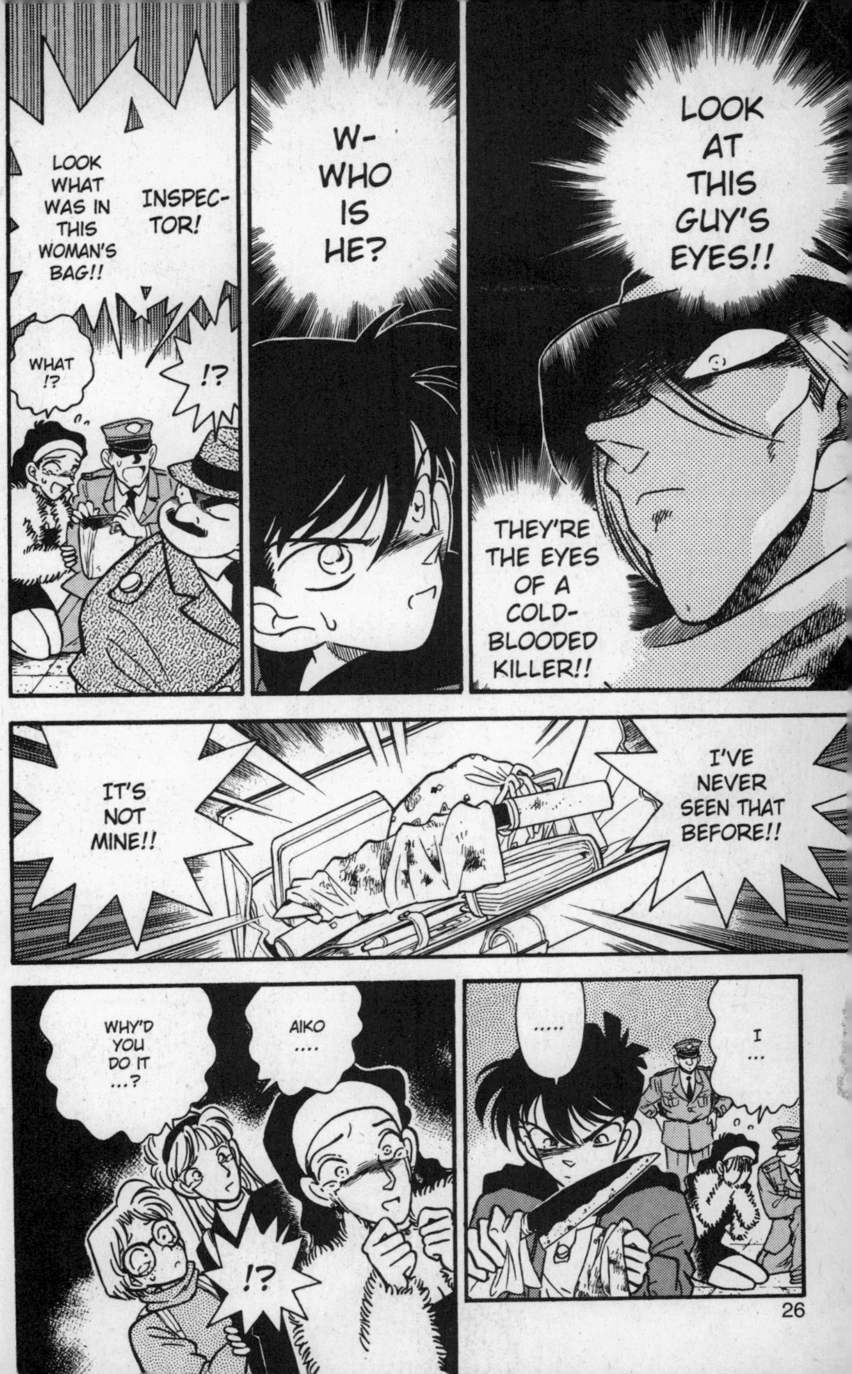

LOOK AT THIS GUY'S EYES!!
THEY'RE THE EYES OF A COLD-BLOODED KILLER!!
W-WHO IS HE?
INSPECTOR!
LOOK WHAT WAS IN THIS WOMAN'S BAG!!
!?
WHAT !?
I'VE NEVER SEEN THAT BEFORE!!
IT'S NOT MINE!!
I ...
.....
AIKO ....
WHY'D YOU DO IT ...?
!?

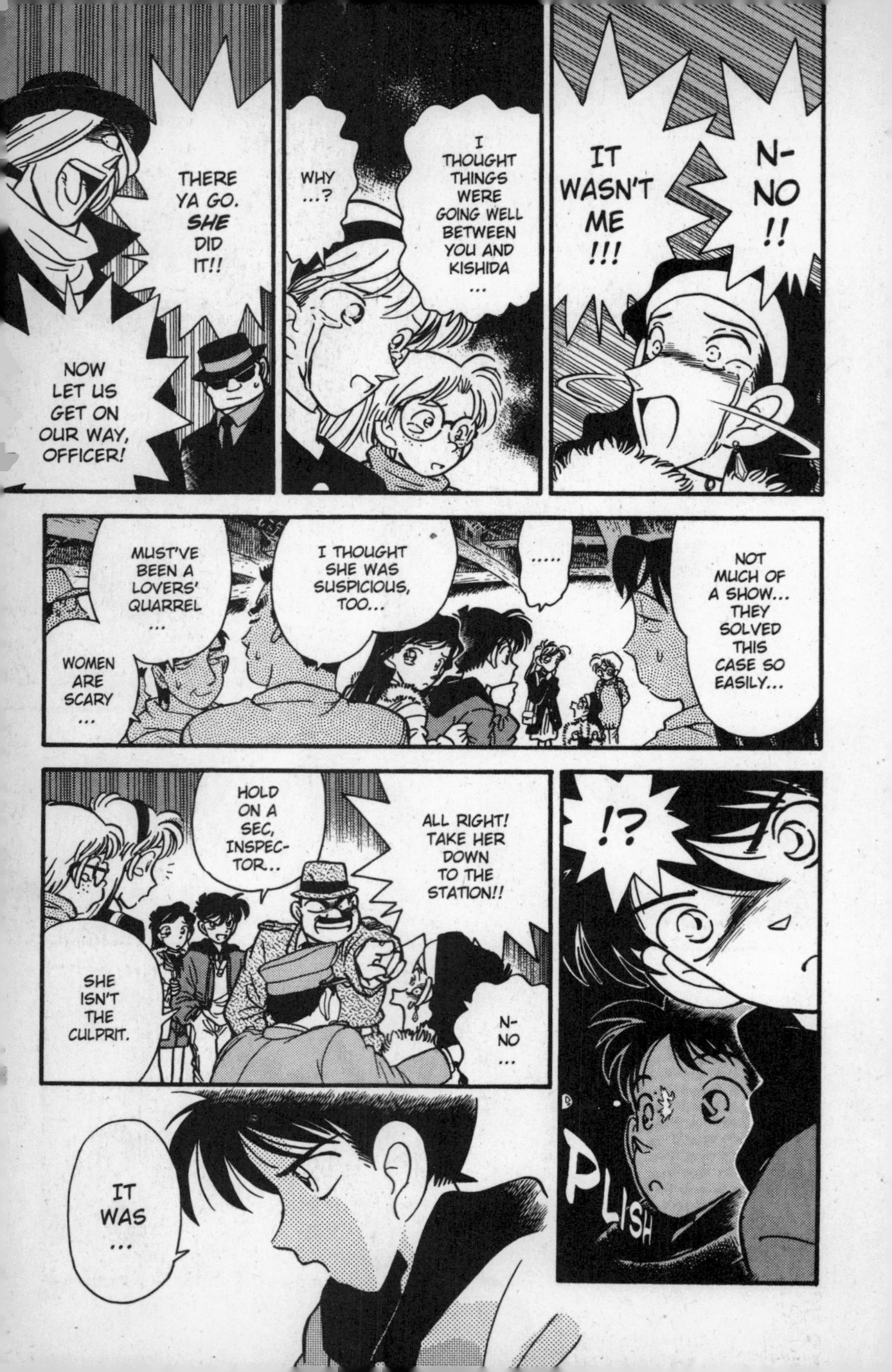
N-NO!!
IT WASN'T ME!!!
I THOUGHT THINGS WERE GOING WELL BETWEEN YOU AND KISHIDA...
WHY...?
THERE YA GO. **SHE** DID IT!!
NOW LET US GET ON OUR WAY, OFFICER!
NOT MUCH OF A SHOW... THEY SOLVED THIS CASE SO EASILY...
.....
I THOUGHT SHE WAS SUSPICIOUS, TOO...
MUST'VE BEEN A LOVERS' QUARREL...
WOMEN ARE SCARY...
!?
PLISH
ALL RIGHT! TAKE HER DOWN TO THE STATION!!
HOLD ON A SEC, INSPECTOR...
N-NO...
SHE ISN'T THE CULPRIT.
IT WAS...

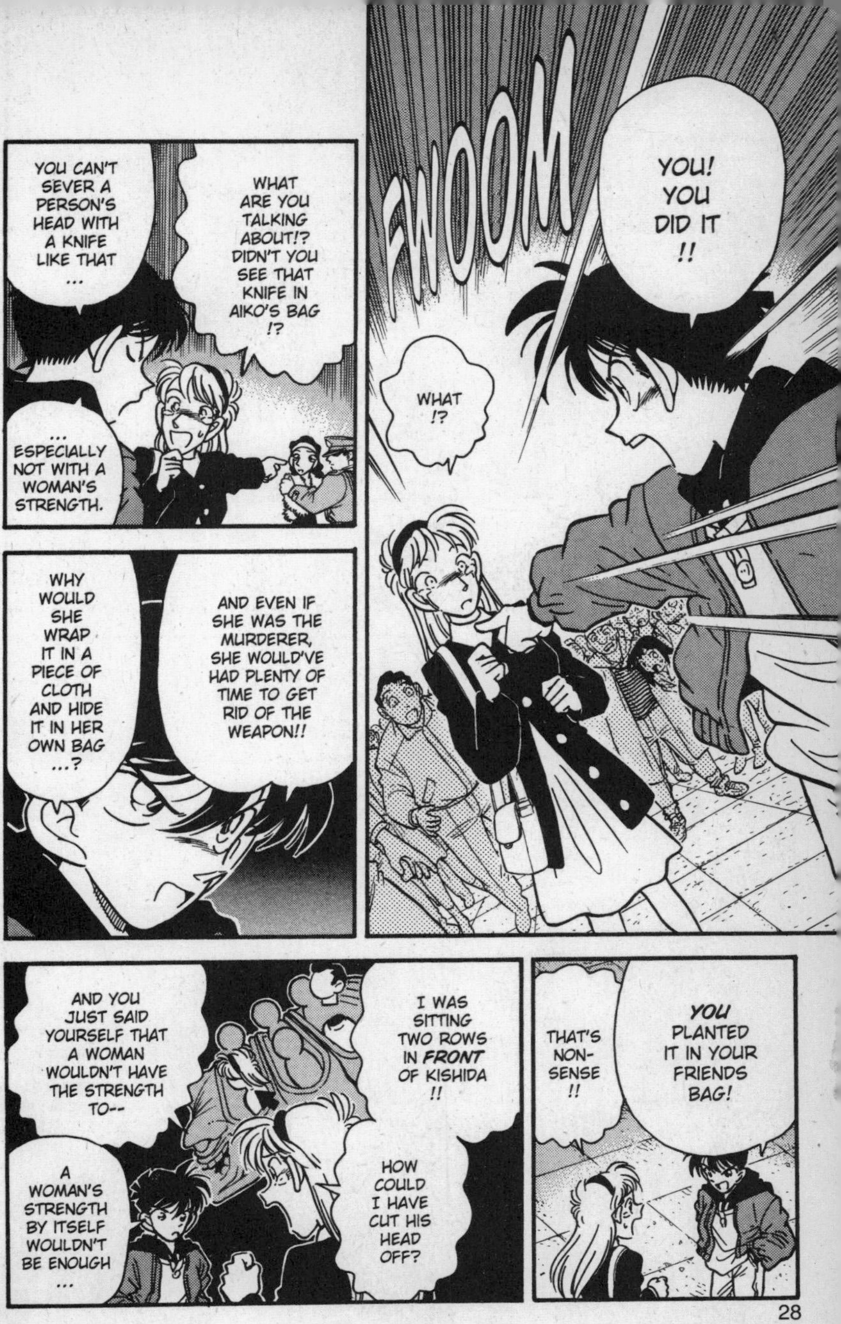
FWOOM
YOU! YOU DID IT !!
WHAT !?
WHAT ARE YOU TALKING ABOUT!? DIDN'T YOU SEE THAT KNIFE IN AIKO'S BAG !?
YOU CAN'T SEVER A PERSON'S HEAD WITH A KNIFE LIKE THAT ...
... ESPECIALLY NOT WITH A WOMAN'S STRENGTH.
AND EVEN IF SHE WAS THE MURDERER, SHE WOULD'VE HAD PLENTY OF TIME TO GET RID OF THE WEAPON!!
WHY WOULD SHE WRAP IT IN A PIECE OF CLOTH AND HIDE IT IN HER OWN BAG ...?
YOU PLANTED IT IN YOUR FRIENDS BAG!
THAT'S NON-SENSE !!
I WAS SITTING TWO ROWS IN *FRONT* OF KISHIDA !!
AND YOU JUST SAID YOURSELF THAT A WOMAN WOULDN'T HAVE THE STRENGTH TO--
HOW COULD I HAVE CUT HIS HEAD OFF?
A WOMAN'S STRENGTH BY ITSELF WOULDN'T BE ENOUGH ...

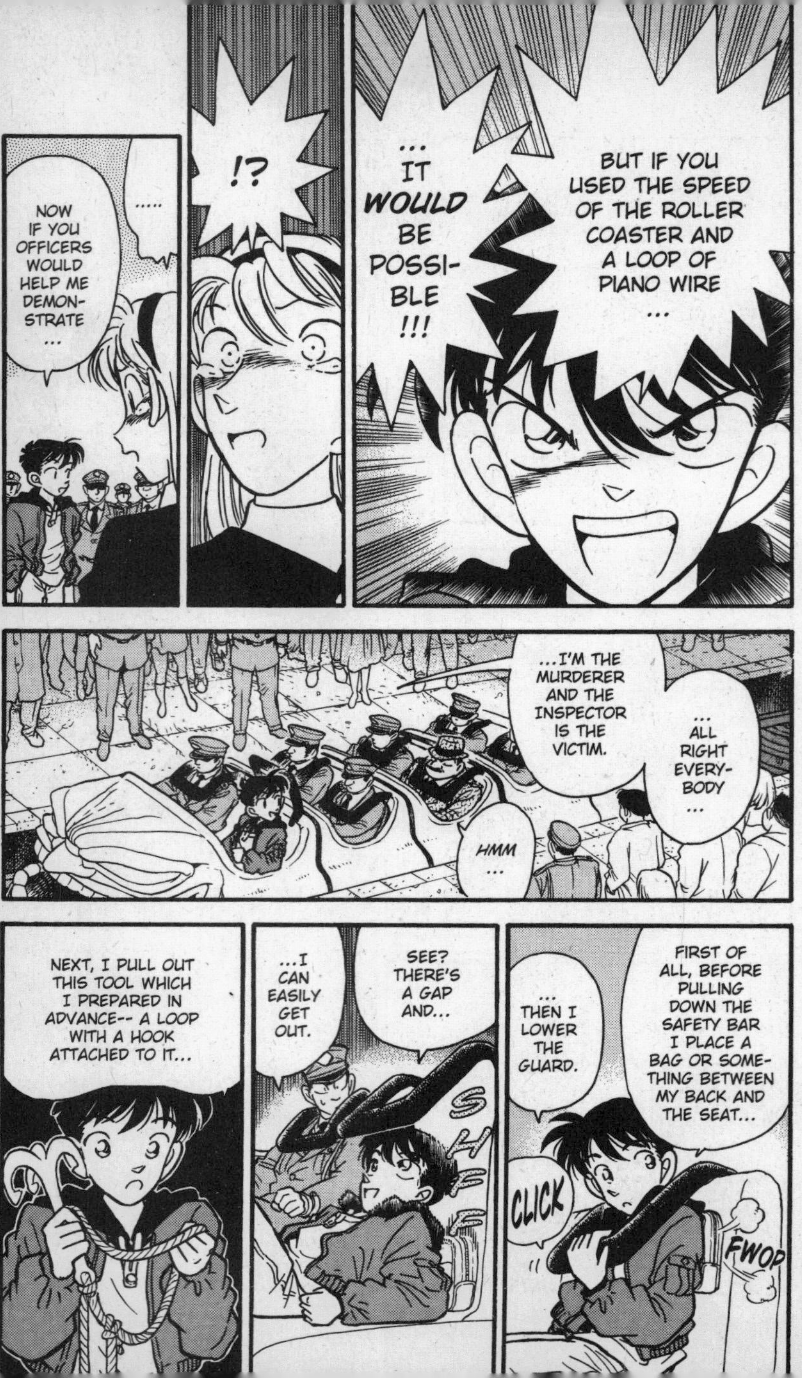
BUT IF YOU USED THE SPEED OF THE ROLLER COASTER AND A LOOP OF PIANO WIRE ...
... IT *WOULD* BE POSSI-BLE !!!
!?
.....
NOW IF YOU OFFICERS WOULD HELP ME DEMON-STRATE ...
... ALL RIGHT EVERY-BODY ...
...I'M THE MURDERER AND THE INSPECTOR IS THE VICTIM.
HMM ...
FIRST OF ALL, BEFORE PULLING DOWN THE SAFETY BAR I PLACE A BAG OR SOME-THING BETWEEN MY BACK AND THE SEAT...
FWOP
... THEN I LOWER THE GUARD.
CLICK
SEE? THERE'S A GAP AND...
...I CAN EASILY GET OUT.
SHFF
NEXT, I PULL OUT THIS TOOL WHICH I PREPARED IN ADVANCE-- A LOOP WITH A HOOK ATTACHED TO IT...

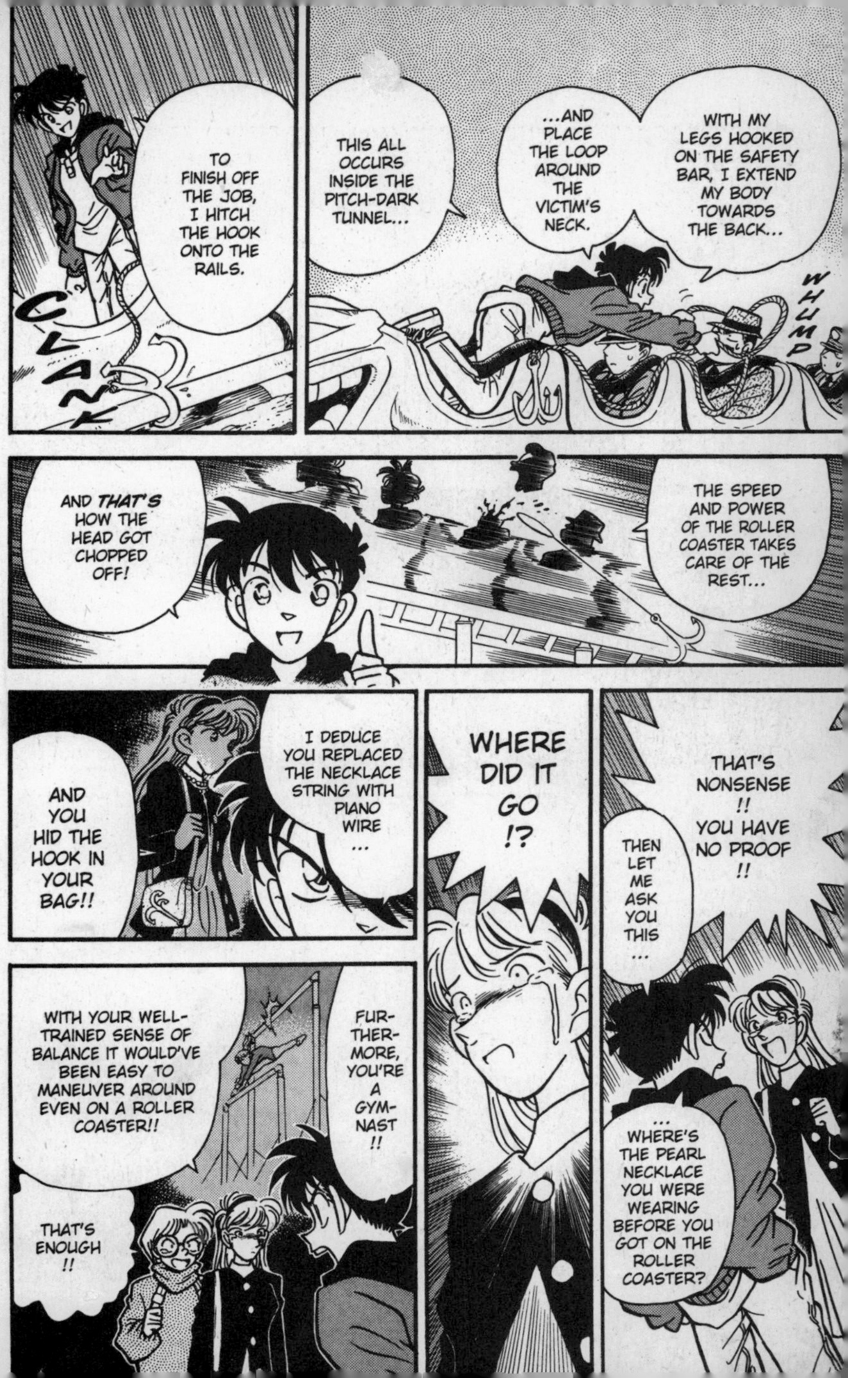
WITH MY LEGS HOOKED ON THE SAFETY BAR, I EXTEND MY BODY TOWARDS THE BACK...
...AND PLACE THE LOOP AROUND THE VICTIM'S NECK.
THIS ALL OCCURS INSIDE THE PITCH-DARK TUNNEL...
WHUMP
TO FINISH OFF THE JOB, I HITCH THE HOOK ONTO THE RAILS.
CLANK
THE SPEED AND POWER OF THE ROLLER COASTER TAKES CARE OF THE REST...
AND *THAT'S* HOW THE HEAD GOT CHOPPED OFF!
THAT'S NONSENSE!! YOU HAVE NO PROOF!!
THEN LET ME ASK YOU THIS...
...WHERE'S THE PEARL NECKLACE YOU WERE WEARING BEFORE YOU GOT ON THE ROLLER COASTER?
WHERE DID IT GO!?
I DEDUCE YOU REPLACED THE NECKLACE STRING WITH PIANO WIRE...
AND YOU HID THE HOOK IN YOUR BAG!!
FUR-THER-MORE, YOU'RE A GYM-NAST!!
WITH YOUR WELL-TRAINED SENSE OF BALANCE IT WOULD'VE BEEN EASY TO MANEUVER AROUND EVEN ON A ROLLER COASTER!!
THAT'S ENOUGH!!

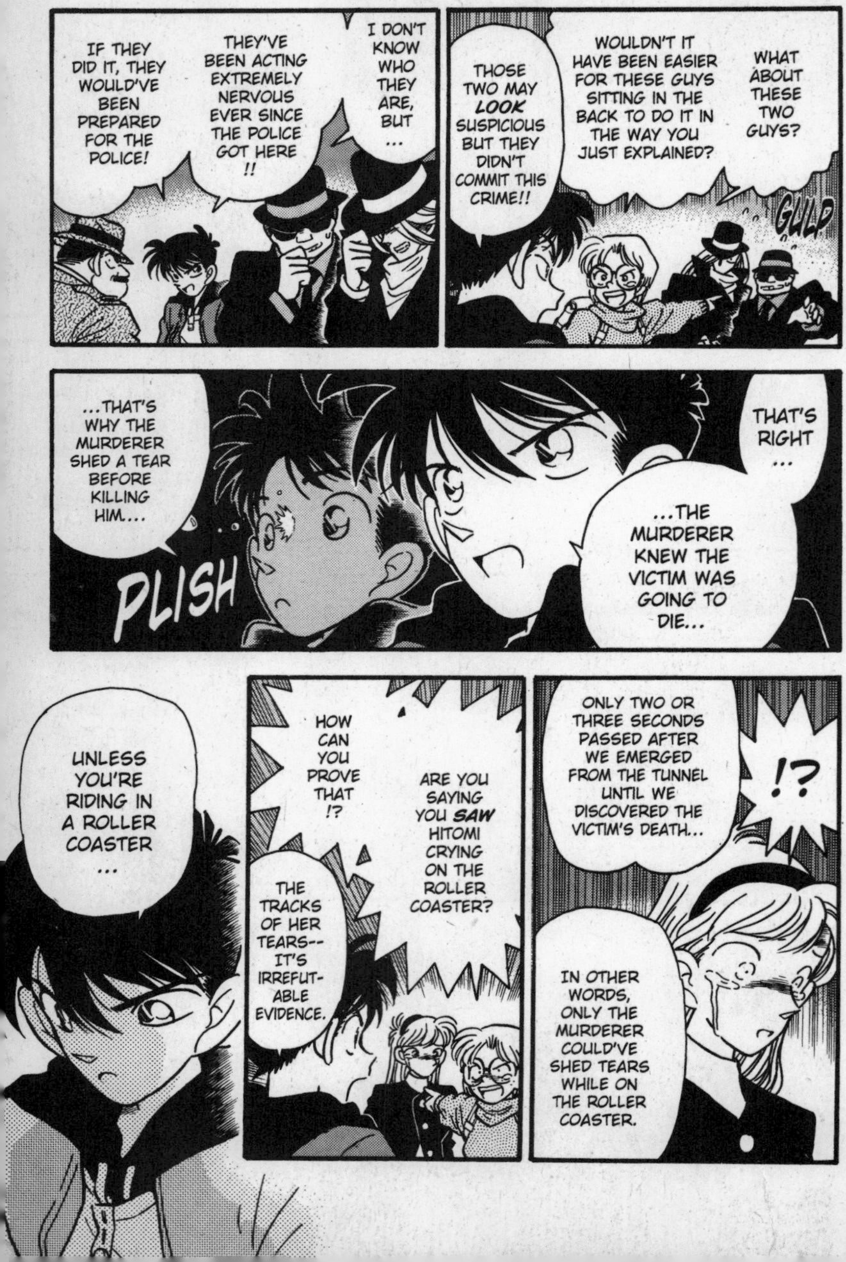
WHAT ABOUT THESE TWO GUYS?
WOULDN'T IT HAVE BEEN EASIER FOR THESE GUYS SITTING IN THE BACK TO DO IT IN THE WAY YOU JUST EXPLAINED?
THOSE TWO MAY *LOOK* SUSPICIOUS BUT THEY DIDN'T COMMIT THIS CRIME!!
GULP
I DON'T KNOW WHO THEY ARE, BUT ...
THEY'VE BEEN ACTING EXTREMELY NERVOUS EVER SINCE THE POLICE GOT HERE !!
IF THEY DID IT, THEY WOULD'VE BEEN PREPARED FOR THE POLICE!
THAT'S RIGHT ...
...THE MURDERER KNEW THE VICTIM WAS GOING TO DIE...
...THAT'S WHY THE MURDERER SHED A TEAR BEFORE KILLING HIM...
PLISH
!?
ONLY TWO OR THREE SECONDS PASSED AFTER WE EMERGED FROM THE TUNNEL UNTIL WE DISCOVERED THE VICTIM'S DEATH...
IN OTHER WORDS, ONLY THE MURDERER COULD'VE SHED TEARS WHILE ON THE ROLLER COASTER.
ARE YOU SAYING YOU *SAW* HITOMI CRYING ON THE ROLLER COASTER?
HOW CAN YOU PROVE THAT !?
THE TRACKS OF HER TEARS-- IT'S IRREFUT-ABLE EVIDENCE.
UNLESS YOU'RE RIDING IN A ROLLER COASTER ...

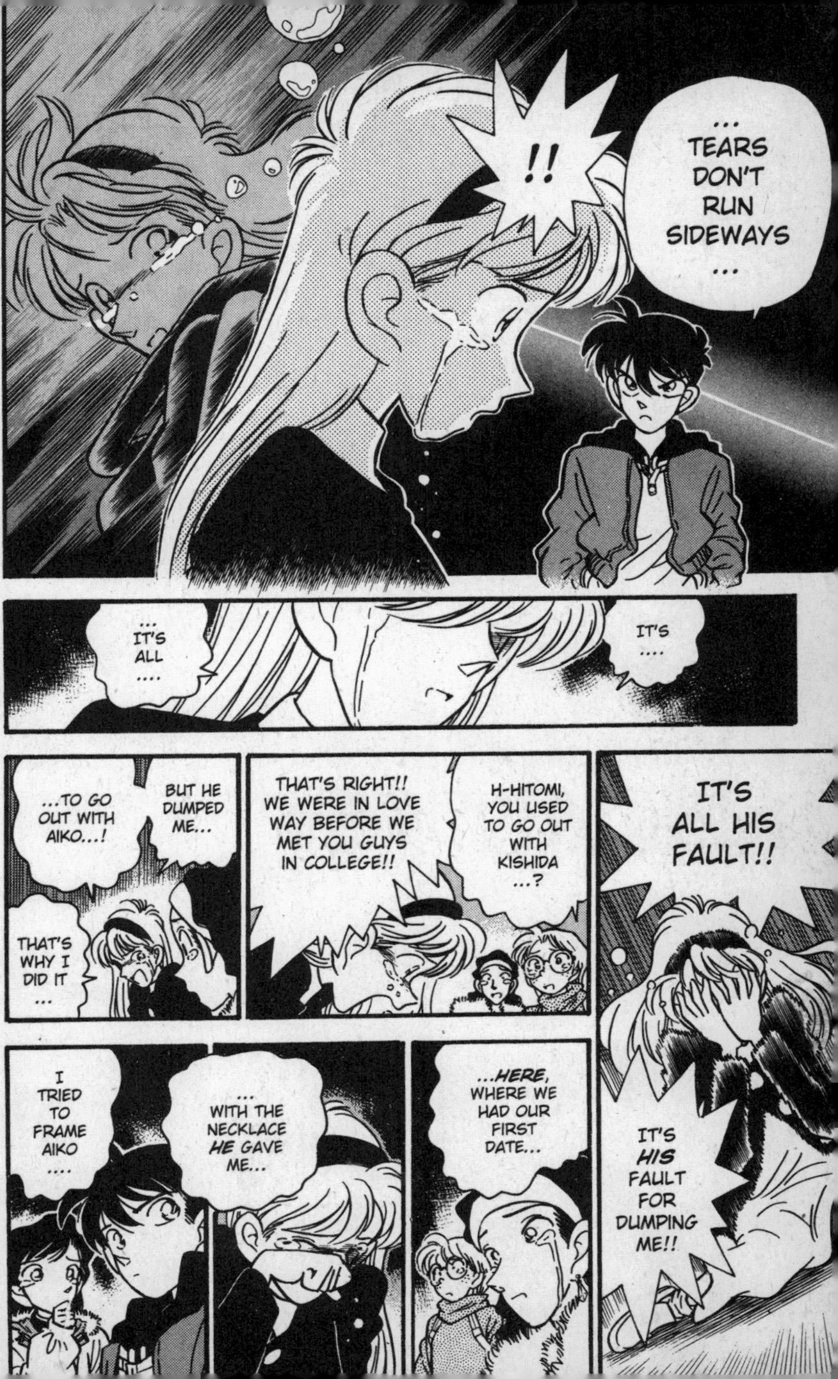
... TEARS DON'T RUN SIDEWAYS ...
!!
IT'S ....
... IT'S ALL ....
IT'S ALL HIS FAULT!!
IT'S *HIS* FAULT FOR DUMPING ME!!
H-HITOMI, YOU USED TO GO OUT WITH KISHIDA ...?
THAT'S RIGHT!! WE WERE IN LOVE WAY BEFORE WE MET YOU GUYS IN COLLEGE!!
BUT HE DUMPED ME...
...TO GO OUT WITH AIKO...!
THAT'S WHY I DID IT ...
...*HERE*, WHERE WE HAD OUR FIRST DATE...
... WITH THE NECKLACE *HE* GAVE ME...
I TRIED TO FRAME AIKO ....

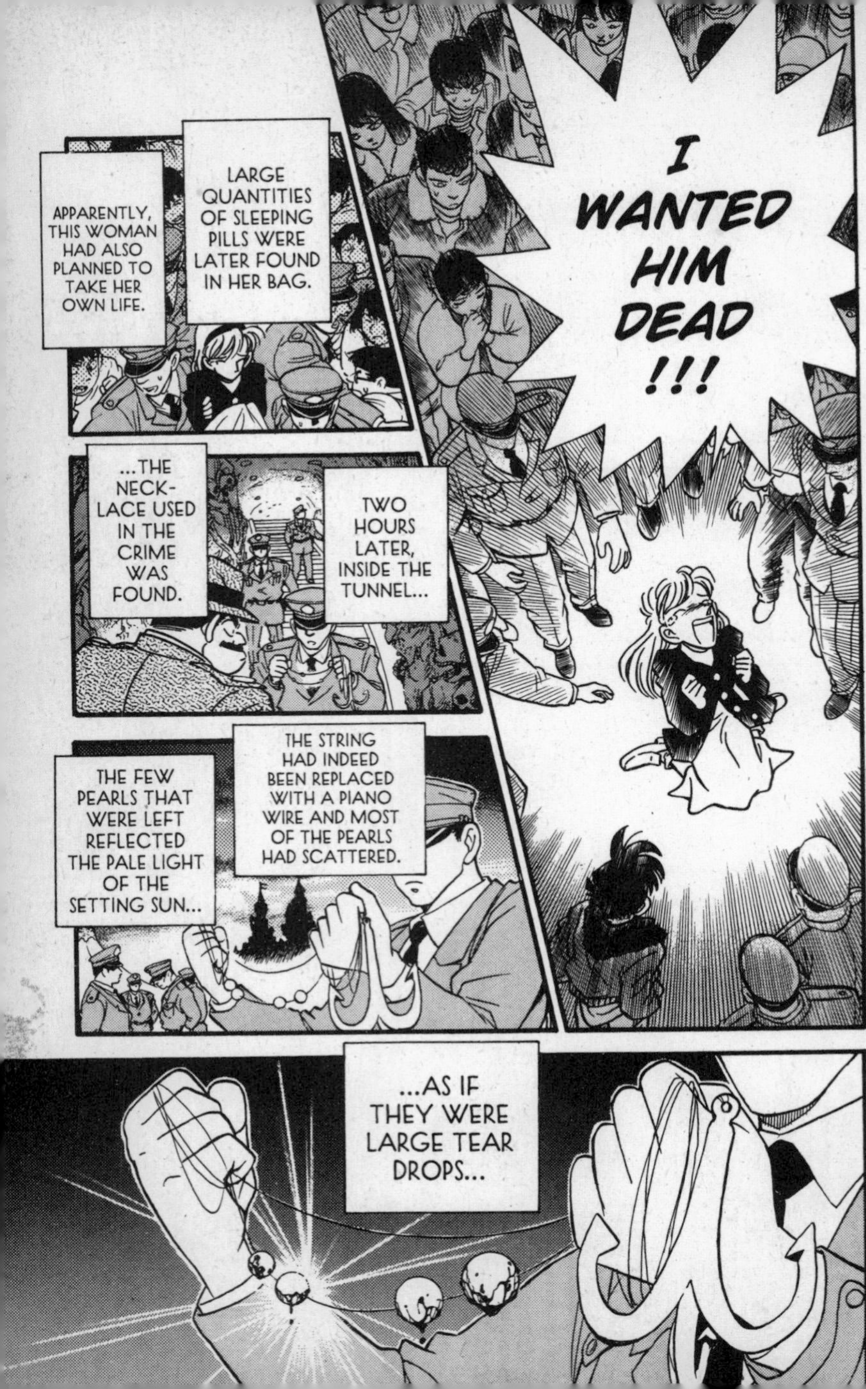
I WANTED HIM DEAD!!!
LARGE QUANTITIES OF SLEEPING PILLS WERE LATER FOUND IN HER BAG.
APPARENTLY, THIS WOMAN HAD ALSO PLANNED TO TAKE HER OWN LIFE.
TWO HOURS LATER, INSIDE THE TUNNEL...
...THE NECKLACE USED IN THE CRIME WAS FOUND.
THE STRING HAD INDEED BEEN REPLACED WITH A PIANO WIRE AND MOST OF THE PEARLS HAD SCATTERED.
THE FEW PEARLS THAT WERE LEFT REFLECTED THE PALE LIGHT OF THE SETTING SUN...
...AS IF THEY WERE LARGE TEAR DROPS...

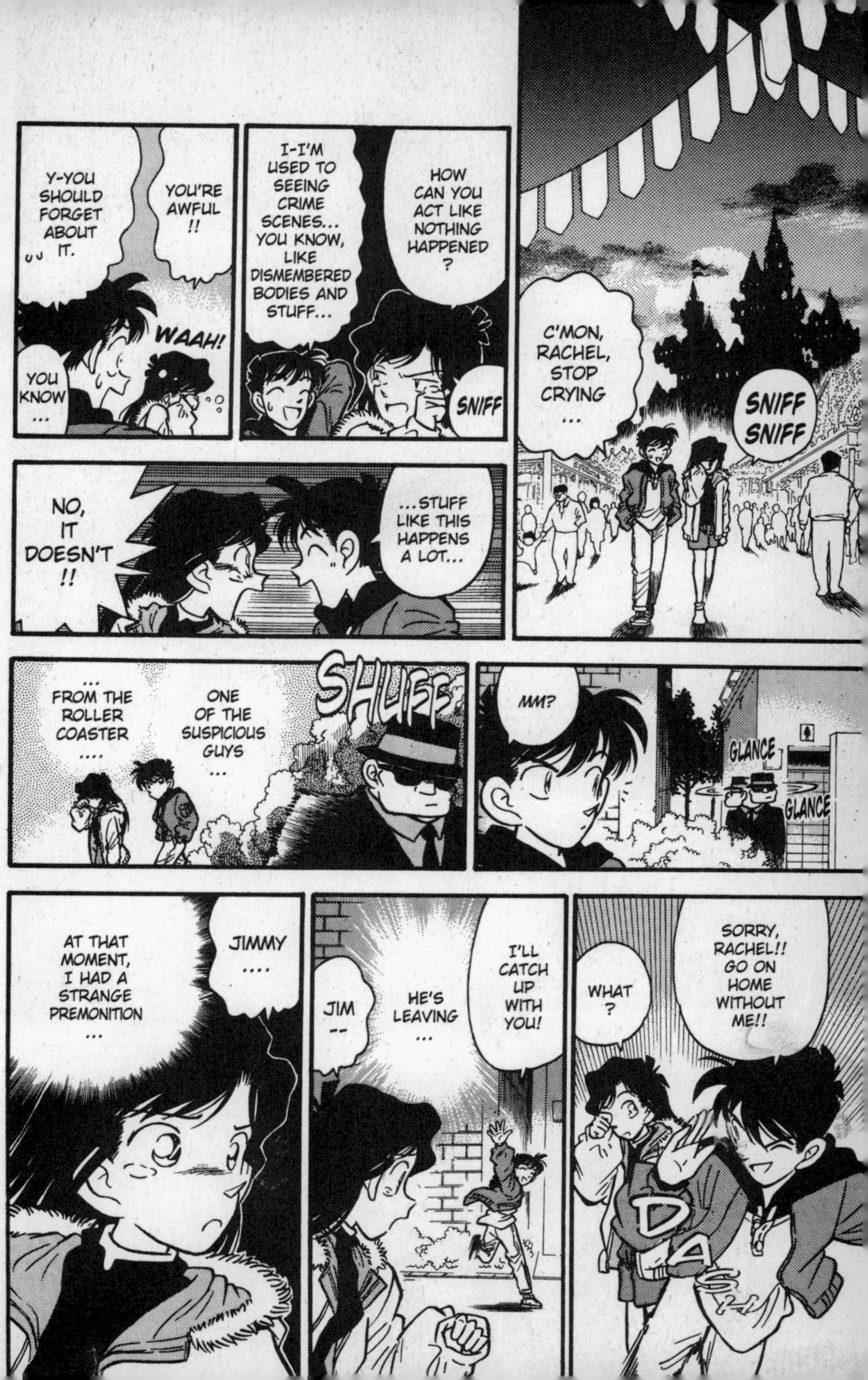
C'MON, RACHEL, STOP CRYING ...
SNIFF SNIFF
HOW CAN YOU ACT LIKE NOTHING HAPPENED ?
I-I'M USED TO SEEING CRIME SCENES... YOU KNOW, LIKE DISMEMBERED BODIES AND STUFF...
SNIFF
YOU'RE AWFUL !!
Y-YOU SHOULD FORGET ABOUT IT.
WAAH!
YOU KNOW ...
...STUFF LIKE THIS HAPPENS A LOT...
NO, IT DOESN'T !!
MM?
GLANCE
GLANCE
SHUFF
ONE OF THE SUSPICIOUS GUYS ...
... FROM THE ROLLER COASTER ....
SORRY, RACHEL!! GO ON HOME WITHOUT ME!!
WHAT ?
I'LL CATCH UP WITH YOU!
HE'S LEAVING ...
JIM --
JIMMY ....
AT THAT MOMENT, I HAD A STRANGE PREMONITION ...

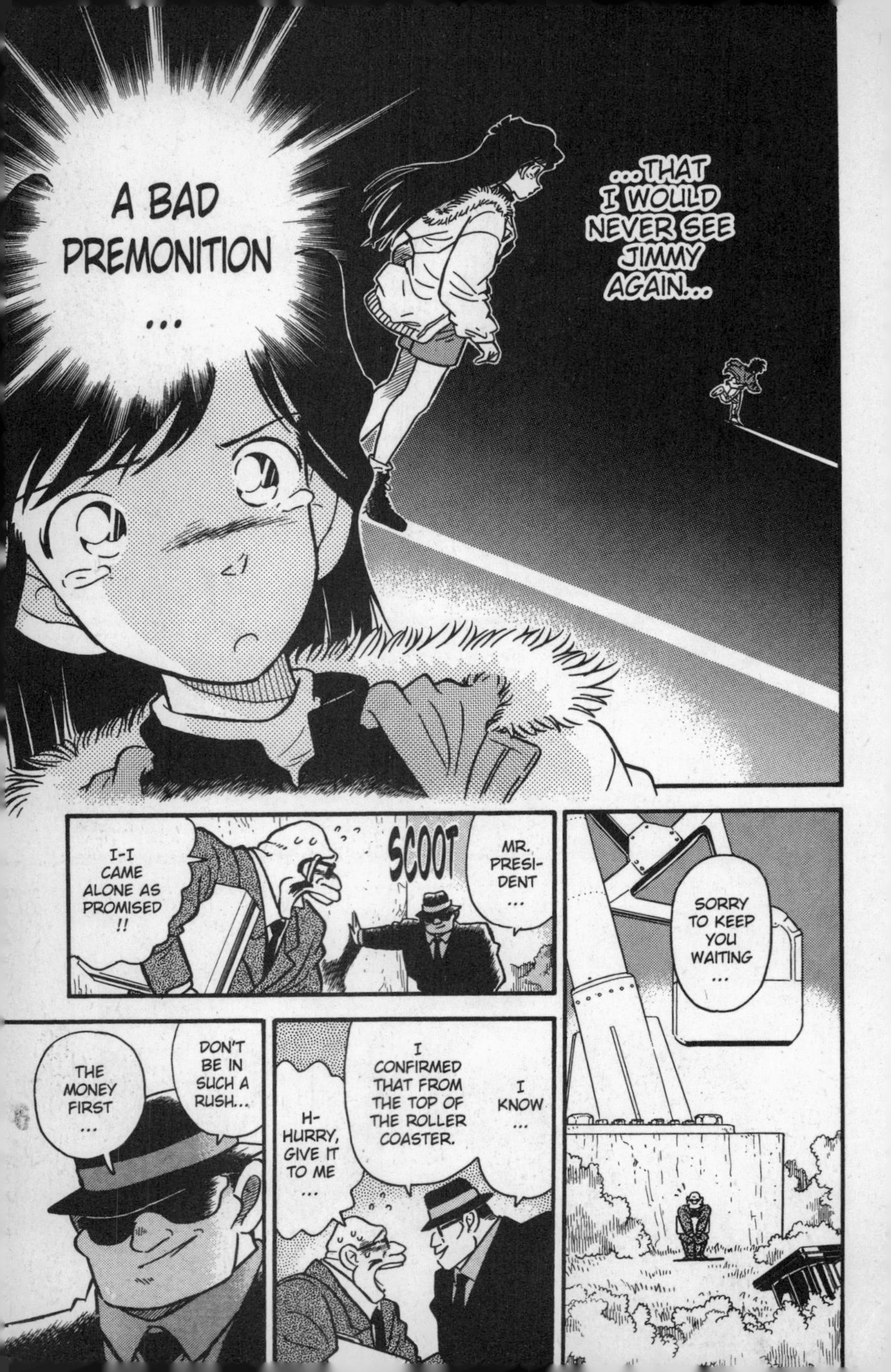
...THAT I WOULD NEVER SEE JIMMY AGAIN...
A BAD PREMONITION ...
SORRY TO KEEP YOU WAITING ...
MR. PRESIDENT ...
SCOOT
I-I CAME ALONE AS PROMISED !!
I KNOW ...
I CONFIRMED THAT FROM THE TOP OF THE ROLLER COASTER.
H-HURRY, GIVE IT TO ME ...
DON'T BE IN SUCH A RUSH...
THE MONEY FIRST ...

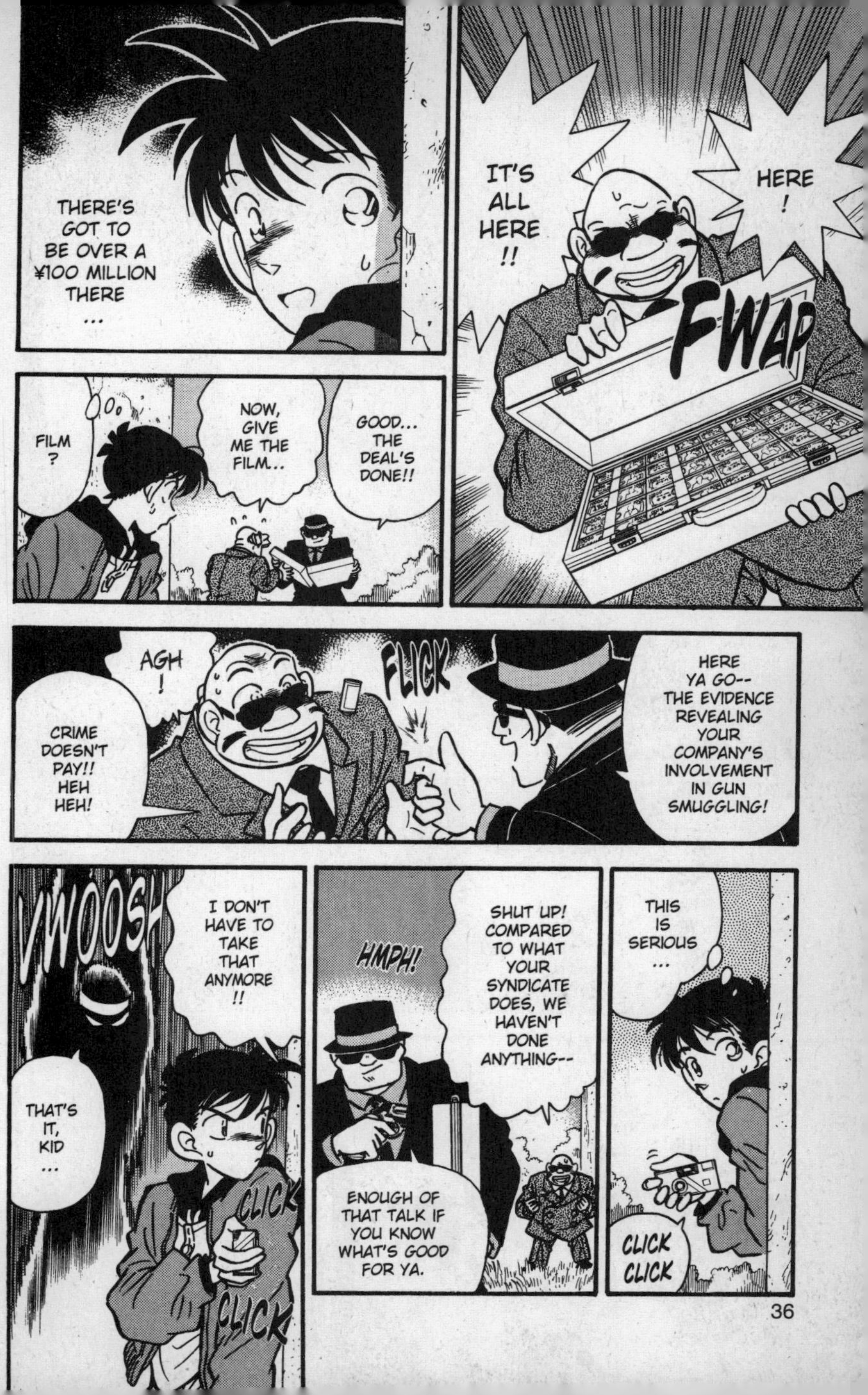
HERE!
IT'S ALL HERE!!
FWAP
THERE'S GOT TO BE OVER A ¥100 MILLION THERE ...
GOOD... THE DEAL'S DONE!!
NOW, GIVE ME THE FILM...
FILM?
HERE YA GO-- THE EVIDENCE REVEALING YOUR COMPANY'S INVOLVEMENT IN GUN SMUGGLING!
FLICK
AGH!
CRIME DOESN'T PAY!! HEH HEH!
THIS IS SERIOUS ...
CLICK CLICK
SHUT UP! COMPARED TO WHAT YOUR SYNDICATE DOES, WE HAVEN'T DONE ANYTHING--
HMPH!
ENOUGH OF THAT TALK IF YOU KNOW WHAT'S GOOD FOR YA.
I DON'T HAVE TO TAKE THAT ANYMORE!!
VWOOSH
THAT'S IT, KID ...
CLICK
CLICK

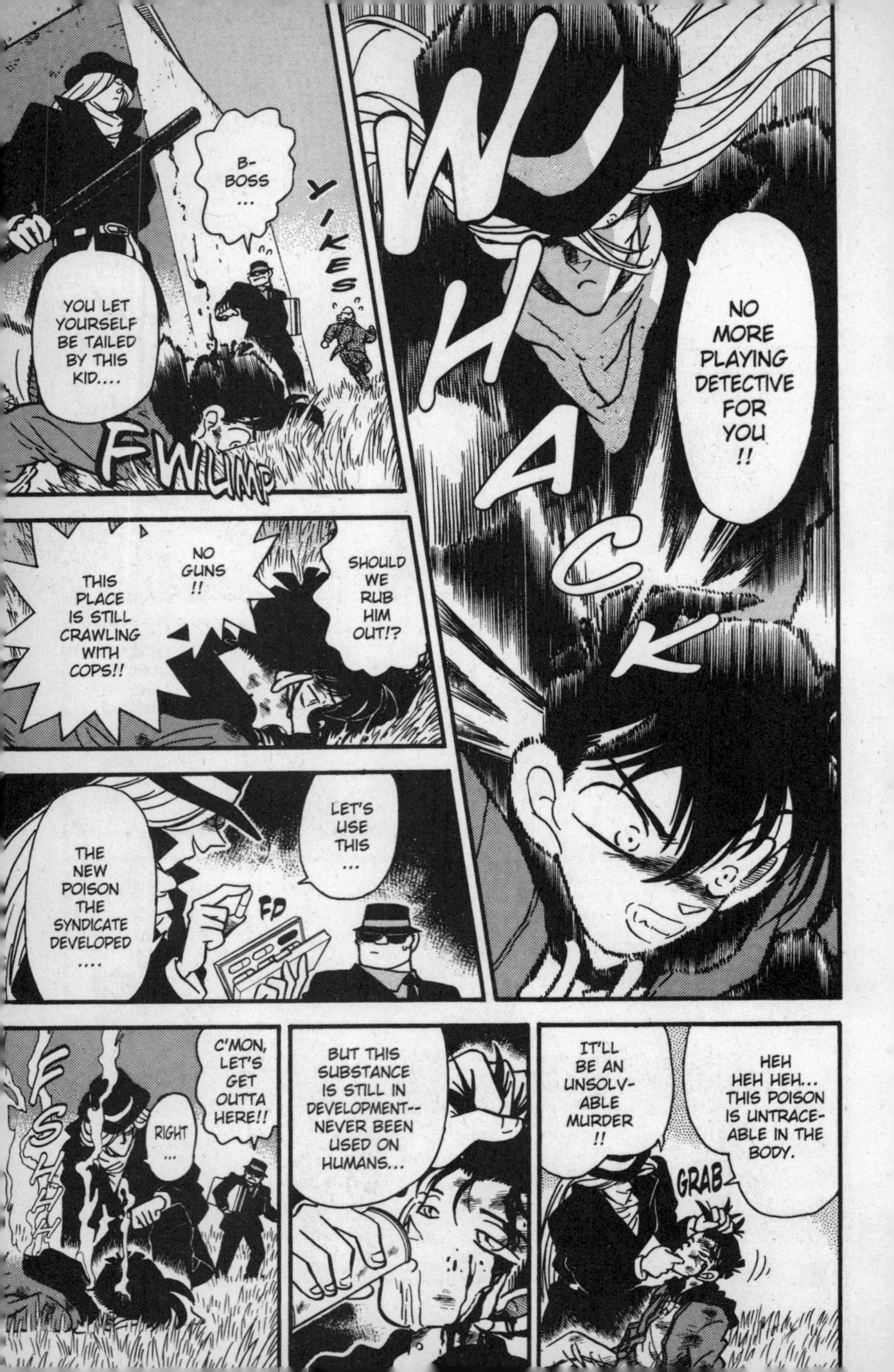
WHACK
NO MORE PLAYING DETECTIVE FOR YOU !!
YIKES
B-BOSS ...
YOU LET YOURSELF BE TAILED BY THIS KID....
FWUMP
SHOULD WE RUB HIM OUT!?
NO GUNS !!
THIS PLACE IS STILL CRAWLING WITH COPS!!
LET'S USE THIS ...
FD
THE NEW POISON THE SYNDICATE DEVELOPED ....
HEH HEH HEH... THIS POISON IS UNTRACE-ABLE IN THE BODY.
IT'LL BE AN UNSOLV-ABLE MURDER !!
GRAB
BUT THIS SUBSTANCE IS STILL IN DEVELOPMENT-- NEVER BEEN USED ON HUMANS...
C'MON, LET'S GET OUTTA HERE!!
RIGHT ...

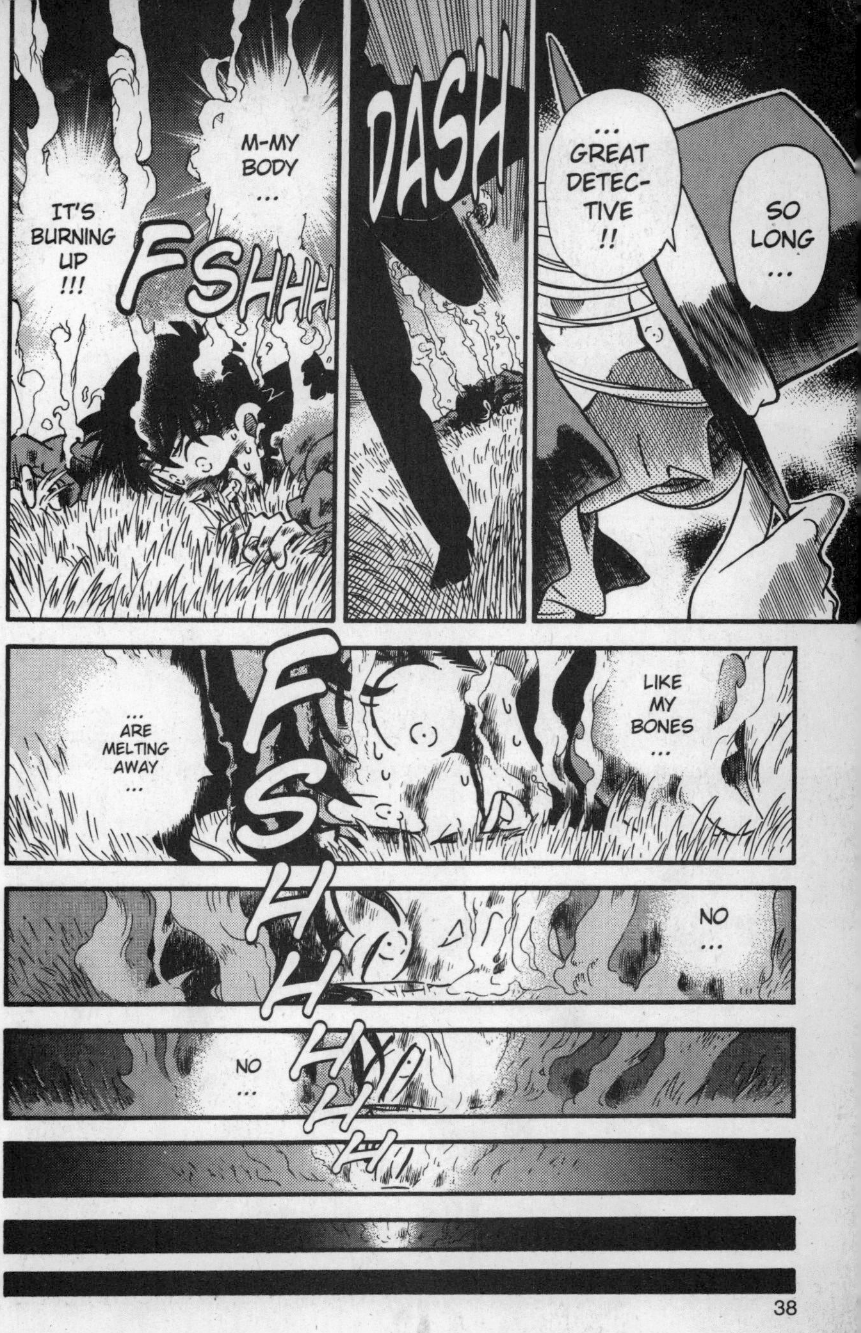
SO LONG ...
... GREAT DETECTIVE !!
DASH
M-MY BODY ...
FSHHH
IT'S BURNING UP !!!
LIKE MY BONES ...
... ARE MELTING AWAY ...
FSSHHHHHH
NO ...
NO ...

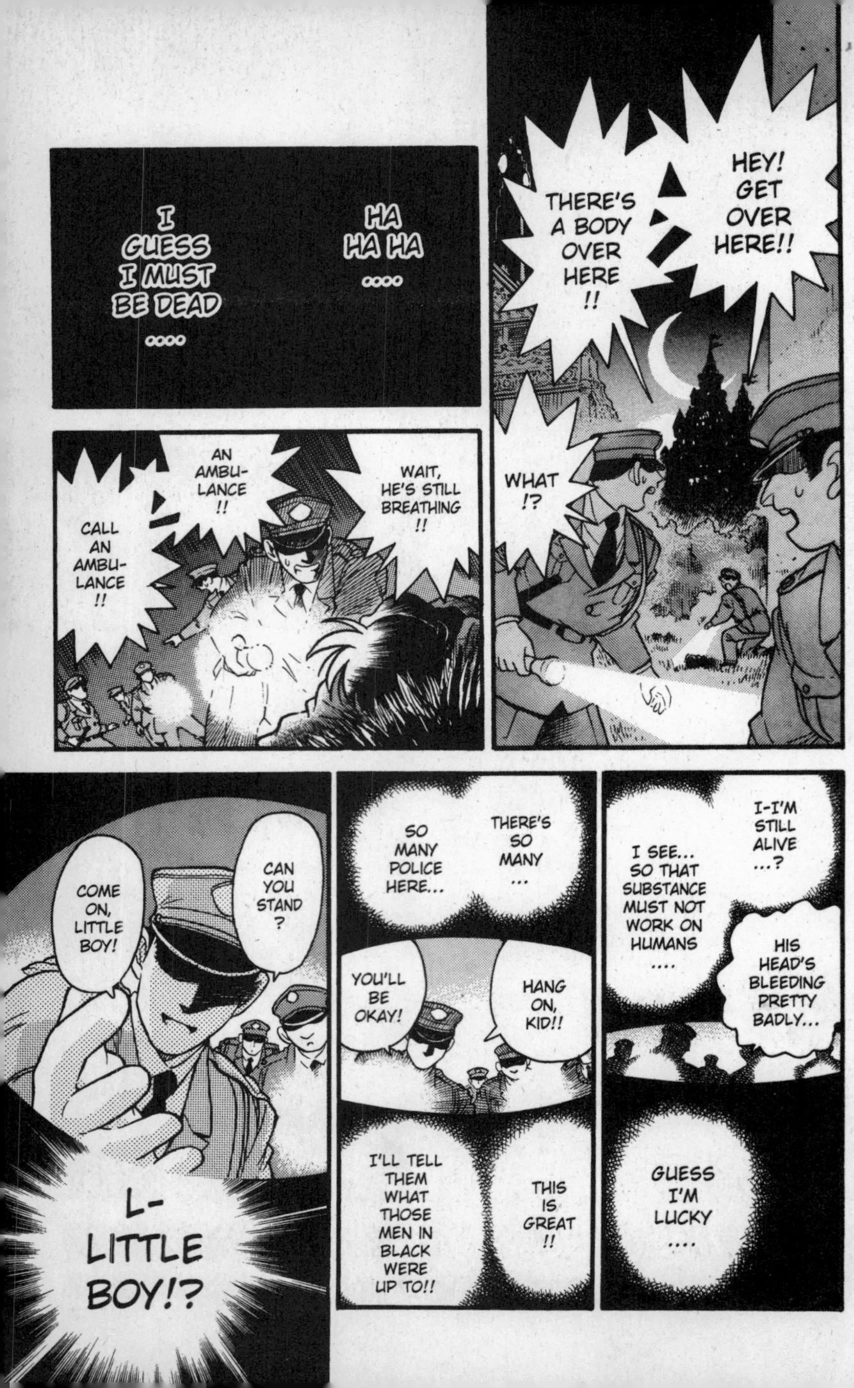
HEY! GET OVER HERE!!
THERE'S A BODY OVER HERE !!
WHAT !?
HA HA HA ....
I GUESS I MUST BE DEAD ....
WAIT, HE'S STILL BREATHING !!
AN AMBULANCE !!
CALL AN AMBULANCE !!
I-I'M STILL ALIVE ...?
I SEE... SO THAT SUBSTANCE MUST NOT WORK ON HUMANS ....
HIS HEAD'S BLEEDING PRETTY BADLY...
GUESS I'M LUCKY ....
THERE'S SO MANY ...
SO MANY POLICE HERE...
HANG ON, KID!!
YOU'LL BE OKAY!
THIS IS GREAT !!
I'LL TELL THEM WHAT THOSE MEN IN BLACK WERE UP TO!!
CAN YOU STAND ?
COME ON, LITTLE BOY!
L- LITTLE BOY!?

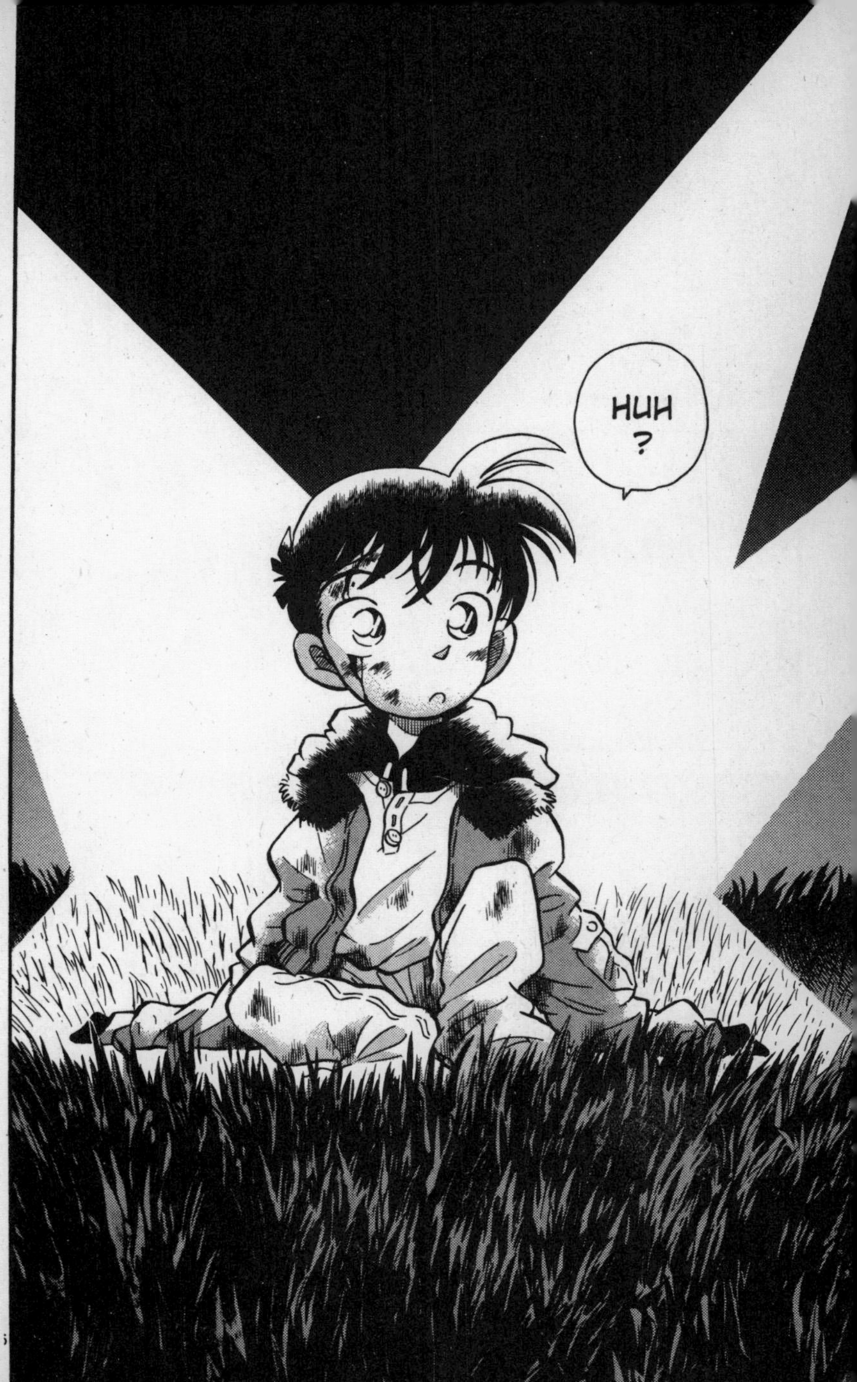
HUH
?

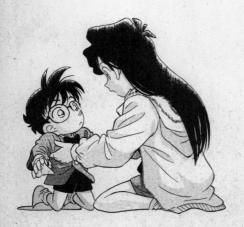

FILE 2: THE GREAT DETECTIVE TURNED SMALL

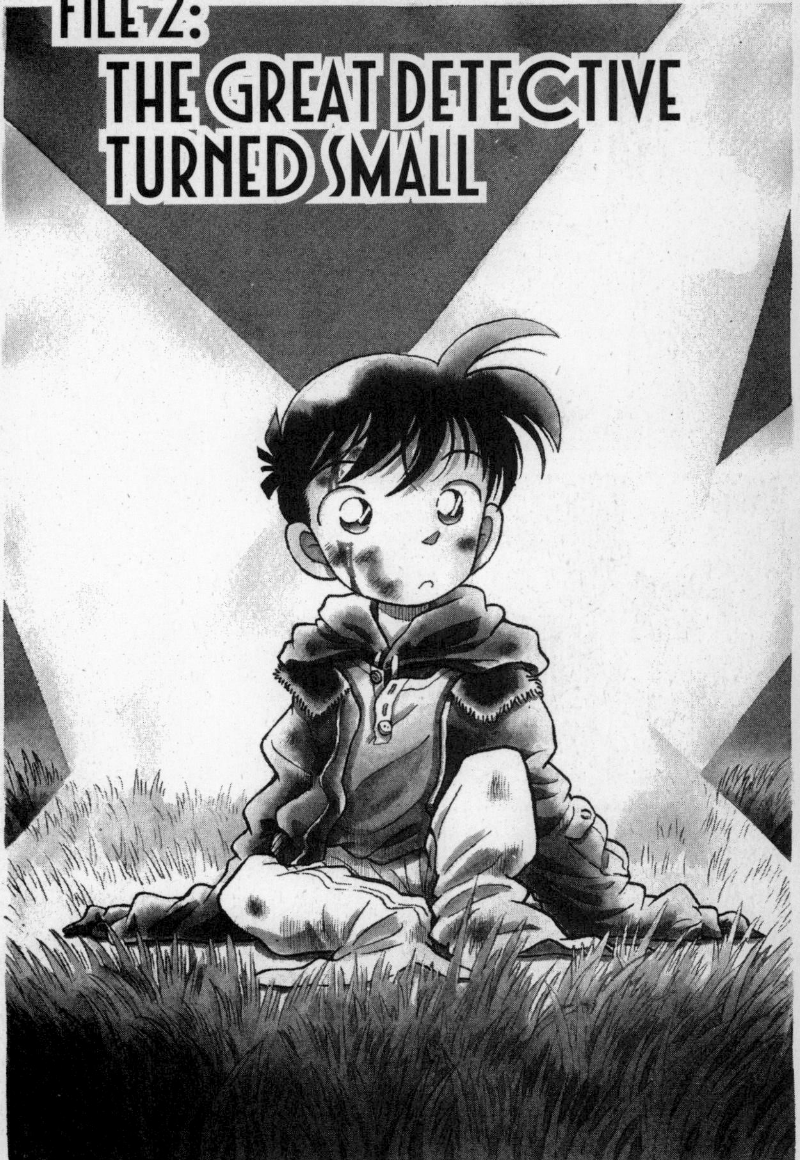

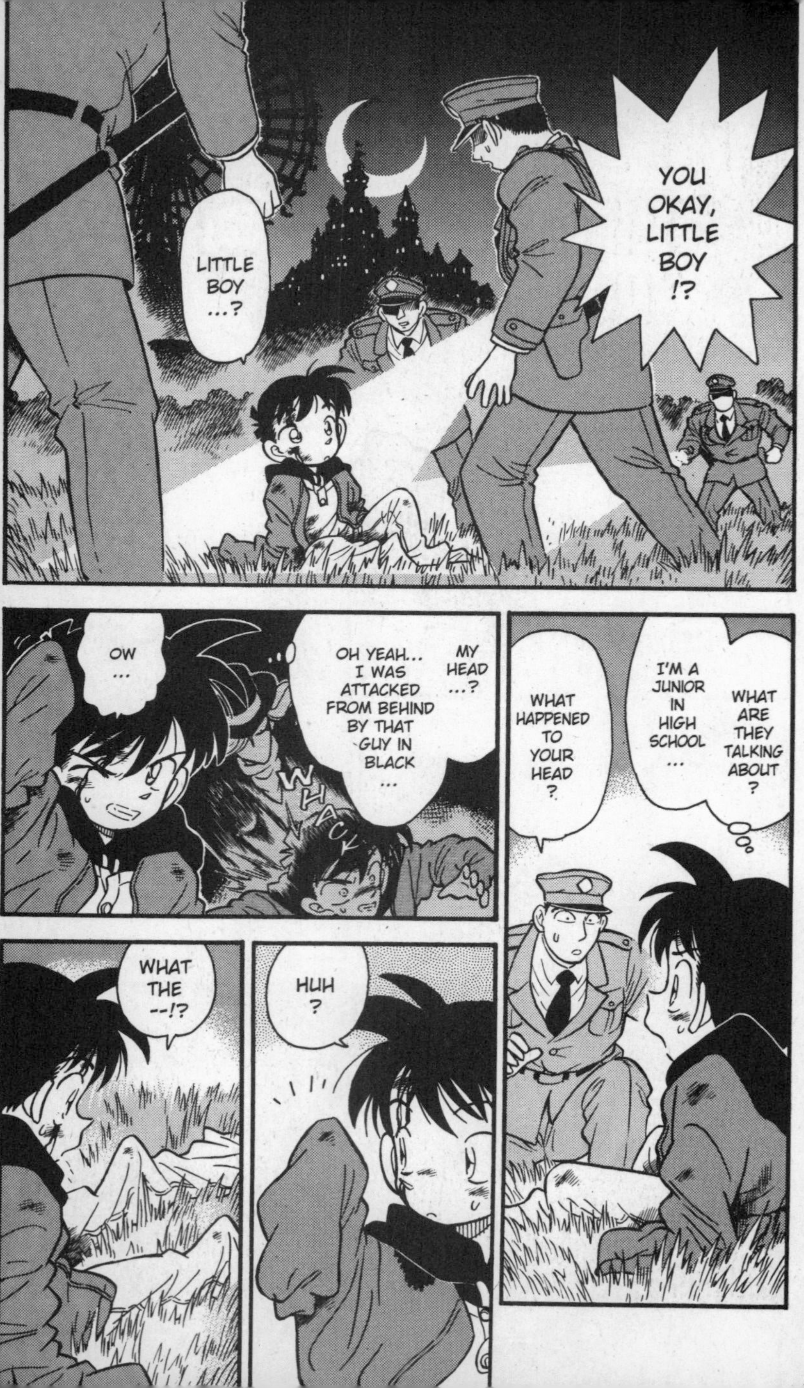
YOU OKAY, LITTLE BOY !?
LITTLE BOY ...?
I'M A JUNIOR IN HIGH SCHOOL ...
WHAT ARE THEY TALKING ABOUT ?
WHAT HAPPENED TO YOUR HEAD ?
MY HEAD ...?
OH YEAH... I WAS ATTACKED FROM BEHIND BY THAT GUY IN BLACK ...
WHACK
OW ...
HUH ?
WHAT THE --!?

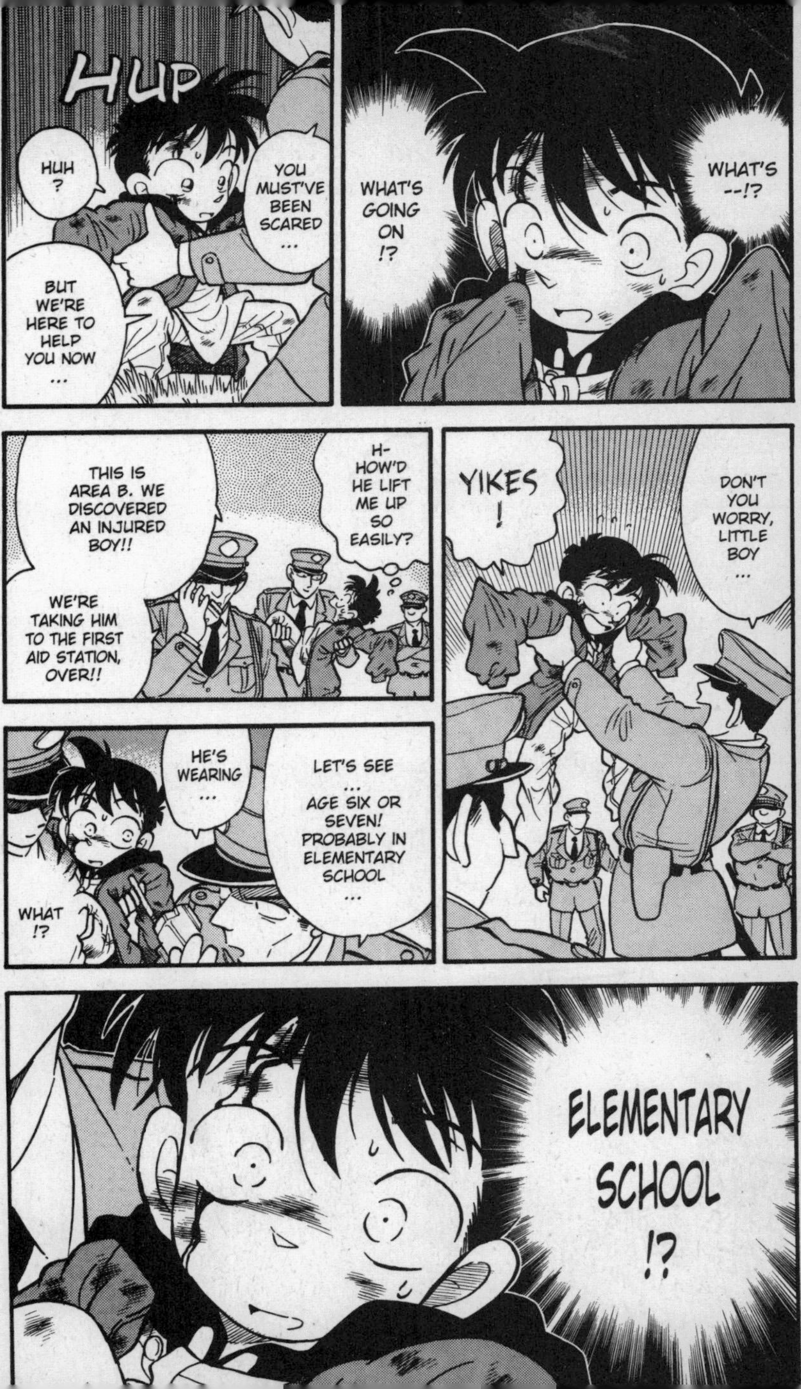
WHAT'S --!?
WHAT'S GOING ON !?
HUP
YOU MUST'VE BEEN SCARED ...
HUH ?
BUT WE'RE HERE TO HELP YOU NOW ...
DON'T YOU WORRY, LITTLE BOY ...
YIKES !
H-HOW'D HE LIFT ME UP SO EASILY?
THIS IS AREA B. WE DISCOVERED AN INJURED BOY!!
WE'RE TAKING HIM TO THE FIRST AID STATION, OVER!!
LET'S SEE ... AGE SIX OR SEVEN! PROBABLY IN ELEMENTARY SCHOOL ...
HE'S WEARING ...
WHAT !?
ELEMENTARY SCHOOL !?

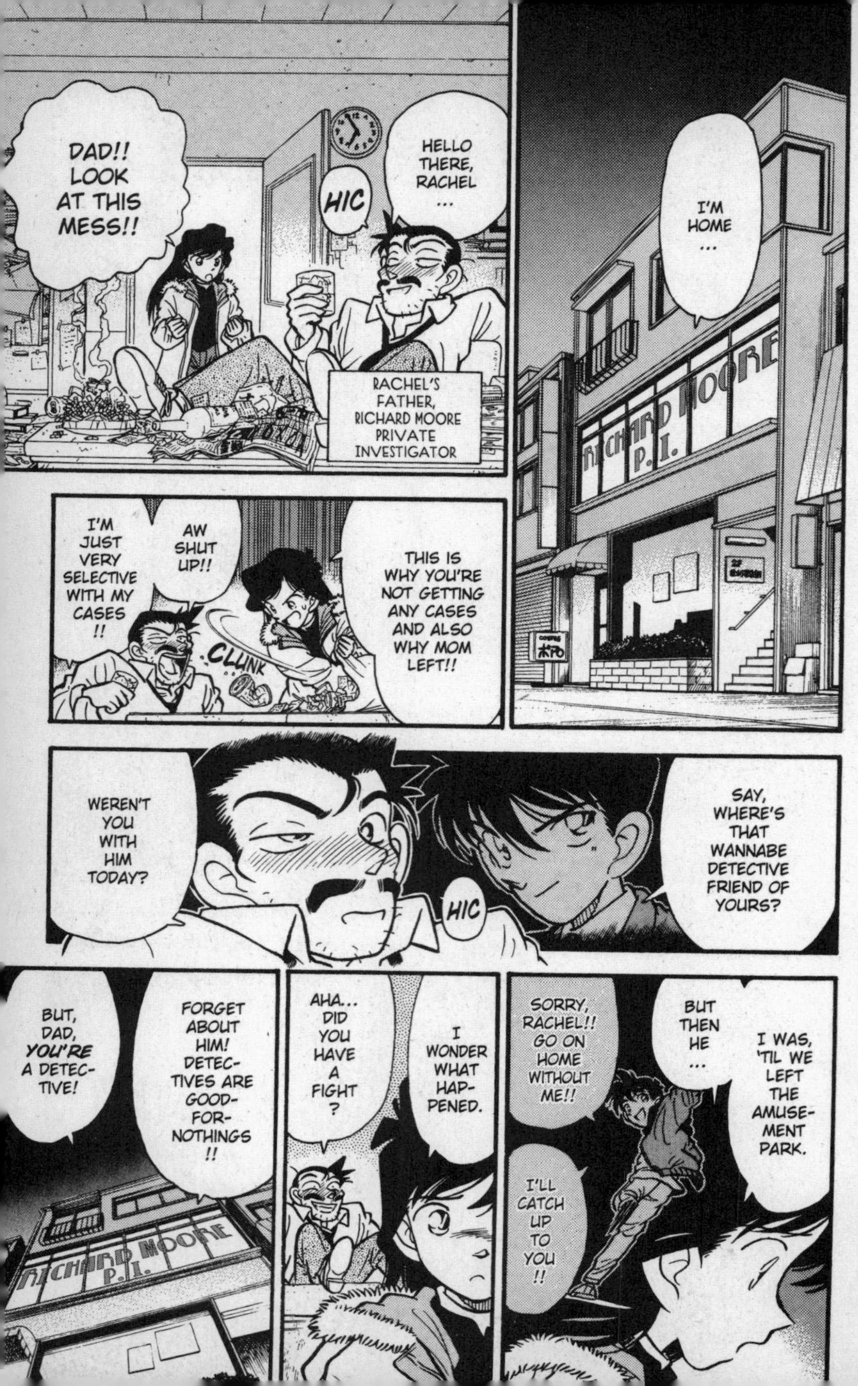
I'M HOME ...
RICHARD MOORE P.I.
HELLO THERE, RACHEL ...
HIC
DAD!! LOOK AT THIS MESS!!
RACHEL'S FATHER, RICHARD MOORE PRIVATE INVESTIGATOR
THIS IS WHY YOU'RE NOT GETTING ANY CASES AND ALSO WHY MOM LEFT!!
AW SHUT UP!!
I'M JUST VERY SELECTIVE WITH MY CASES !!
CLUNK
SAY, WHERE'S THAT WANNABE DETECTIVE FRIEND OF YOURS?
HIC
WEREN'T YOU WITH HIM TODAY?
I WAS, 'TIL WE LEFT THE AMUSEMENT PARK.
BUT THEN HE ...
SORRY, RACHEL!! GO ON HOME WITHOUT ME!!
I'LL CATCH UP TO YOU !!
I WONDER WHAT HAPPENED.
AHA... DID YOU HAVE A FIGHT ?
FORGET ABOUT HIM! DETECTIVES ARE GOOD-FOR-NOTHINGS !!
BUT, DAD, ***YOU'RE*** A DETECTIVE!
RICHARD MOORE P.I.

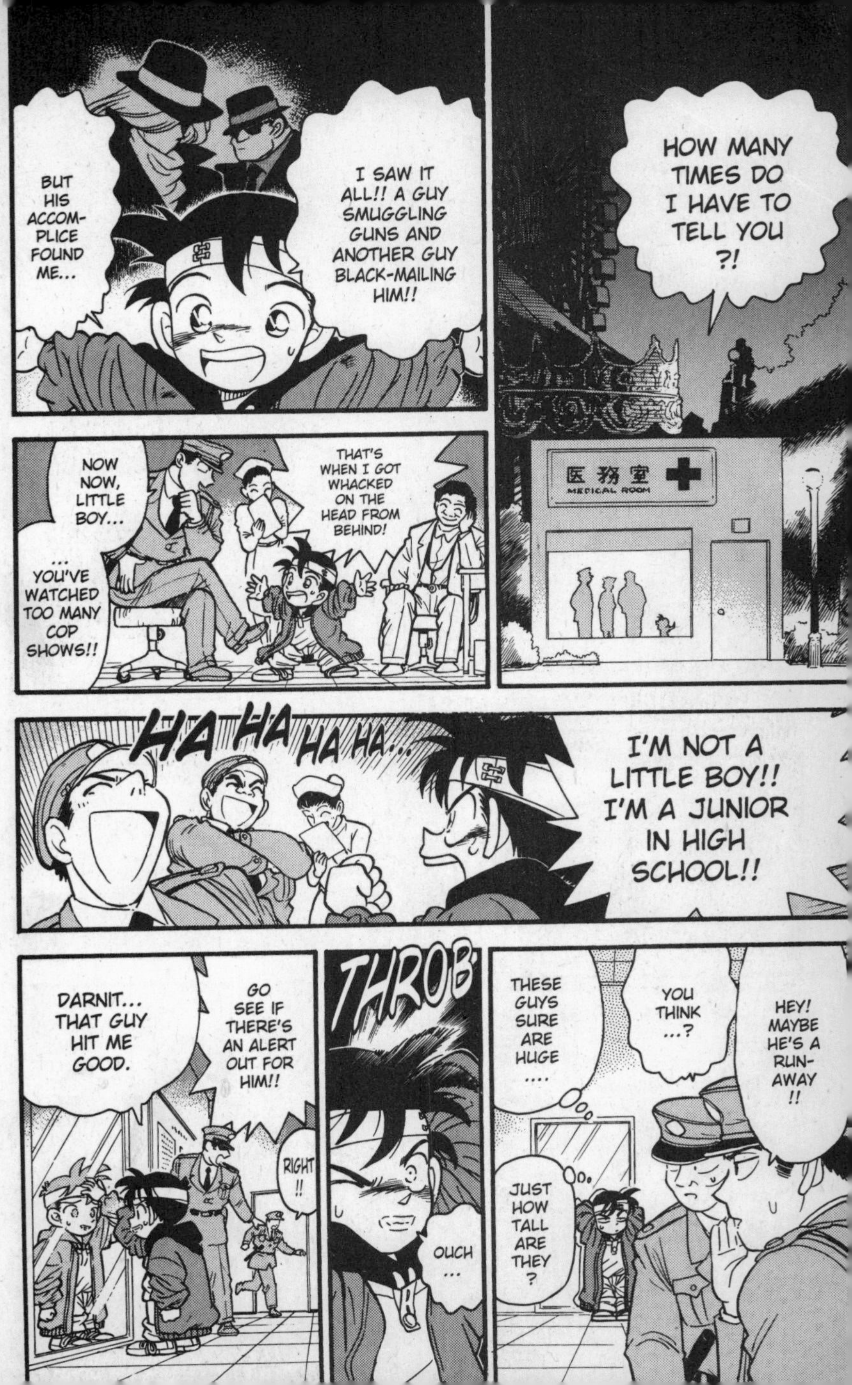
HOW MANY TIMES DO I HAVE TO TELL YOU ?!
I SAW IT ALL!! A GUY SMUGGLING GUNS AND ANOTHER GUY BLACK-MAILING HIM!!
BUT HIS ACCOM-PLICE FOUND ME...
THAT'S WHEN I GOT WHACKED ON THE HEAD FROM BEHIND!
NOW NOW, LITTLE BOY...
... YOU'VE WATCHED TOO MANY COP SHOWS!!
医務室
MEDICAL ROOM
I'M NOT A LITTLE BOY!! I'M A JUNIOR IN HIGH SCHOOL!!
HA HA HA HA...
HEY! MAYBE HE'S A RUN-AWAY !!
YOU THINK ...?
THESE GUYS SURE ARE HUGE ....
JUST HOW TALL ARE THEY ?
THROB
OUCH ...
GO SEE IF THERE'S AN ALERT OUT FOR HIM!!
DARNIT... THAT GUY HIT ME GOOD.
RIGHT !!

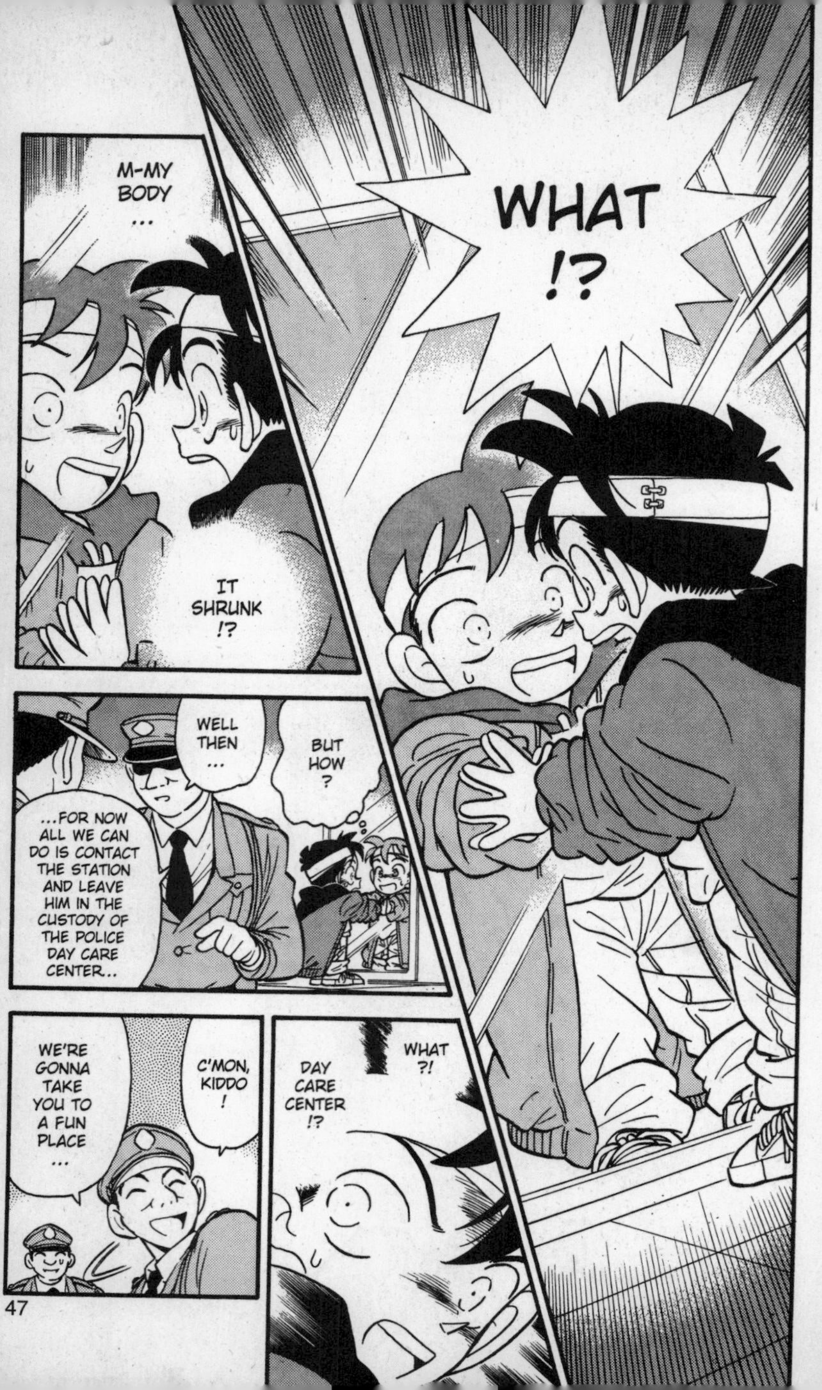
WHAT !?
M-MY BODY ...
IT SHRUNK !?
BUT HOW ?
WELL THEN ...
...FOR NOW ALL WE CAN DO IS CONTACT THE STATION AND LEAVE HIM IN THE CUSTODY OF THE POLICE DAY CARE CENTER...
WHAT ?!
DAY CARE CENTER !?
C'MON, KIDDO !
WE'RE GONNA TAKE YOU TO A FUN PLACE ...

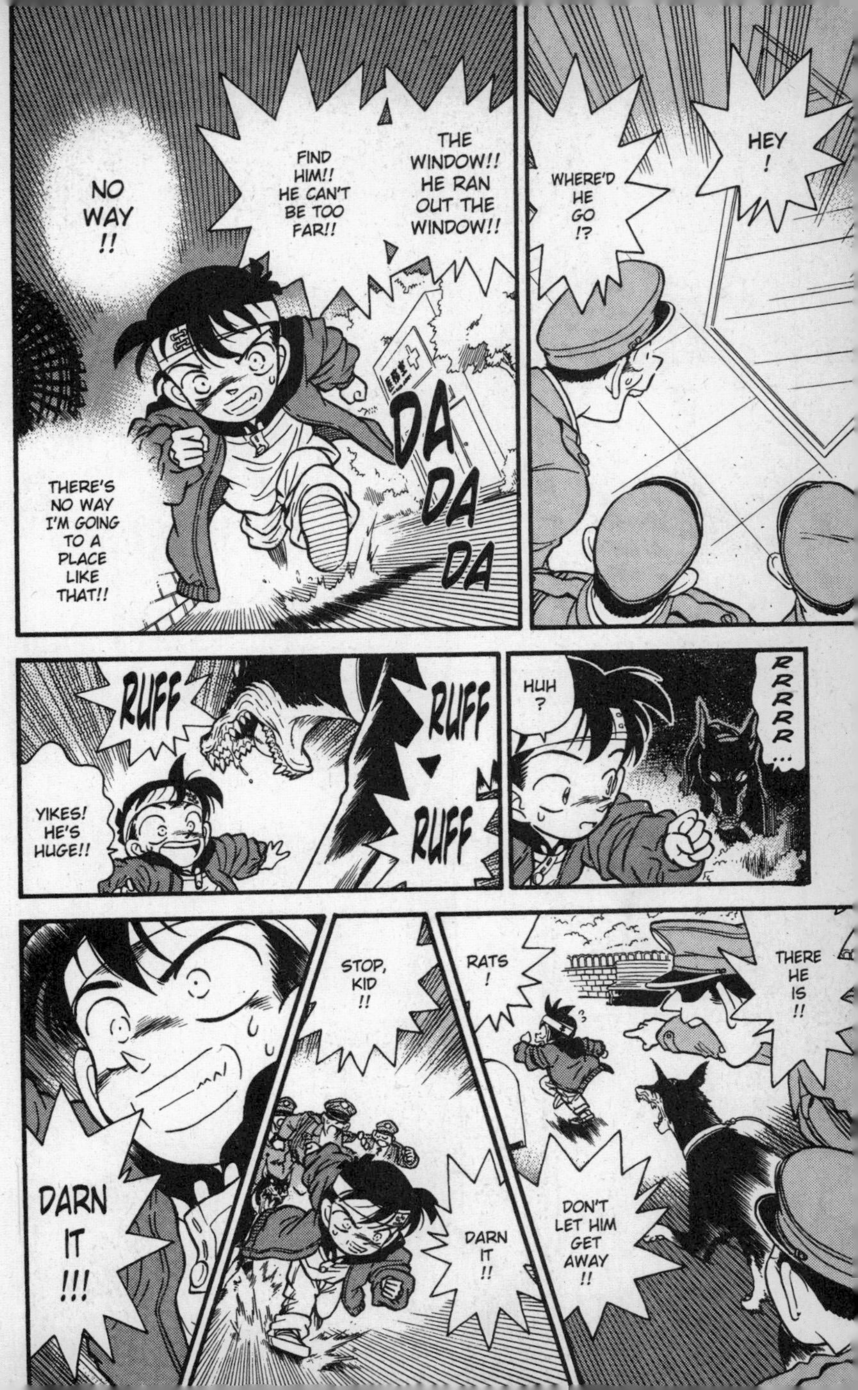
HEY!
WHERE'D HE GO!?
THE WINDOW!! HE RAN OUT THE WINDOW!!
FIND HIM!! HE CAN'T BE TOO FAR!!
NO WAY!!
DA DA DA
THERE'S NO WAY I'M GOING TO A PLACE LIKE THAT!!
RRRRR...
HUH?
RUFF
RUFF
RUFF
YIKES! HE'S HUGE!!
THERE HE IS!!
RATS!
DON'T LET HIM GET AWAY!!
STOP, KID!!
DARN IT!!
DARN IT!!!

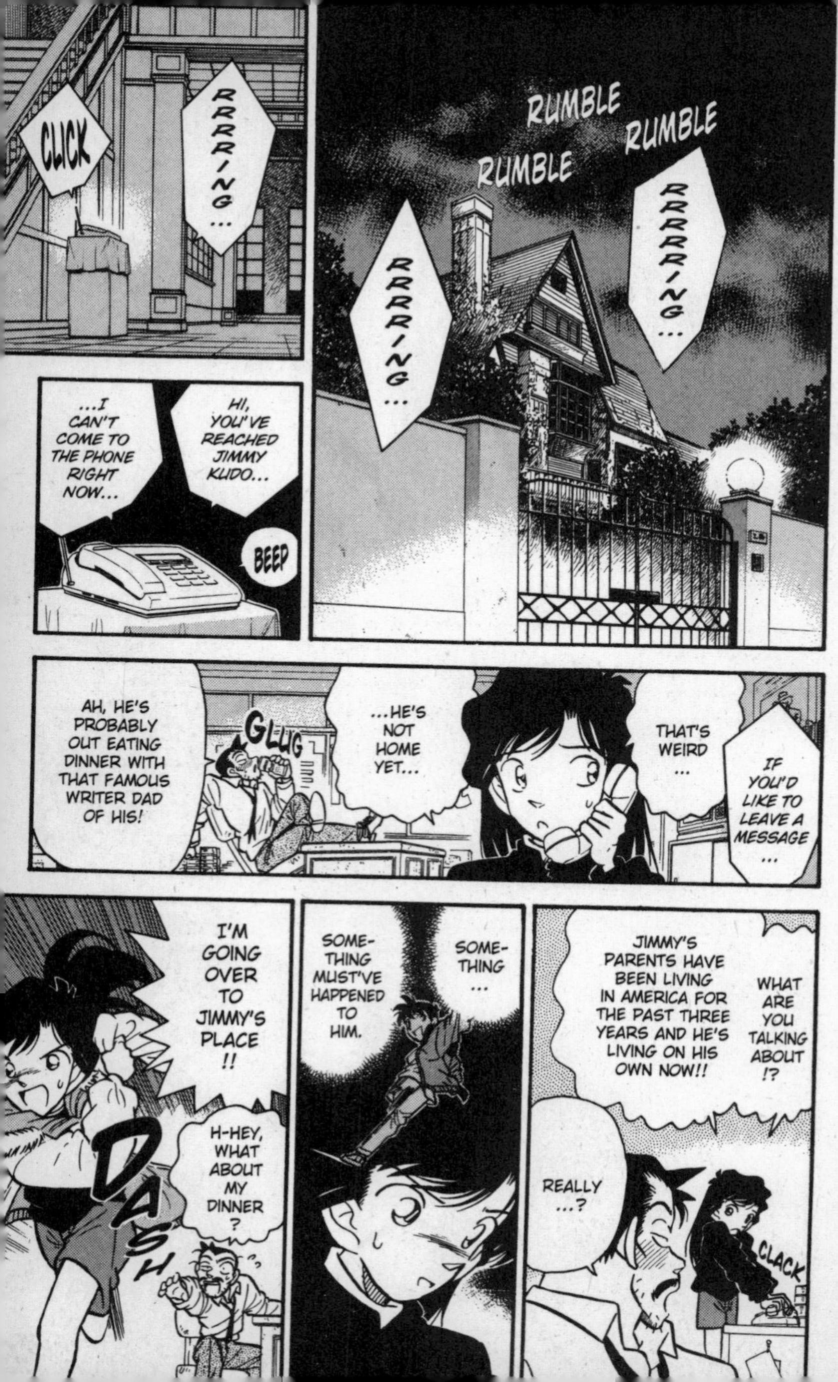
RUMBLE
RUMBLE
RUMBLE
RRRRRING...
RRRRING...
RRRRING...
CLICK
HI, YOU'VE REACHED JIMMY KUDO...
...I CAN'T COME TO THE PHONE RIGHT NOW...
BEEP
IF YOU'D LIKE TO LEAVE A MESSAGE...
THAT'S WEIRD...
...HE'S NOT HOME YET...
GLUG
AH, HE'S PROBABLY OUT EATING DINNER WITH THAT FAMOUS WRITER DAD OF HIS!
WHAT ARE YOU TALKING ABOUT!?
JIMMY'S PARENTS HAVE BEEN LIVING IN AMERICA FOR THE PAST THREE YEARS AND HE'S LIVING ON HIS OWN NOW!!
REALLY...?
CLACK
SOME-THING...
SOME-THING MUST'VE HAPPENED TO HIM.
I'M GOING OVER TO JIMMY'S PLACE!!
DASH
H-HEY, WHAT ABOUT MY DINNER?

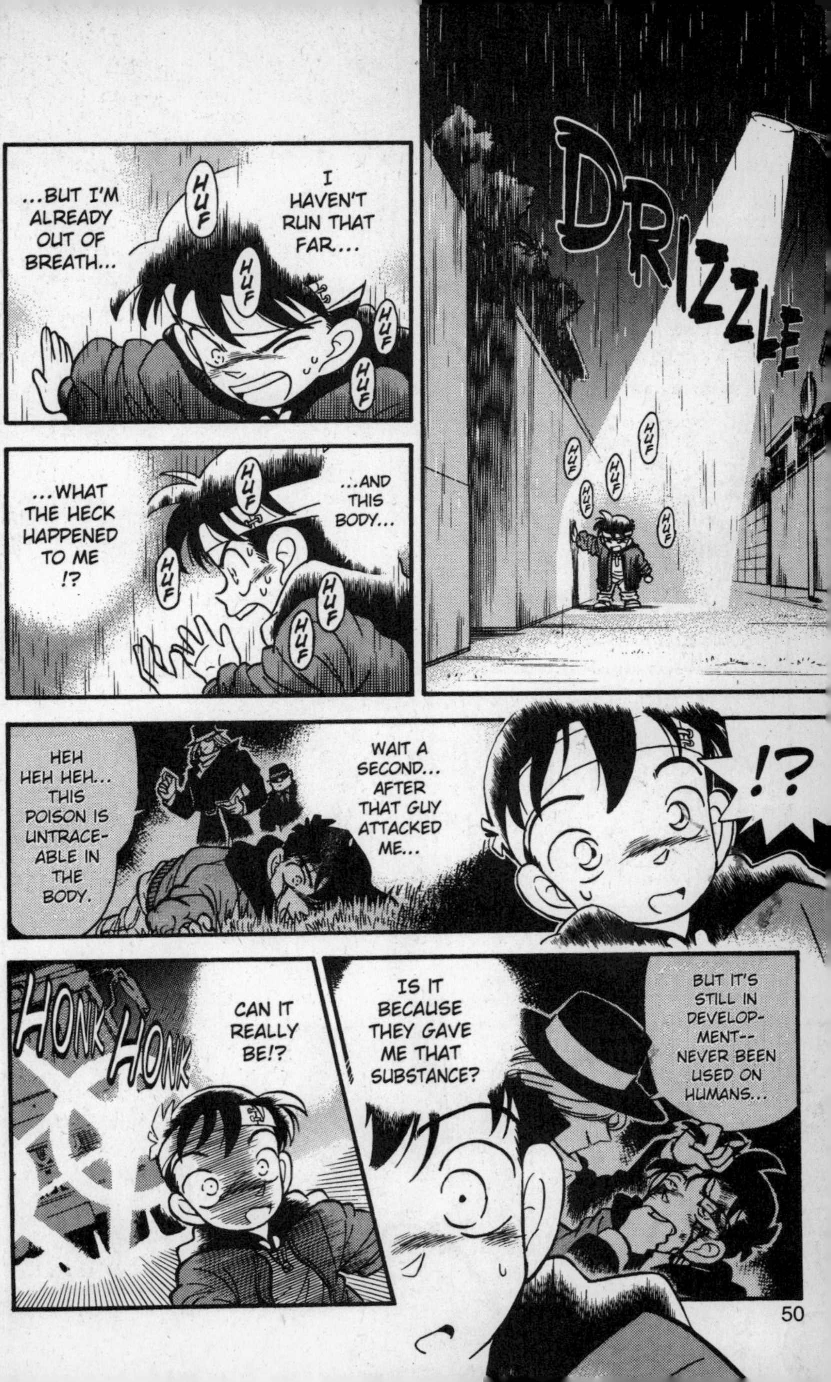
DRIZZLE
HUF HUF HUF HUF HUF HUF
I HAVEN'T RUN THAT FAR...
...BUT I'M ALREADY OUT OF BREATH...
HUF HUF HUF HUF
...AND THIS BODY...
...WHAT THE HECK HAPPENED TO ME !?
HUF HUF HUF
!?
WAIT A SECOND... AFTER THAT GUY ATTACKED ME...
HEH HEH HEH... THIS POISON IS UNTRACE-ABLE IN THE BODY.
BUT IT'S STILL IN DEVELOP-MENT-- NEVER BEEN USED ON HUMANS...
IS IT BECAUSE THEY GAVE ME THAT SUBSTANCE?
CAN IT REALLY BE!?
HONK HONK

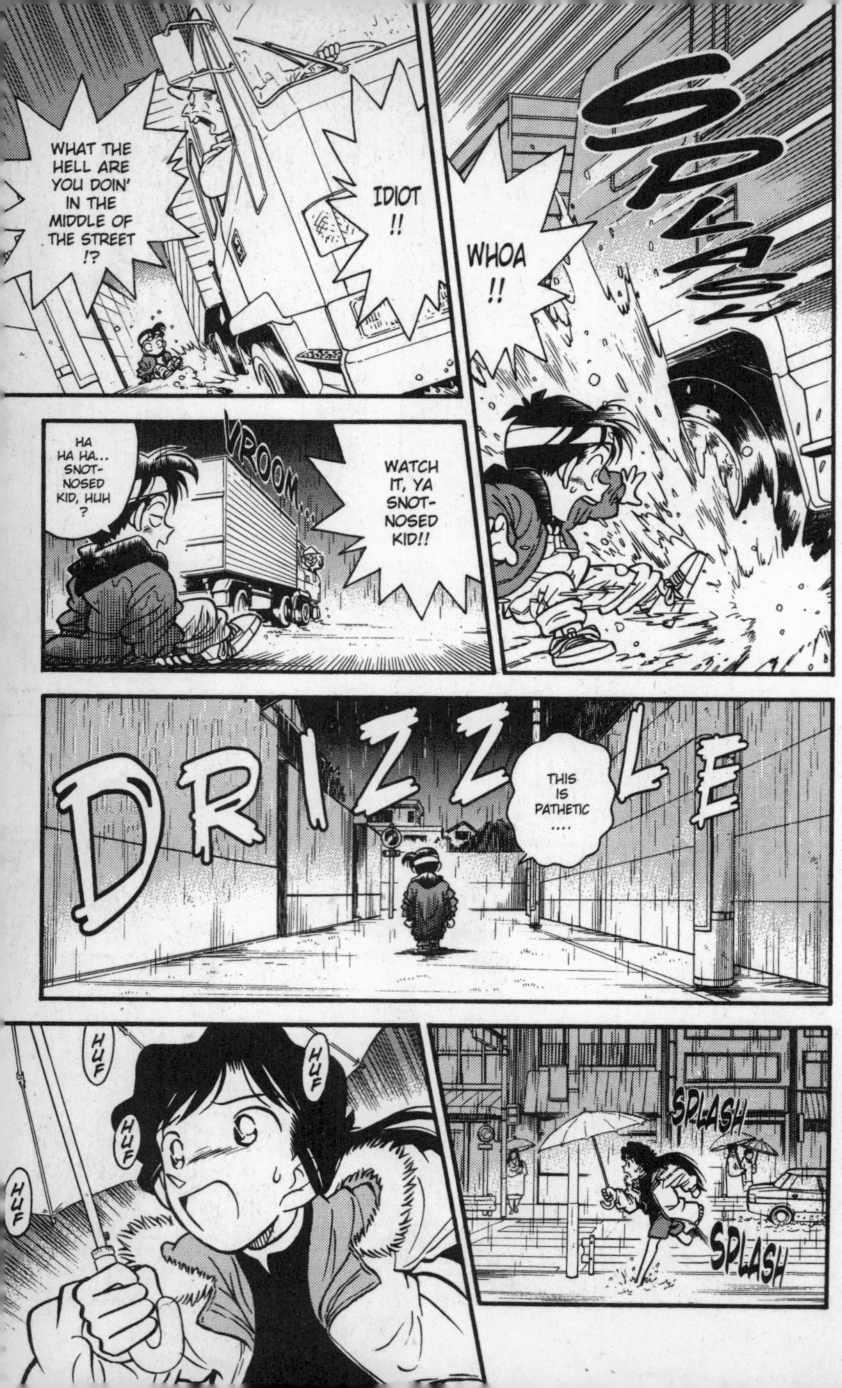
SPLASH!!
WHOA !!
IDIOT !!
WHAT THE HELL ARE YOU DOIN' IN THE MIDDLE OF THE STREET !?
WATCH IT, YA SNOT-NOSED KID!!
VROOM...
HA HA HA... SNOT-NOSED KID, HUH ?
DRIZZLE
THIS IS PATHETIC ....
SPLASH
SPLASH
HUF
HUF
HUF
HUF

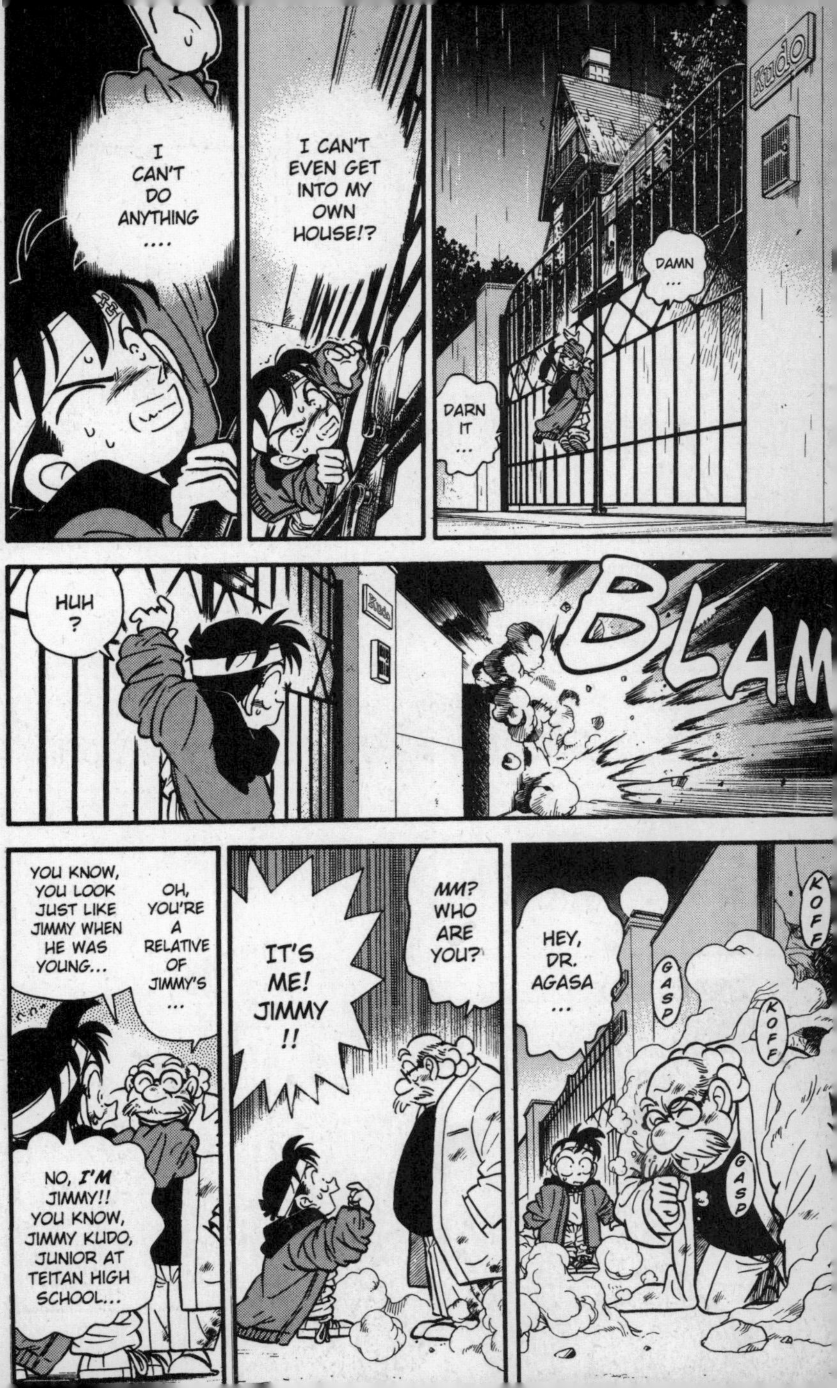
DAMN ...
DARN IT ...
I CAN'T EVEN GET INTO MY OWN HOUSE!?
I CAN'T DO ANYTHING ....
BLAM
HUH ?
KOFF
HEY, DR. AGASA ...
GASP
KOFF
GASP
MM? WHO ARE YOU?
IT'S ME! JIMMY !!
OH, YOU'RE A RELATIVE OF JIMMY'S ...
YOU KNOW, YOU LOOK JUST LIKE JIMMY WHEN HE WAS YOUNG...
NO, *I'M* JIMMY!! YOU KNOW, JIMMY KUDO, JUNIOR AT TEITAN HIGH SCHOOL...

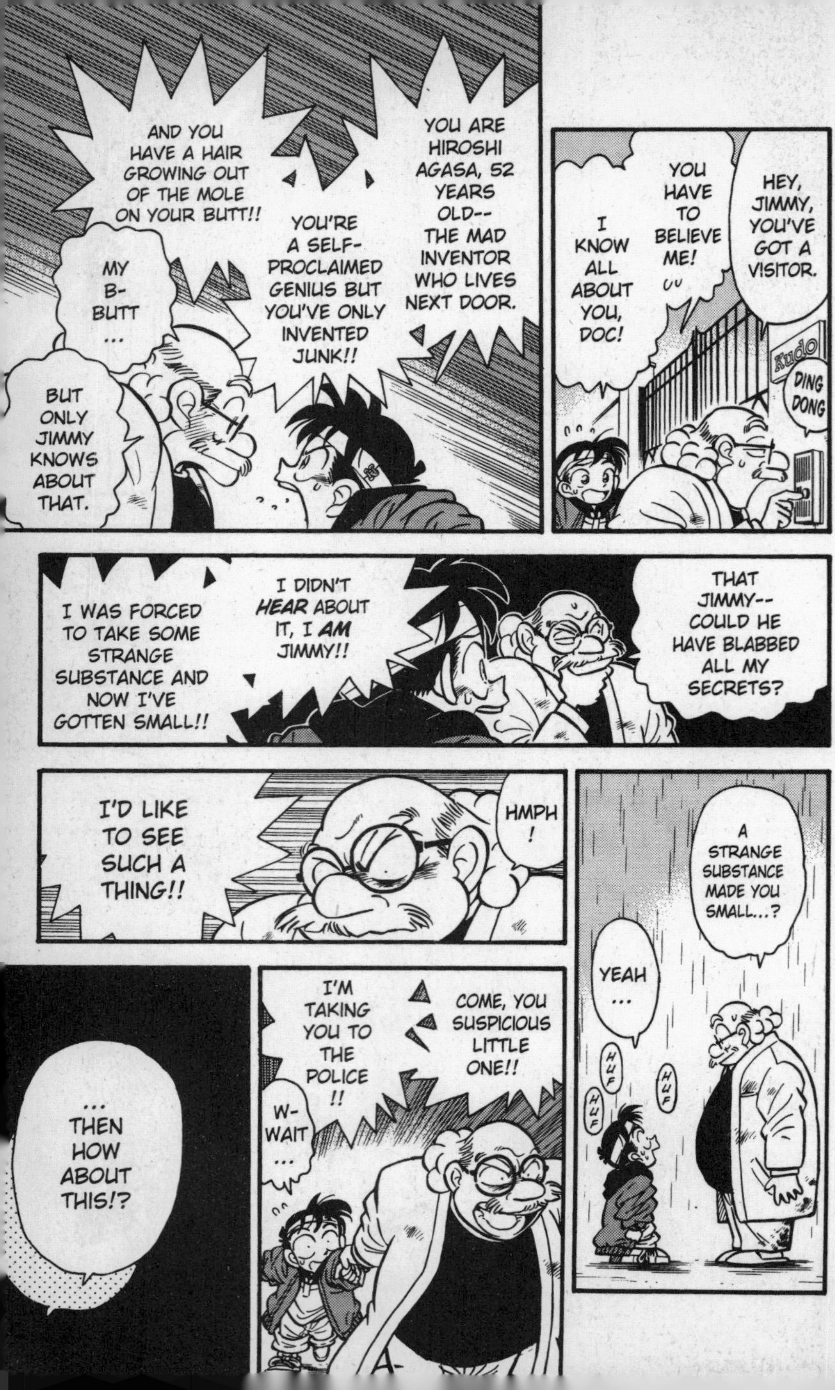
HEY, JIMMY, YOU'VE GOT A VISITOR.
Kudo
DING DONG
YOU HAVE TO BELIEVE ME!
I KNOW ALL ABOUT YOU, DOC!
YOU ARE HIROSHI AGASA, 52 YEARS OLD-- THE MAD INVENTOR WHO LIVES NEXT DOOR.
YOU'RE A SELF-PROCLAIMED GENIUS BUT YOU'VE ONLY INVENTED JUNK!!
AND YOU HAVE A HAIR GROWING OUT OF THE MOLE ON YOUR BUTT!!
MY B-BUTT ...
BUT ONLY JIMMY KNOWS ABOUT THAT.
THAT JIMMY-- COULD HE HAVE BLABBED ALL MY SECRETS?
I DIDN'T **HEAR** ABOUT IT, I **AM** JIMMY!!
I WAS FORCED TO TAKE SOME STRANGE SUBSTANCE AND NOW I'VE GOTTEN SMALL!!
A STRANGE SUBSTANCE MADE YOU SMALL...?
YEAH ...
HUF
HUF
HUF
HMPH !
I'D LIKE TO SEE SUCH A THING!!
COME, YOU SUSPICIOUS LITTLE ONE!!
I'M TAKING YOU TO THE POLICE !!
W-WAIT ...
... THEN HOW ABOUT THIS!?

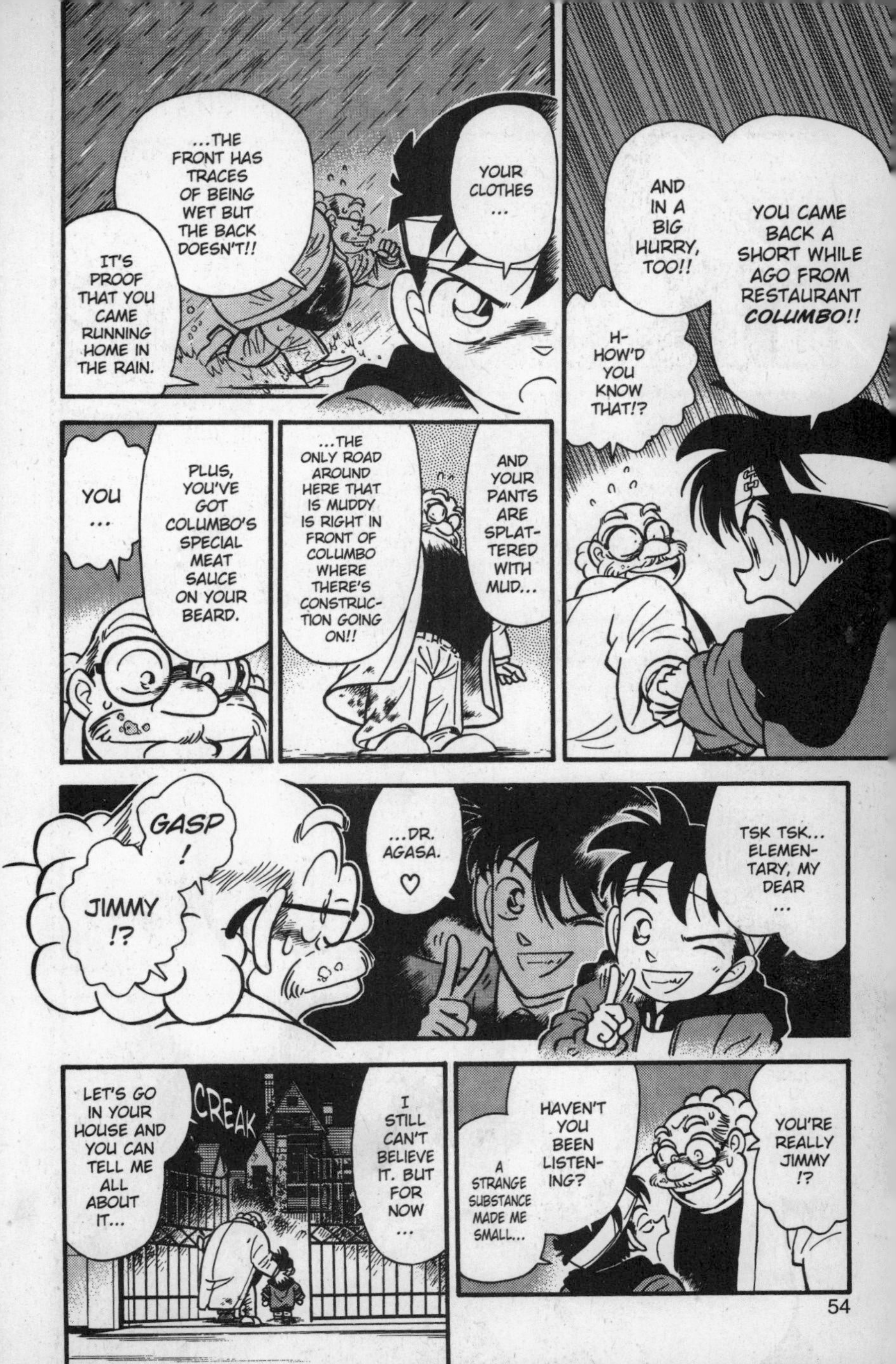
YOU CAME BACK A SHORT WHILE AGO FROM RESTAURANT *COLUMBO*!!
AND IN A BIG HURRY, TOO!!
H-HOW'D YOU KNOW THAT!?
YOUR CLOTHES ...
...THE FRONT HAS TRACES OF BEING WET BUT THE BACK DOESN'T!!
IT'S PROOF THAT YOU CAME RUNNING HOME IN THE RAIN.
AND YOUR PANTS ARE SPLATTERED WITH MUD...
...THE ONLY ROAD AROUND HERE THAT IS MUDDY IS RIGHT IN FRONT OF COLUMBO WHERE THERE'S CONSTRUCTION GOING ON!!
PLUS, YOU'VE GOT COLUMBO'S SPECIAL MEAT SAUCE ON YOUR BEARD.
YOU ...
TSK TSK... ELEMENTARY, MY DEAR ...
...DR. AGASA. ♡
GASP!
JIMMY!?
YOU'RE REALLY JIMMY!?
HAVEN'T YOU BEEN LISTENING?
A STRANGE SUBSTANCE MADE ME SMALL...
I STILL CAN'T BELIEVE IT. BUT FOR NOW ...
LET'S GO IN YOUR HOUSE AND YOU CAN TELL ME ALL ABOUT IT...
CREAK

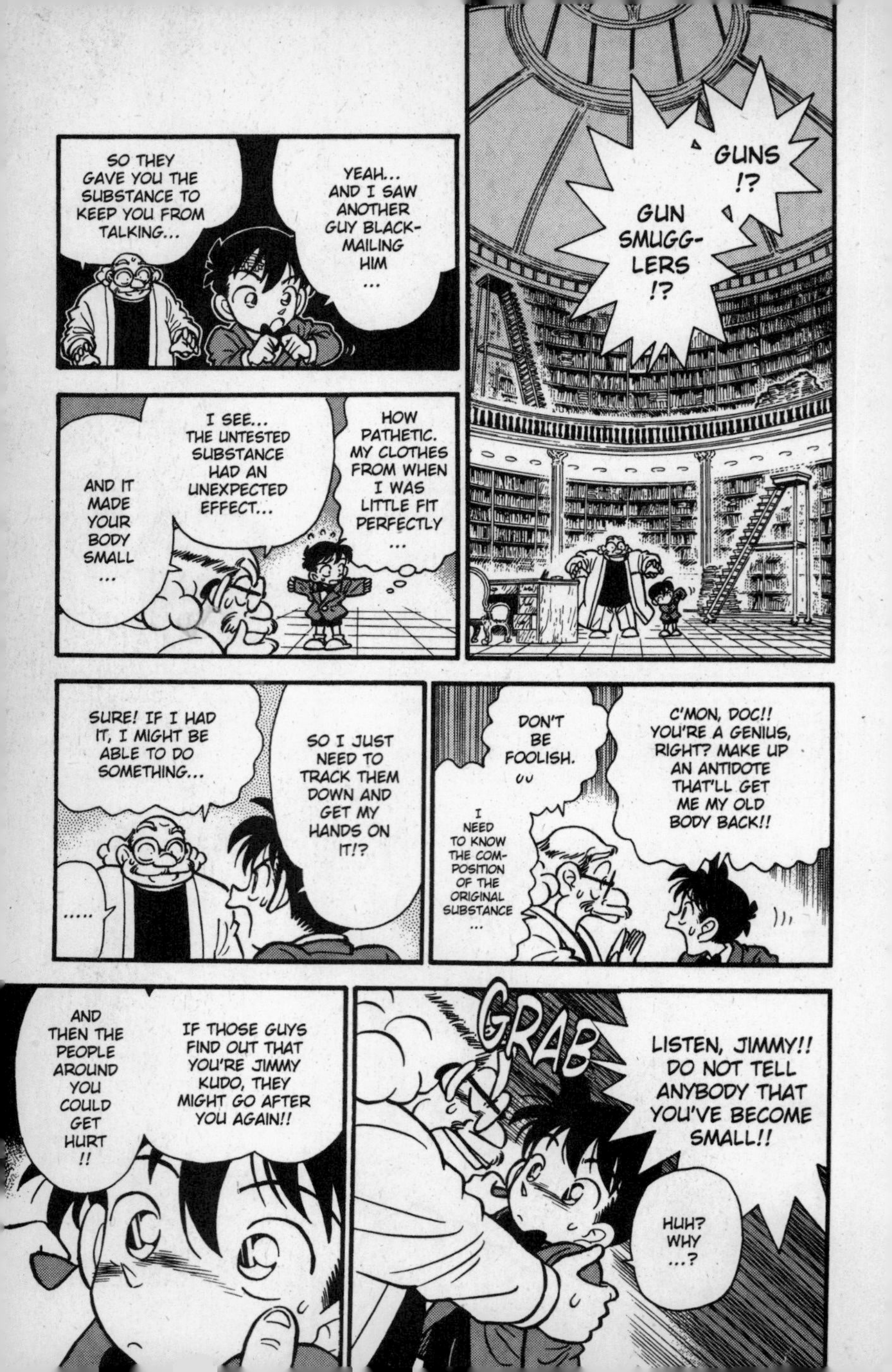
GUNS !?
GUN SMUGGLERS !?
YEAH... AND I SAW ANOTHER GUY BLACKMAILING HIM ...
SO THEY GAVE YOU THE SUBSTANCE TO KEEP YOU FROM TALKING...
HOW PATHETIC. MY CLOTHES FROM WHEN I WAS LITTLE FIT PERFECTLY ...
I SEE... THE UNTESTED SUBSTANCE HAD AN UNEXPECTED EFFECT...
AND IT MADE YOUR BODY SMALL ...
C'MON, DOC!! YOU'RE A GENIUS, RIGHT? MAKE UP AN ANTIDOTE THAT'LL GET ME MY OLD BODY BACK!!
DON'T BE FOOLISH.
I NEED TO KNOW THE COMPOSITION OF THE ORIGINAL SUBSTANCE ...
SO I JUST NEED TO TRACK THEM DOWN AND GET MY HANDS ON IT!?
SURE! IF I HAD IT, I MIGHT BE ABLE TO DO SOMETHING...
.....
GRAB
LISTEN, JIMMY!! DO NOT TELL ANYBODY THAT YOU'VE BECOME SMALL!!
HUH? WHY ...?
IF THOSE GUYS FIND OUT THAT YOU'RE JIMMY KUDO, THEY MIGHT GO AFTER YOU AGAIN!!
AND THEN THE PEOPLE AROUND YOU COULD GET HURT !!

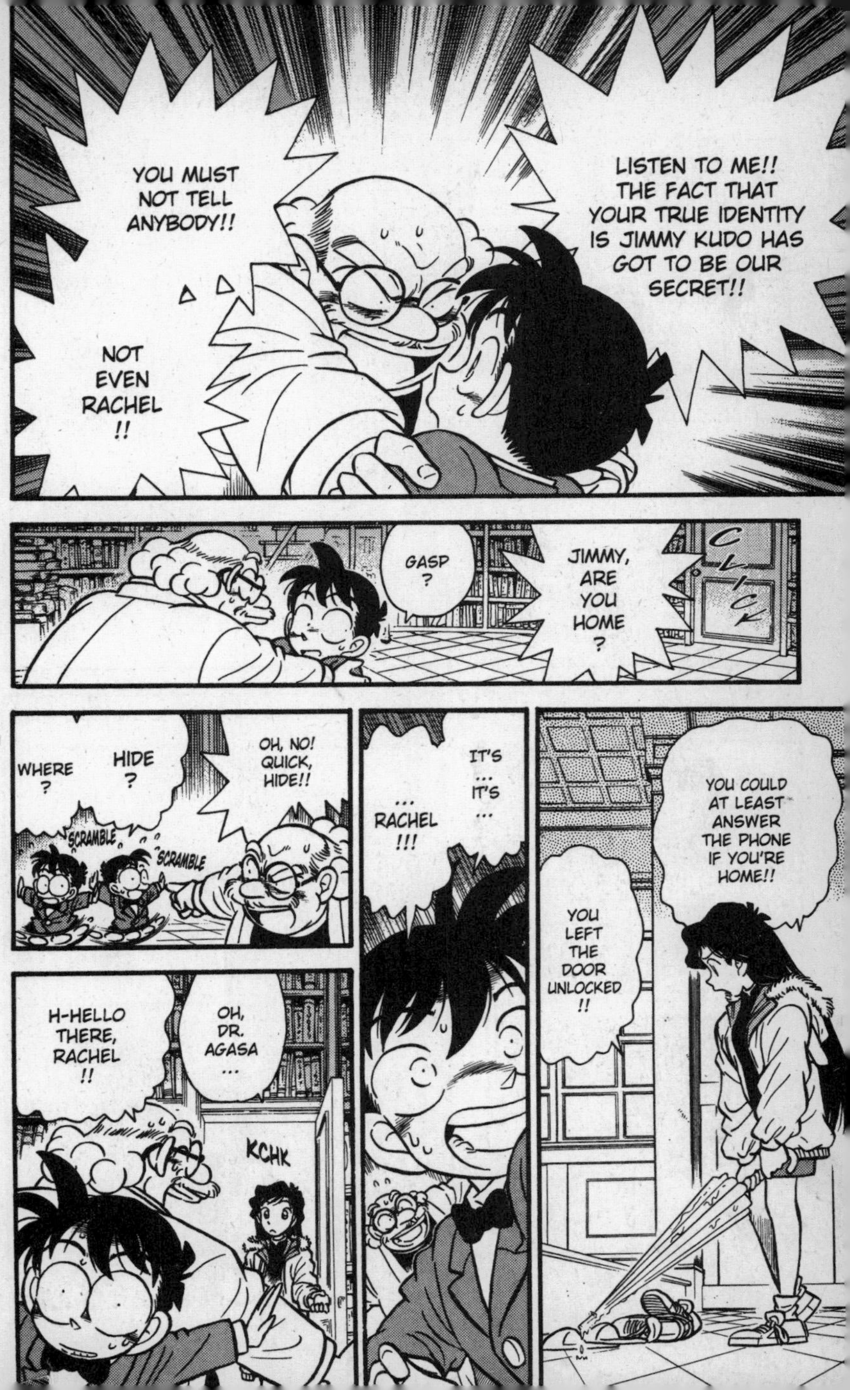
LISTEN TO ME!! THE FACT THAT YOUR TRUE IDENTITY IS JIMMY KUDO HAS GOT TO BE OUR SECRET!!
YOU MUST NOT TELL ANYBODY!!
NOT EVEN RACHEL !!
CLICK
JIMMY, ARE YOU HOME ?
GASP ?
YOU COULD AT LEAST ANSWER THE PHONE IF YOU'RE HOME!!
YOU LEFT THE DOOR UNLOCKED !!
IT'S ... IT'S ...
... RACHEL !!!
OH, NO! QUICK, HIDE!!
HIDE ?
WHERE ?
SCRAMBLE
SCRAMBLE
OH, DR. AGASA ...
H-HELLO THERE, RACHEL !!
KCHK

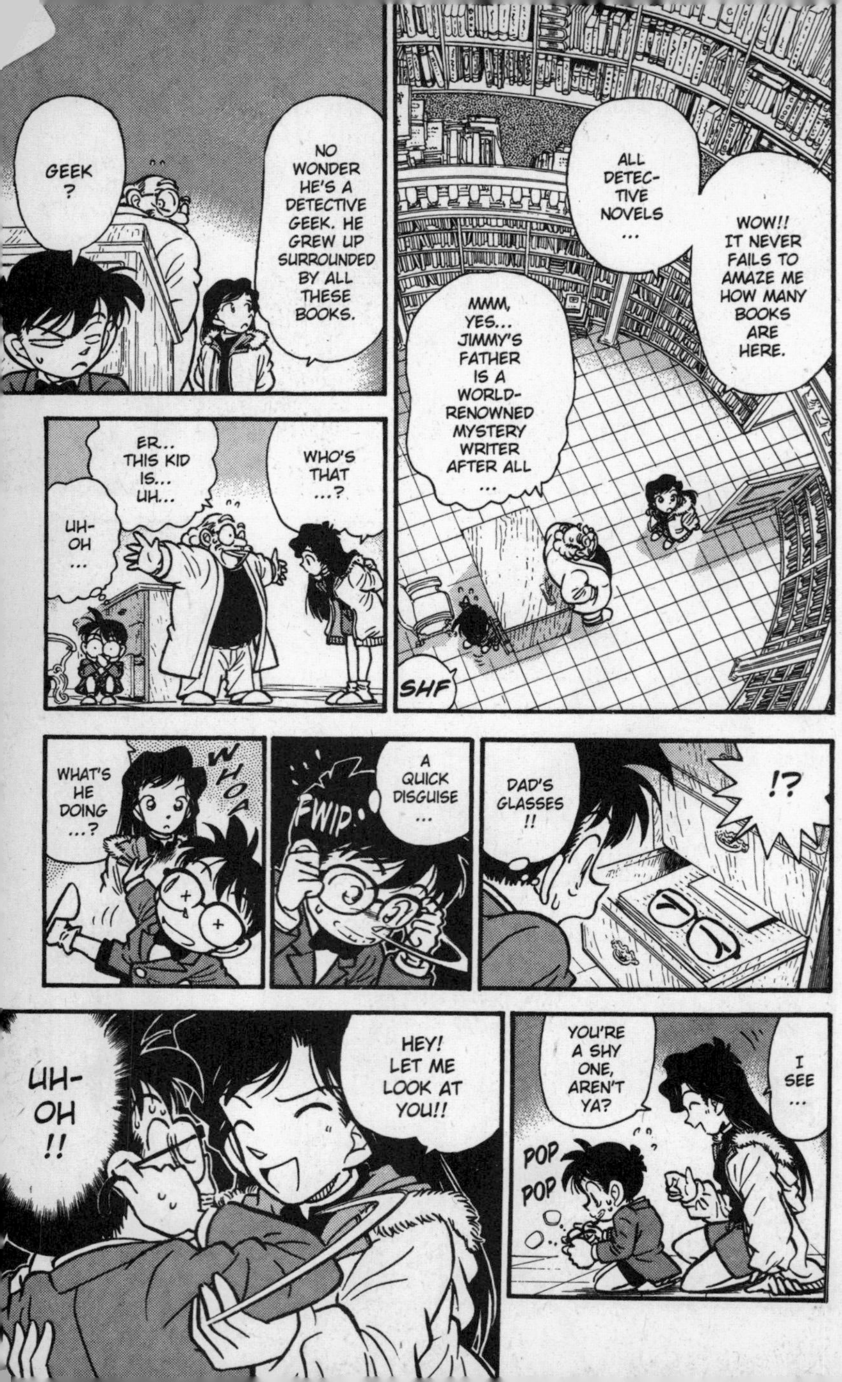
WOW!! IT NEVER FAILS TO AMAZE ME HOW MANY BOOKS ARE HERE.
ALL DETECTIVE NOVELS...
MMM, YES... JIMMY'S FATHER IS A WORLD-RENOWNED MYSTERY WRITER AFTER ALL...
SHF
NO WONDER HE'S A DETECTIVE GEEK. HE GREW UP SURROUNDED BY ALL THESE BOOKS.
GEEK?
WHO'S THAT...?
ER... THIS KID IS... UH...
UH-OH...
!?
DAD'S GLASSES!!
A QUICK DISGUISE...
FWIP
WHAT'S HE DOING...?
WHOA
I SEE...
YOU'RE A SHY ONE, AREN'T YA?
POP
POP
HEY! LET ME LOOK AT YOU!!
UH-OH!!

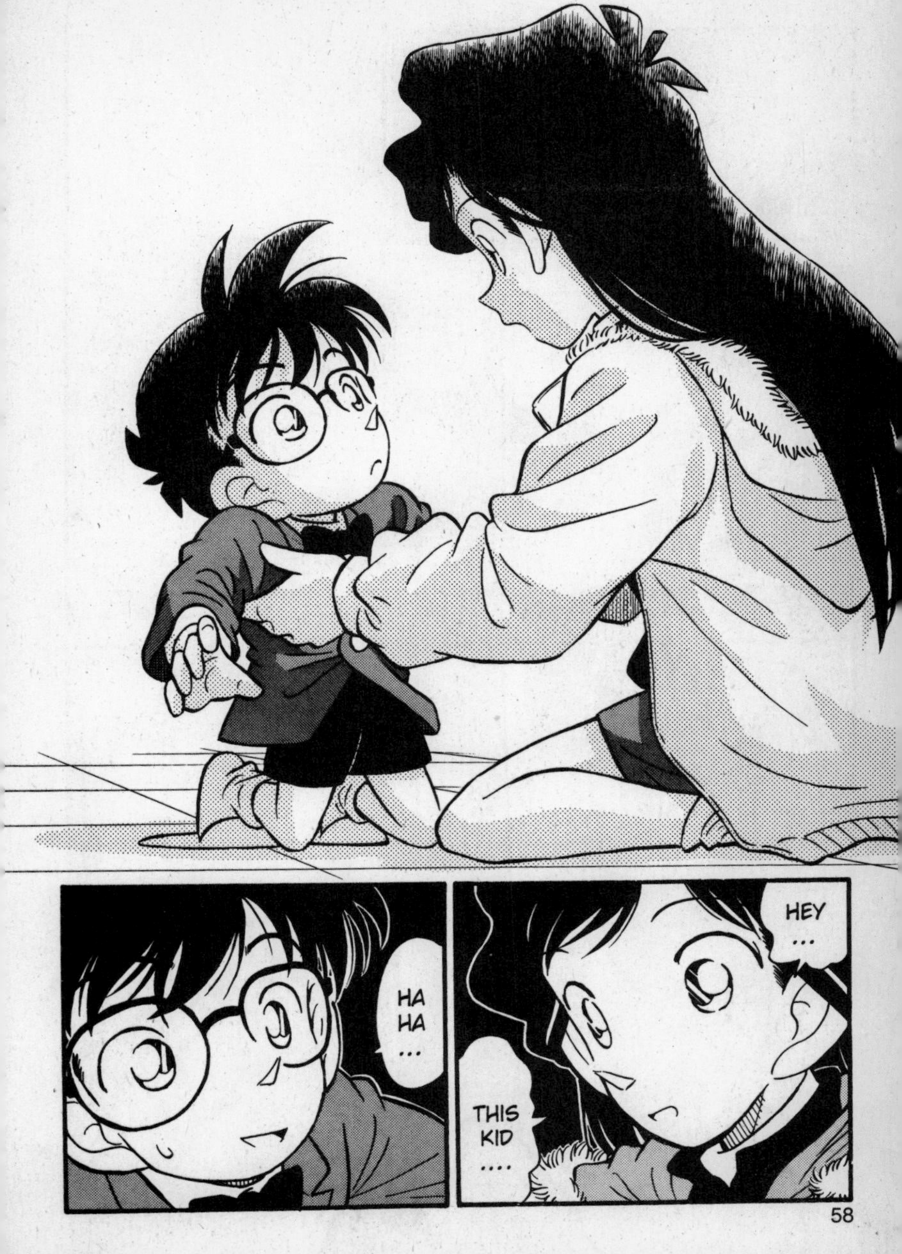
HEY ...
THIS KID ....
HA HA ...

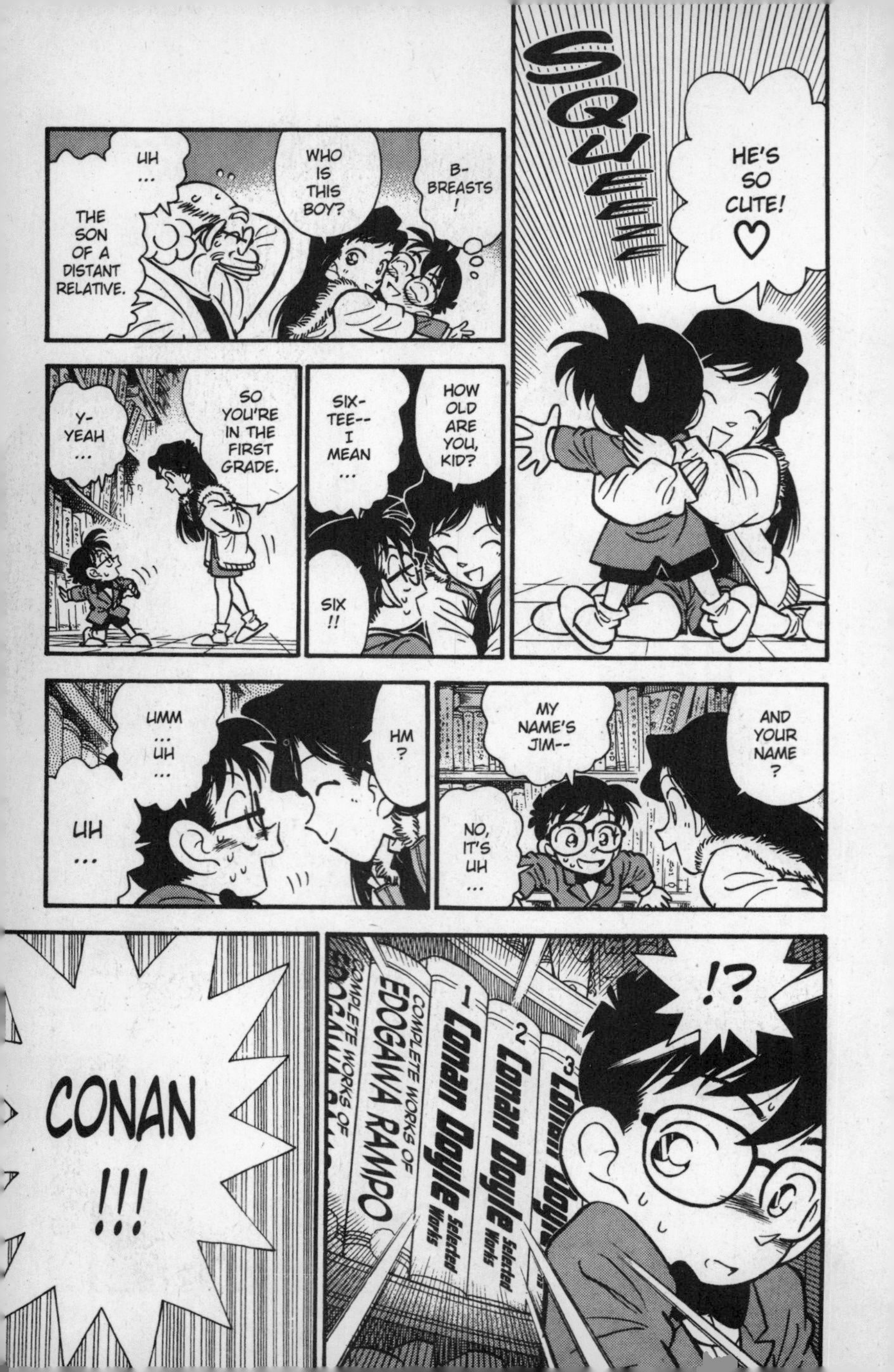
SQUEEEE
HE'S SO CUTE! ♥
B-BREASTS!
WHO IS THIS BOY?
UH ...
THE SON OF A DISTANT RELATIVE.
HOW OLD ARE YOU, KID?
SIX-TEE-- I MEAN ...
SIX!!
SO YOU'RE IN THE FIRST GRADE.
Y-YEAH ...
AND YOUR NAME?
MY NAME'S JIM--
NO, IT'S UH ...
HM?
UMM ... UH ...
UH ...
!?
1 Conan Doyle Selected Works
2 Conan Doyle Selected Works
3
COMPLETE WORKS OF EDOGAWA RAMPO
COMPLETE WORKS OF
CONAN!!!

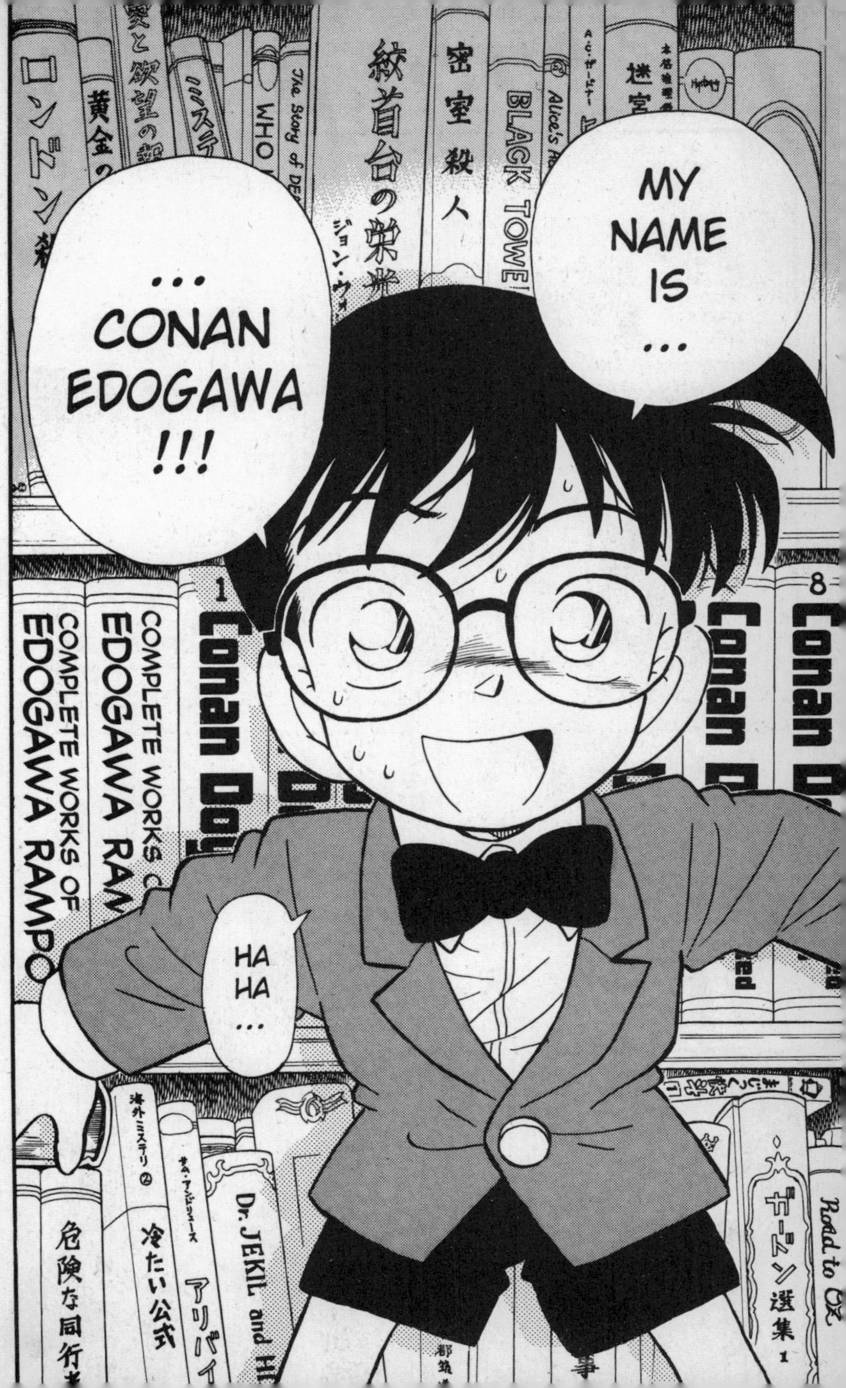
MY NAME IS ...
... CONAN EDOGAWA !!!
HA HA ...
COMPLETE WORKS OF EDOGAWA RAMPO

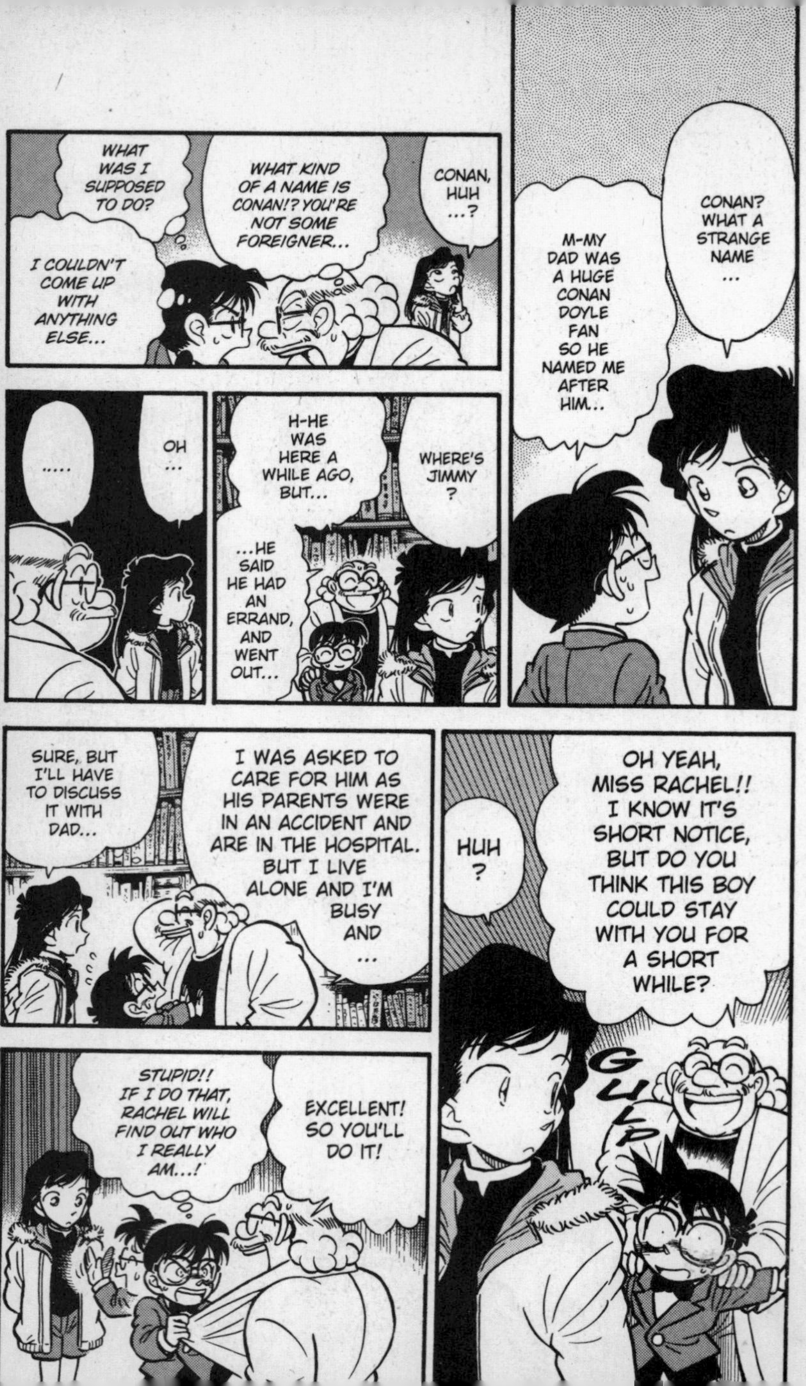
CONAN? WHAT A STRANGE NAME ...
M-MY DAD WAS A HUGE CONAN DOYLE FAN SO HE NAMED ME AFTER HIM...
CONAN, HUH ...?
WHAT KIND OF A NAME IS CONAN!? YOU'RE NOT SOME FOREIGNER...
WHAT WAS I SUPPOSED TO DO?
I COULDN'T COME UP WITH ANYTHING ELSE...
WHERE'S JIMMY?
H-HE WAS HERE A WHILE AGO, BUT...
...HE SAID HE HAD AN ERRAND, AND WENT OUT...
OH ...
.....
OH YEAH, MISS RACHEL!! I KNOW IT'S SHORT NOTICE, BUT DO YOU THINK THIS BOY COULD STAY WITH YOU FOR A SHORT WHILE?
HUH ?
GULP
I WAS ASKED TO CARE FOR HIM AS HIS PARENTS WERE IN AN ACCIDENT AND ARE IN THE HOSPITAL. BUT I LIVE ALONE AND I'M BUSY AND ...
SURE, BUT I'LL HAVE TO DISCUSS IT WITH DAD...
EXCELLENT! SO YOU'LL DO IT!
STUPID!! IF I DO THAT, RACHEL WILL FIND OUT WHO I REALLY AM...!

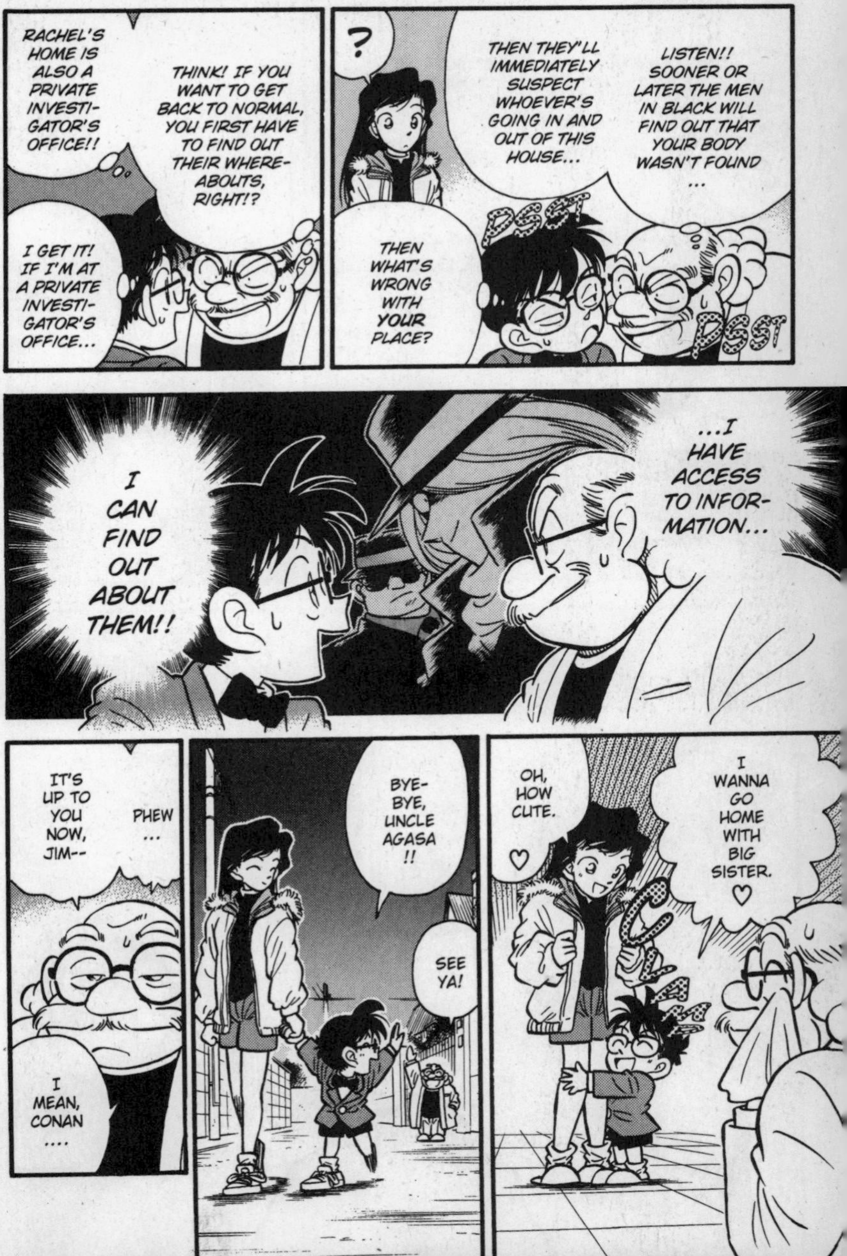
?
THEN WHAT'S WRONG WITH YOUR PLACE?
LISTEN!! SOONER OR LATER THE MEN IN BLACK WILL FIND OUT THAT YOUR BODY WASN'T FOUND...
THEN THEY'LL IMMEDIATELY SUSPECT WHOEVER'S GOING IN AND OUT OF THIS HOUSE...
PSST
PSST
THINK! IF YOU WANT TO GET BACK TO NORMAL, YOU FIRST HAVE TO FIND OUT THEIR WHERE-ABOUTS, RIGHT!?
RACHEL'S HOME IS ALSO A PRIVATE INVESTI-GATOR'S OFFICE!!
I GET IT! IF I'M AT A PRIVATE INVESTI-GATOR'S OFFICE...
...I HAVE ACCESS TO INFOR-MATION...
I CAN FIND OUT ABOUT THEM!!
I WANNA GO HOME WITH BIG SISTER. ♥
OH, HOW CUTE. ♥
BYE-BYE, UNCLE AGASA!!
SEE YA!
PHEW...
IT'S UP TO YOU NOW, JIM--
I MEAN, CONAN....

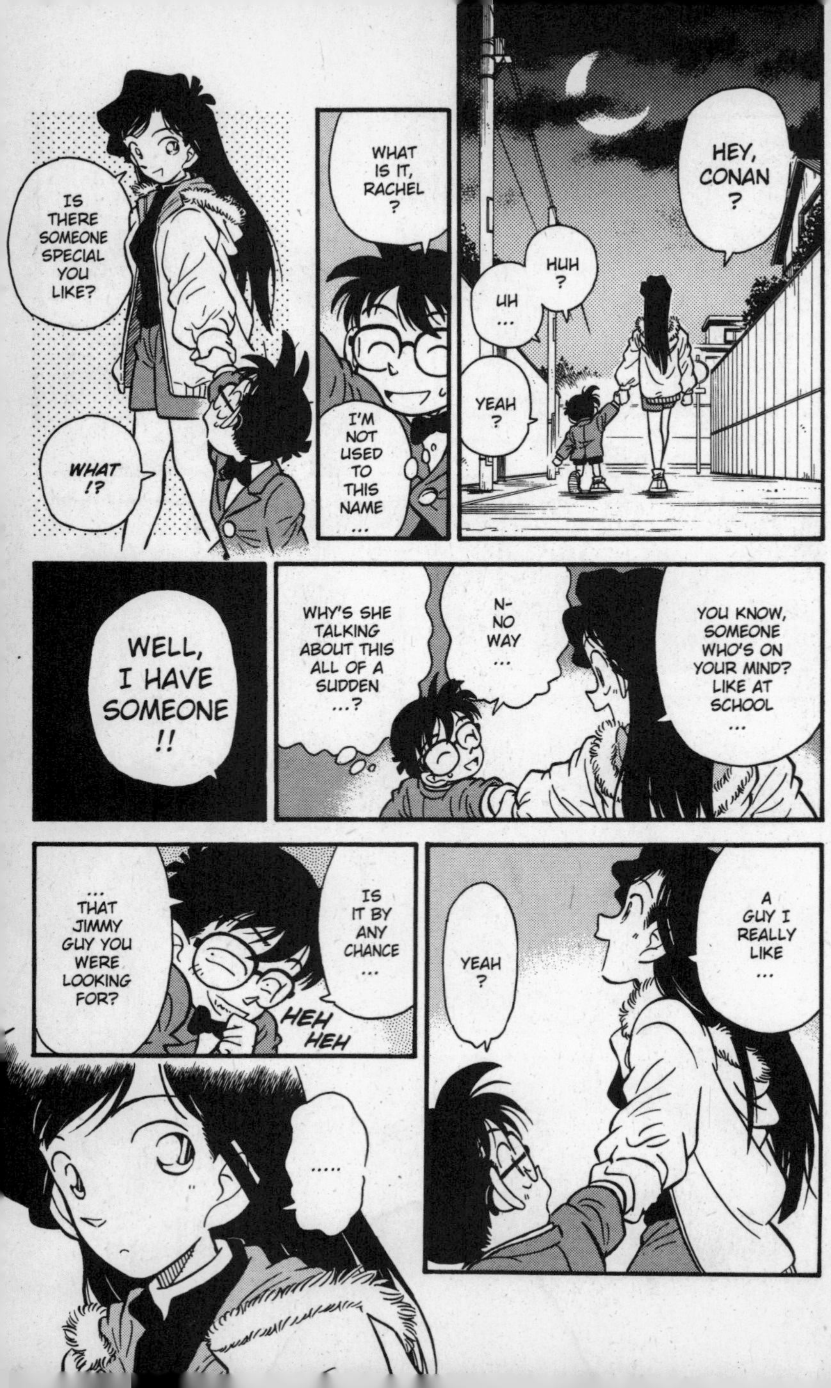
HEY, CONAN ?
HUH ?
UH ...
YEAH ?
WHAT IS IT, RACHEL ?
I'M NOT USED TO THIS NAME ...
IS THERE SOMEONE SPECIAL YOU LIKE?
WHAT !?
YOU KNOW, SOMEONE WHO'S ON YOUR MIND? LIKE AT SCHOOL ...
N- NO WAY ...
WHY'S SHE TALKING ABOUT THIS ALL OF A SUDDEN ...?
WELL, I HAVE SOMEONE !!
A GUY I REALLY LIKE ...
YEAH ?
IS IT BY ANY CHANCE ...
... THAT JIMMY GUY YOU WERE LOOKING FOR?
HEH HEH
......

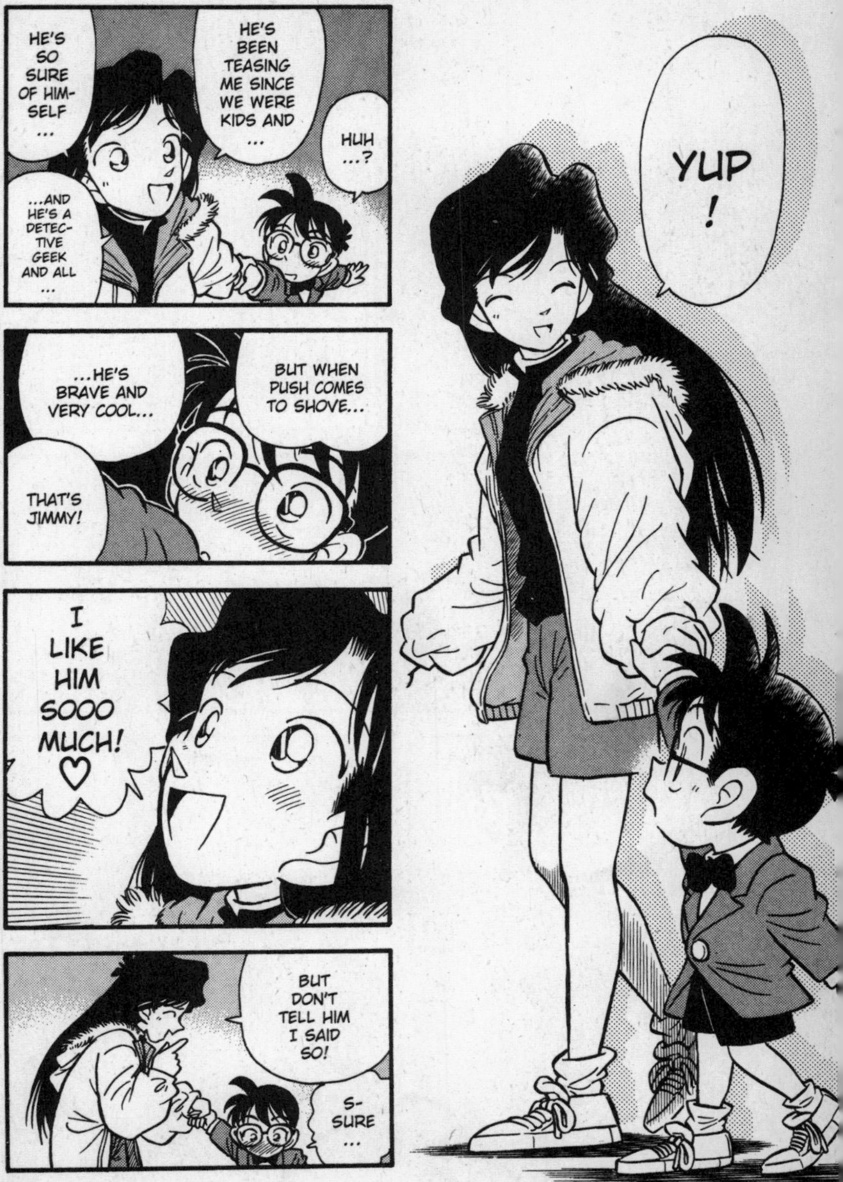
YUP!
HUH ...?
HE'S BEEN TEASING ME SINCE WE WERE KIDS AND ...
HE'S SO SURE OF HIM-SELF ...
...AND HE'S A DETEC-TIVE GEEK AND ALL ...
BUT WHEN PUSH COMES TO SHOVE...
...HE'S BRAVE AND VERY COOL...
THAT'S JIMMY!
I LIKE HIM SOOO MUCH! ♡
BUT DON'T TELL HIM I SAID SO!
S-SURE ...

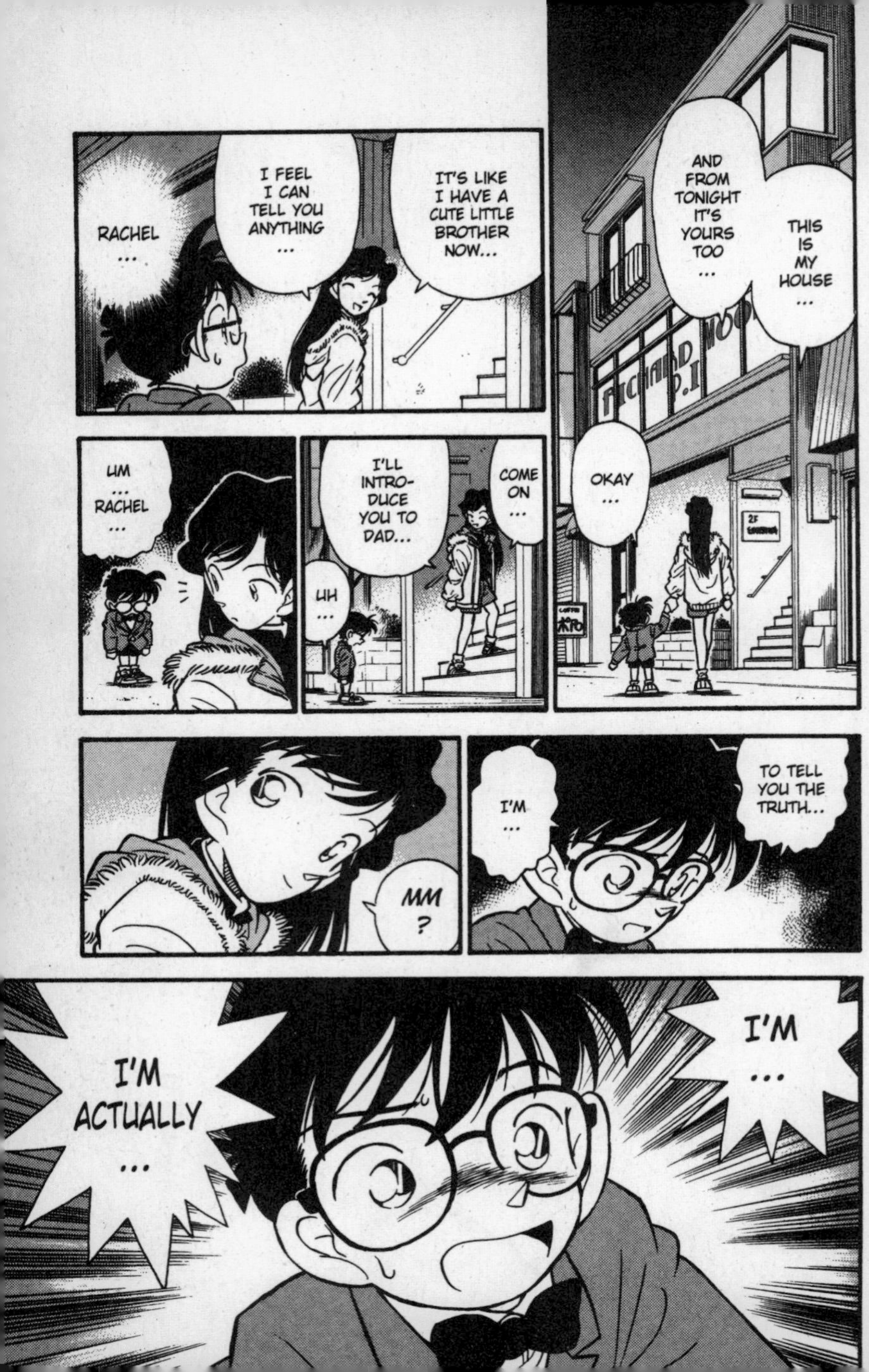

THIS IS MY HOUSE ...
AND FROM TONIGHT IT'S YOURS TOO ...
OKAY ...
IT'S LIKE I HAVE A CUTE LITTLE BROTHER NOW...
I FEEL I CAN TELL YOU ANYTHING ...
RACHEL ...
COME ON ...
I'LL INTRODUCE YOU TO DAD...
UH ...
UM ... RACHEL ...
TO TELL YOU THE TRUTH...
I'M ...
MM ?
I'M ...
I'M ACTUALLY ...

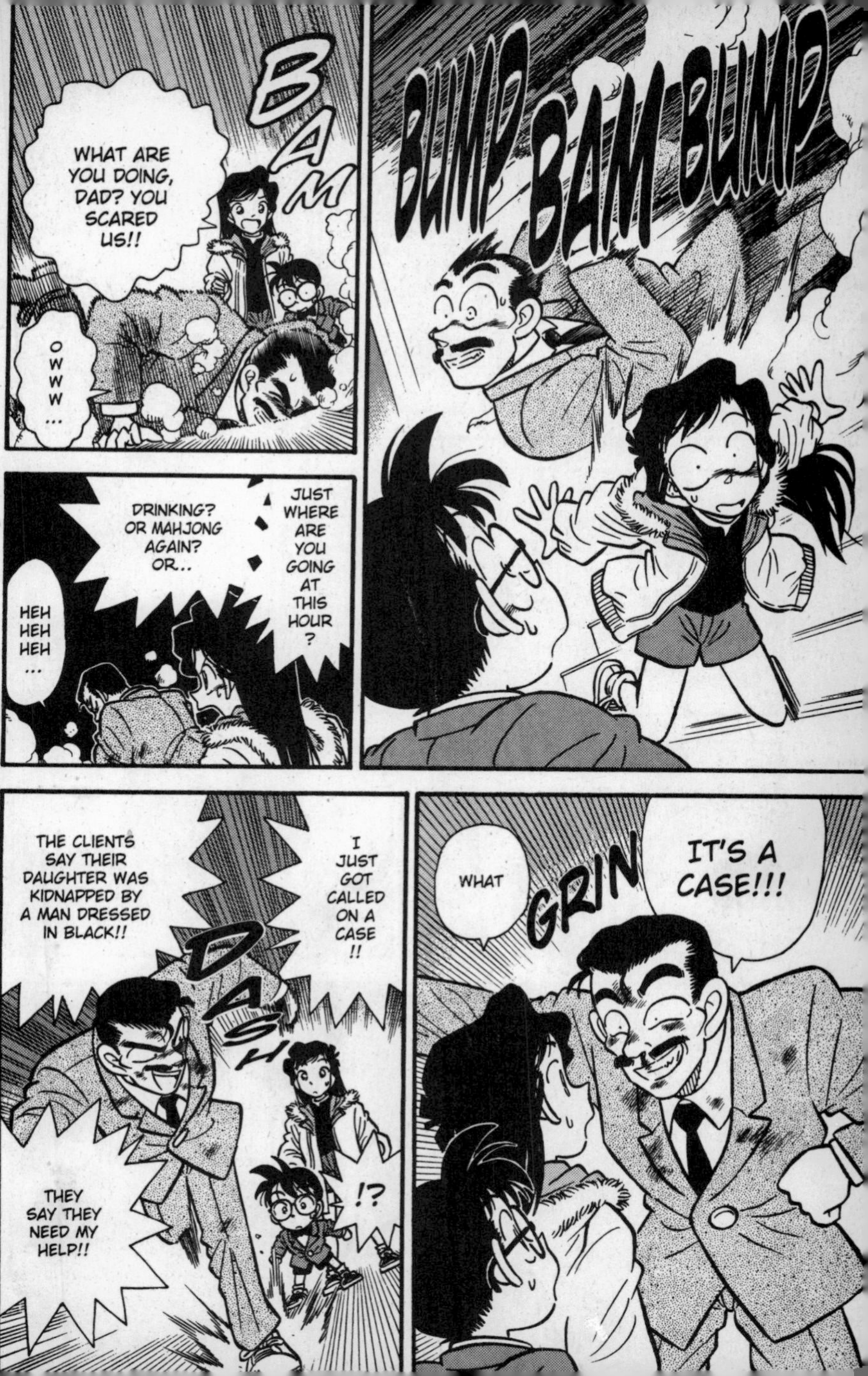
BUMP BAM BUMP
BAM
WHAT ARE YOU DOING, DAD? YOU SCARED US!!
OWWW...
JUST WHERE ARE YOU GOING AT THIS HOUR?
DRINKING? OR MAHJONG AGAIN? OR...
HEH HEH HEH...
IT'S A CASE!!!
GRIN
WHAT
I JUST GOT CALLED ON A CASE!!
THE CLIENTS SAY THEIR DAUGHTER WAS KIDNAPPED BY A MAN DRESSED IN BLACK!!
DASH
THEY SAY THEY NEED MY HELP!!
!?

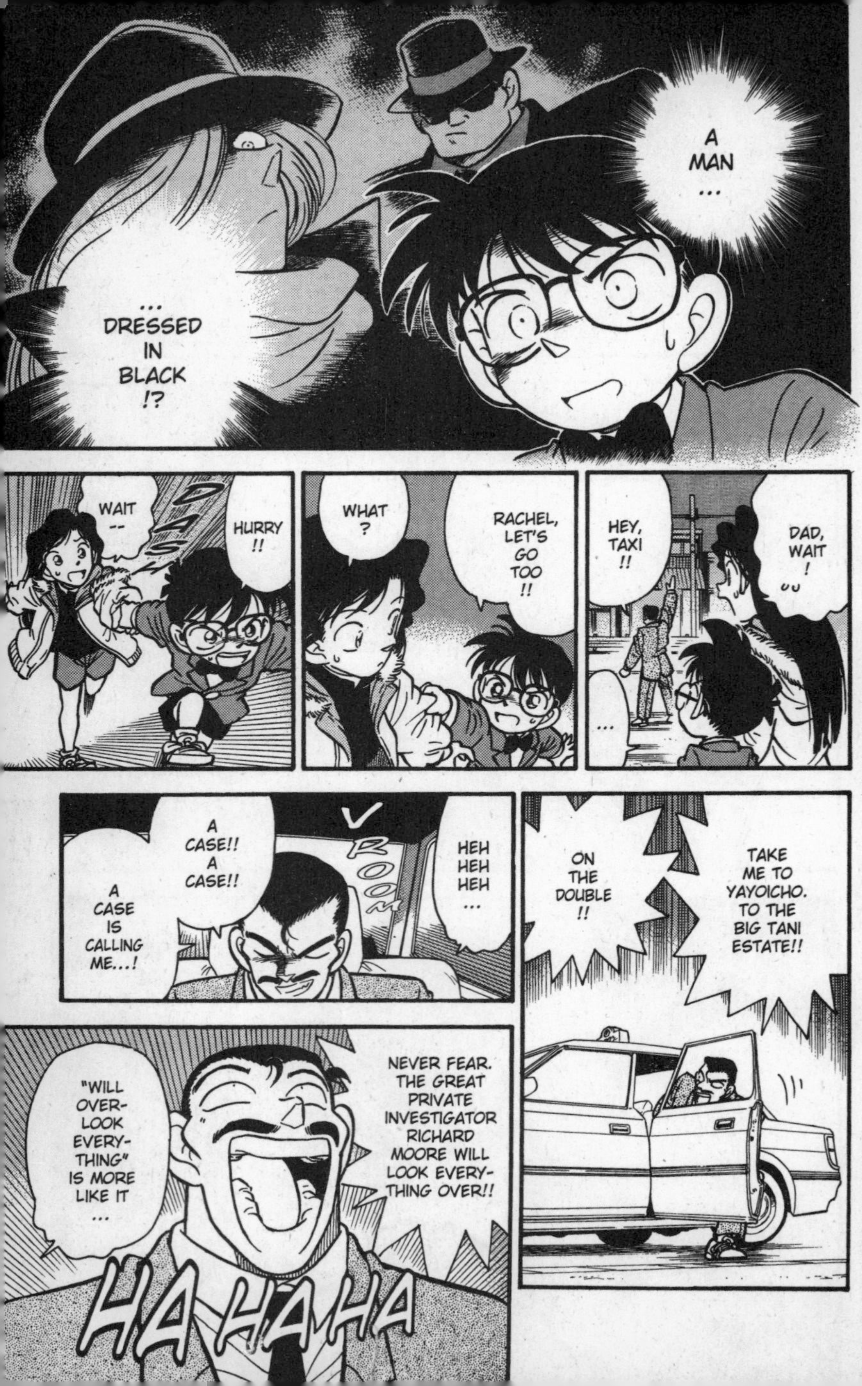
A MAN ...
... DRESSED IN BLACK !?
DAD, WAIT !
HEY, TAXI !!
...
RACHEL, LET'S GO TOO !!
WHAT ?
HURRY !!
WAIT --
TAKE ME TO YAYOICHO. TO THE BIG TANI ESTATE!!
ON THE DOUBLE !!
HEH HEH HEH ...
VROOM
A CASE!! A CASE!!
A CASE IS CALLING ME...!
NEVER FEAR. THE GREAT PRIVATE INVESTIGATOR RICHARD MOORE WILL LOOK EVERY-THING OVER!!
"WILL OVER-LOOK EVERY-THING" IS MORE LIKE IT ...
HA HA HA HA

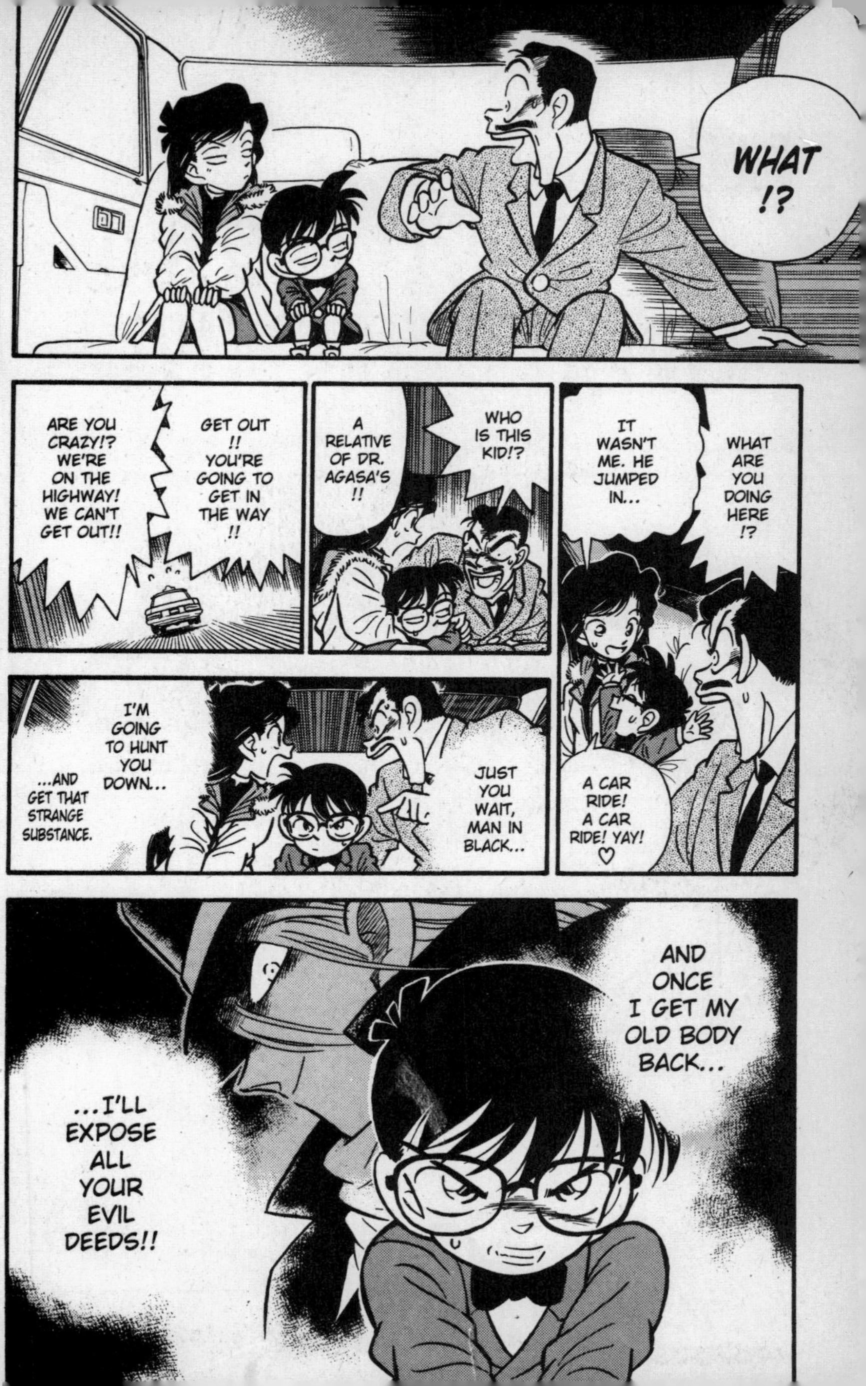
WHAT !?
WHAT ARE YOU DOING HERE !?
IT WASN'T ME. HE JUMPED IN...
A CAR RIDE! A CAR RIDE! YAY! ♡
WHO IS THIS KID!?
A RELATIVE OF DR. AGASA'S !!
GET OUT !! YOU'RE GOING TO GET IN THE WAY !!
ARE YOU CRAZY!? WE'RE ON THE HIGHWAY! WE CAN'T GET OUT!!
JUST YOU WAIT, MAN IN BLACK...
I'M GOING TO HUNT YOU DOWN...
...AND GET THAT STRANGE SUBSTANCE.
AND ONCE I GET MY OLD BODY BACK...
...I'LL EXPOSE ALL YOUR EVIL DEEDS!!

FILE 3:
THE UNWELCOME GREAT DETECTIVE

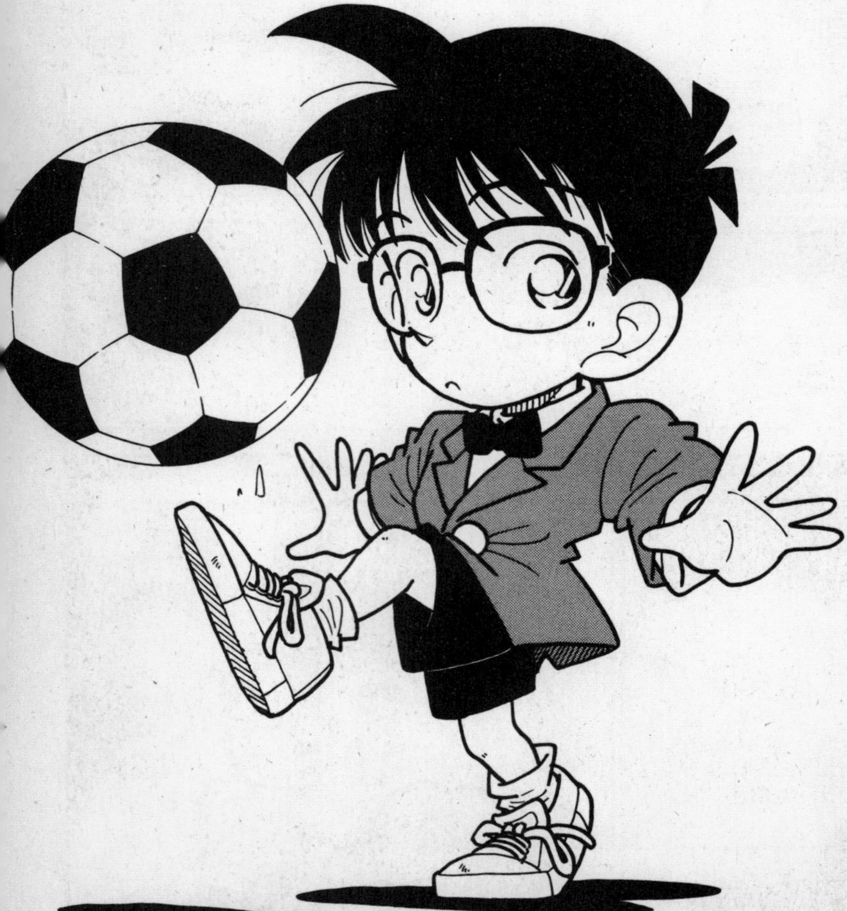

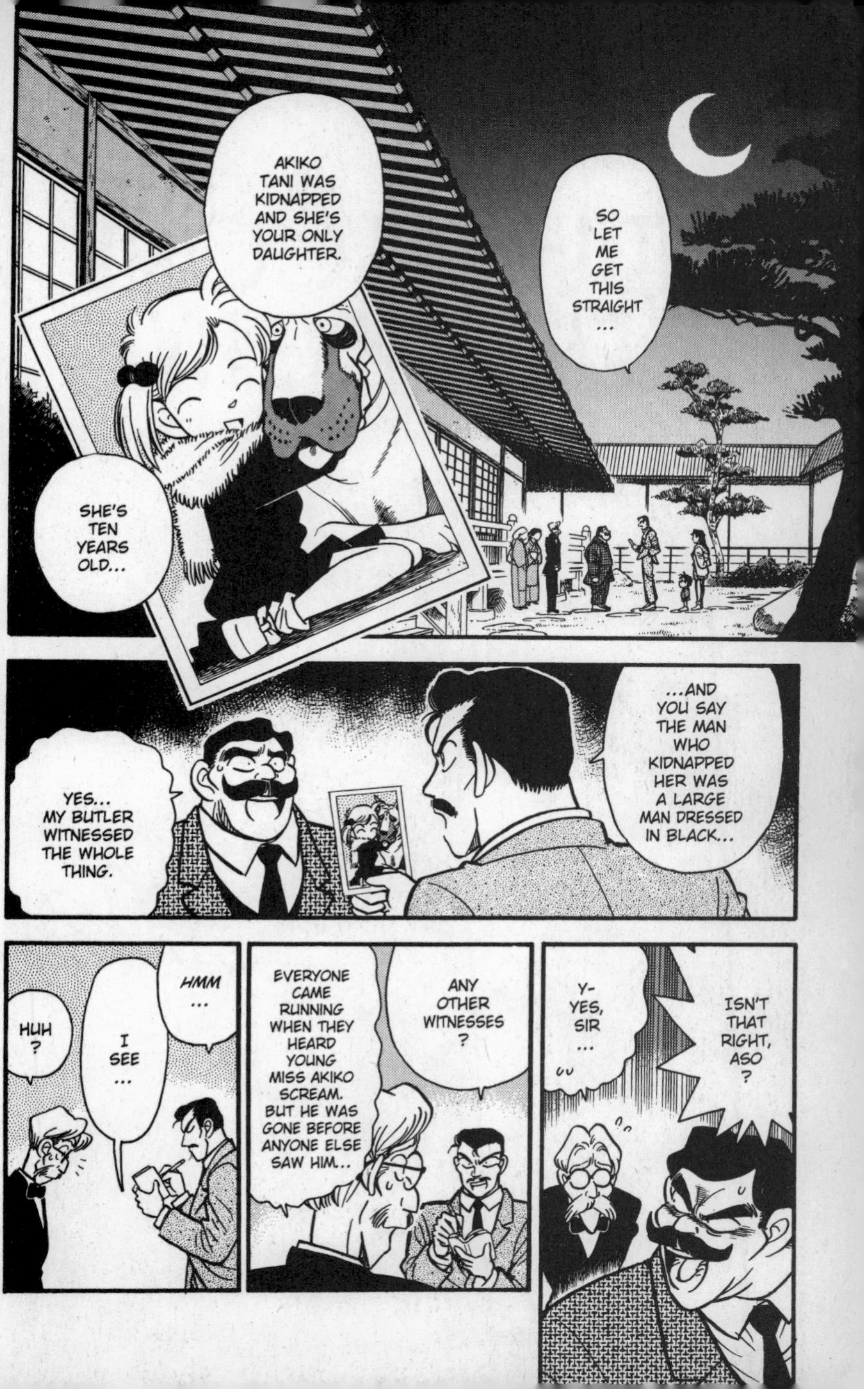
SO LET ME GET THIS STRAIGHT...
AKIKO TANI WAS KIDNAPPED AND SHE'S YOUR ONLY DAUGHTER.
SHE'S TEN YEARS OLD...
...AND YOU SAY THE MAN WHO KIDNAPPED HER WAS A LARGE MAN DRESSED IN BLACK...
YES... MY BUTLER WITNESSED THE WHOLE THING.
ISN'T THAT RIGHT, ASO?
Y-YES, SIR...
ANY OTHER WITNESSES?
EVERYONE CAME RUNNING WHEN THEY HEARD YOUNG MISS AKIKO SCREAM. BUT HE WAS GONE BEFORE ANYONE ELSE SAW HIM...
HMM...
I SEE...
HUH?

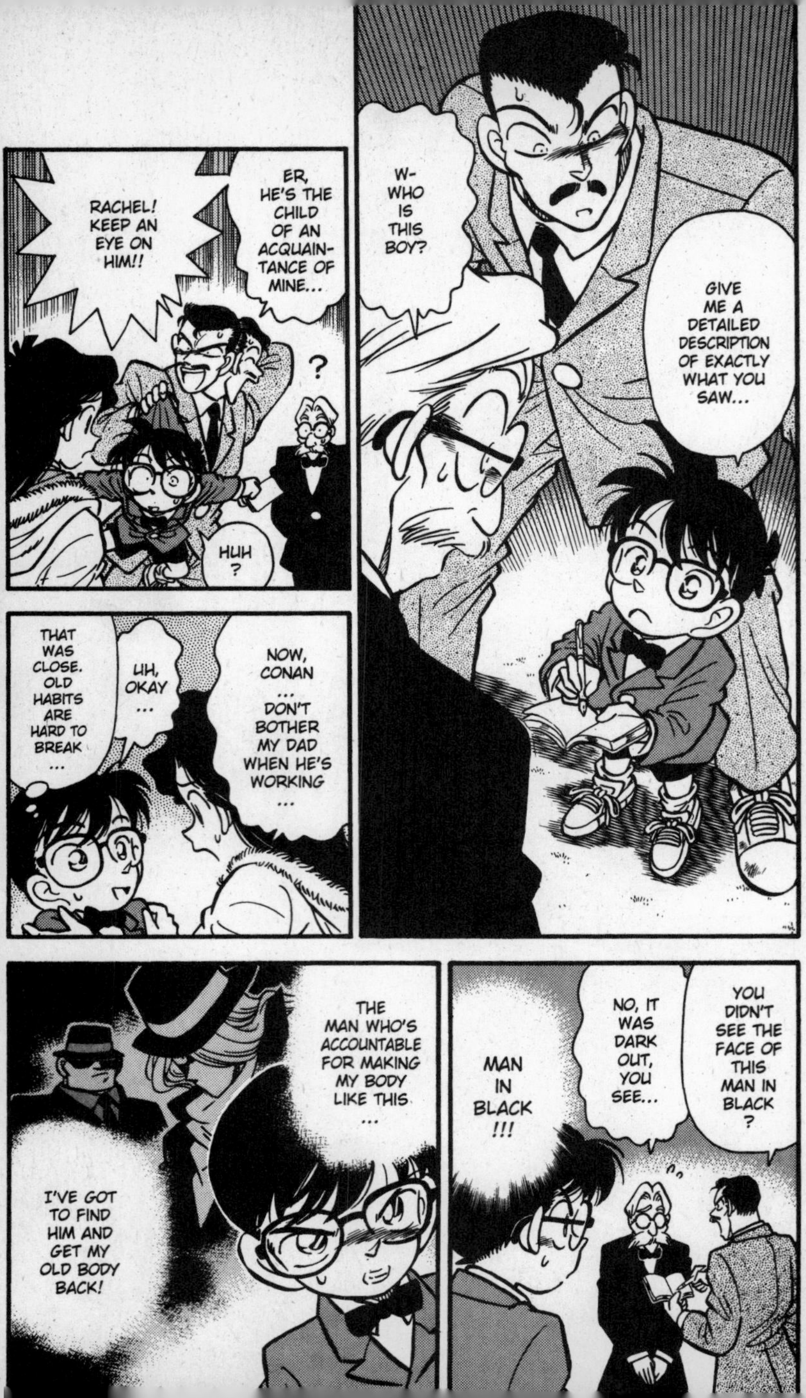
W- WHO IS THIS BOY?
GIVE ME A DETAILED DESCRIPTION OF EXACTLY WHAT YOU SAW...
ER, HE'S THE CHILD OF AN ACQUAIN-TANCE OF MINE...
RACHEL! KEEP AN EYE ON HIM!!
?
HUH ?
NOW, CONAN ... DON'T BOTHER MY DAD WHEN HE'S WORKING ...
UH, OKAY ...
THAT WAS CLOSE. OLD HABITS ARE HARD TO BREAK ...
YOU DIDN'T SEE THE FACE OF THIS MAN IN BLACK ?
NO, IT WAS DARK OUT, YOU SEE...
MAN IN BLACK !!!
THE MAN WHO'S ACCOUNTABLE FOR MAKING MY BODY LIKE THIS ...
I'VE GOT TO FIND HIM AND GET MY OLD BODY BACK!

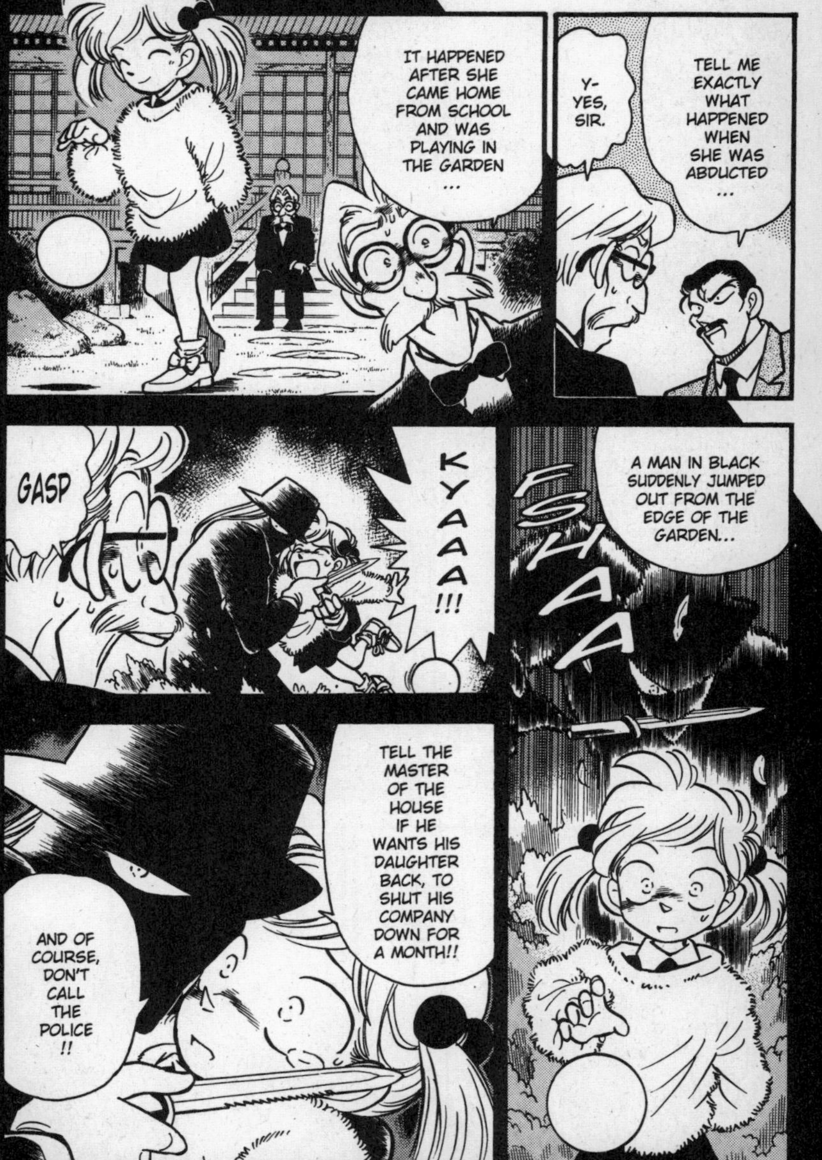
TELL ME EXACTLY WHAT HAPPENED WHEN SHE WAS ABDUCTED ...
Y- YES, SIR.
IT HAPPENED AFTER SHE CAME HOME FROM SCHOOL AND WAS PLAYING IN THE GARDEN ...
A MAN IN BLACK SUDDENLY JUMPED OUT FROM THE EDGE OF THE GARDEN...
FSHAAA
KYAAAA!!!
GASP
TELL THE MASTER OF THE HOUSE IF HE WANTS HIS DAUGHTER BACK, TO SHUT HIS COMPANY DOWN FOR A MONTH!!
AND OF COURSE, DON'T CALL THE POLICE !!

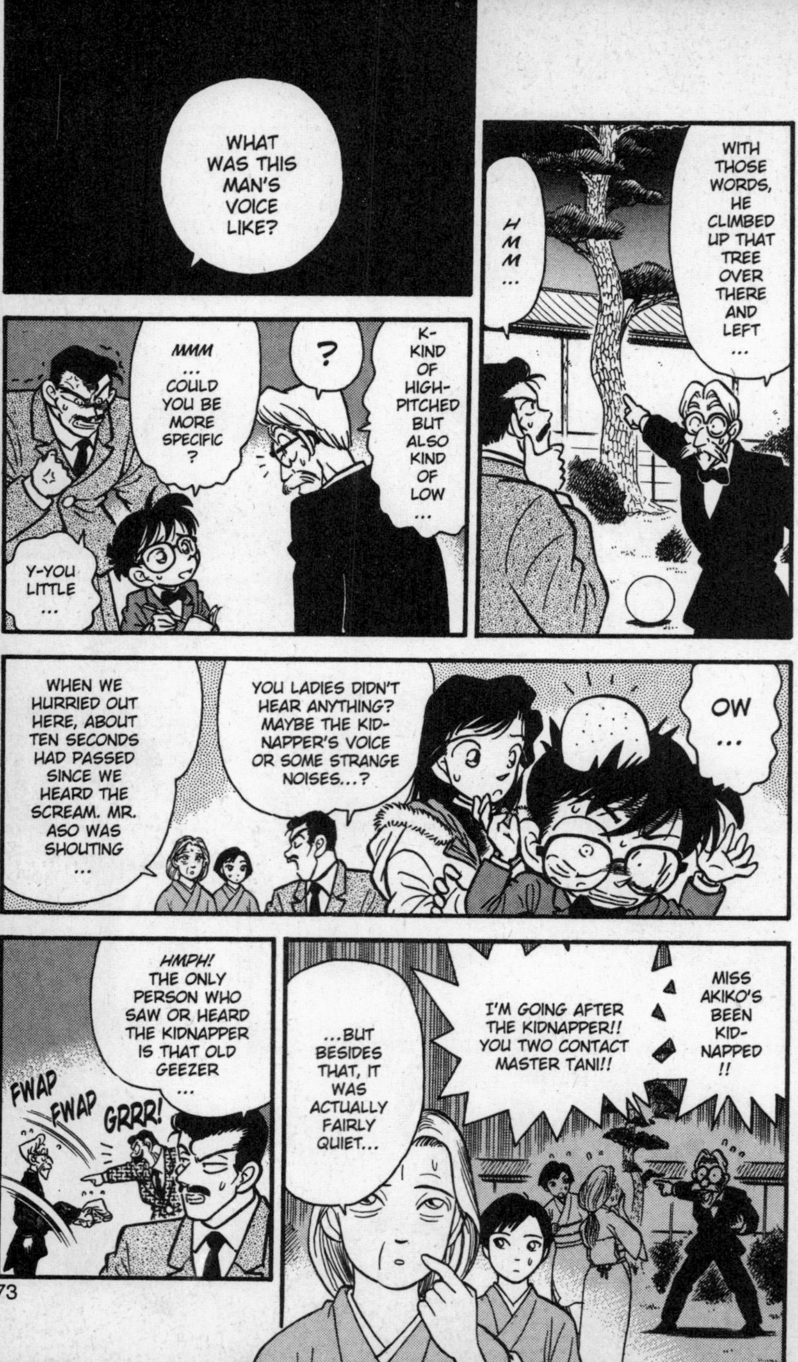
WITH THOSE WORDS, HE CLIMBED UP THAT TREE OVER THERE AND LEFT...
HMM...
WHAT WAS THIS MAN'S VOICE LIKE?
K-KIND OF HIGH-PITCHED BUT ALSO KIND OF LOW...
?
MMM... COULD YOU BE MORE SPECIFIC?
Y-YOU LITTLE...
OW...
YOU LADIES DIDN'T HEAR ANYTHING? MAYBE THE KIDNAPPER'S VOICE OR SOME STRANGE NOISES...?
WHEN WE HURRIED OUT HERE, ABOUT TEN SECONDS HAD PASSED SINCE WE HEARD THE SCREAM. MR. ASO WAS SHOUTING...
MISS AKIKO'S BEEN KID-NAPPED!!
I'M GOING AFTER THE KIDNAPPER!! YOU TWO CONTACT MASTER TANI!!
...BUT BESIDES THAT, IT WAS ACTUALLY FAIRLY QUIET...
HMPH! THE ONLY PERSON WHO SAW OR HEARD THE KIDNAPPER IS THAT OLD GEEZER...
GRRR!
FWAP FWAP

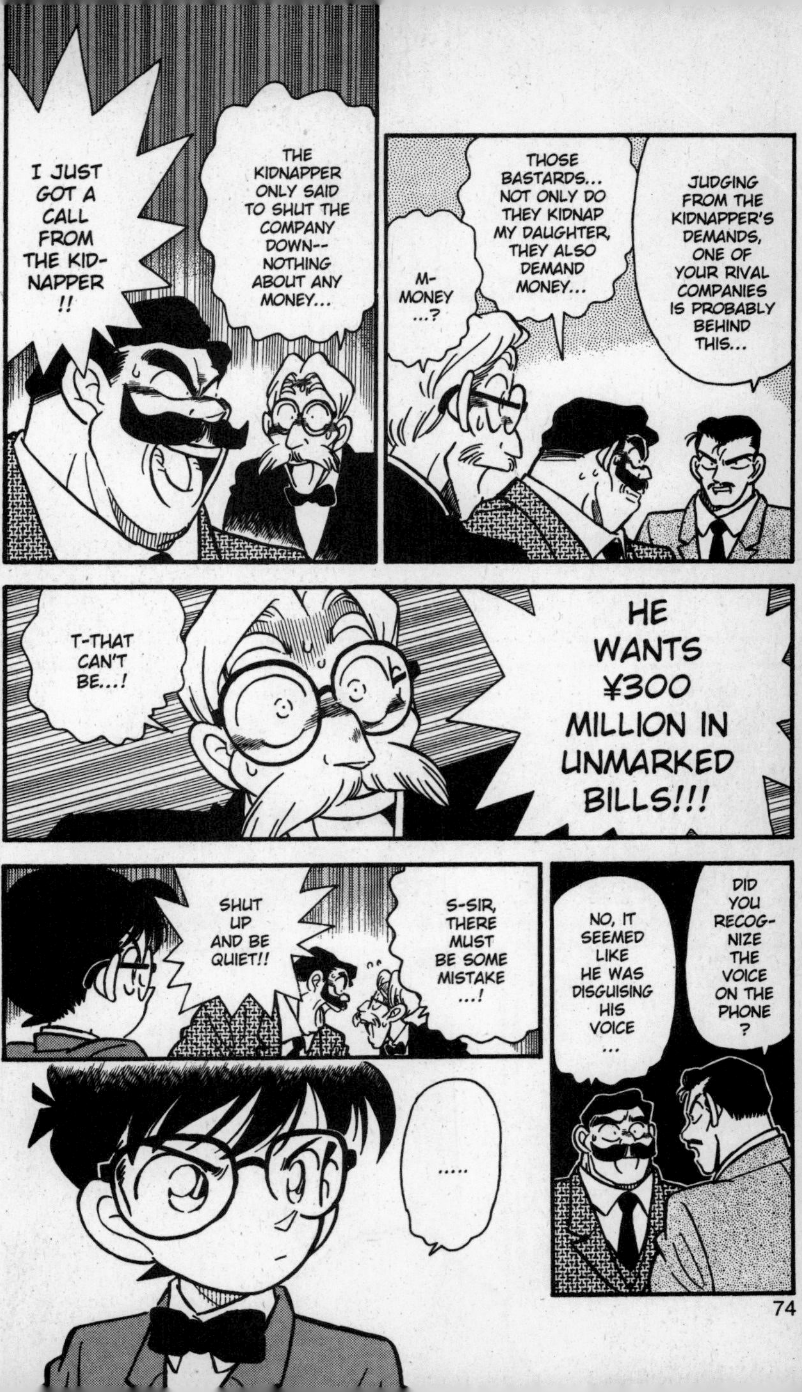

JUDGING FROM THE KIDNAPPER'S DEMANDS, ONE OF YOUR RIVAL COMPANIES IS PROBABLY BEHIND THIS...
THOSE BASTARDS... NOT ONLY DO THEY KIDNAP MY DAUGHTER, THEY ALSO DEMAND MONEY...
M-MONEY ...?
THE KIDNAPPER ONLY SAID TO SHUT THE COMPANY DOWN--NOTHING ABOUT ANY MONEY...
I JUST GOT A CALL FROM THE KID-NAPPER !!
HE WANTS ¥300 MILLION IN UNMARKED BILLS!!!
T-THAT CAN'T BE...!
DID YOU RECOG-NIZE THE VOICE ON THE PHONE ?
NO, IT SEEMED LIKE HE WAS DISGUISING HIS VOICE ...
S-SIR, THERE MUST BE SOME MISTAKE ...!
SHUT UP AND BE QUIET!!
.....

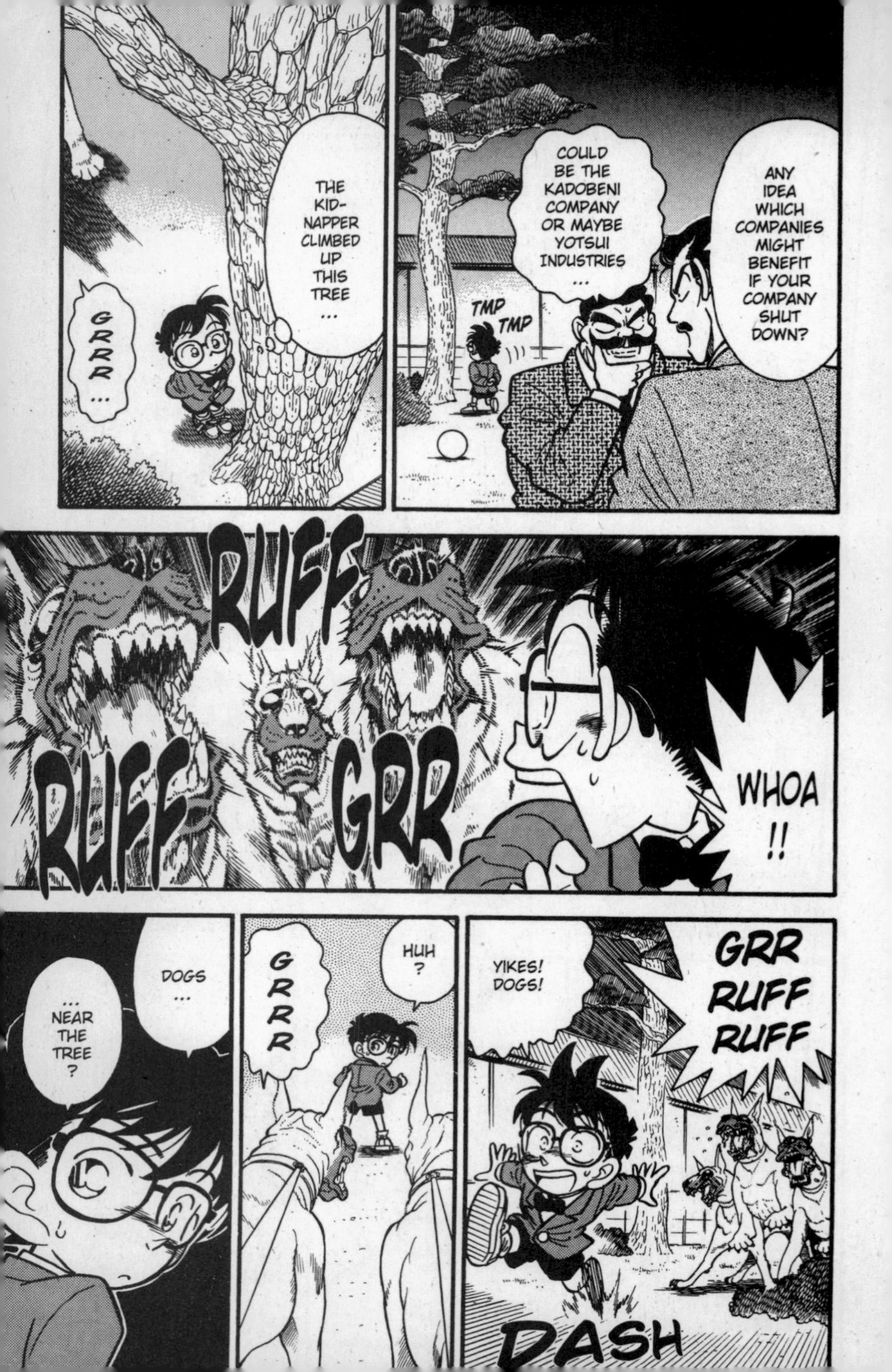
ANY IDEA WHICH COMPANIES MIGHT BENEFIT IF YOUR COMPANY SHUT DOWN?
COULD BE THE KADOBENI COMPANY OR MAYBE YOTSUI INDUSTRIES ...
TMP TMP
THE KID-NAPPER CLIMBED UP THIS TREE ...
GRRR ...
WHOA !!
RUFF
GRR
RUFF
GRR RUFF RUFF
YIKES! DOGS!
DASH
HUH ?
GRRR
DOGS ...
... NEAR THE TREE ?

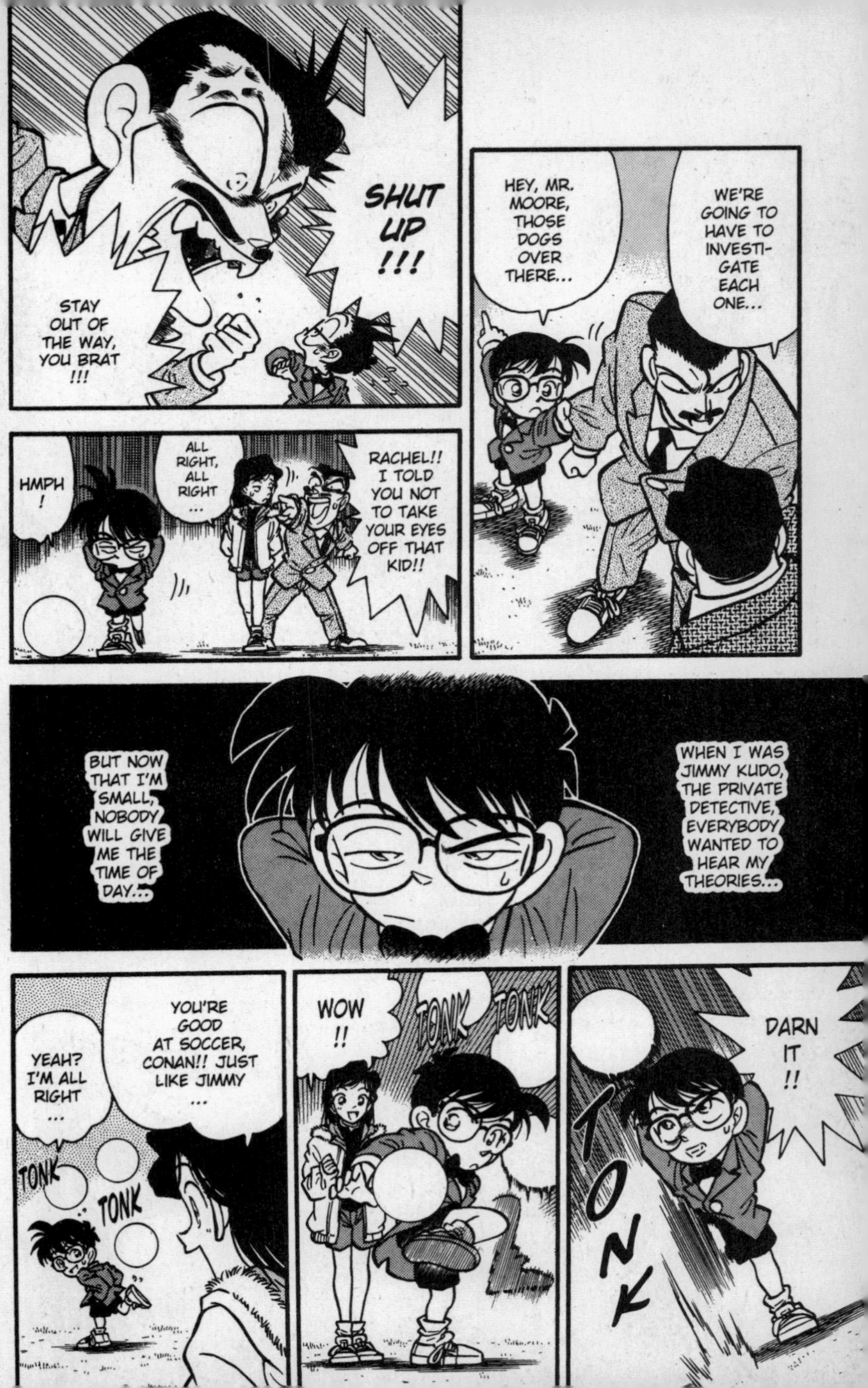
WE'RE GOING TO HAVE TO INVESTI-GATE EACH ONE...
HEY, MR. MOORE, THOSE DOGS OVER THERE...
SHUT UP !!!
STAY OUT OF THE WAY, YOU BRAT !!!
RACHEL!! I TOLD YOU NOT TO TAKE YOUR EYES OFF THAT KID!!
ALL RIGHT, ALL RIGHT ...
HMPH !
WHEN I WAS JIMMY KUDO, THE PRIVATE DETECTIVE, EVERYBODY WANTED TO HEAR MY THEORIES...
BUT NOW THAT I'M SMALL, NOBODY WILL GIVE ME THE TIME OF DAY...
DARN IT !!
TONK
TONK
TONK
WOW !!
YOU'RE GOOD AT SOCCER, CONAN!! JUST LIKE JIMMY ...
YEAH? I'M ALL RIGHT ...
TONK
TONK

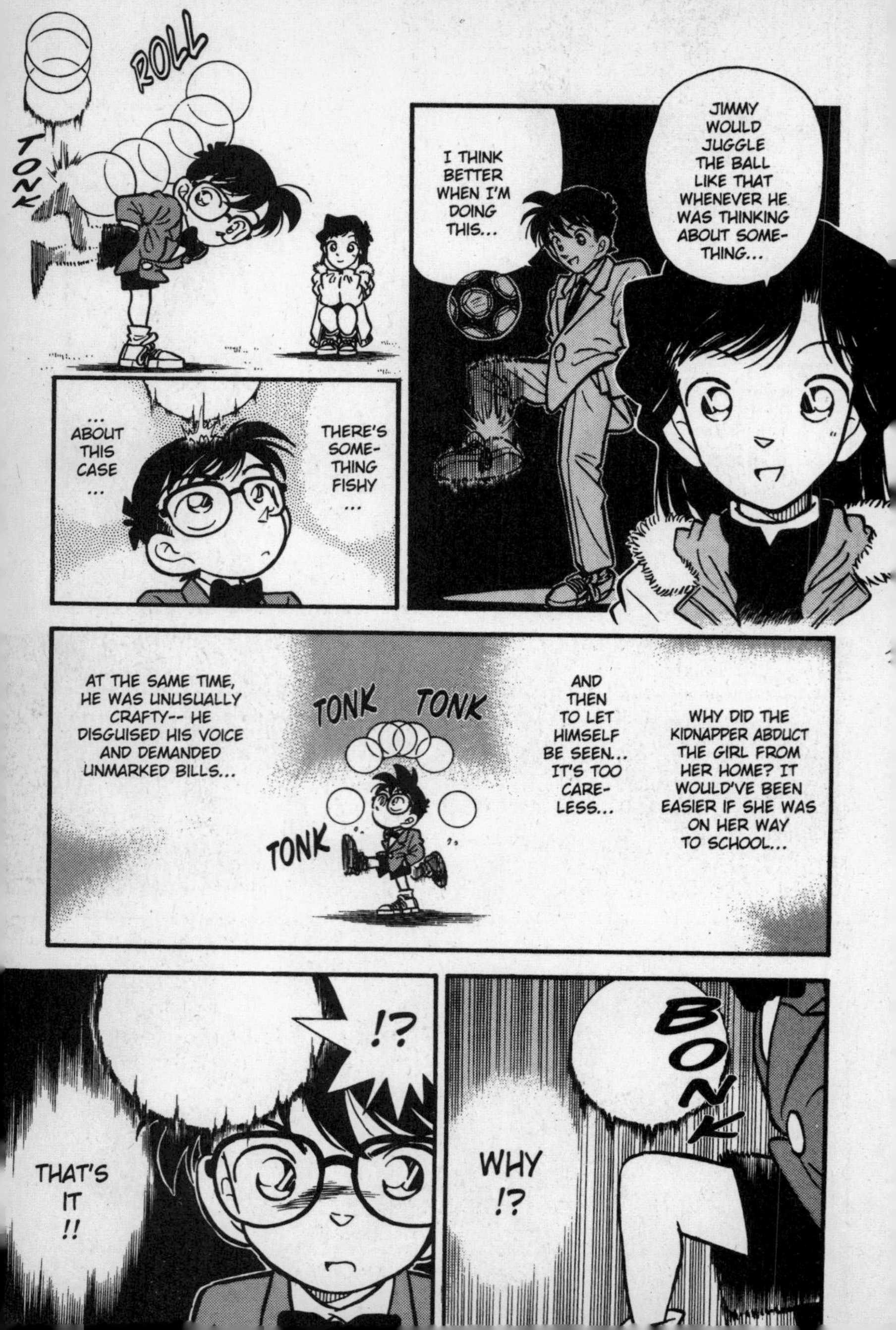
JIMMY WOULD JUGGLE THE BALL LIKE THAT WHENEVER HE WAS THINKING ABOUT SOME-THING...
I THINK BETTER WHEN I'M DOING THIS...
ROLL
TONK
THERE'S SOME-THING FISHY...
...ABOUT THIS CASE...
WHY DID THE KIDNAPPER ABDUCT THE GIRL FROM HER HOME? IT WOULD'VE BEEN EASIER IF SHE WAS ON HER WAY TO SCHOOL...
AND THEN TO LET HIMSELF BE SEEN... IT'S TOO CARE-LESS...
TONK TONK
TONK
AT THE SAME TIME, HE WAS UNUSUALLY CRAFTY-- HE DISGUISED HIS VOICE AND DEMANDED UNMARKED BILLS...
BONK
WHY!?
!?
THAT'S IT!!

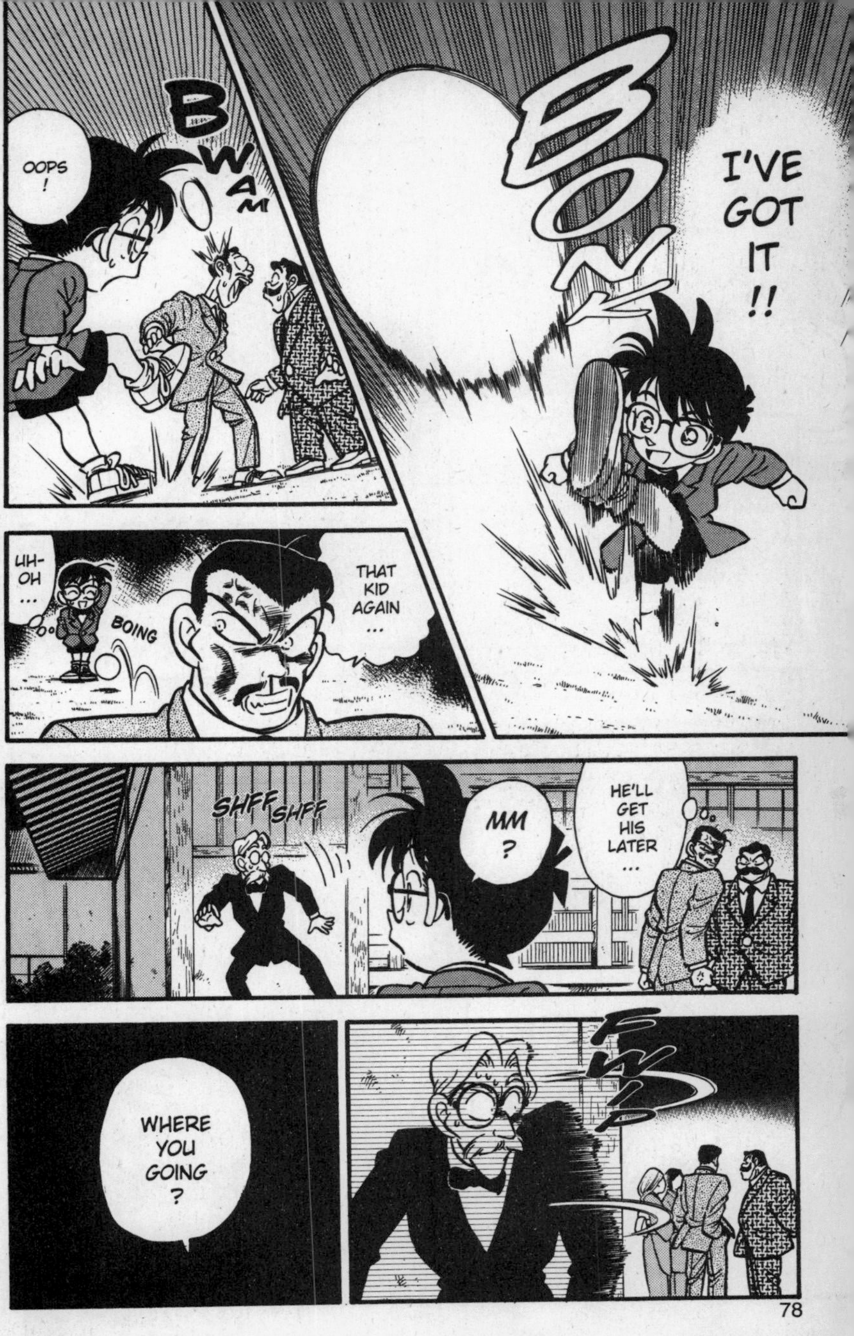
BOM
I'VE GOT IT !!
BWAM
OOPS !
THAT KID AGAIN ...
UH-OH ...
BOING
HE'LL GET HIS LATER ...
MM ?
SHFF SHFF
FWIP
WHERE YOU GOING ?

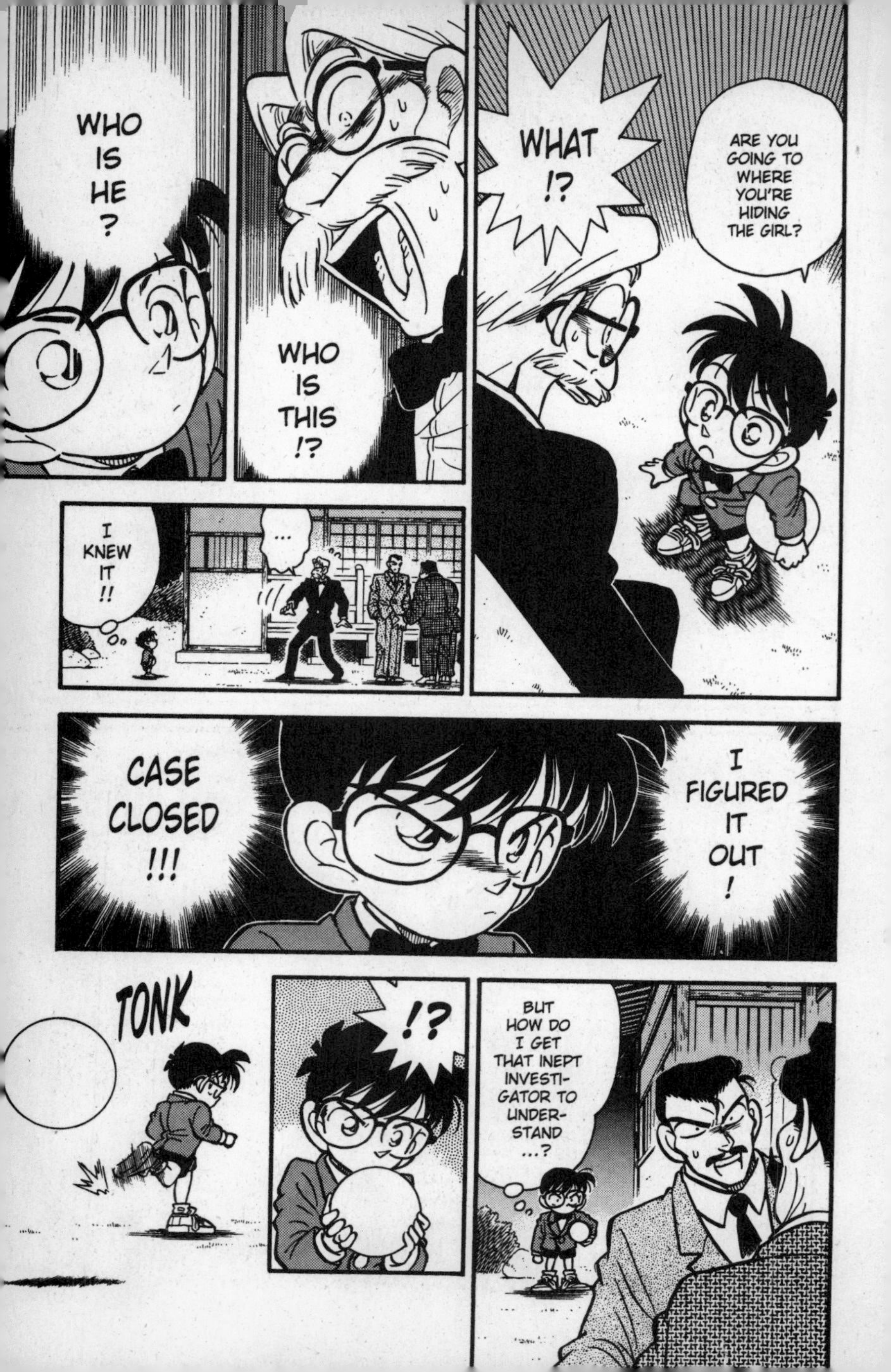
ARE YOU GOING TO WHERE YOU'RE HIDING THE GIRL?
WHAT !?
WHO IS THIS !?
WHO IS HE ?
...
I KNEW IT !!
I FIGURED IT OUT !
CASE CLOSED !!!
BUT HOW DO I GET THAT INEPT INVESTI-GATOR TO UNDER-STAND ...?
!?
TONK

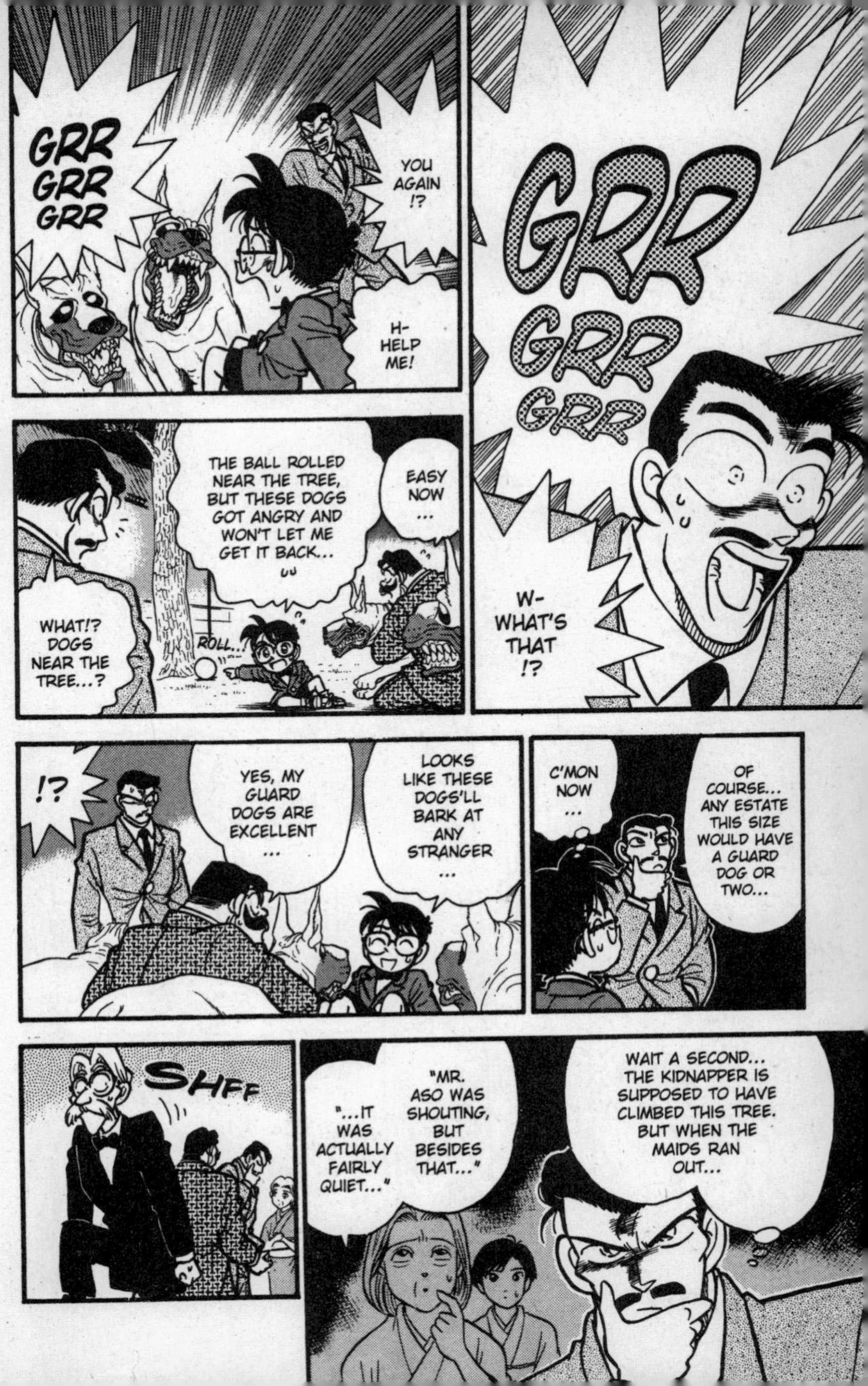
GRR
GRR
GRR
W-WHAT'S THAT!?
YOU AGAIN!?
GRR GRR GRR
H-HELP ME!
EASY NOW...
THE BALL ROLLED NEAR THE TREE, BUT THESE DOGS GOT ANGRY AND WON'T LET ME GET IT BACK...
ROLL...
WHAT!? DOGS NEAR THE TREE...?
OF COURSE... ANY ESTATE THIS SIZE WOULD HAVE A GUARD DOG OR TWO...
C'MON NOW...
LOOKS LIKE THESE DOGS'LL BARK AT ANY STRANGER...
YES, MY GUARD DOGS ARE EXCELLENT...
!?
WAIT A SECOND... THE KIDNAPPER IS SUPPOSED TO HAVE CLIMBED THIS TREE. BUT WHEN THE MAIDS RAN OUT...
"MR. ASO WAS SHOUTING, BUT BESIDES THAT..."
"...IT WAS ACTUALLY FAIRLY QUIET..."
SHFF

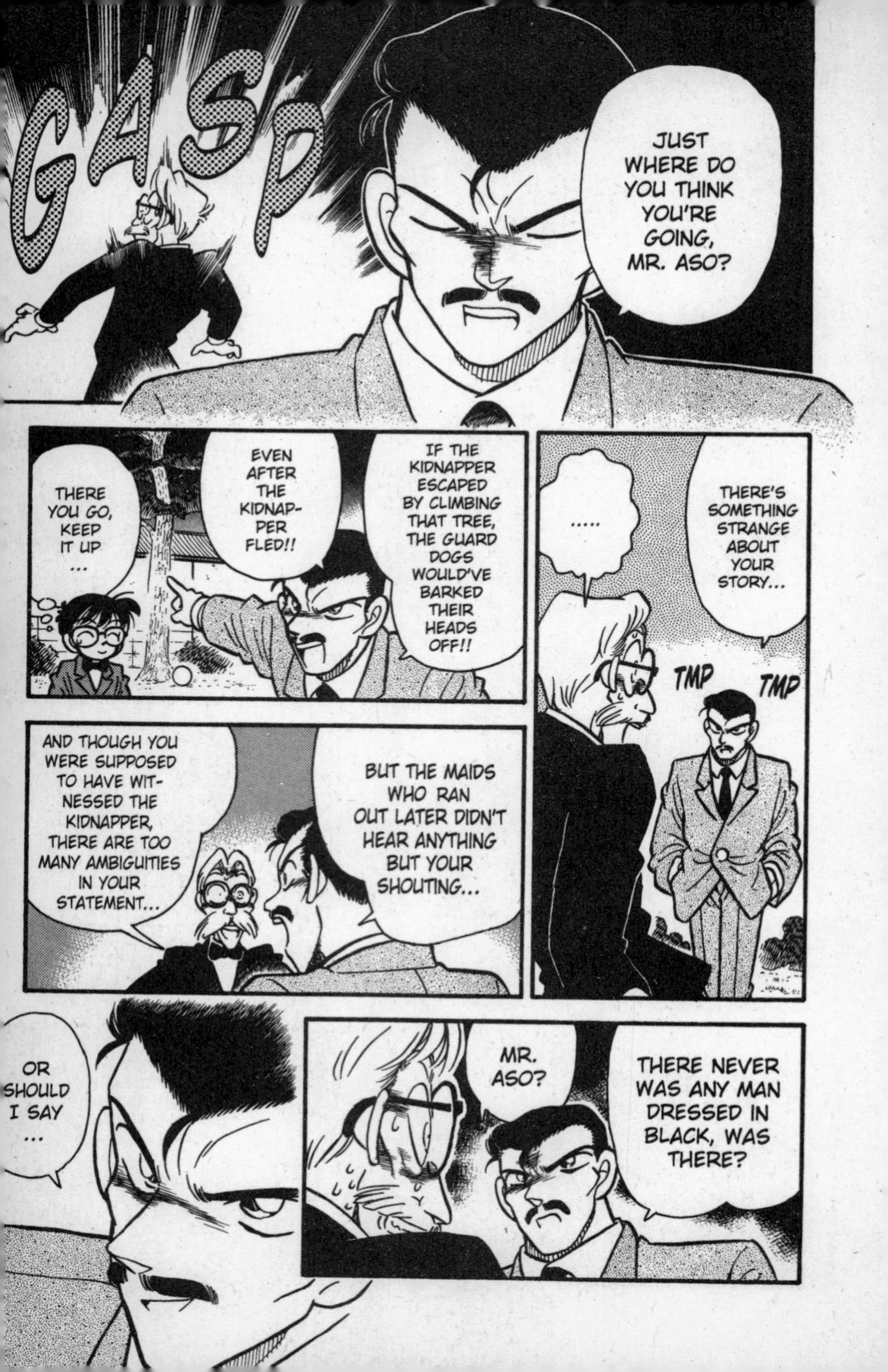
JUST WHERE DO YOU THINK YOU'RE GOING, MR. ASO?
GASP
THERE'S SOMETHING STRANGE ABOUT YOUR STORY...
.....
TMP
TMP
IF THE KIDNAPPER ESCAPED BY CLIMBING THAT TREE, THE GUARD DOGS WOULD'VE BARKED THEIR HEADS OFF!!
EVEN AFTER THE KIDNAP-PER FLED!!
THERE YOU GO, KEEP IT UP ...
BUT THE MAIDS WHO RAN OUT LATER DIDN'T HEAR ANYTHING BUT YOUR SHOUTING...
AND THOUGH YOU WERE SUPPOSED TO HAVE WIT-NESSED THE KIDNAPPER, THERE ARE TOO MANY AMBIGUITIES IN YOUR STATEMENT...
THERE NEVER WAS ANY MAN DRESSED IN BLACK, WAS THERE?
MR. ASO?
OR SHOULD I SAY ...

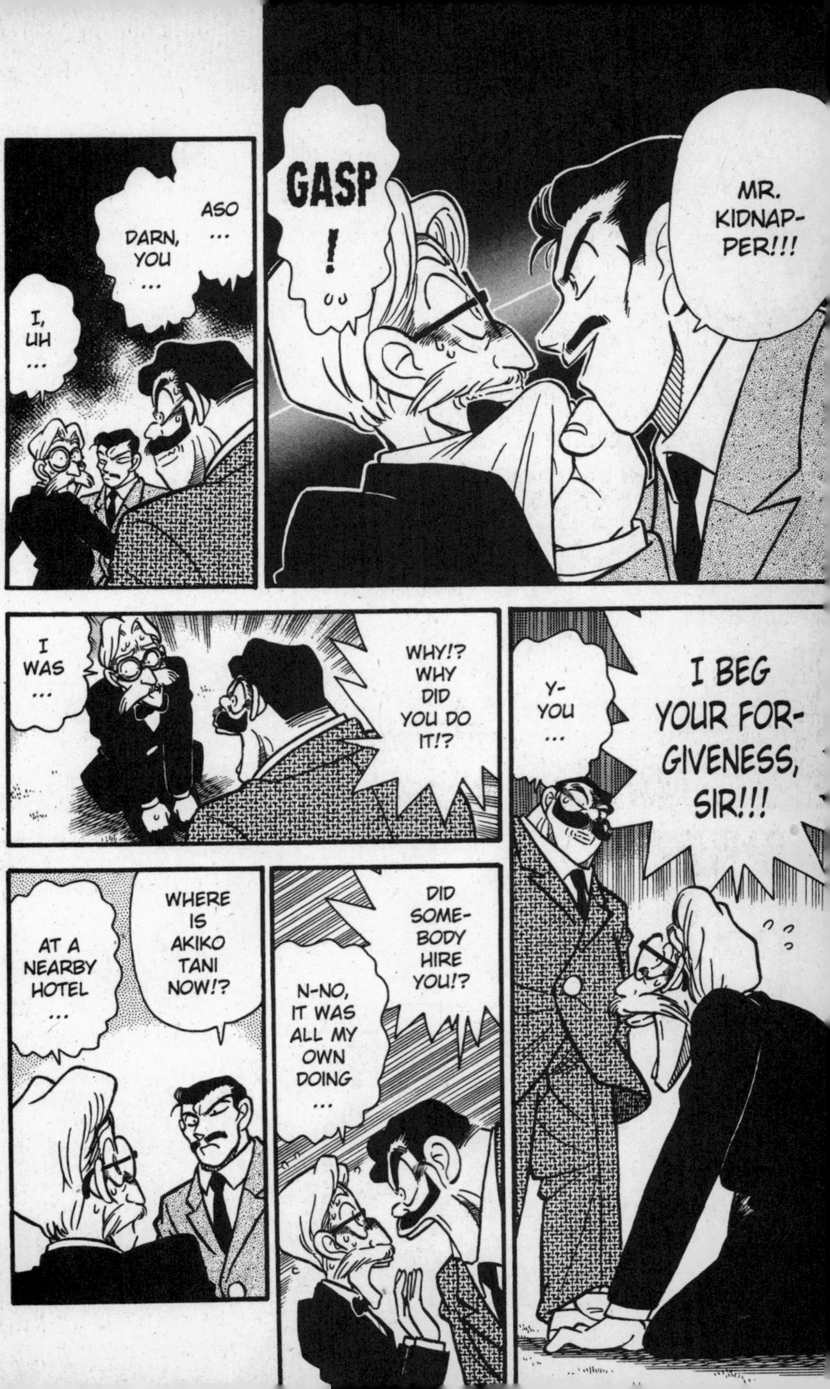
MR. KIDNAPPER!!!
GASP !
ASO ...
DARN, YOU ...
I, UH ...
I BEG YOUR FORGIVENESS, SIR!!!
Y-YOU ...
WHY!? WHY DID YOU DO IT!?
I WAS ...
DID SOMEBODY HIRE YOU!?
N-NO, IT WAS ALL MY OWN DOING ...
WHERE IS AKIKO TANI NOW!?
AT A NEARBY HOTEL ...

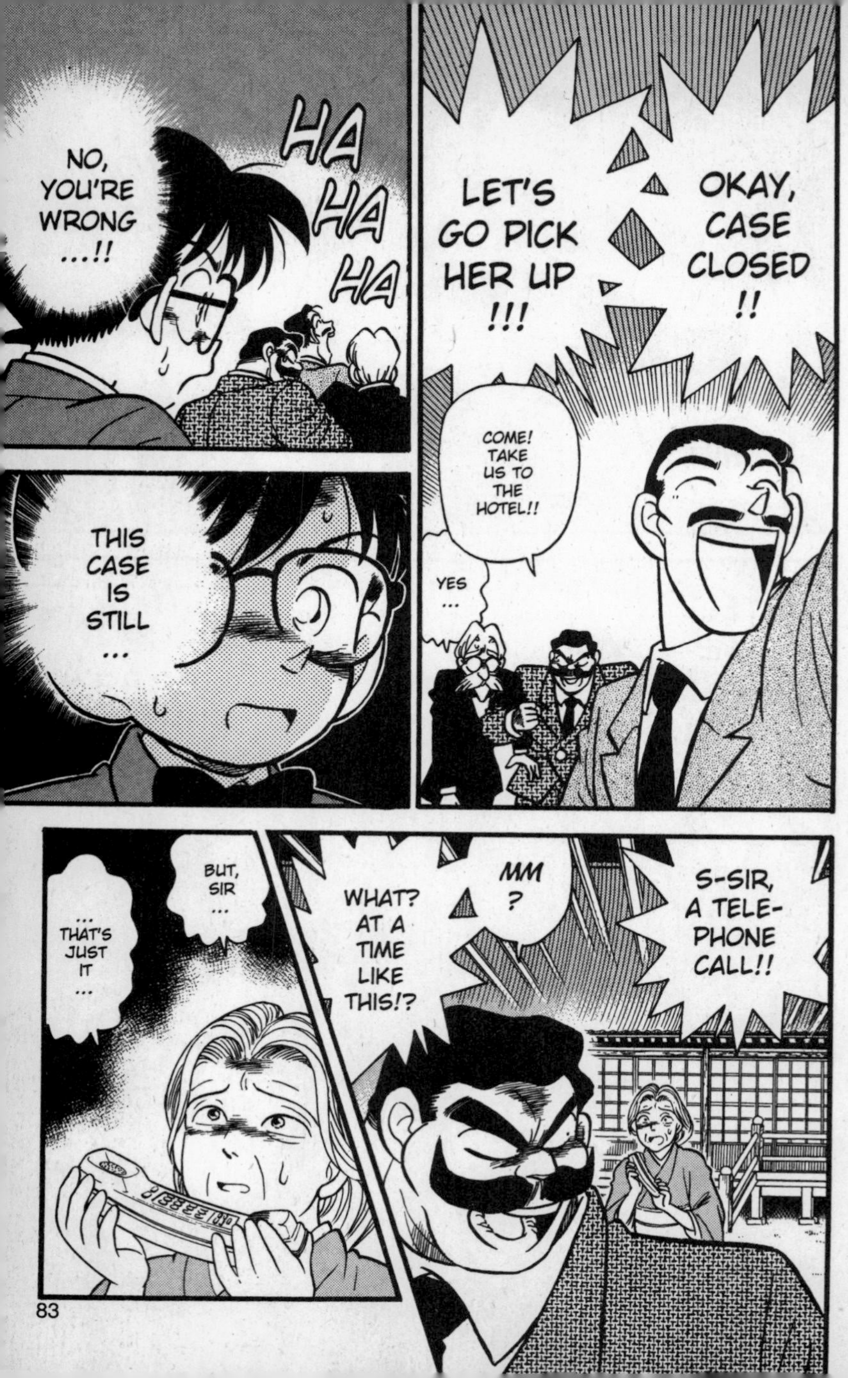
OKAY, CASE CLOSED!!
LET'S GO PICK HER UP!!!
COME! TAKE US TO THE HOTEL!!
YES...
HA HA HA
NO, YOU'RE WRONG...!!
THIS CASE IS STILL...
S-SIR, A TELE-PHONE CALL!!
MM?
WHAT? AT A TIME LIKE THIS!?
BUT, SIR...
...THAT'S JUST IT...

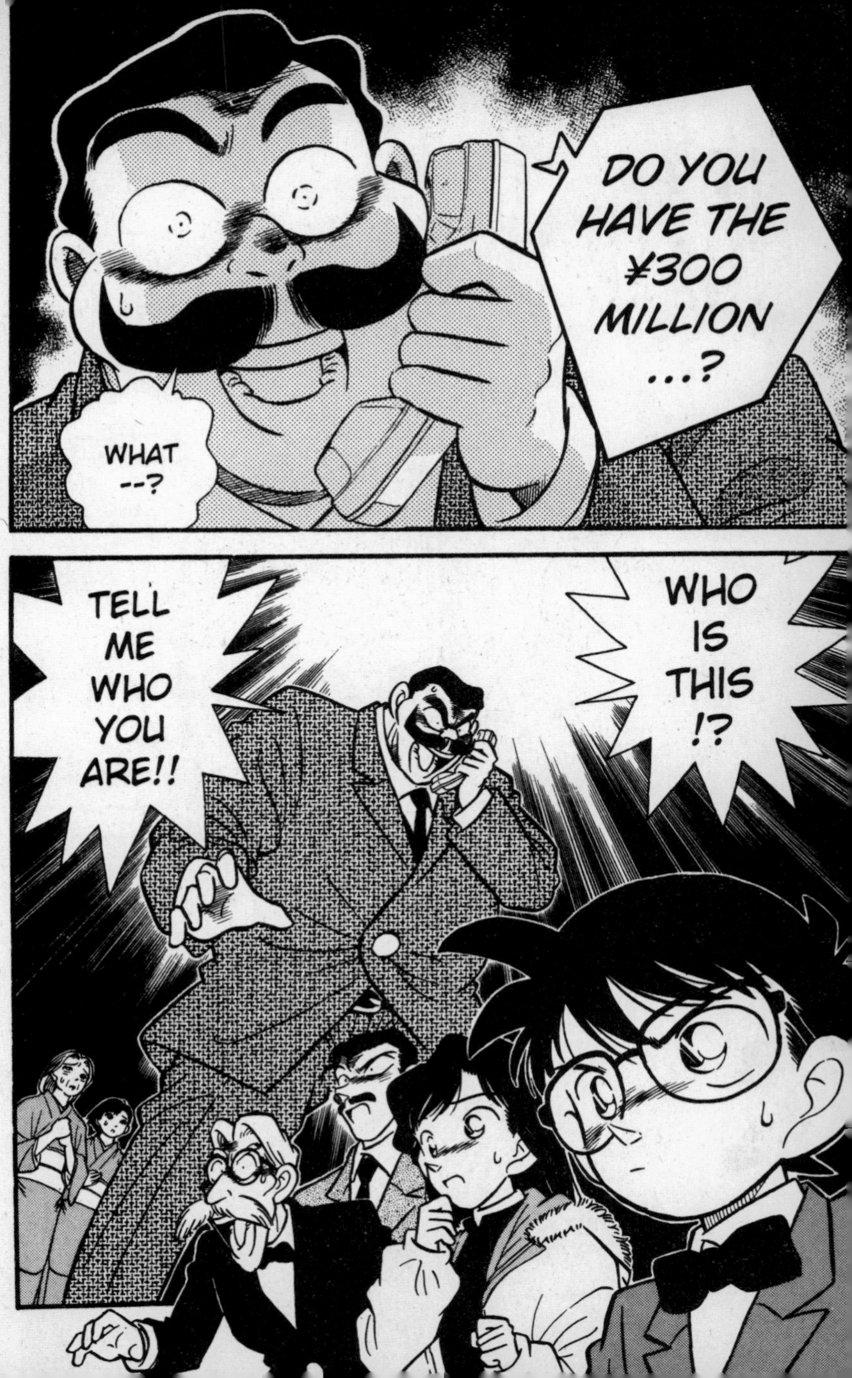
DO YOU HAVE THE ¥300 MILLION ...?
WHAT --?
WHO IS THIS !?
TELL ME WHO YOU ARE!!

FILE 4:
THE SIXTH SMOKESTACK

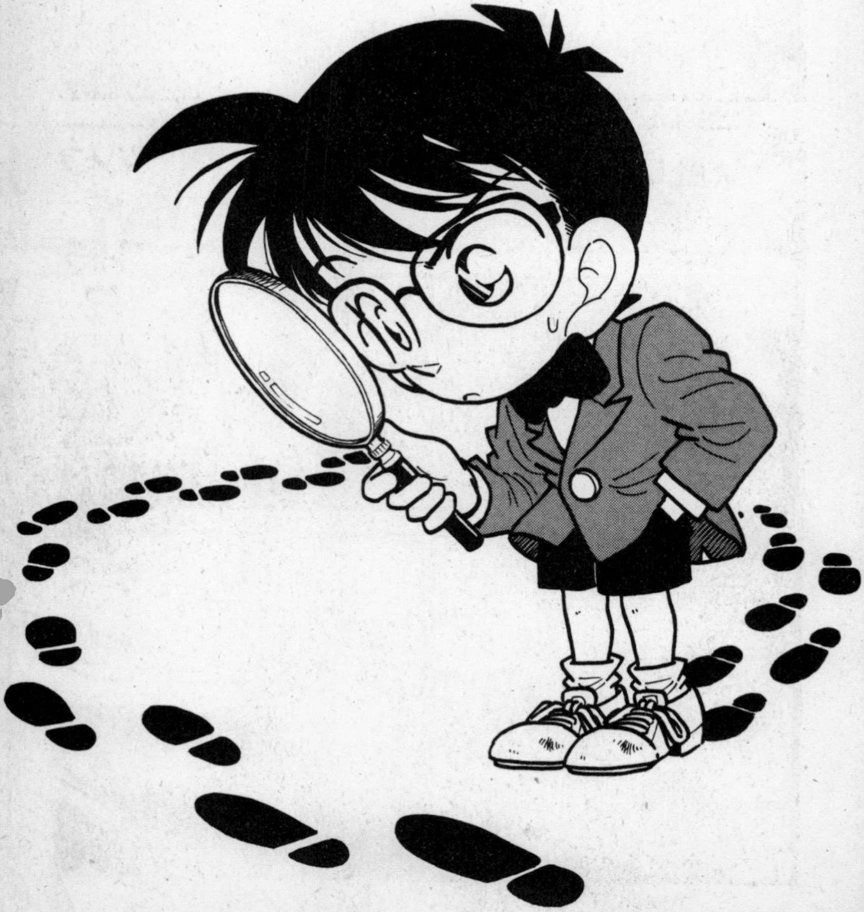

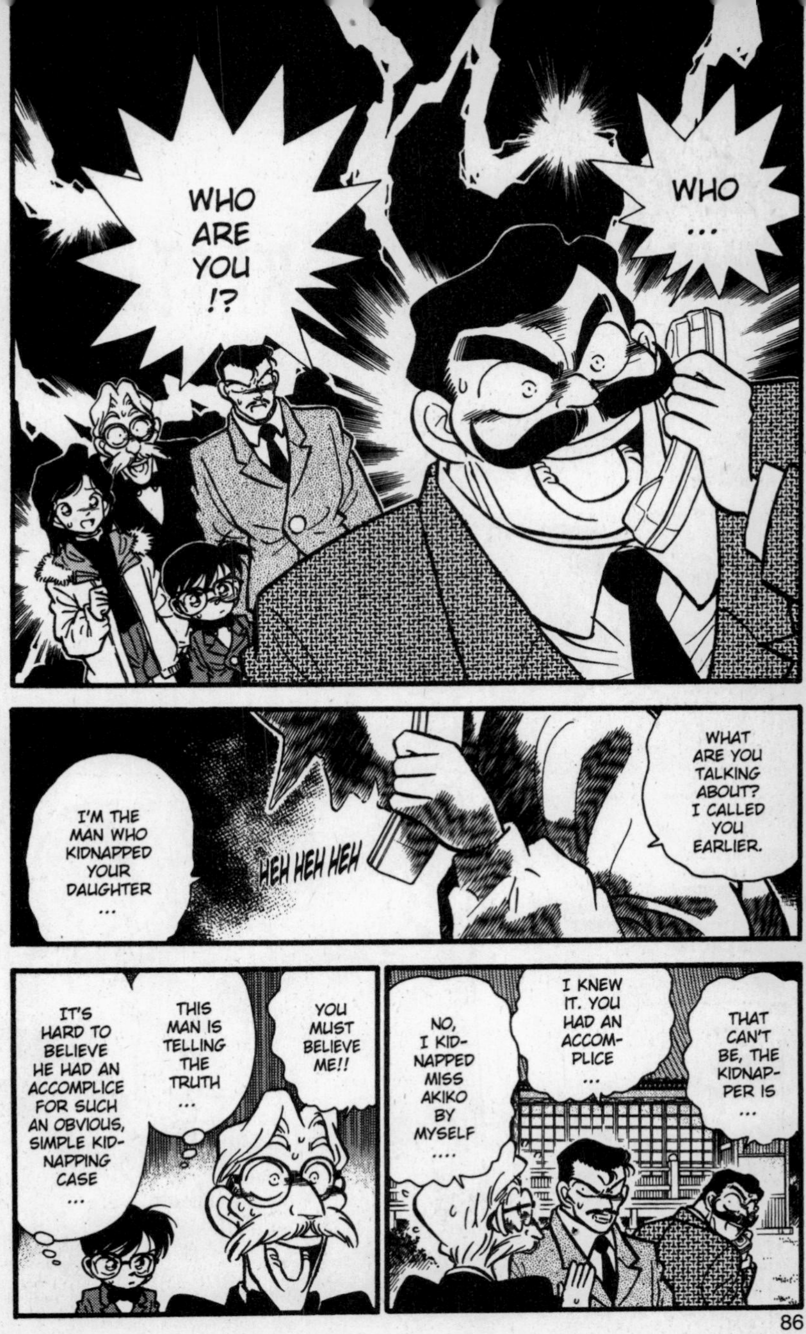
WHO ...
WHO ARE YOU !?
WHAT ARE YOU TALKING ABOUT? I CALLED YOU EARLIER.
HEH HEH HEH
I'M THE MAN WHO KIDNAPPED YOUR DAUGHTER ...
THAT CAN'T BE, THE KIDNAPPER IS ...
I KNEW IT. YOU HAD AN ACCOMPLICE ...
NO, I KIDNAPPED MISS AKIKO BY MYSELF ....
YOU MUST BELIEVE ME!!
THIS MAN IS TELLING THE TRUTH ...
IT'S HARD TO BELIEVE HE HAD AN ACCOMPLICE FOR SUCH AN OBVIOUS, SIMPLE KIDNAPPING CASE ...

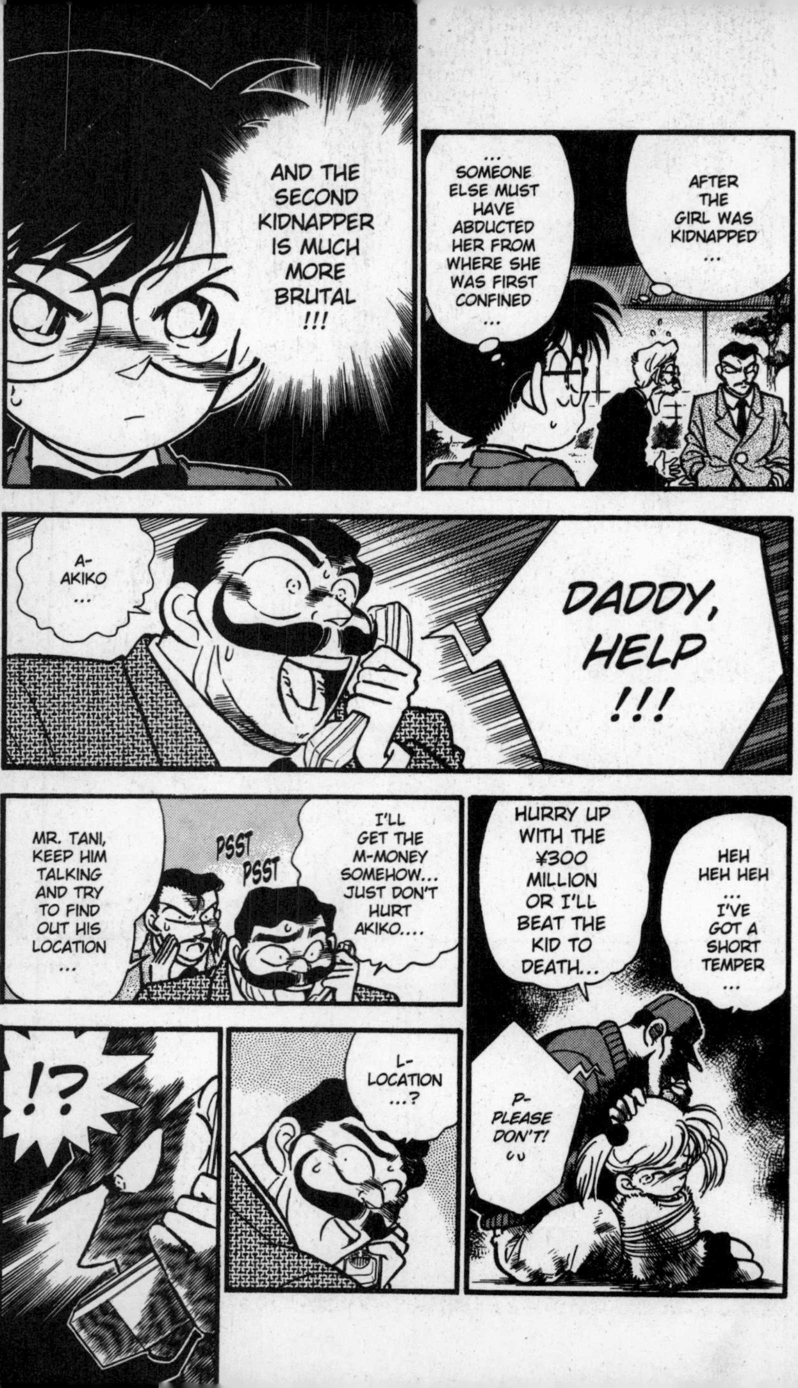
AFTER THE GIRL WAS KIDNAPPED ...
... SOMEONE ELSE MUST HAVE ABDUCTED HER FROM WHERE SHE WAS FIRST CONFINED ...
AND THE SECOND KIDNAPPER IS MUCH MORE BRUTAL !!!
DADDY, HELP !!!
A- AKIKO ...
HEH HEH HEH ... I'VE GOT A SHORT TEMPER ...
HURRY UP WITH THE ¥300 MILLION OR I'LL BEAT THE KID TO DEATH...
P- PLEASE DON'T!
I'LL GET THE M-MONEY SOMEHOW... JUST DON'T HURT AKIKO....
PSST PSST
MR. TANI, KEEP HIM TALKING AND TRY TO FIND OUT HIS LOCATION ...
L- LOCATION ...?
!?

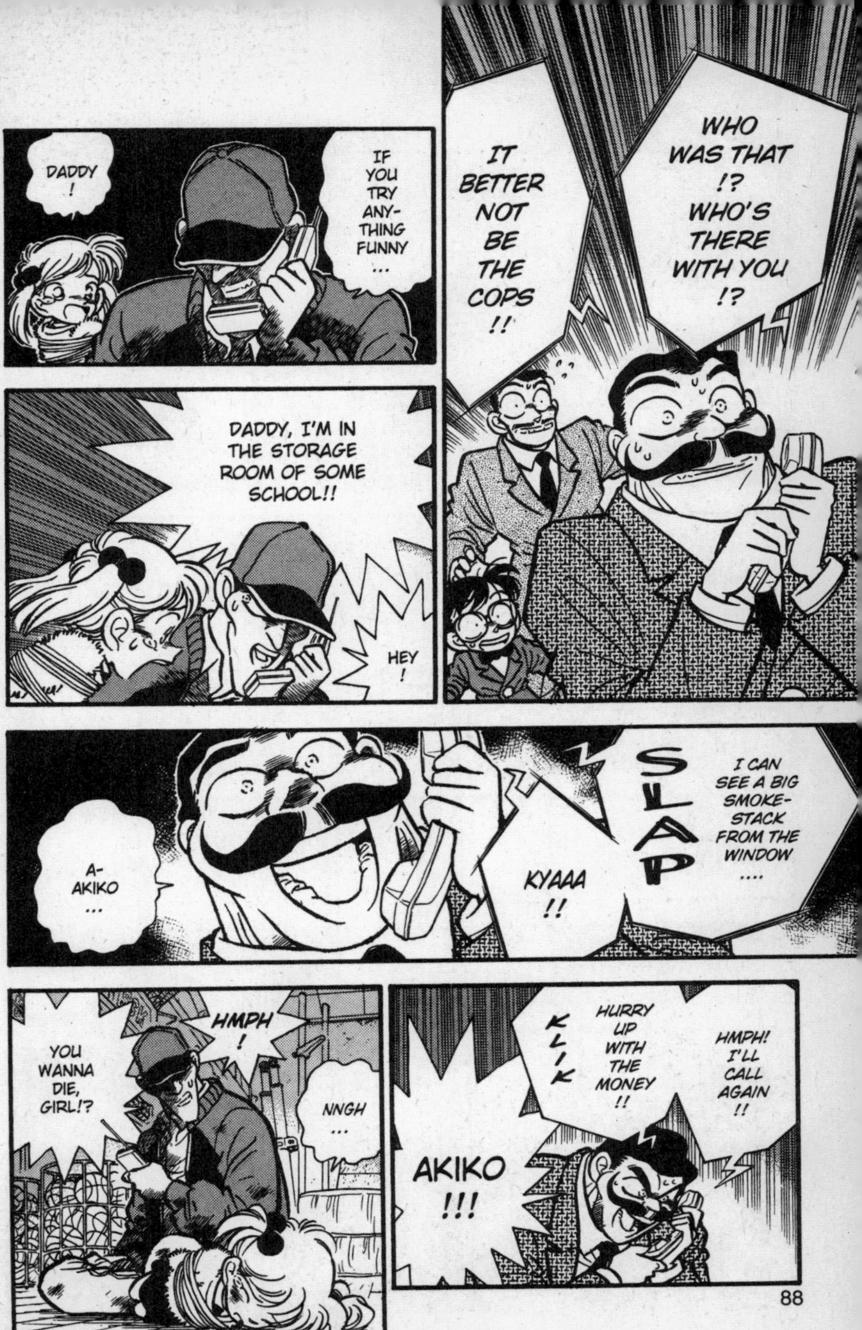
WHO WAS THAT!? WHO'S THERE WITH YOU!?
IT BETTER NOT BE THE COPS!!
IF YOU TRY ANY-THING FUNNY ...
DADDY!
DADDY, I'M IN THE STORAGE ROOM OF SOME SCHOOL!!
HEY!
I CAN SEE A BIG SMOKE-STACK FROM THE WINDOW ....
SLAP
KYAAA!!
A-AKIKO ...
HMPH! I'LL CALL AGAIN!!
HURRY UP WITH THE MONEY!!
KLIK
AKIKO!!!
HMPH!
NNGH ...
YOU WANNA DIE, GIRL!?

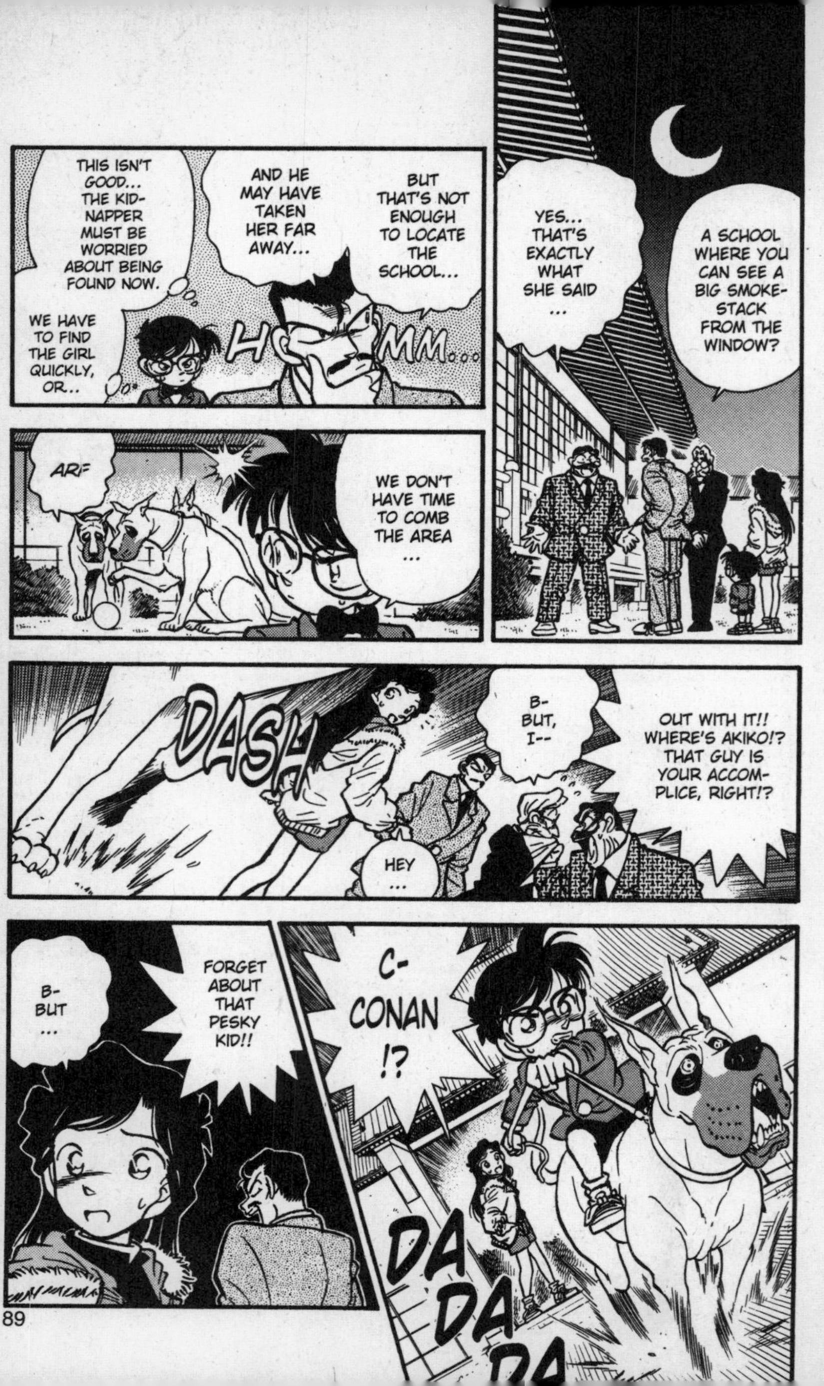
A SCHOOL WHERE YOU CAN SEE A BIG SMOKE-STACK FROM THE WINDOW?
YES... THAT'S EXACTLY WHAT SHE SAID...
BUT THAT'S NOT ENOUGH TO LOCATE THE SCHOOL...
AND HE MAY HAVE TAKEN HER FAR AWAY...
HMMM...
THIS ISN'T GOOD... THE KID-NAPPER MUST BE WORRIED ABOUT BEING FOUND NOW.
WE HAVE TO FIND THE GIRL QUICKLY, OR...
WE DON'T HAVE TIME TO COMB THE AREA...
ARF
OUT WITH IT!! WHERE'S AKIKO!? THAT GUY IS YOUR ACCOM-PLICE, RIGHT!?
B-BUT, I--
HEY...
DASH
C-CONAN!?
DA DA DA DA
FORGET ABOUT THAT PESKY KID!!
B-BUT...

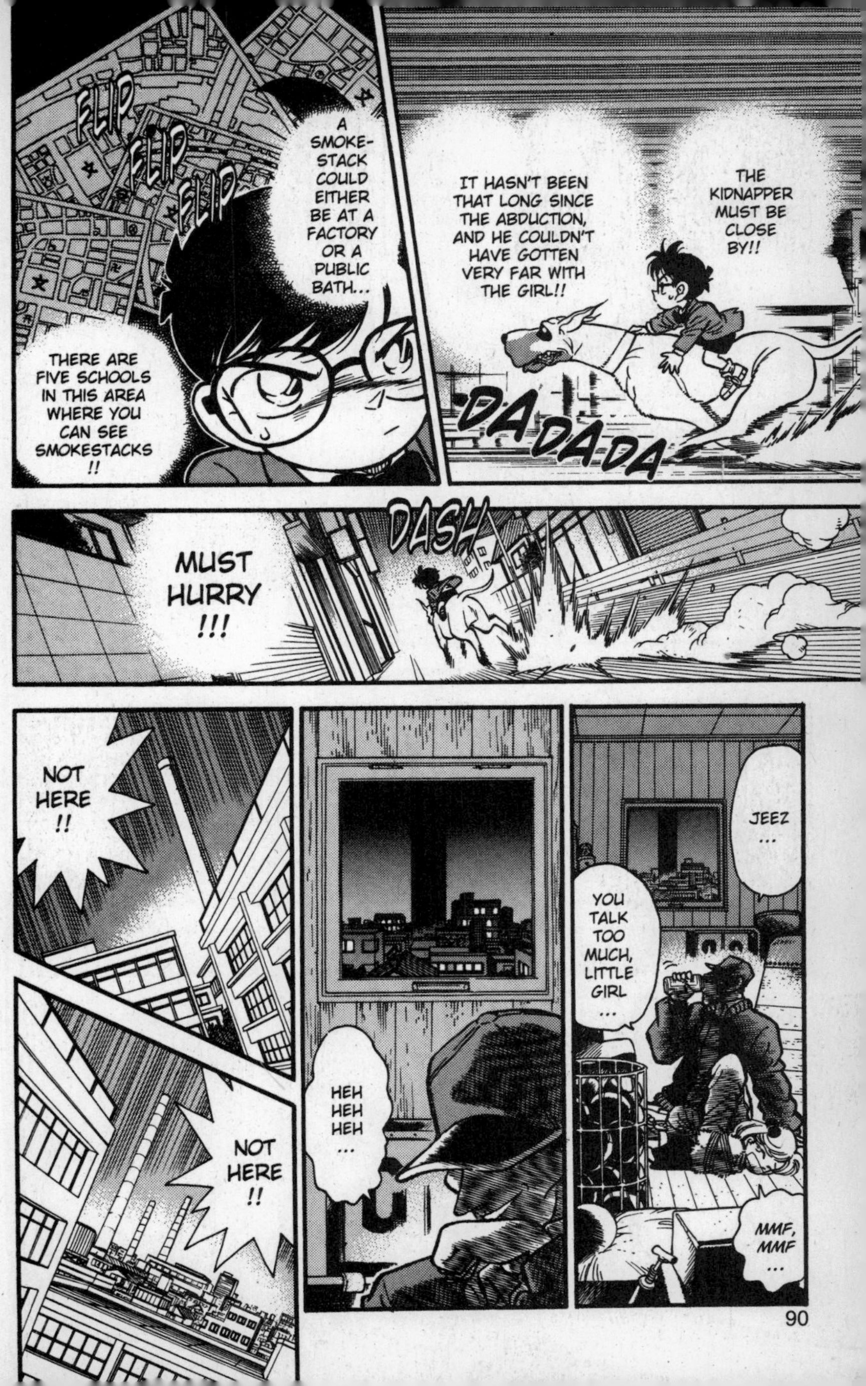
THE KIDNAPPER MUST BE CLOSE BY!!
IT HASN'T BEEN THAT LONG SINCE THE ABDUCTION, AND HE COULDN'T HAVE GOTTEN VERY FAR WITH THE GIRL!!
DA DA DA DA
A SMOKE-STACK COULD EITHER BE AT A FACTORY OR A PUBLIC BATH...
FLIP FLIP FLIP
THERE ARE FIVE SCHOOLS IN THIS AREA WHERE YOU CAN SEE SMOKESTACKS !!
DASH
MUST HURRY !!!
JEEZ ...
YOU TALK TOO MUCH, LITTLE GIRL ...
MMF, MMF ...
HEH HEH HEH ...
NOT HERE !!
NOT HERE !!

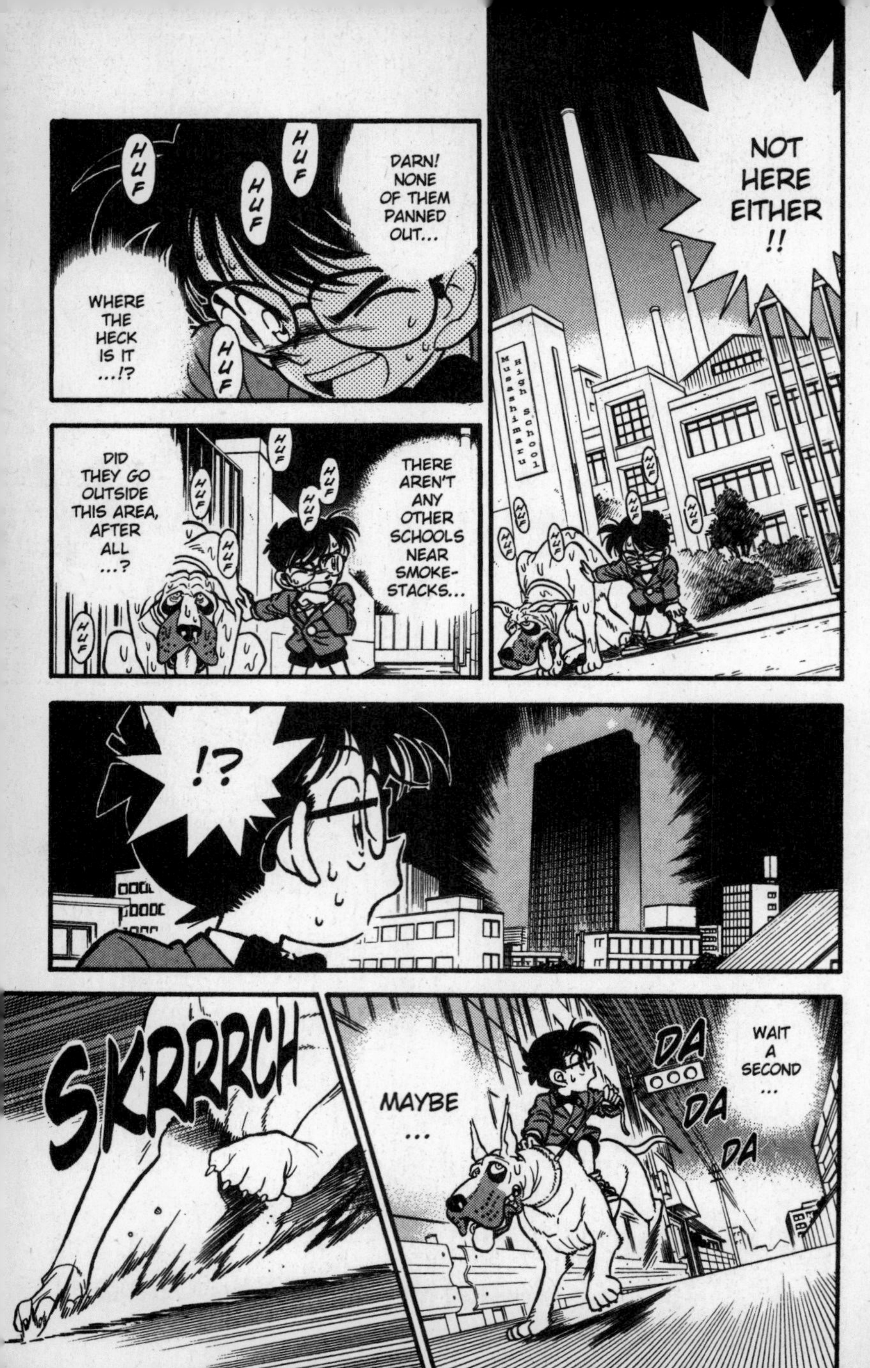
NOT HERE EITHER !!
Musashimaru High School
HUF
HUF
HUF
HUF
HUF
DARN! NONE OF THEM PANNED OUT...
HUF
HUF
WHERE THE HECK IS IT ...!?
HUF
THERE AREN'T ANY OTHER SCHOOLS NEAR SMOKE-STACKS...
HUF
HUF
HUF
HUF
DID THEY GO OUTSIDE THIS AREA, AFTER ALL ...?
HUF
!?
WAIT A SECOND ...
DA
DA
DA
MAYBE ...
SKRRRCH

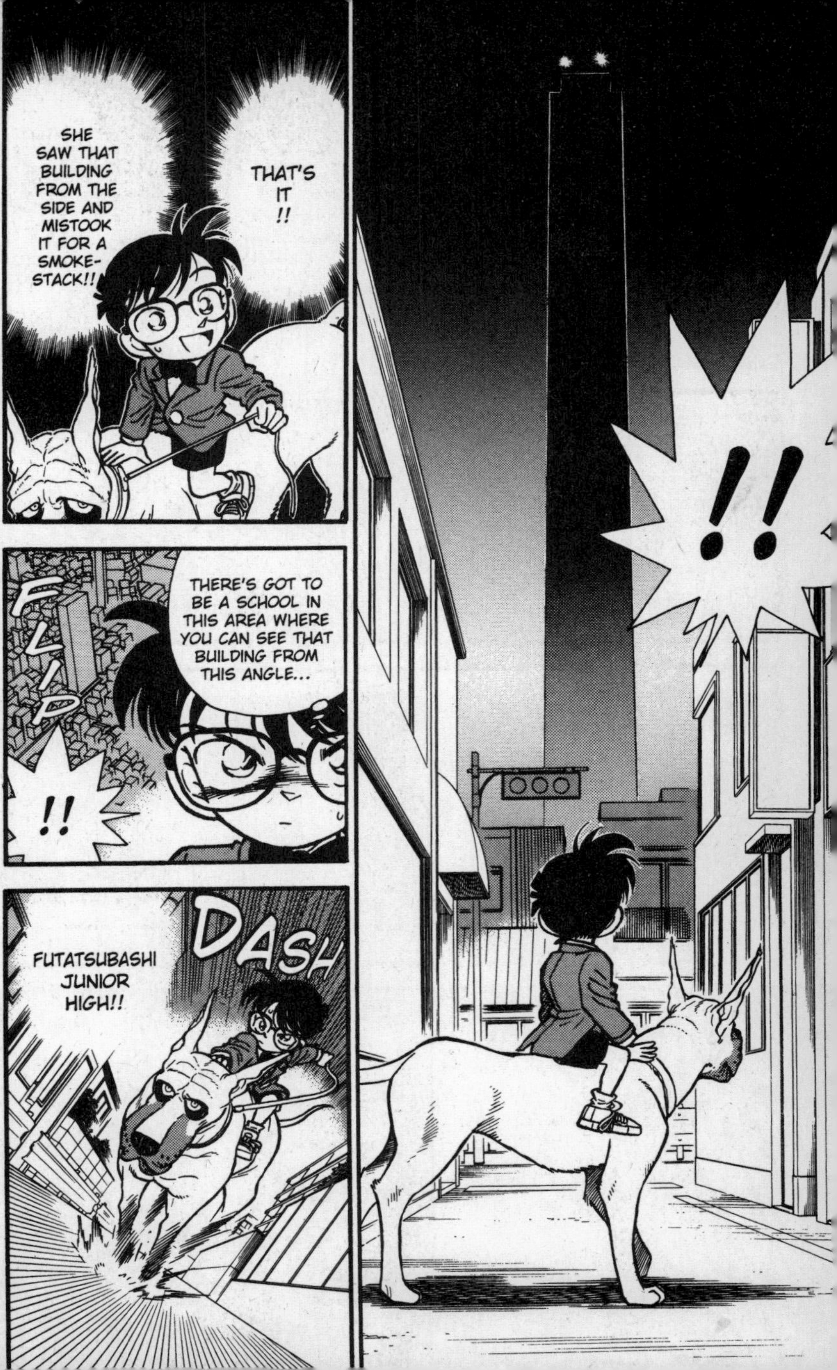
!!
THAT'S IT !!
SHE SAW THAT BUILDING FROM THE SIDE AND MISTOOK IT FOR A SMOKE-STACK!!
THERE'S GOT TO BE A SCHOOL IN THIS AREA WHERE YOU CAN SEE THAT BUILDING FROM THIS ANGLE...
FLIP
!!
DASH
FUTATSUBASHI JUNIOR HIGH!!

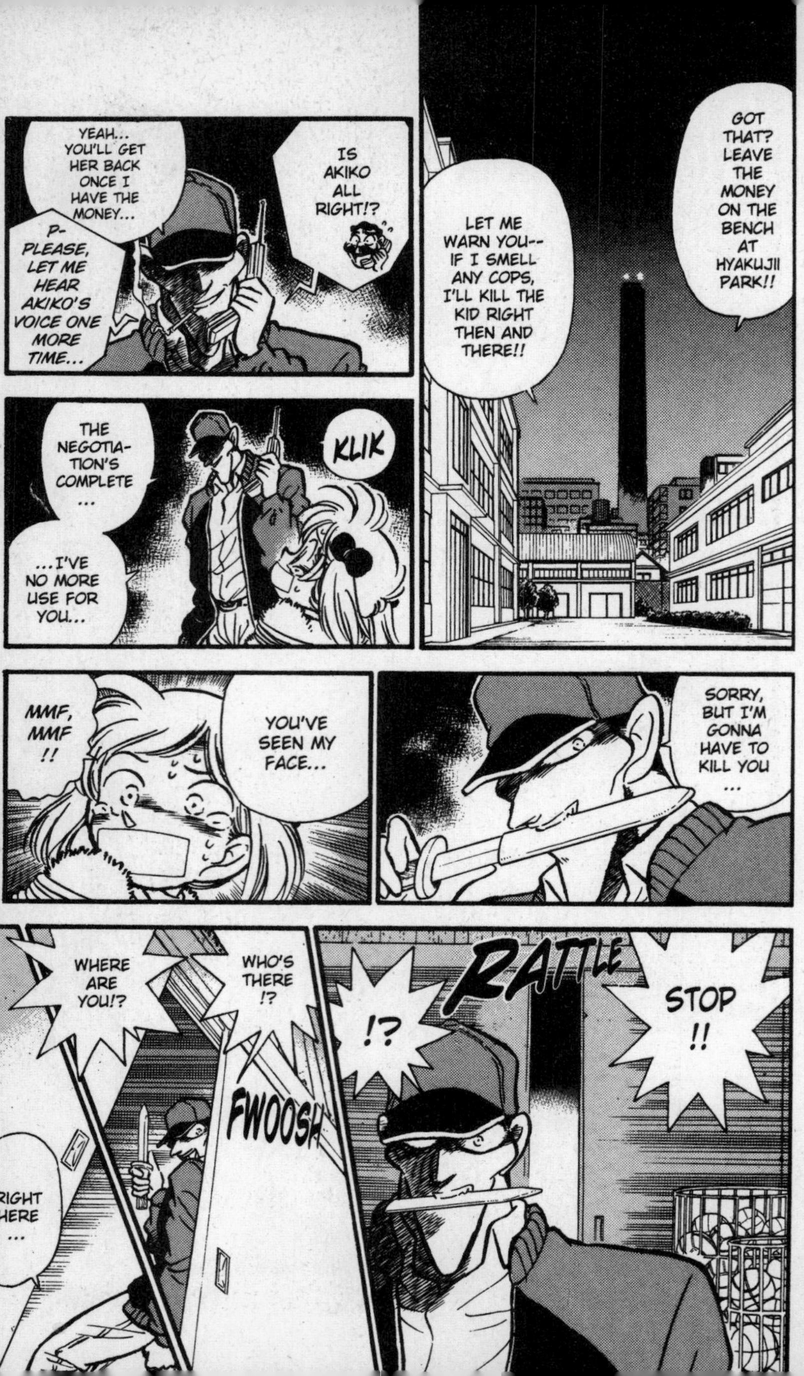
GOT THAT? LEAVE THE MONEY ON THE BENCH AT HYAKUJII PARK!!
LET ME WARN YOU-- IF I SMELL ANY COPS, I'LL KILL THE KID RIGHT THEN AND THERE!!
IS AKIKO ALL RIGHT!?
YEAH... YOU'LL GET HER BACK ONCE I HAVE THE MONEY...
P-PLEASE, LET ME HEAR AKIKO'S VOICE ONE MORE TIME...
KLIK
THE NEGOTIATION'S COMPLETE...
...I'VE NO MORE USE FOR YOU...
SORRY, BUT I'M GONNA HAVE TO KILL YOU...
YOU'VE SEEN MY FACE...
MMF, MMF!!
STOP!!
RATTLE
!?
WHO'S THERE!?
WHERE ARE YOU!?
FWOOSH
RIGHT HERE...

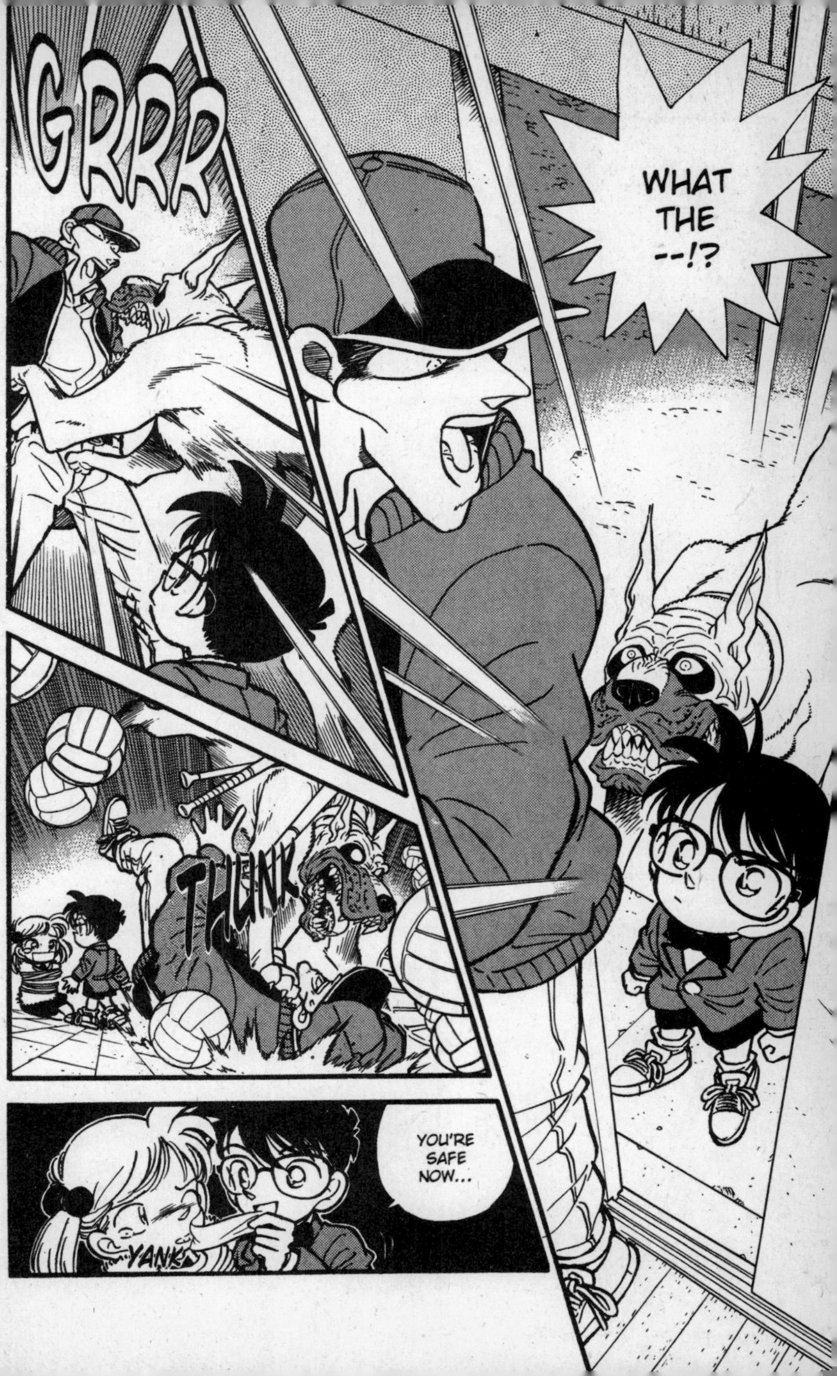
WHAT THE --!?
GRRR
THUNK
YOU'RE SAFE NOW...
YANK

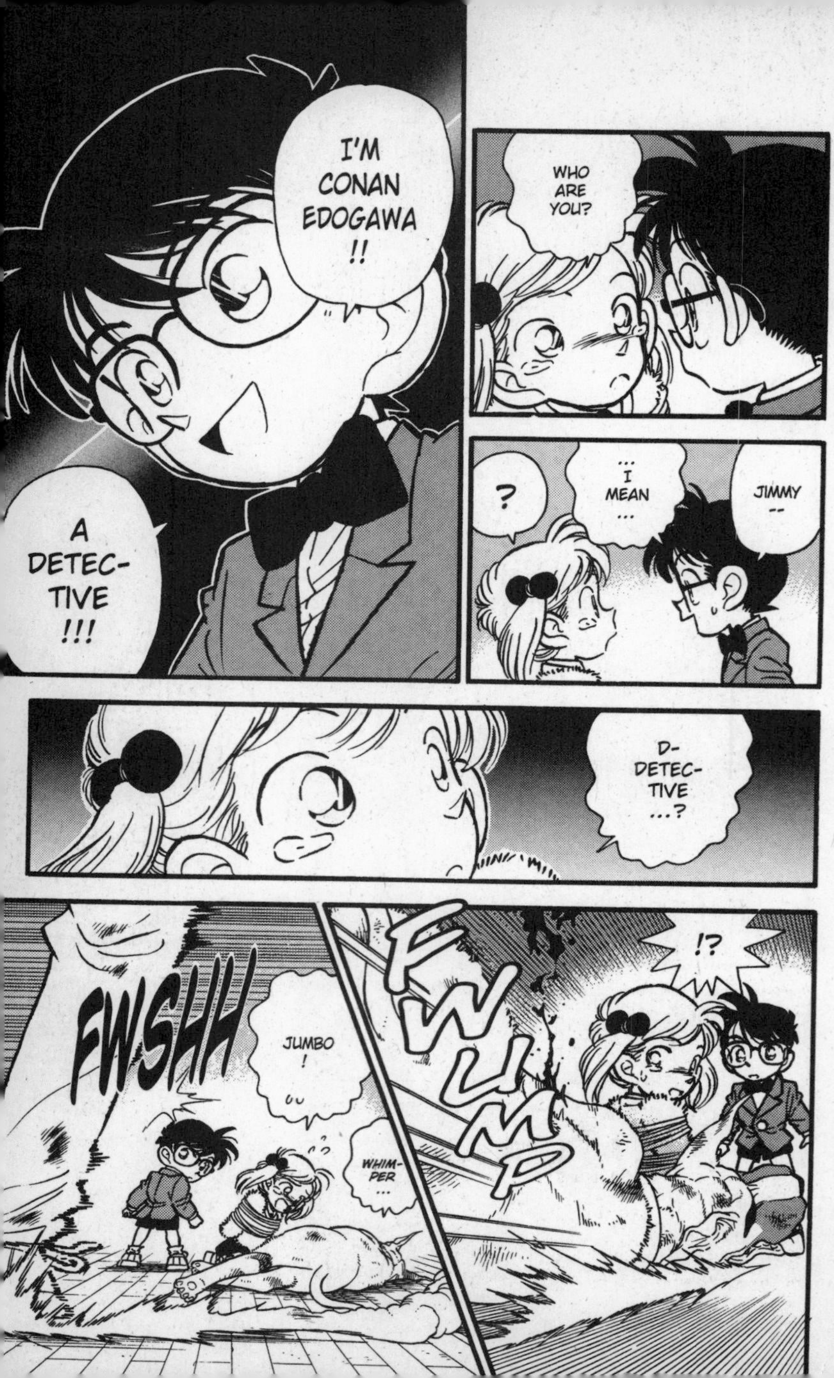
WHO ARE YOU?
JIMMY --
... I MEAN ...
?
I'M CONAN EDOGAWA !!
A DETECTIVE !!!
D-DETECTIVE ...?
!?
FWUMP
FWSHH
JUMBO !
WHIMPER ...

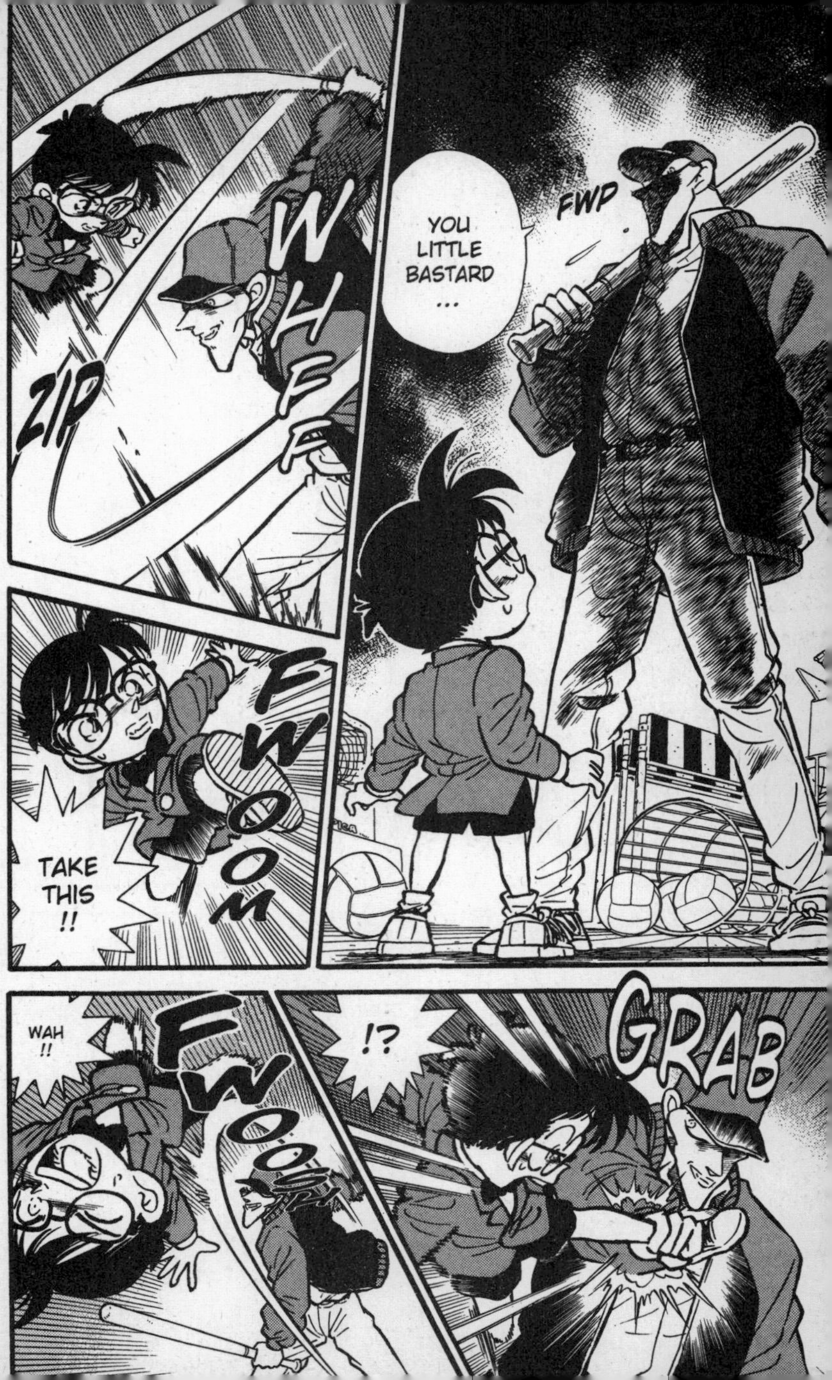
YOU LITTLE BASTARD ...
FWP
WHFF
ZIP
FWOOM
TAKE THIS !!
GRAB
!?
FWOOOM
WAH !!

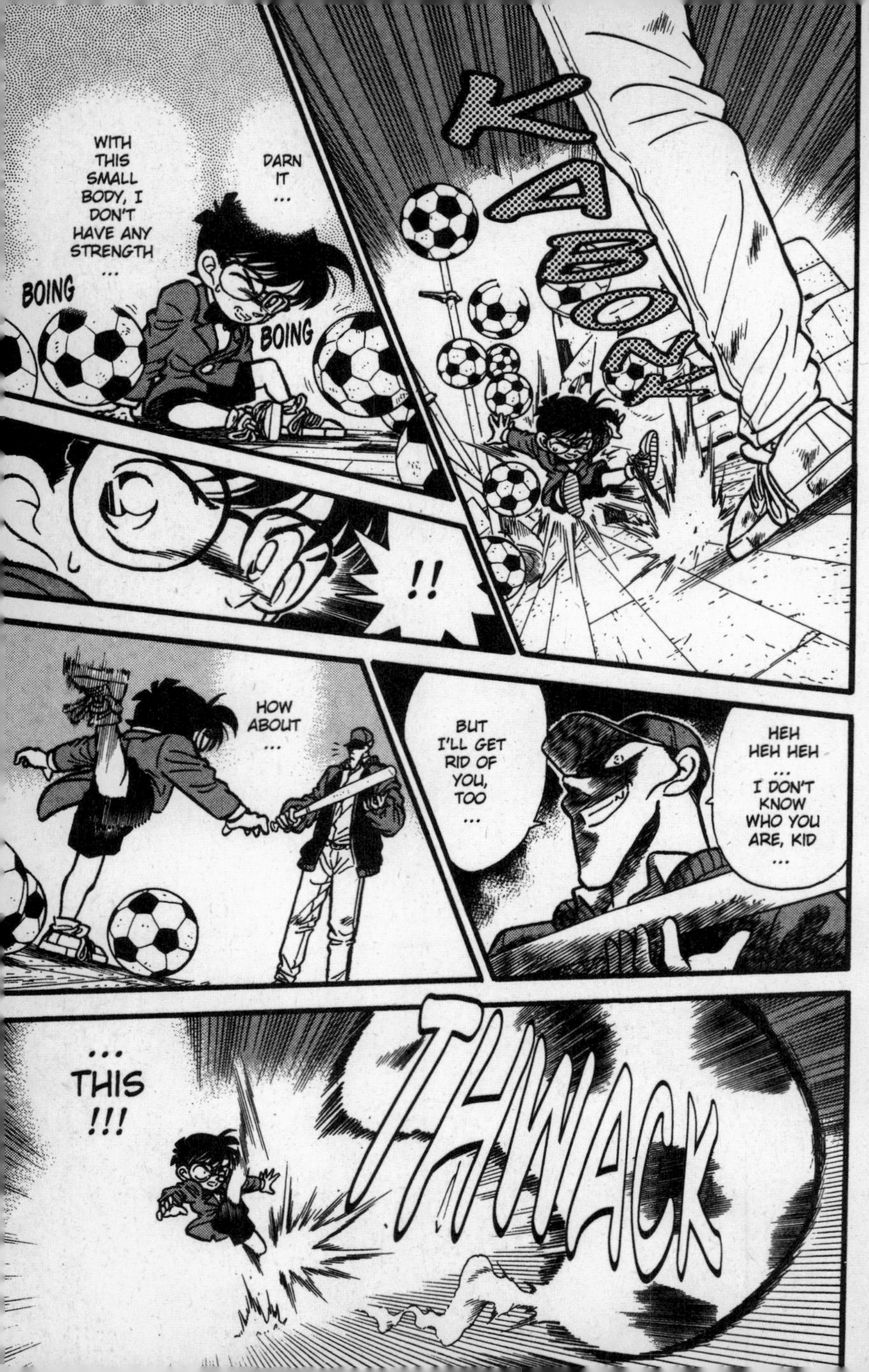
KABOOM
DARN IT ...
WITH THIS SMALL BODY, I DON'T HAVE ANY STRENGTH ...
BOING
BOING
!!
HEH HEH HEH ... I DON'T KNOW WHO YOU ARE, KID ...
BUT I'LL GET RID OF YOU, TOO ...
HOW ABOUT ...
... THIS !!!
THWACK

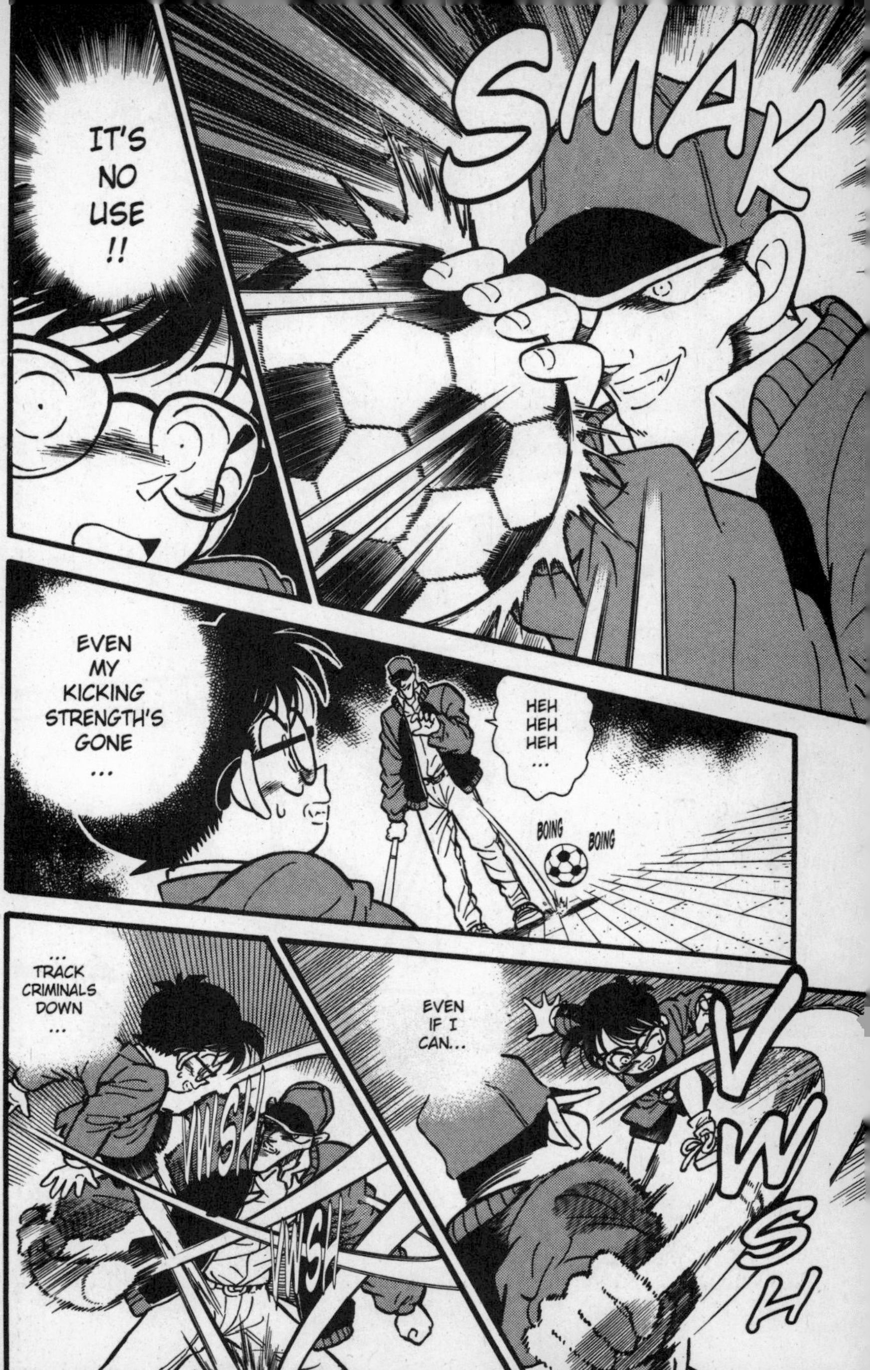
SMAK
IT'S NO USE !!
HEH HEH HEH ...
BOING BOING
EVEN MY KICKING STRENGTH'S GONE ...
EVEN IF I CAN...
VWSH
... TRACK CRIMINALS DOWN ...
VWSH
VWSH

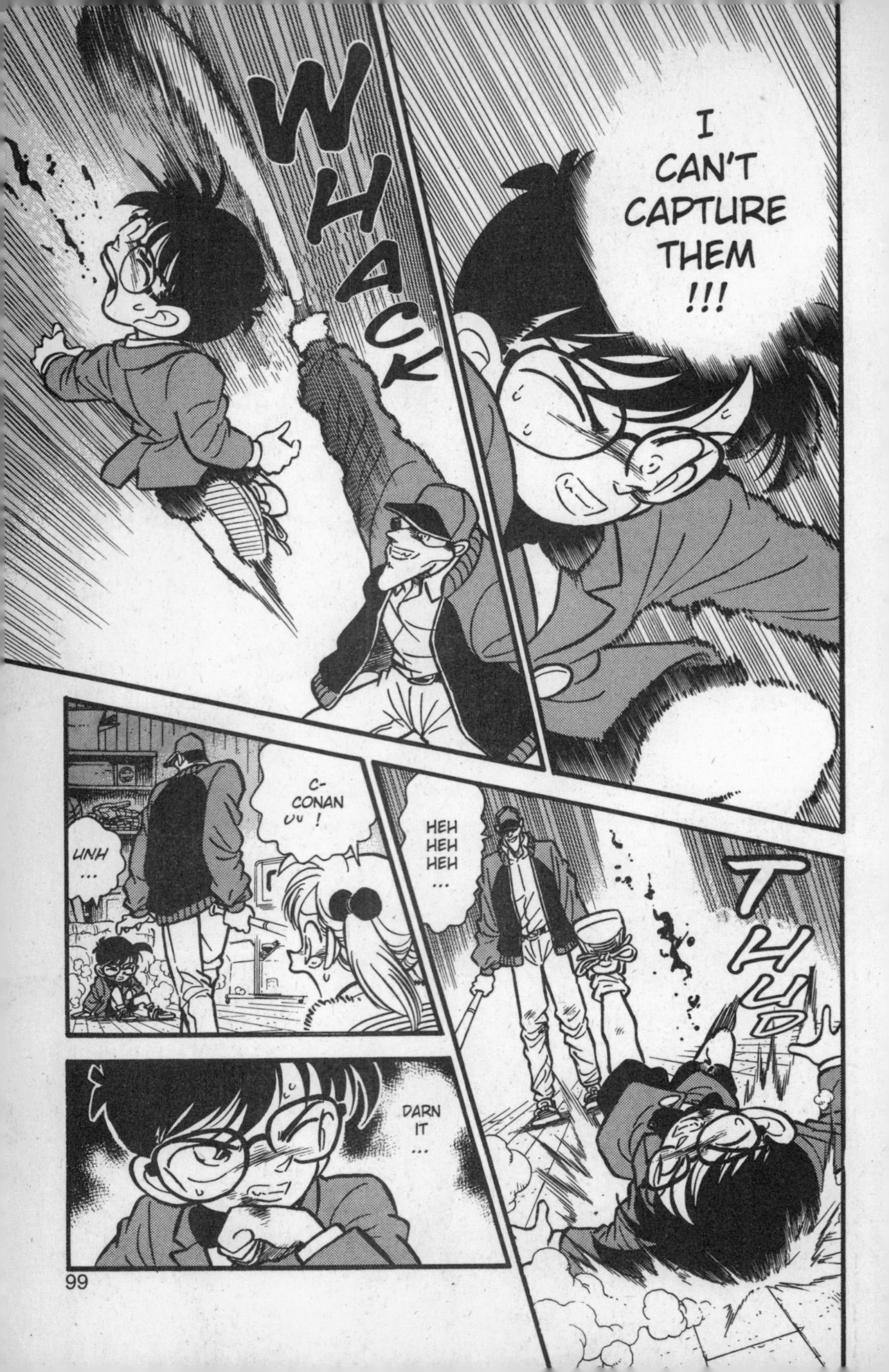
I CAN'T CAPTURE THEM !!!
WHACK
HEH HEH HEH ...
THUD
C- CONAN UU !
UNH ...
DARN IT ...

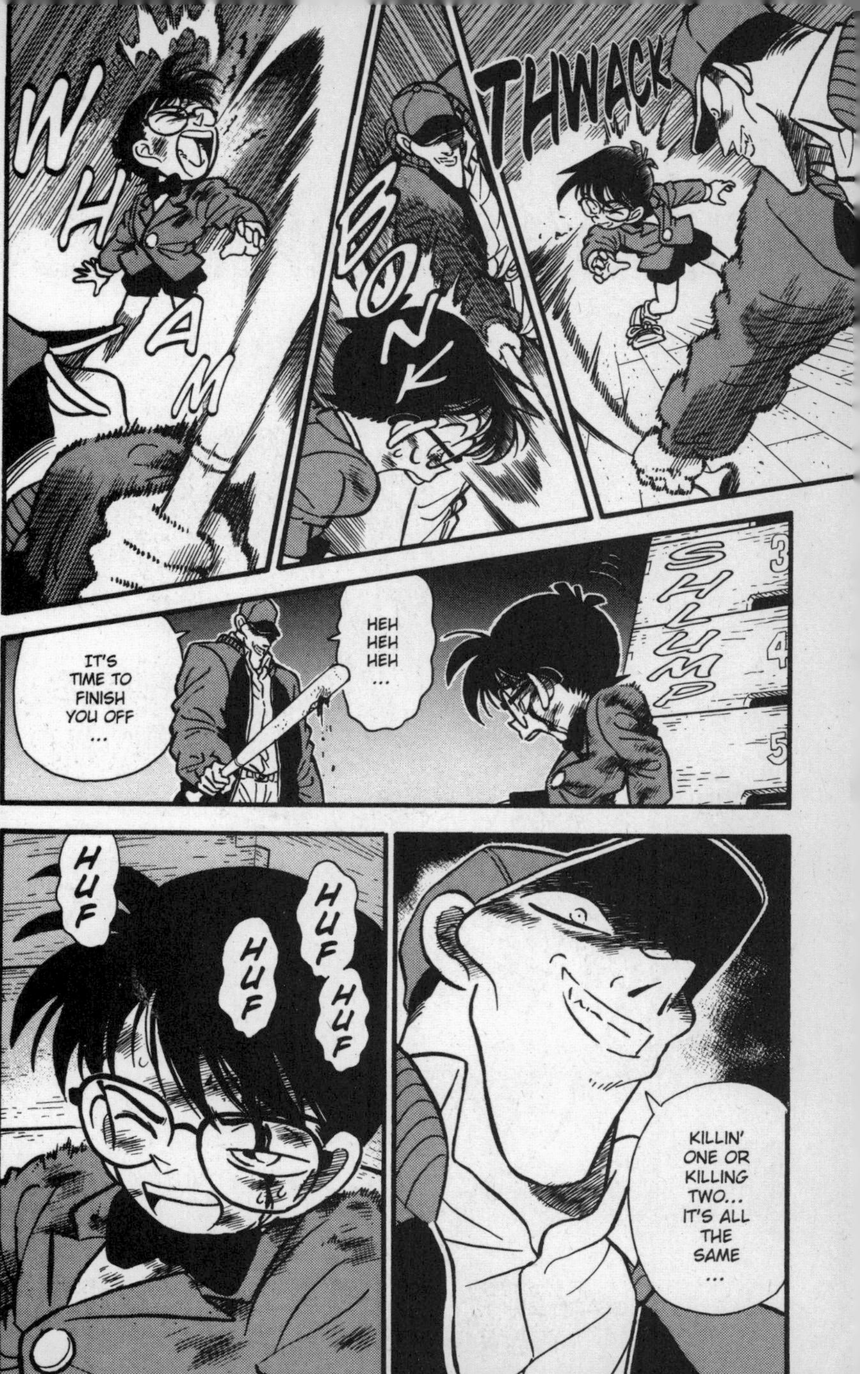
THWACK
BONK
WHAM
SHUMP
HEH HEH HEH ...
IT'S TIME TO FINISH YOU OFF ...
KILLIN' ONE OR KILLING TWO... IT'S ALL THE SAME ...
HUF HUF
HUF HUF

FILE 5: THE OTHER PERPETRATOR

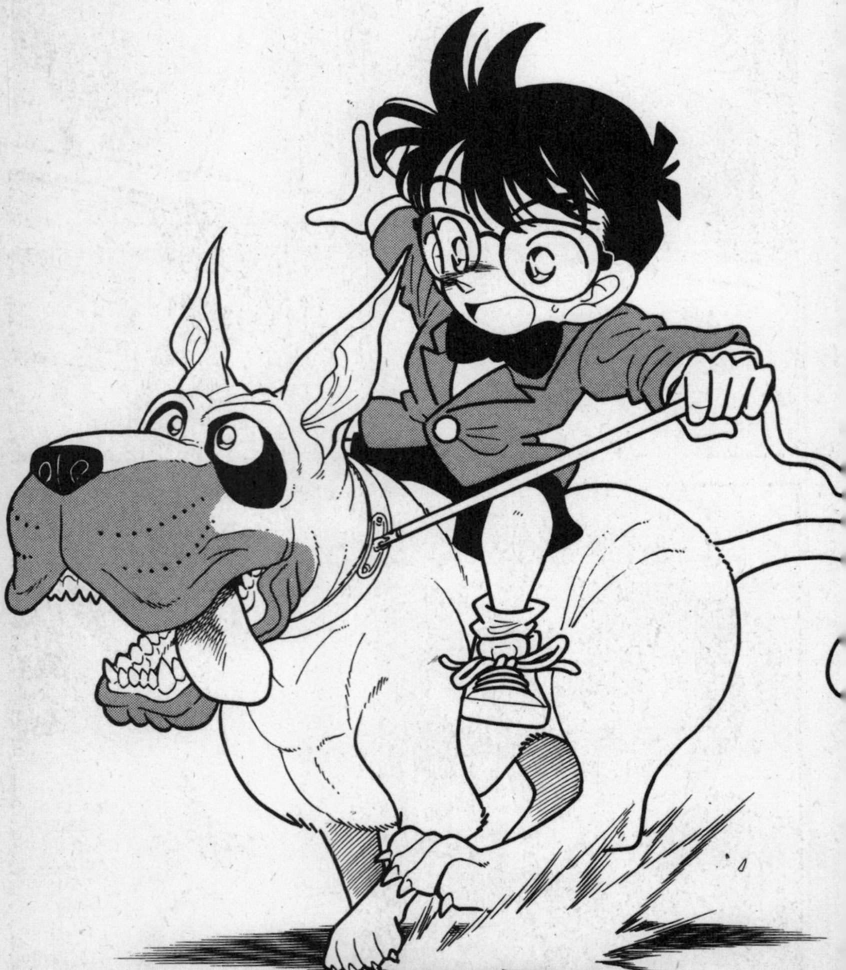

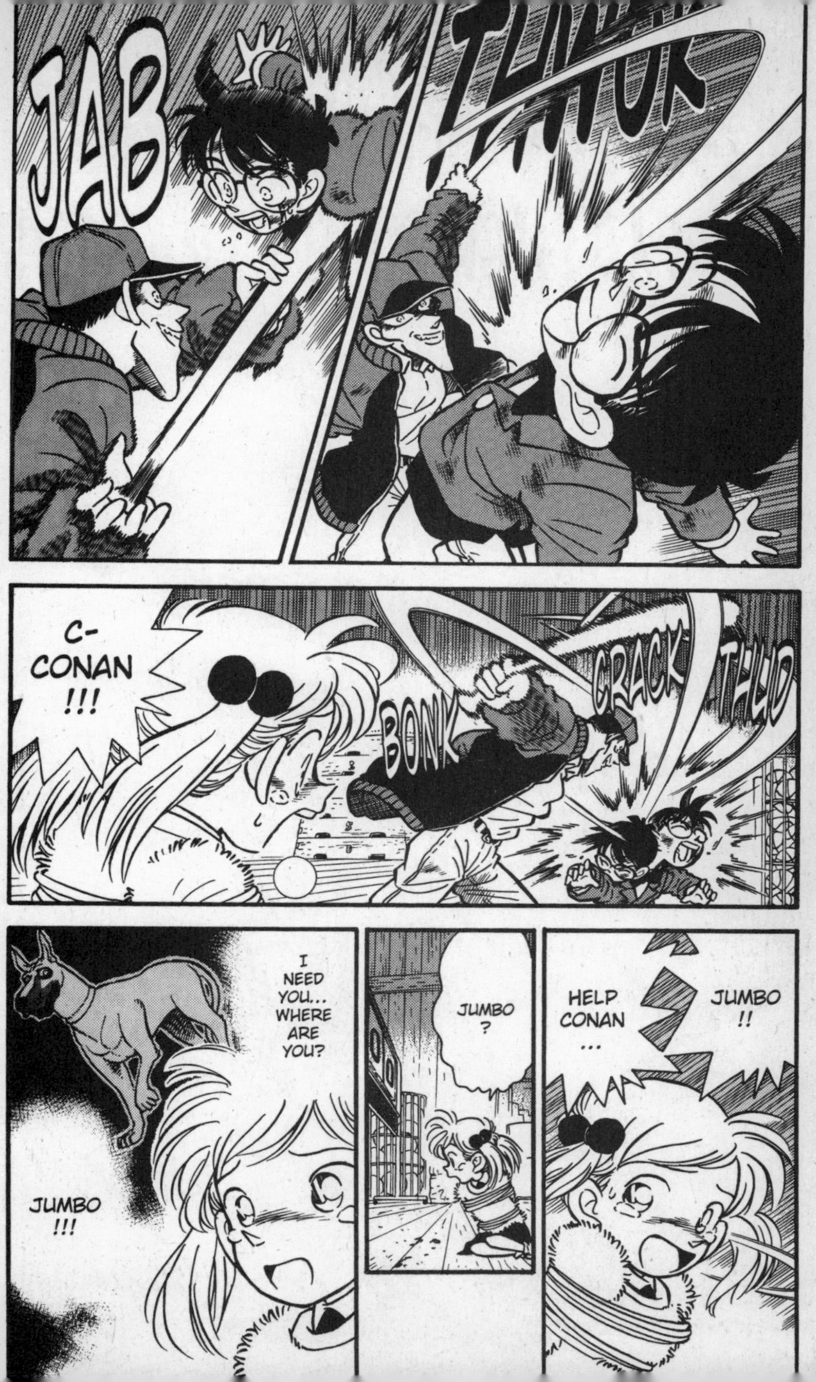
JAB
THUD
CRACK
BONK
C-
CONAN
!!!
JUMBO
!!
HELP
CONAN
...
JUMBO
?
I
NEED
YOU...
WHERE
ARE
YOU?
JUMBO
!!!

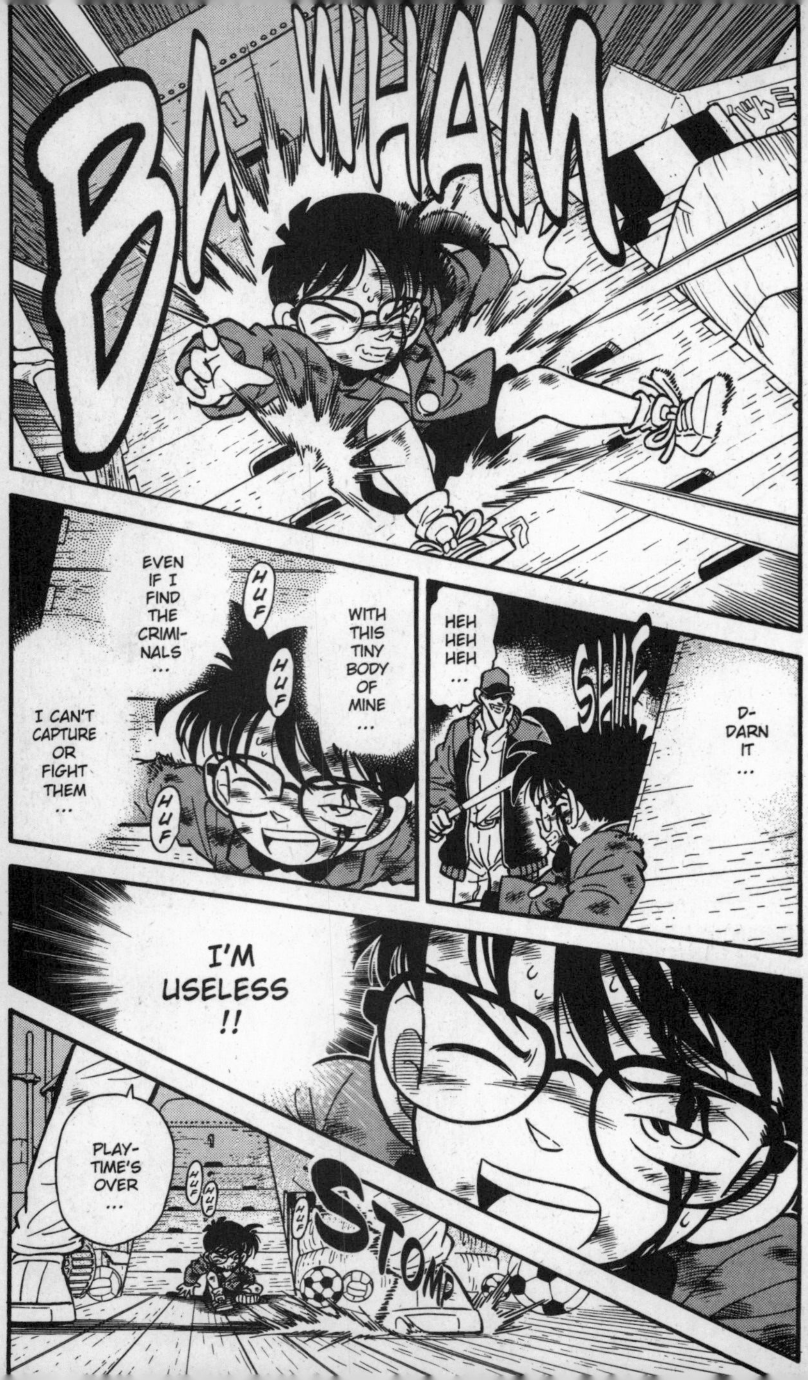
BA-WHAM
HEH HEH HEH ...
D-DARN IT ...
HUF HUF
WITH THIS TINY BODY OF MINE ...
EVEN IF I FIND THE CRIMINALS ...
I CAN'T CAPTURE OR FIGHT THEM ...
HUF HUF
I'M USELESS !!
PLAY-TIME'S OVER ...
HUF HUF
HUF
STOMP

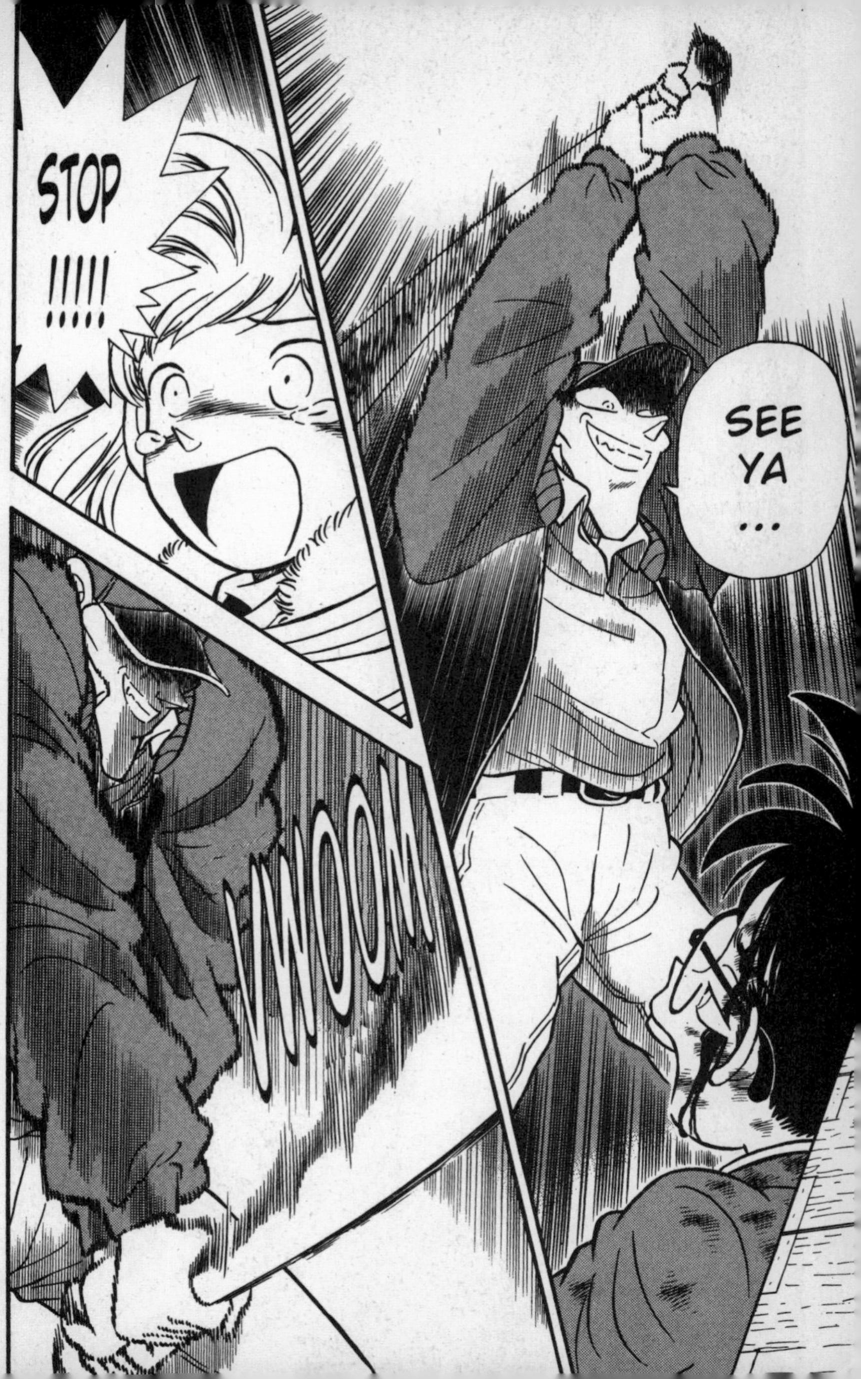
SEE YA ...
STOP !!!!!
VWOOM

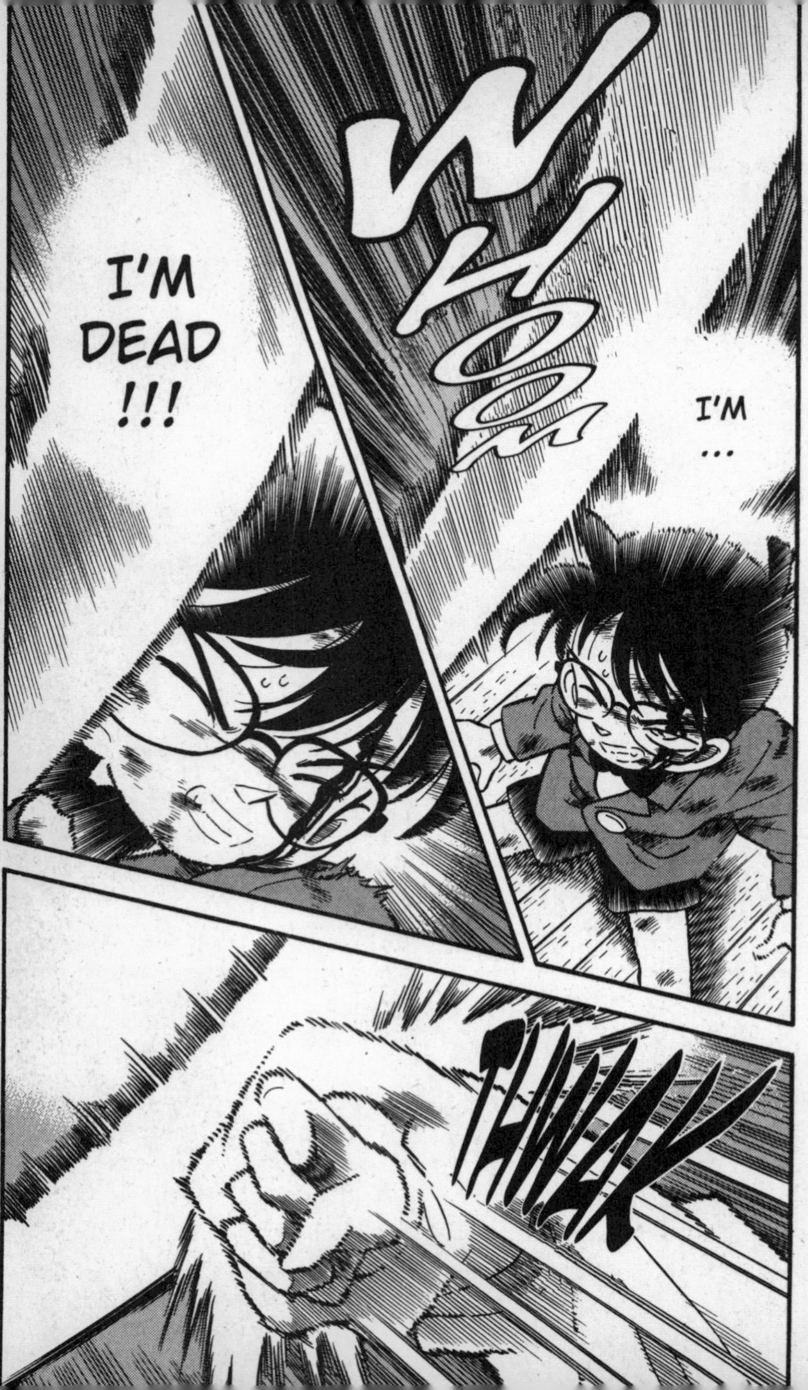
WHOOSH
I'M ...
I'M DEAD !!!
THWAK

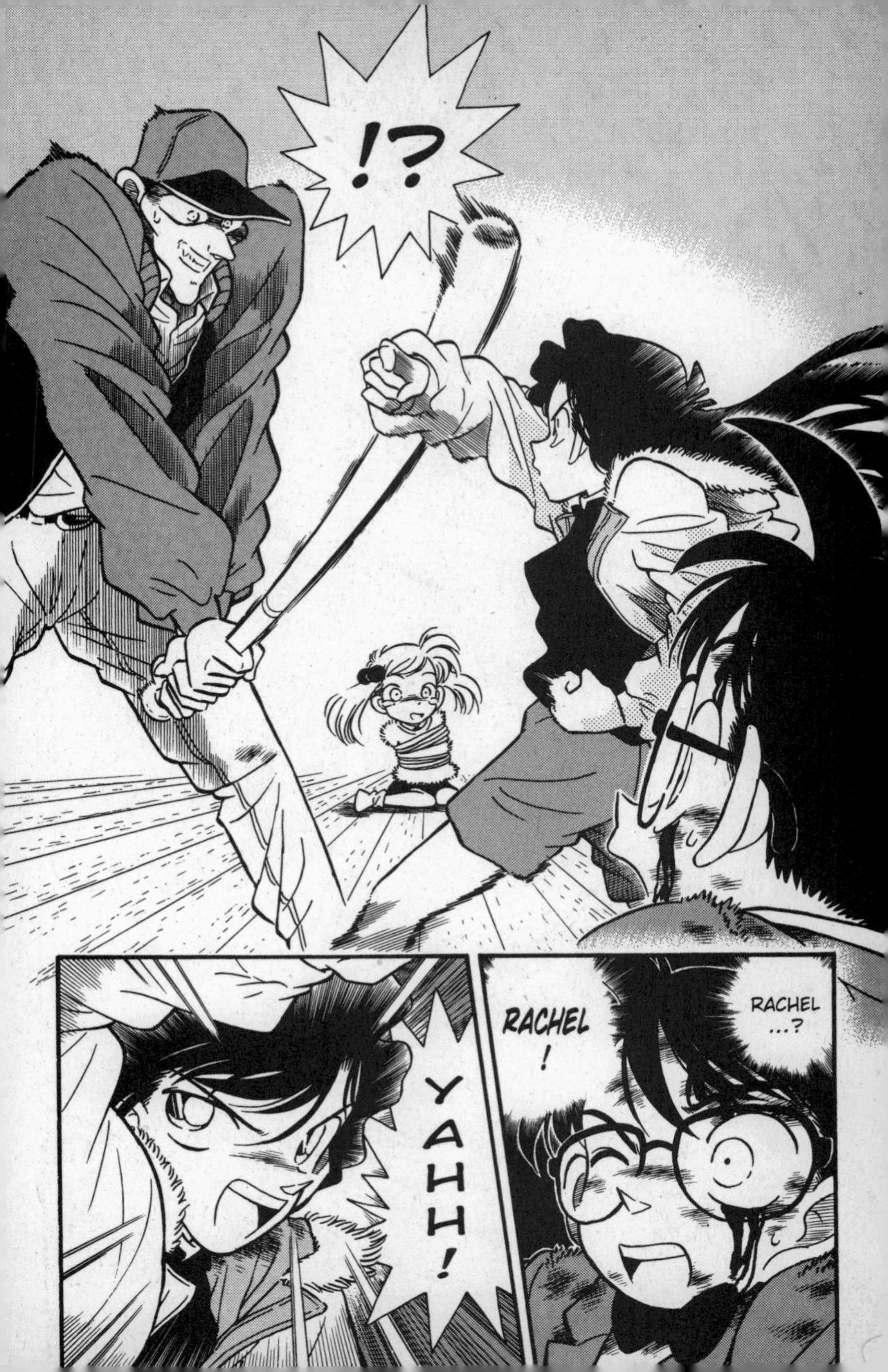
!?
RACHEL ...?
RACHEL !
YAHH!

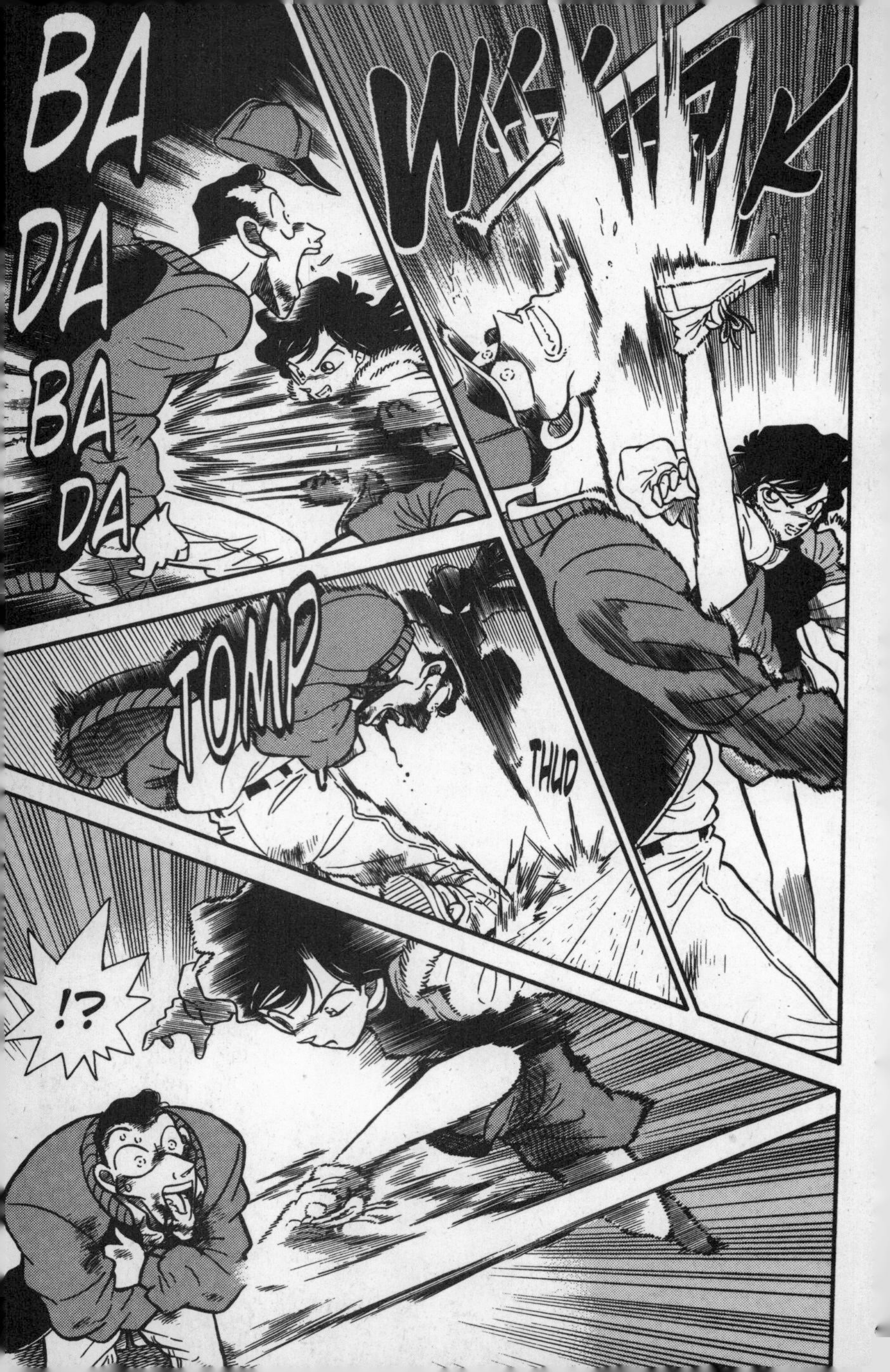
BA DA DA BA DA DA
TOMP
THUD
!?

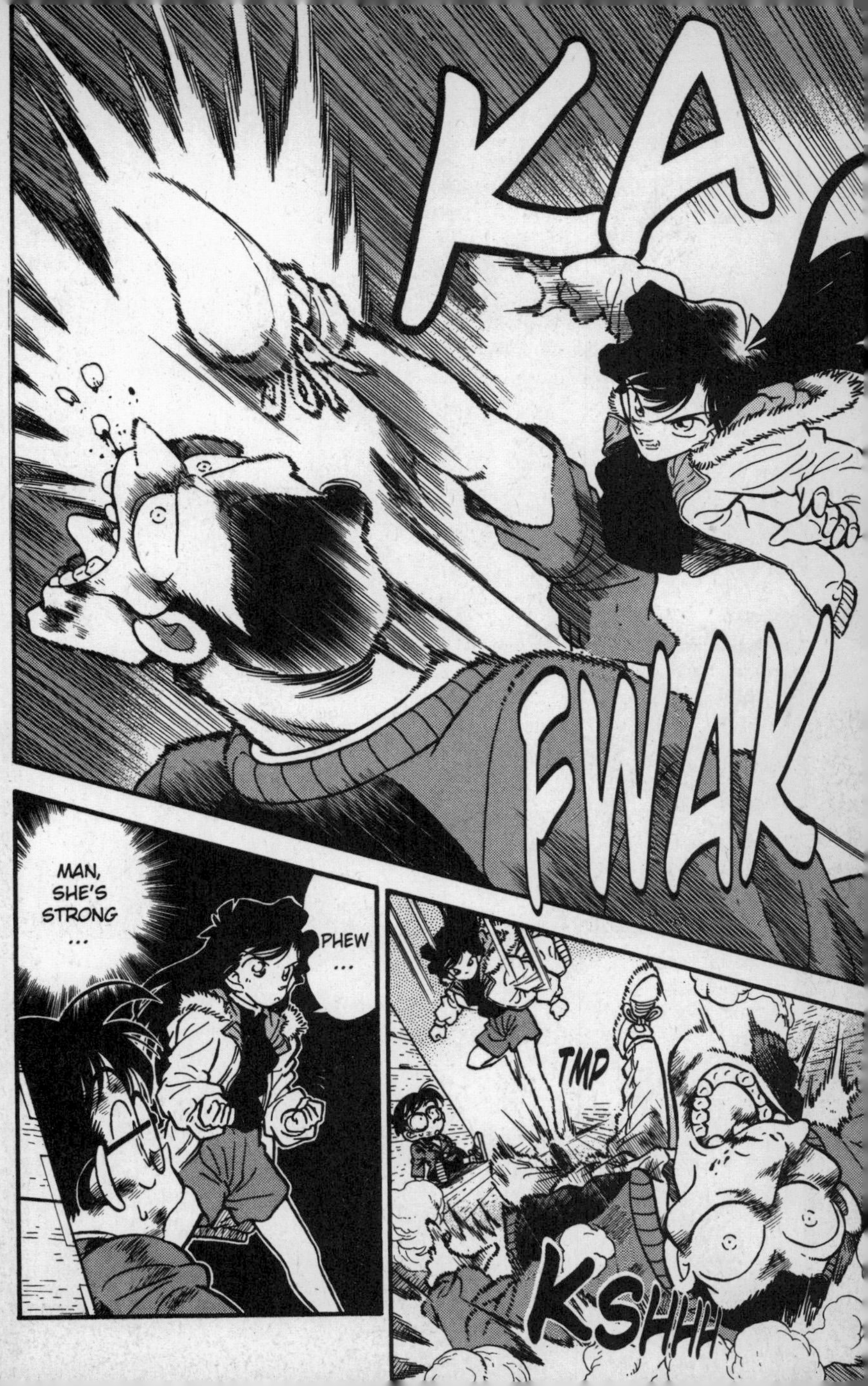
KA...
FWAK
TMP
KSHHH
PHEW ...
MAN, SHE'S STRONG ...

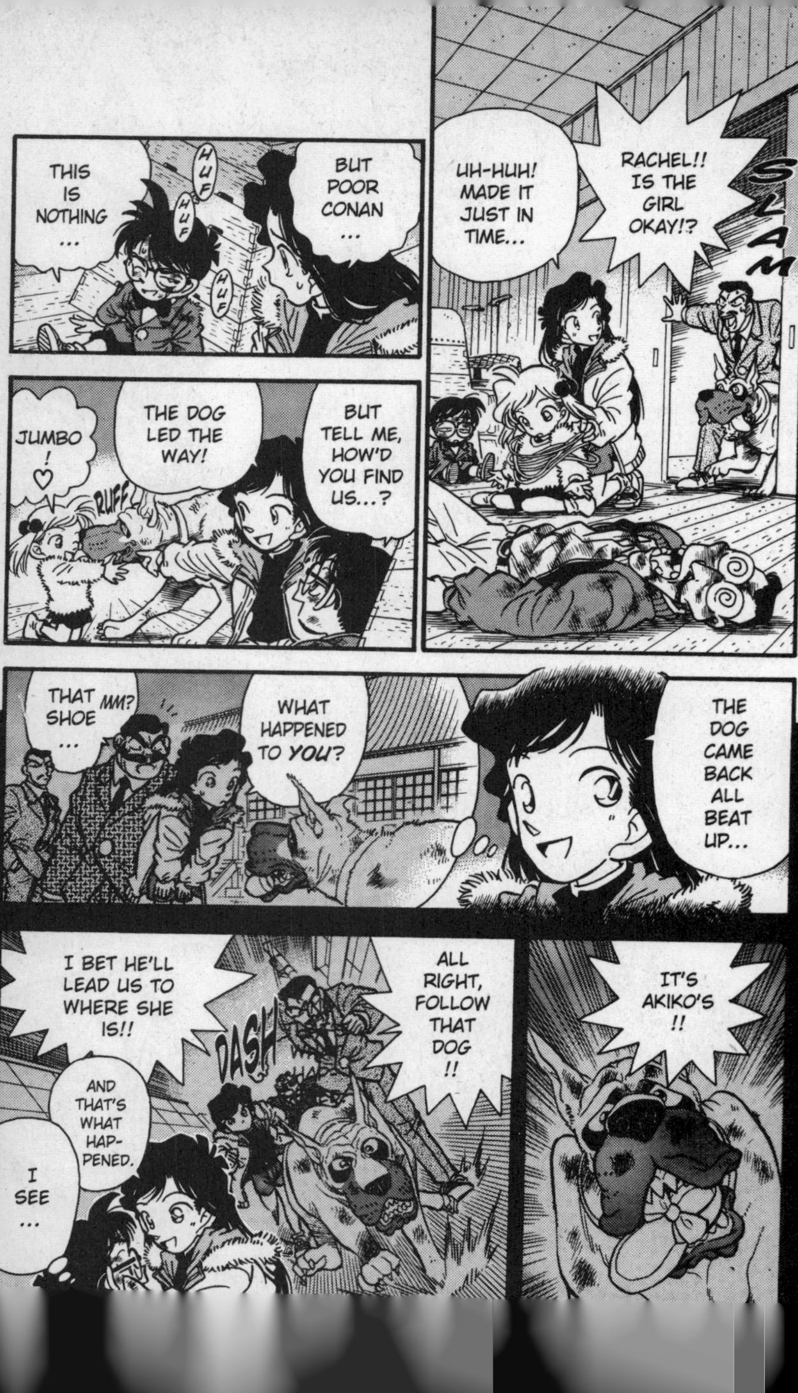

RACHEL!! IS THE GIRL OKAY!?
SLAM
UH-HUH! MADE IT JUST IN TIME...
BUT POOR CONAN ...
HUF
HUF
HUF
THIS IS NOTHING ...
BUT TELL ME, HOW'D YOU FIND US...?
THE DOG LED THE WAY!
RUFF
JUMBO! ♡
THE DOG CAME BACK ALL BEAT UP...
WHAT HAPPENED TO *YOU*?
MM?
THAT SHOE ...
IT'S AKIKO'S !!
ALL RIGHT, FOLLOW THAT DOG !!
I BET HE'LL LEAD US TO WHERE SHE IS!!
DASH
AND THAT'S WHAT HAP-PENED.
I SEE ...

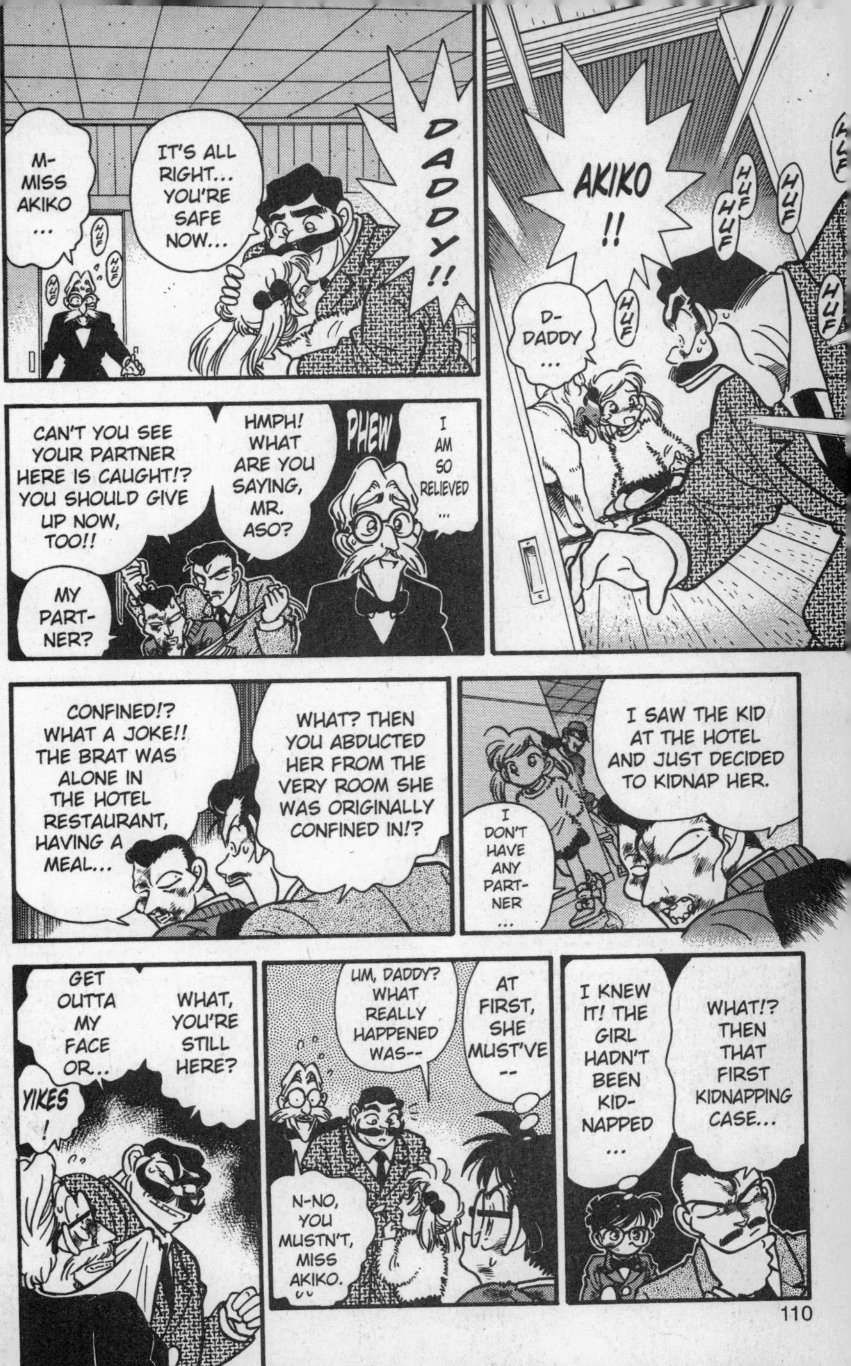
AKIKO !!
HUF HUF HUF HUF HUF HUF
D-DADDY ...
DADDY!!
IT'S ALL RIGHT... YOU'RE SAFE NOW...
M-MISS AKIKO ...
HUF HUF HUF
I AM SO RELIEVED ...
PHEW
HMPH! WHAT ARE YOU SAYING, MR. ASO?
CAN'T YOU SEE YOUR PARTNER HERE IS CAUGHT!? YOU SHOULD GIVE UP NOW, TOO!!
MY PARTNER?
I SAW THE KID AT THE HOTEL AND JUST DECIDED TO KIDNAP HER.
I DON'T HAVE ANY PARTNER ...
WHAT? THEN YOU ABDUCTED HER FROM THE VERY ROOM SHE WAS ORIGINALLY CONFINED IN!?
CONFINED!? WHAT A JOKE!! THE BRAT WAS ALONE IN THE HOTEL RESTAURANT, HAVING A MEAL...
WHAT!? THEN THAT FIRST KIDNAPPING CASE...
I KNEW IT! THE GIRL HADN'T BEEN KIDNAPPED ...
AT FIRST, SHE MUST'VE --
UM, DADDY? WHAT REALLY HAPPENED WAS--
N-NO, YOU MUSTN'T, MISS AKIKO.
WHAT, YOU'RE STILL HERE?
GET OUTTA MY FACE OR...
YIKES !

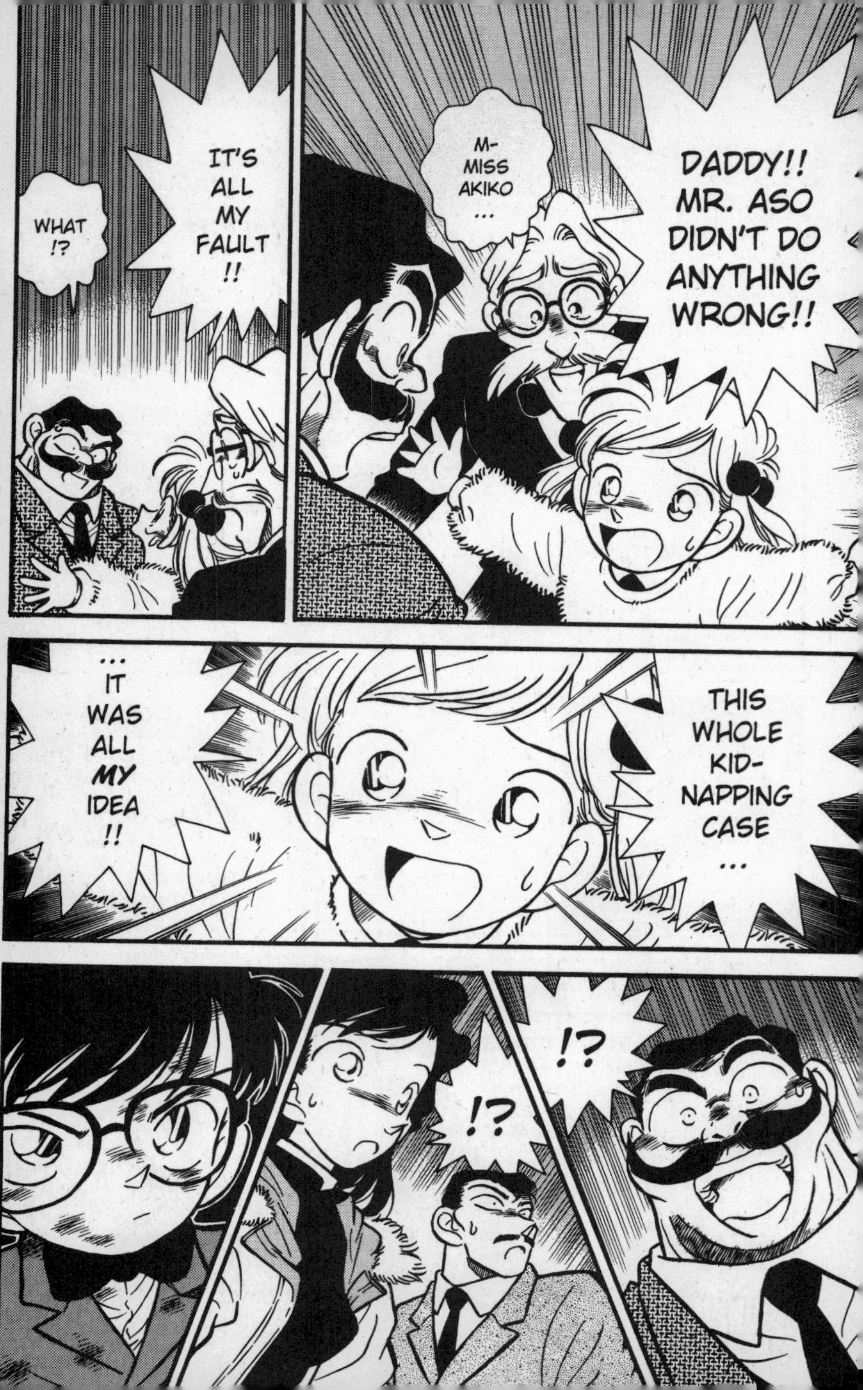
DADDY!! MR. ASO DIDN'T DO ANYTHING WRONG!!
M-MISS AKIKO ...
IT'S ALL MY FAULT !!
WHAT !?
THIS WHOLE KID-NAPPING CASE ...
... IT WAS ALL *MY* IDEA !!
!?
!?

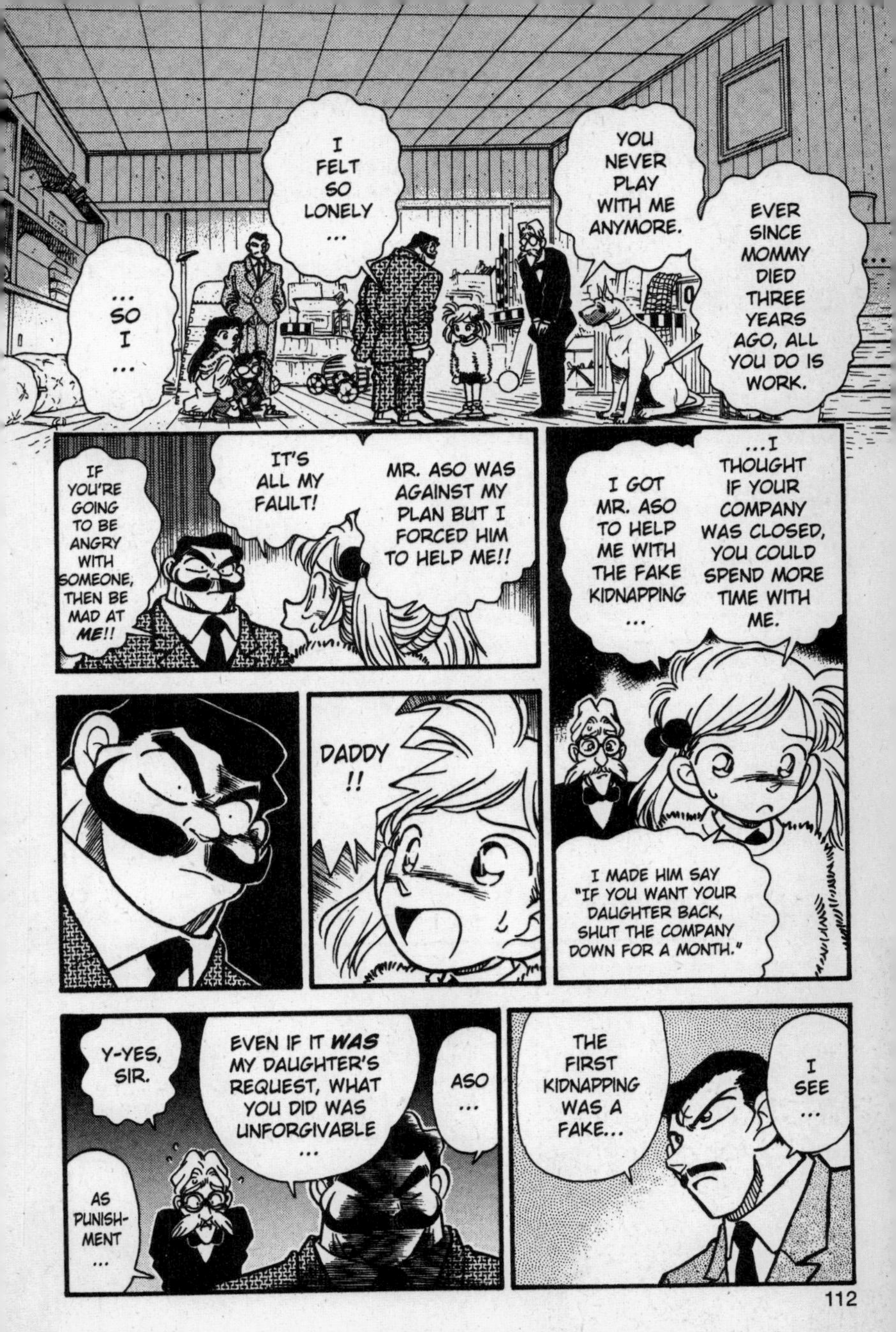
EVER SINCE MOMMY DIED THREE YEARS AGO, ALL YOU DO IS WORK.
YOU NEVER PLAY WITH ME ANYMORE.
I FELT SO LONELY ...
... SO I ...
...I THOUGHT IF YOUR COMPANY WAS CLOSED, YOU COULD SPEND MORE TIME WITH ME.
I GOT MR. ASO TO HELP ME WITH THE FAKE KIDNAPPING ...
I MADE HIM SAY "IF YOU WANT YOUR DAUGHTER BACK, SHUT THE COMPANY DOWN FOR A MONTH."
MR. ASO WAS AGAINST MY PLAN BUT I FORCED HIM TO HELP ME!!
IT'S ALL MY FAULT!
IF YOU'RE GOING TO BE ANGRY WITH SOMEONE, THEN BE MAD AT *ME*!!
DADDY !!
I SEE ...
THE FIRST KIDNAPPING WAS A FAKE...
ASO ...
EVEN IF IT ***WAS*** MY DAUGHTER'S REQUEST, WHAT YOU DID WAS UNFORGIVABLE ...
Y-YES, SIR.
AS PUNISH-MENT ...

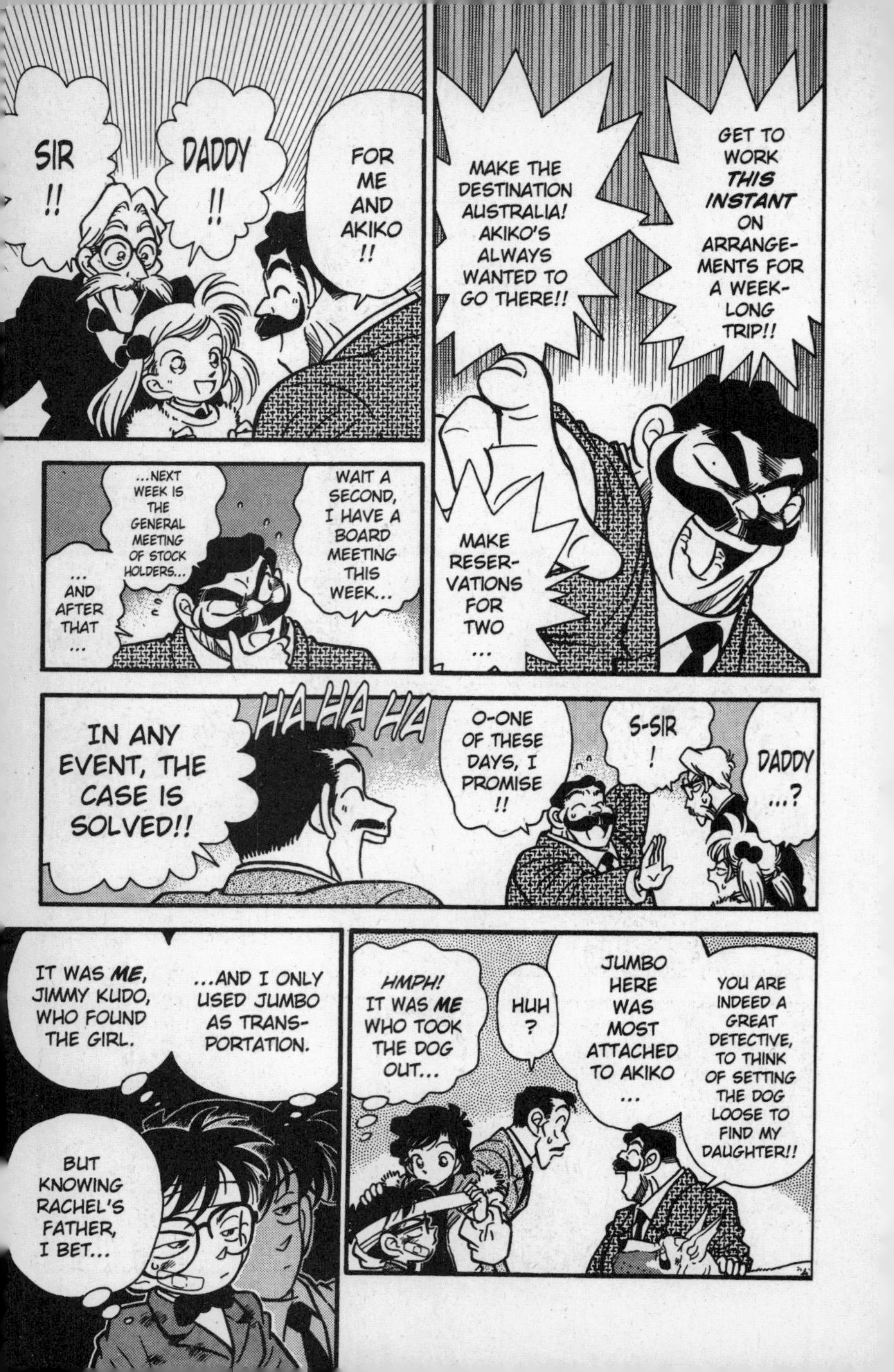
GET TO WORK *THIS INSTANT* ON ARRANGE-MENTS FOR A WEEK-LONG TRIP!!
MAKE THE DESTINATION AUSTRALIA! AKIKO'S ALWAYS WANTED TO GO THERE!!
MAKE RESER-VATIONS FOR TWO ...
FOR ME AND AKIKO !!
DADDY !!
SIR !!
WAIT A SECOND, I HAVE A BOARD MEETING THIS WEEK...
...NEXT WEEK IS THE GENERAL MEETING OF STOCK HOLDERS...
... AND AFTER THAT ...
DADDY ...?
S-SIR !
O-ONE OF THESE DAYS, I PROMISE !!
HA HA HA
IN ANY EVENT, THE CASE IS SOLVED!!
YOU ARE INDEED A GREAT DETECTIVE, TO THINK OF SETTING THE DOG LOOSE TO FIND MY DAUGHTER!!
JUMBO HERE WAS MOST ATTACHED TO AKIKO ...
HUH ?
HMPH! IT WAS *ME* WHO TOOK THE DOG OUT...
...AND I ONLY USED JUMBO AS TRANS-PORTATION.
IT WAS *ME*, JIMMY KUDO, WHO FOUND THE GIRL.
BUT KNOWING RACHEL'S FATHER, I BET...

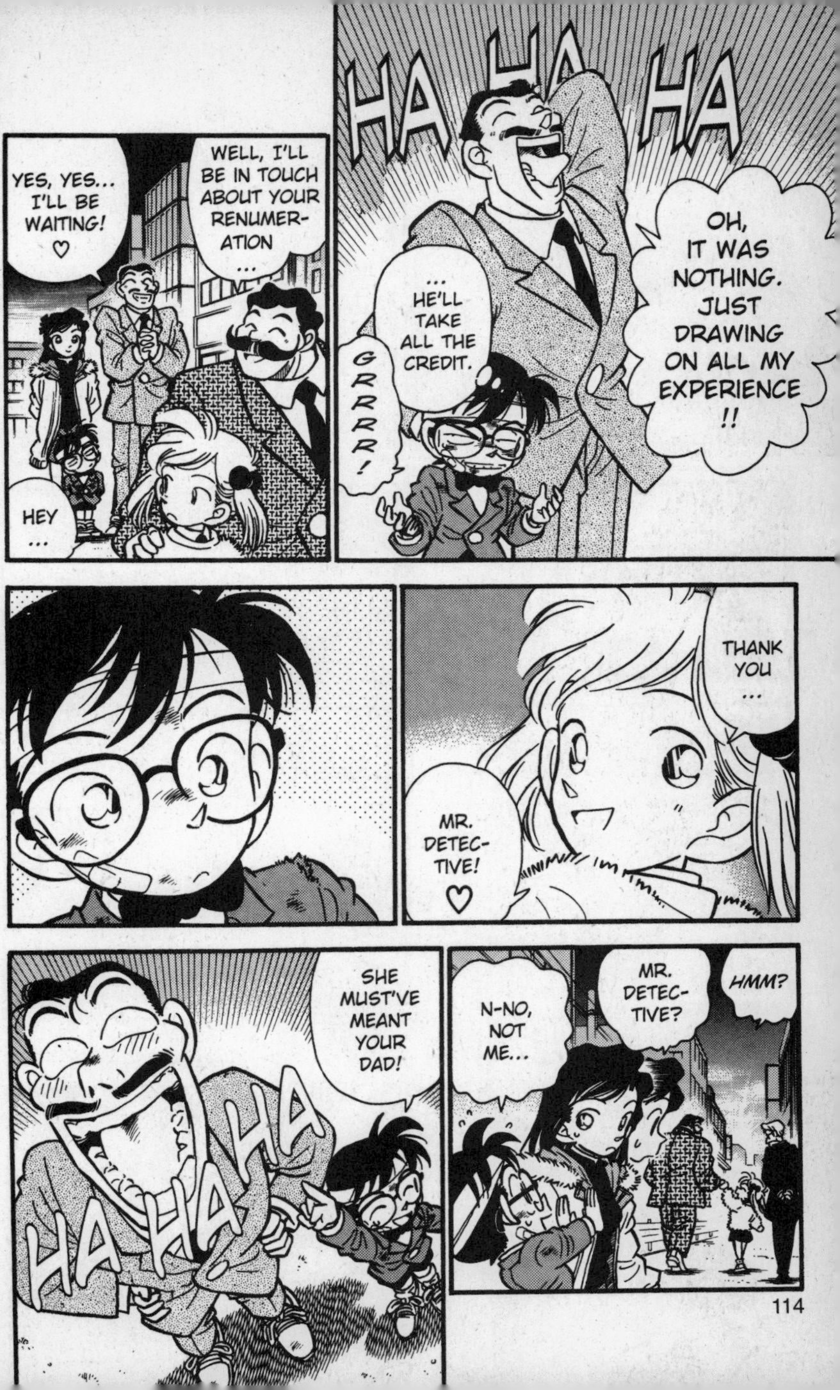

HA HA HA HA
OH, IT WAS NOTHING. JUST DRAWING ON ALL MY EXPERIENCE !!
... HE'LL TAKE ALL THE CREDIT.
GRRRR!
WELL, I'LL BE IN TOUCH ABOUT YOUR RENUMERATION ...
YES, YES... I'LL BE WAITING! ♡
HEY ...
THANK YOU ...
MR. DETECTIVE! ♡
HMM?
MR. DETECTIVE?
N-NO, NOT ME...
SHE MUST'VE MEANT YOUR DAD!
HA HA HA HA

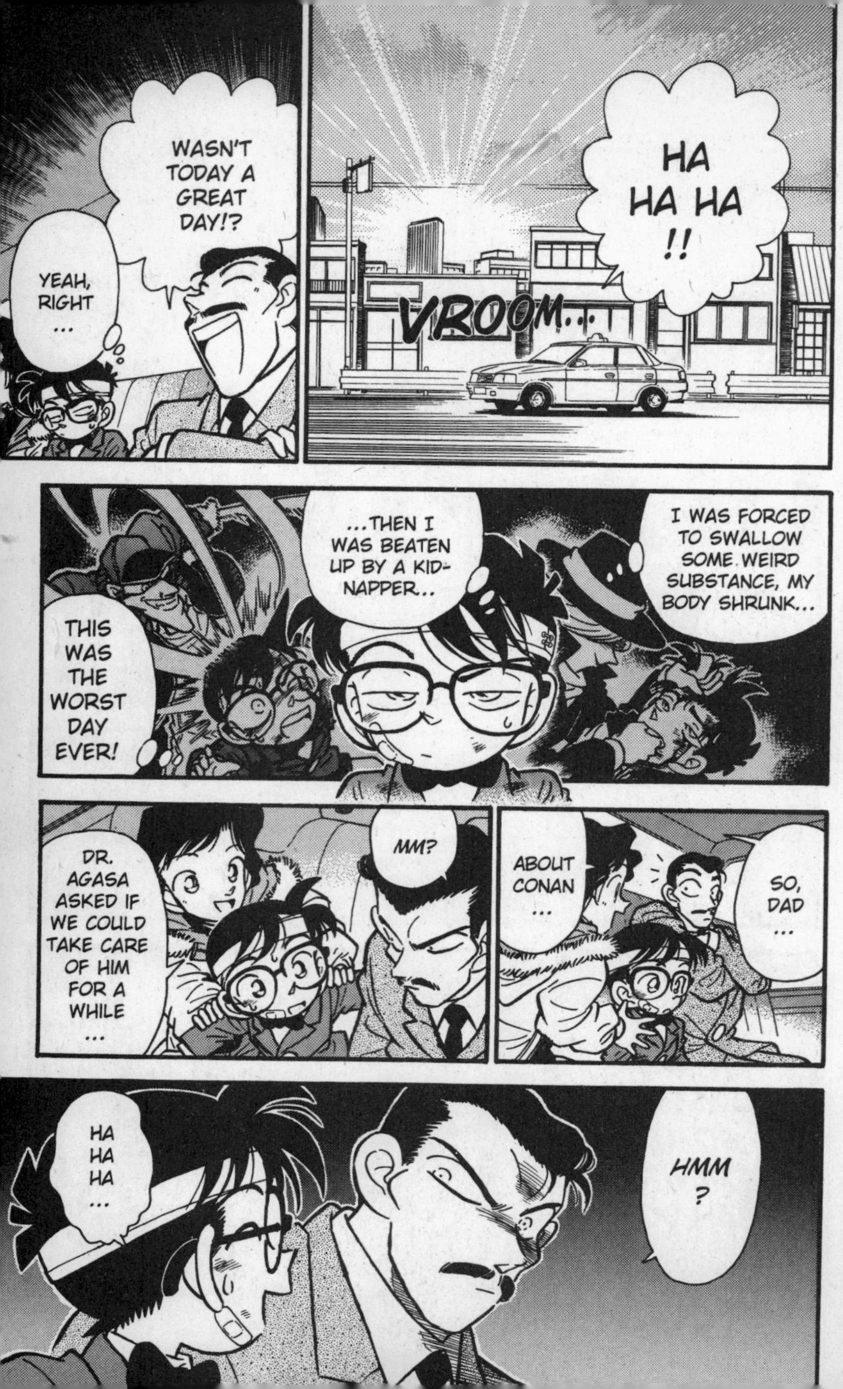
HA HA HA !!
VROOM...
WASN'T TODAY A GREAT DAY!?
YEAH, RIGHT ...
I WAS FORCED TO SWALLOW SOME WEIRD SUBSTANCE, MY BODY SHRUNK...
...THEN I WAS BEATEN UP BY A KID-NAPPER...
THIS WAS THE WORST DAY EVER!
SO, DAD ...
ABOUT CONAN ...
MM?
DR. AGASA ASKED IF WE COULD TAKE CARE OF HIM FOR A WHILE ...
HMM ?
HA HA HA ...

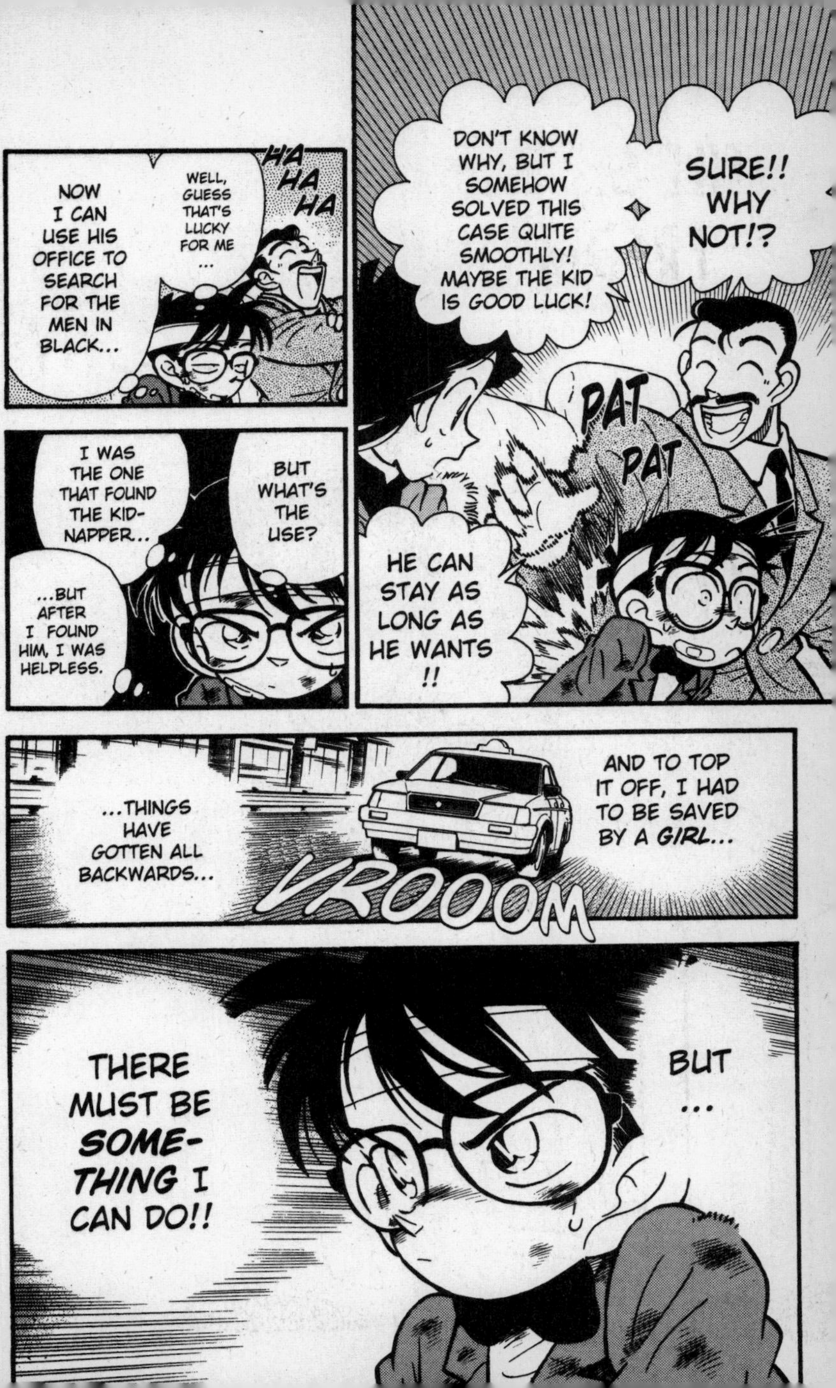
DON'T KNOW WHY, BUT I SOMEHOW SOLVED THIS CASE QUITE SMOOTHLY! MAYBE THE KID IS GOOD LUCK!
SURE!! WHY NOT!?
PAT PAT
HE CAN STAY AS LONG AS HE WANTS !!
HA HA HA
WELL, GUESS THAT'S LUCKY FOR ME ...
NOW I CAN USE HIS OFFICE TO SEARCH FOR THE MEN IN BLACK...
BUT WHAT'S THE USE?
I WAS THE ONE THAT FOUND THE KID-NAPPER...
...BUT AFTER I FOUND HIM, I WAS HELPLESS.
AND TO TOP IT OFF, I HAD TO BE SAVED BY A *GIRL*...
VROOOM
...THINGS HAVE GOTTEN ALL BACKWARDS...
BUT ...
THERE MUST BE ***SOME-THING*** I CAN DO!!

FILE 6: FROM THIRD-RATE TO GREAT DETECTIVE

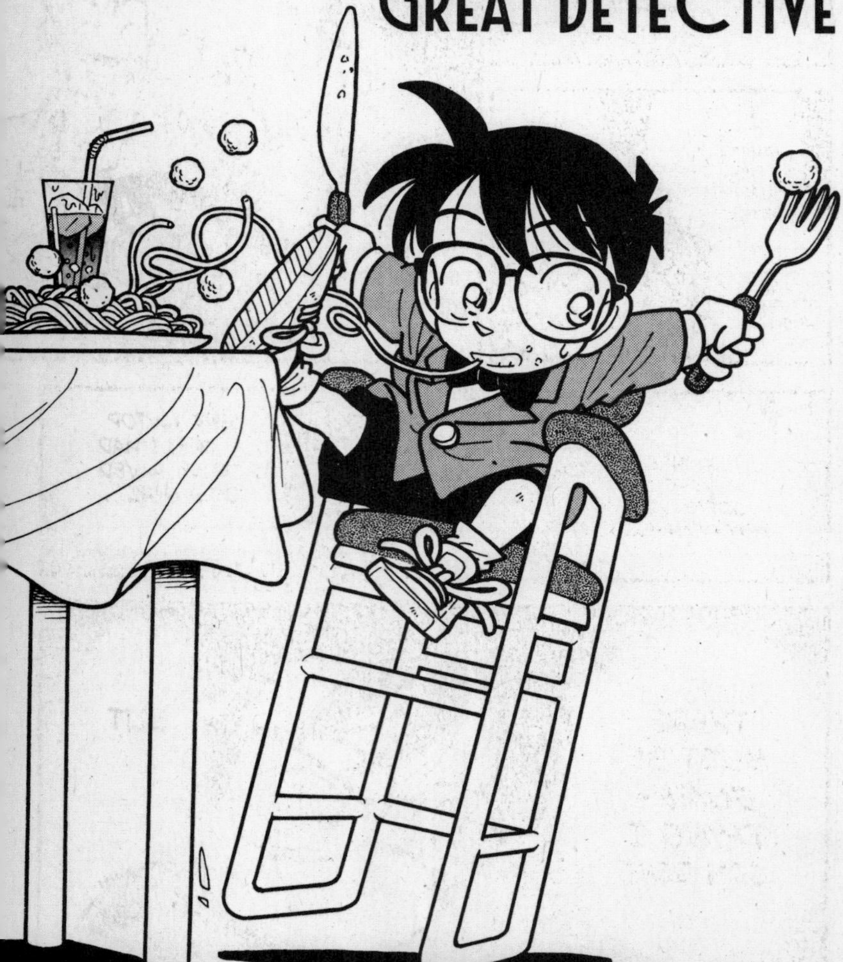

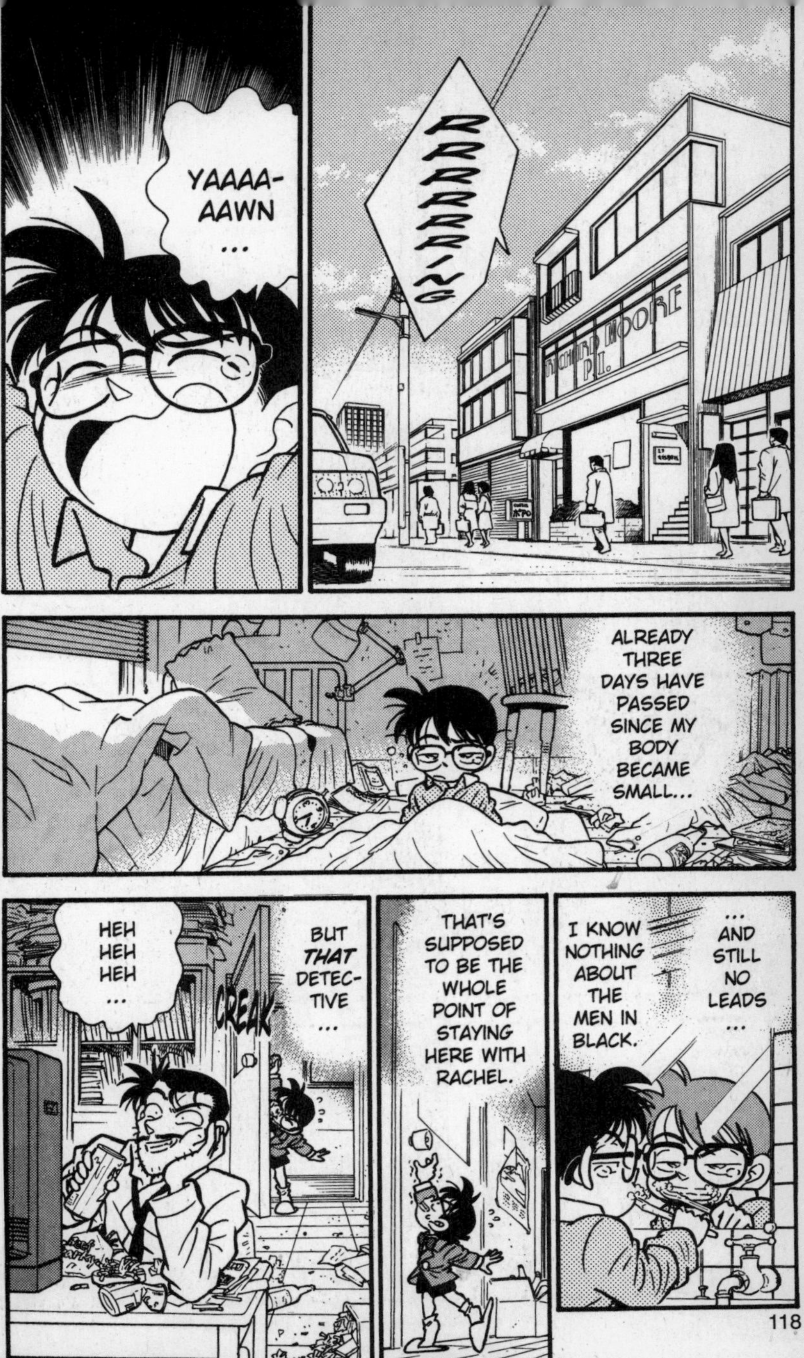
RRRRRRING
RICHARD MOORE P.I.
YAAAA-AAWN ...
ALREADY THREE DAYS HAVE PASSED SINCE MY BODY BECAME SMALL...
... AND STILL NO LEADS ...
I KNOW NOTHING ABOUT THE MEN IN BLACK.
THAT'S SUPPOSED TO BE THE WHOLE POINT OF STAYING HERE WITH RACHEL.
BUT *THAT* DETECTIVE ...
CREAK
HEH HEH HEH ...

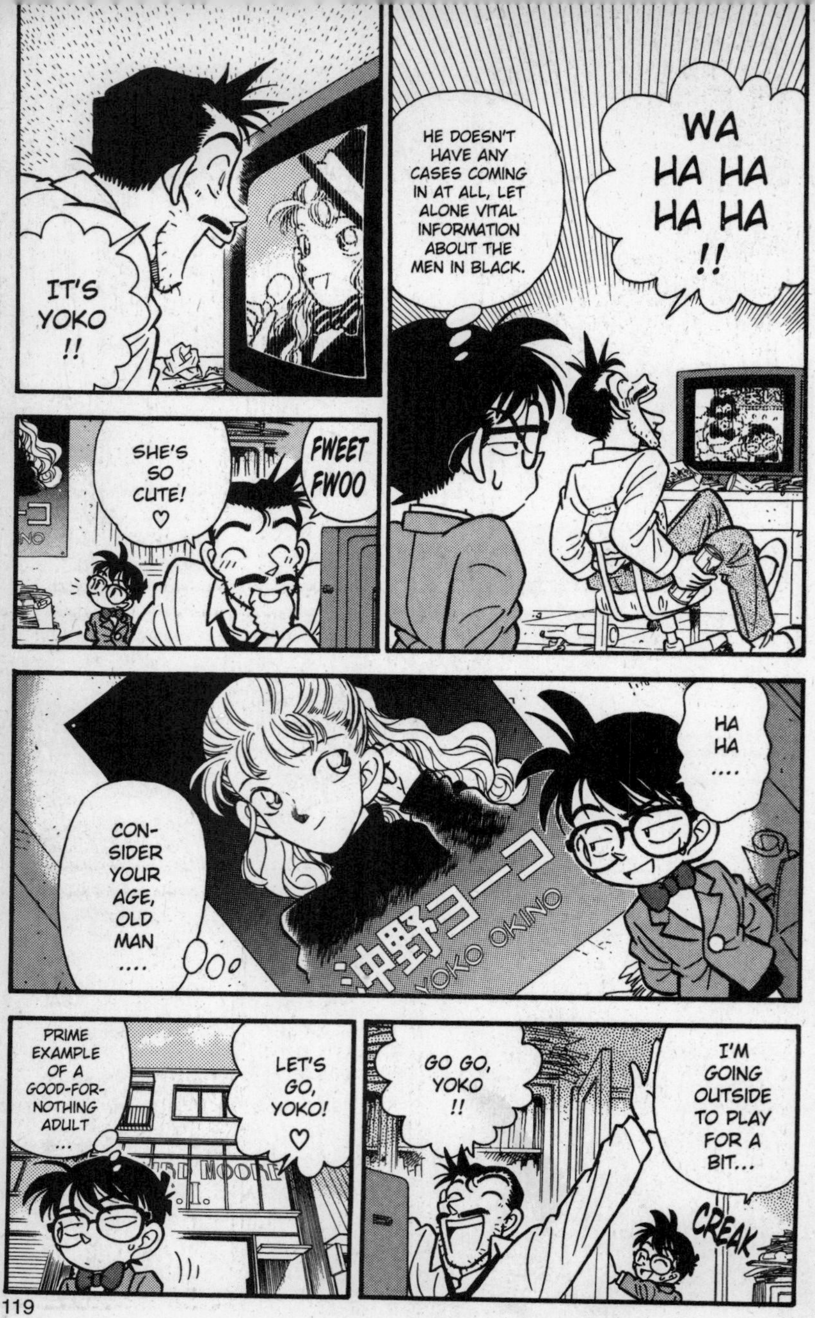
WA HA HA HA HA !!
HE DOESN'T HAVE ANY CASES COMING IN AT ALL, LET ALONE VITAL INFORMATION ABOUT THE MEN IN BLACK.
IT'S YOKO !!
FWEET FWOO
SHE'S SO CUTE! ♡
HA HA ....
CONSIDER YOUR AGE, OLD MAN ....
YOKO OKINO
I'M GOING OUTSIDE TO PLAY FOR A BIT...
GO GO, YOKO !!
CREAK
LET'S GO, YOKO! ♡
PRIME EXAMPLE OF A GOOD-FOR-NOTHING ADULT ...

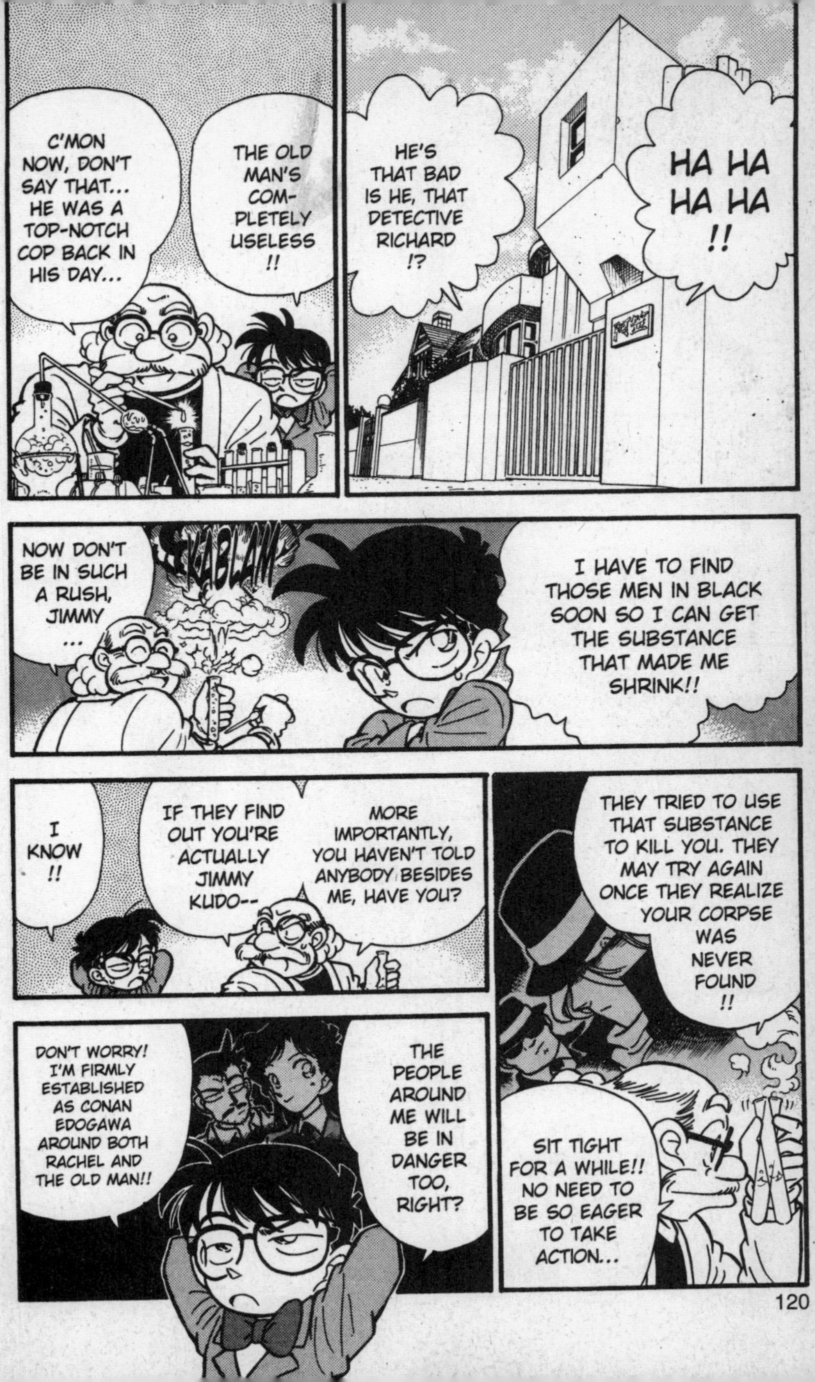
HA HA HA HA !!
HE'S THAT BAD IS HE, THAT DETECTIVE RICHARD !?
THE OLD MAN'S COM-PLETELY USELESS !!
C'MON NOW, DON'T SAY THAT... HE WAS A TOP-NOTCH COP BACK IN HIS DAY...
I HAVE TO FIND THOSE MEN IN BLACK SOON SO I CAN GET THE SUBSTANCE THAT MADE ME SHRINK!!
KABLAM
NOW DON'T BE IN SUCH A RUSH, JIMMY ...
THEY TRIED TO USE THAT SUBSTANCE TO KILL YOU. THEY MAY TRY AGAIN ONCE THEY REALIZE YOUR CORPSE WAS NEVER FOUND !!
SIT TIGHT FOR A WHILE!! NO NEED TO BE SO EAGER TO TAKE ACTION...
MORE IMPORTANTLY, YOU HAVEN'T TOLD ANYBODY BESIDES ME, HAVE YOU?
IF THEY FIND OUT YOU'RE ACTUALLY JIMMY KUDO--
I KNOW !!
THE PEOPLE AROUND ME WILL BE IN DANGER TOO, RIGHT?
DON'T WORRY! I'M FIRMLY ESTABLISHED AS CONAN EDOGAWA AROUND BOTH RACHEL AND THE OLD MAN!!

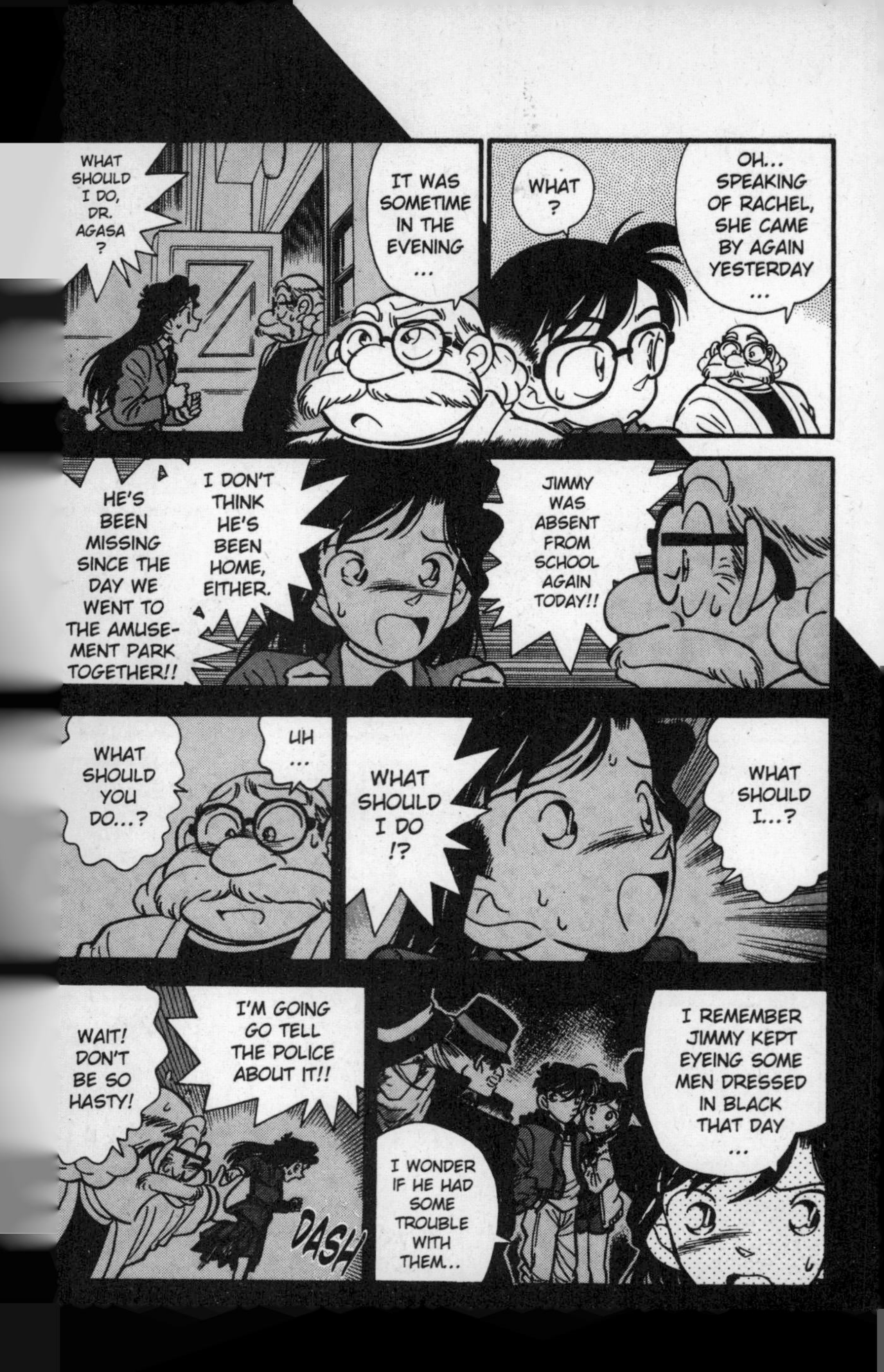
OH... SPEAKING OF RACHEL, SHE CAME BY AGAIN YESTERDAY ...
WHAT ?
IT WAS SOMETIME IN THE EVENING ...
WHAT SHOULD I DO, DR. AGASA ?
JIMMY WAS ABSENT FROM SCHOOL AGAIN TODAY!!
I DON'T THINK HE'S BEEN HOME, EITHER.
HE'S BEEN MISSING SINCE THE DAY WE WENT TO THE AMUSEMENT PARK TOGETHER!!
WHAT SHOULD I...?
WHAT SHOULD I DO !?
UH ...
WHAT SHOULD YOU DO...?
I REMEMBER JIMMY KEPT EYEING SOME MEN DRESSED IN BLACK THAT DAY ...
I WONDER IF HE HAD SOME TROUBLE WITH THEM..
I'M GOING GO TELL THE POLICE ABOUT IT!!
WAIT! DON'T BE SO HASTY!
DASH

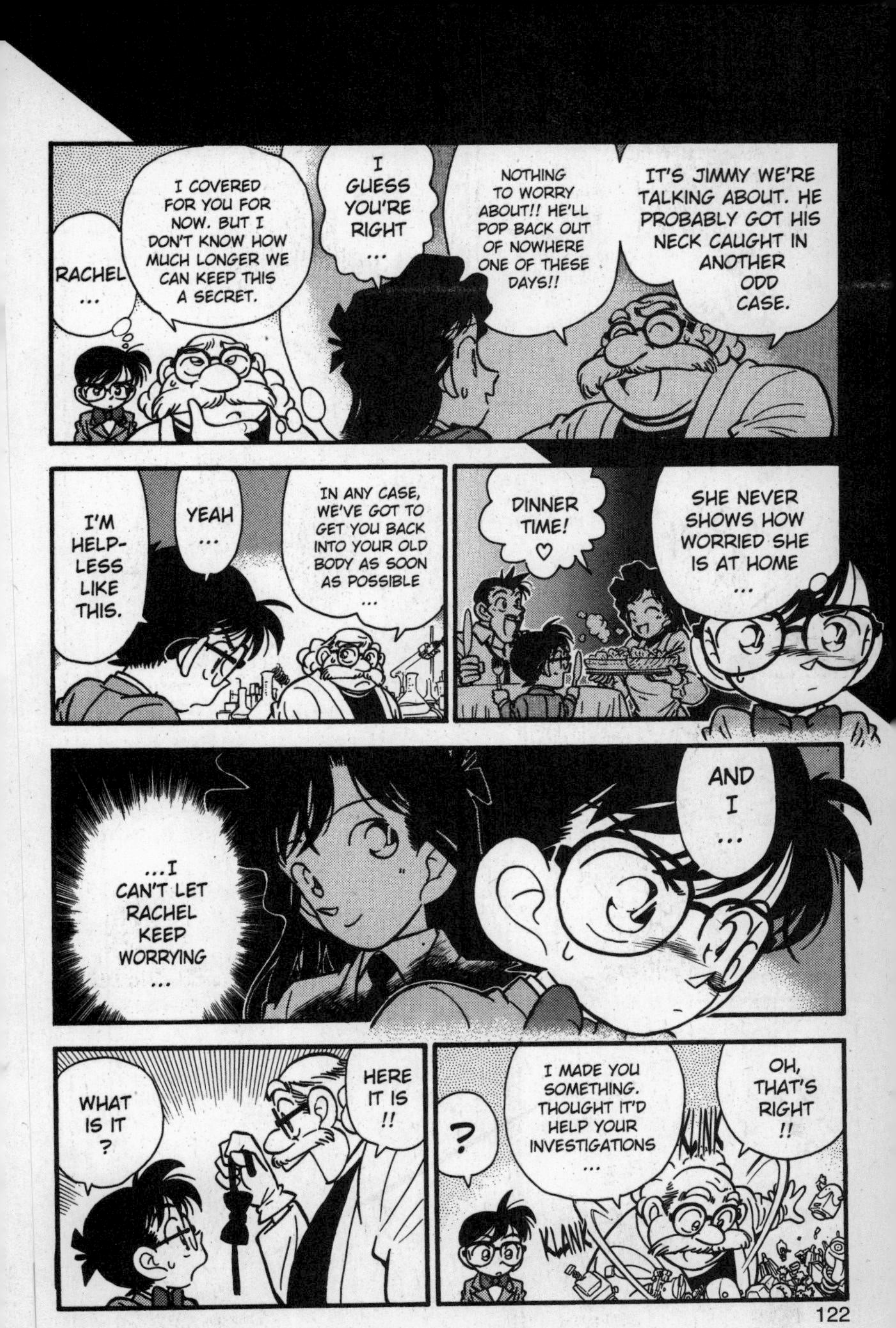
IT'S JIMMY WE'RE TALKING ABOUT. HE PROBABLY GOT HIS NECK CAUGHT IN ANOTHER ODD CASE.
NOTHING TO WORRY ABOUT!! HE'LL POP BACK OUT OF NOWHERE ONE OF THESE DAYS!!
I GUESS YOU'RE RIGHT ...
I COVERED FOR YOU FOR NOW. BUT I DON'T KNOW HOW MUCH LONGER WE CAN KEEP THIS A SECRET.
RACHEL ...
SHE NEVER SHOWS HOW WORRIED SHE IS AT HOME ...
DINNER TIME! ♡
IN ANY CASE, WE'VE GOT TO GET YOU BACK INTO YOUR OLD BODY AS SOON AS POSSIBLE ...
YEAH ...
I'M HELP-LESS LIKE THIS.
AND I ...
...I CAN'T LET RACHEL KEEP WORRYING ...
OH, THAT'S RIGHT !!
KLINK
I MADE YOU SOMETHING. THOUGHT IT'D HELP YOUR INVESTIGATIONS ...
?
KLANK
HERE IT IS !!
WHAT IS IT ?

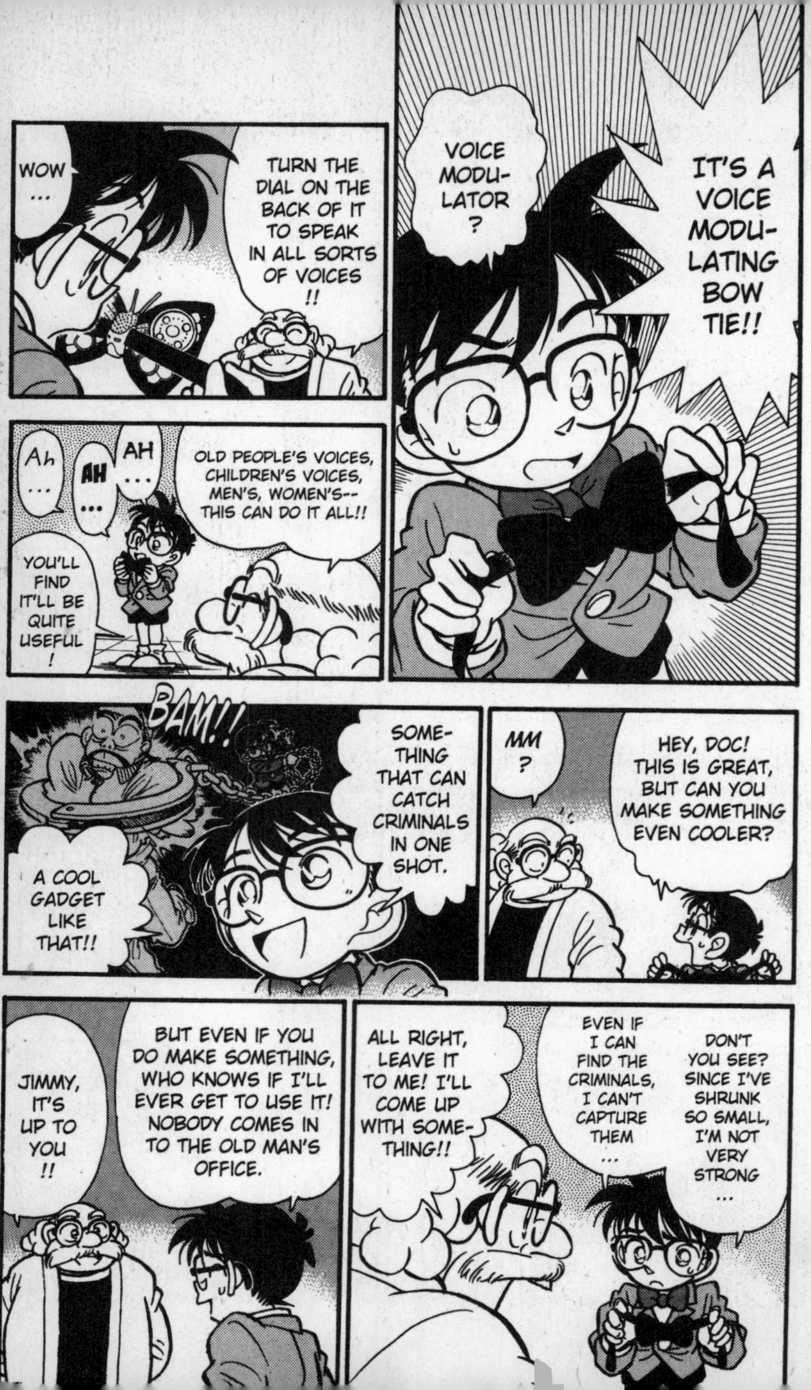
VOICE MODULATOR?
IT'S A VOICE MODULATING BOW TIE!!
TURN THE DIAL ON THE BACK OF IT TO SPEAK IN ALL SORTS OF VOICES!!
WOW...
OLD PEOPLE'S VOICES, CHILDREN'S VOICES, MEN'S, WOMEN'S-- THIS CAN DO IT ALL!!
AH...
AH...
Ah...
YOU'LL FIND IT'LL BE QUITE USEFUL!
HEY, DOC! THIS IS GREAT, BUT CAN YOU MAKE SOMETHING EVEN COOLER?
MM?
SOMETHING THAT CAN CATCH CRIMINALS IN ONE SHOT.
BAM!!
A COOL GADGET LIKE THAT!!
DON'T YOU SEE? SINCE I'VE SHRUNK SO SMALL, I'M NOT VERY STRONG...
EVEN IF I CAN FIND THE CRIMINALS, I CAN'T CAPTURE THEM...
ALL RIGHT, LEAVE IT TO ME! I'LL COME UP WITH SOMETHING!!
BUT EVEN IF YOU DO MAKE SOMETHING, WHO KNOWS IF I'LL EVER GET TO USE IT! NOBODY COMES IN TO THE OLD MAN'S OFFICE.
JIMMY, IT'S UP TO YOU!!

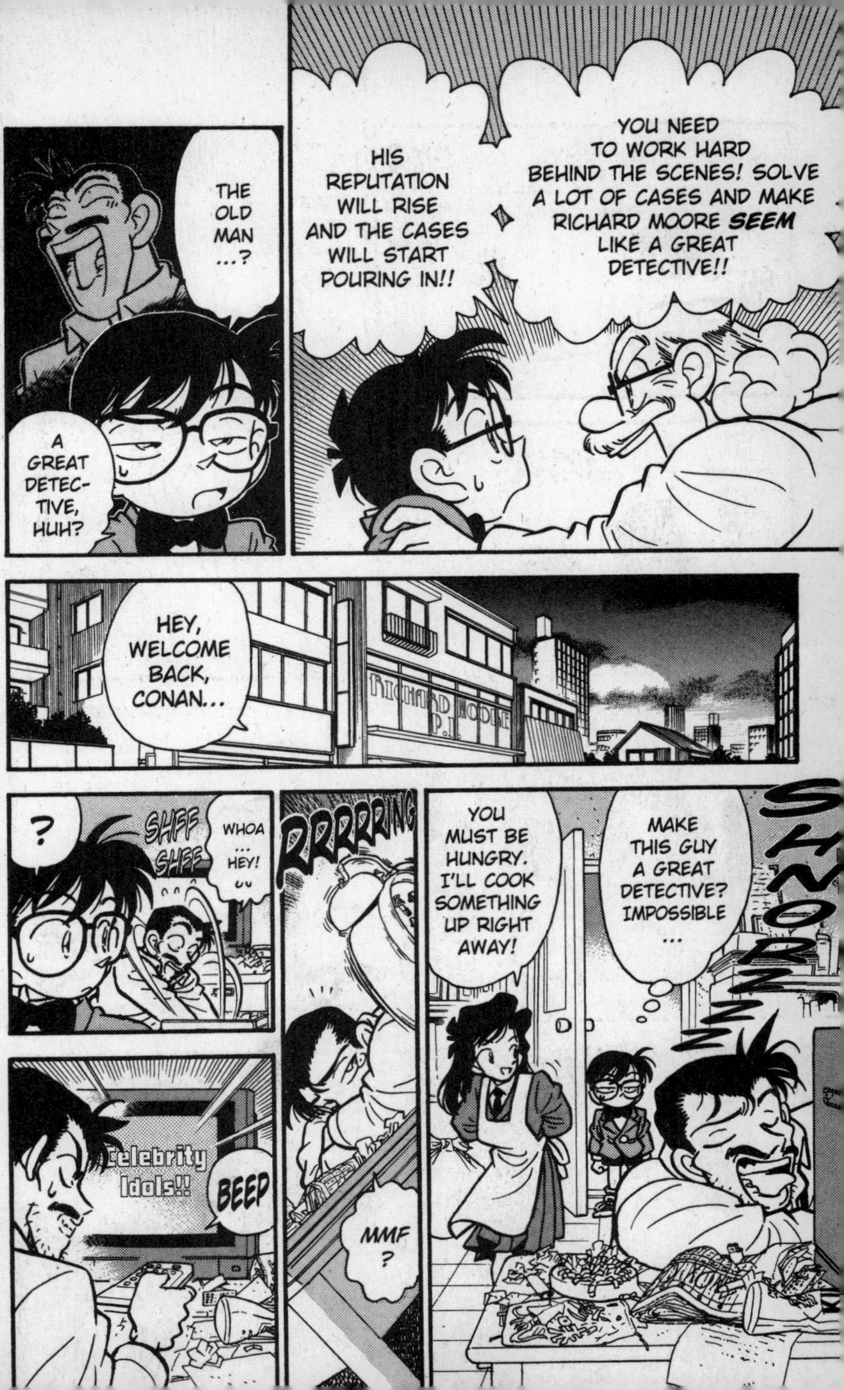
YOU NEED TO WORK HARD BEHIND THE SCENES! SOLVE A LOT OF CASES AND MAKE RICHARD MOORE *SEEM* LIKE A GREAT DETECTIVE!!
HIS REPUTATION WILL RISE AND THE CASES WILL START POURING IN!!
THE OLD MAN ...?
A GREAT DETECTIVE, HUH?
HEY, WELCOME BACK, CONAN...
RICHARD MOORE P.I.
SHNORZZZ
MAKE THIS GUY A GREAT DETECTIVE? IMPOSSIBLE ...
YOU MUST BE HUNGRY. I'LL COOK SOMETHING UP RIGHT AWAY!
RRRRRING
MMF?
?
SHFF SHFF
WHOA ... HEY!
Celebrity Idols!!
BEEP

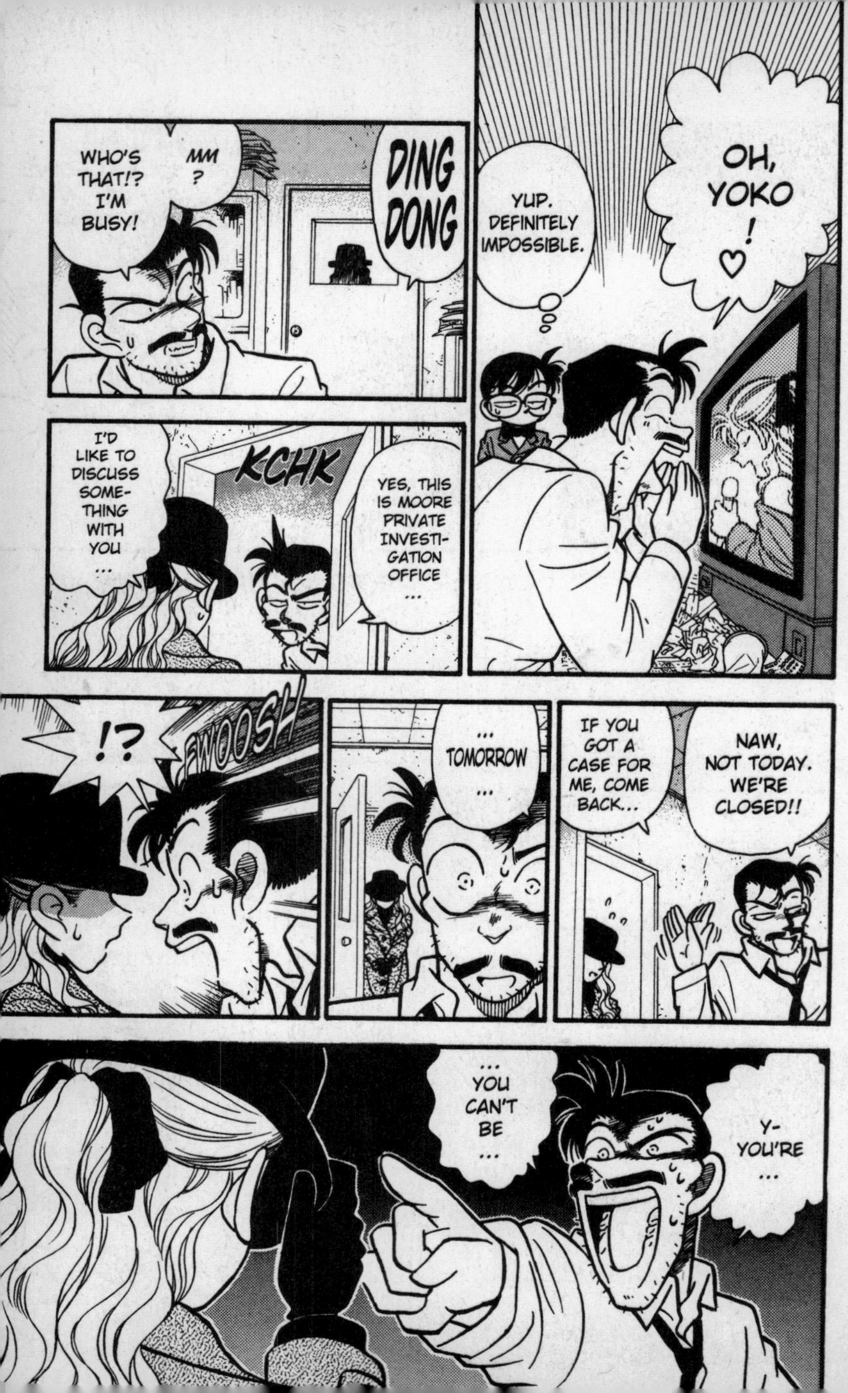
OH, YOKO! ♥
YUP. DEFINITELY IMPOSSIBLE.
DING DONG
MM ?
WHO'S THAT!? I'M BUSY!
YES, THIS IS MOORE PRIVATE INVESTIGATION OFFICE ...
KCHK
I'D LIKE TO DISCUSS SOMETHING WITH YOU ...
NAW, NOT TODAY. WE'RE CLOSED!!
IF YOU GOT A CASE FOR ME, COME BACK...
... TOMORROW ...
FWOOSH
!?
Y- YOU'RE ...
... YOU CAN'T BE ...

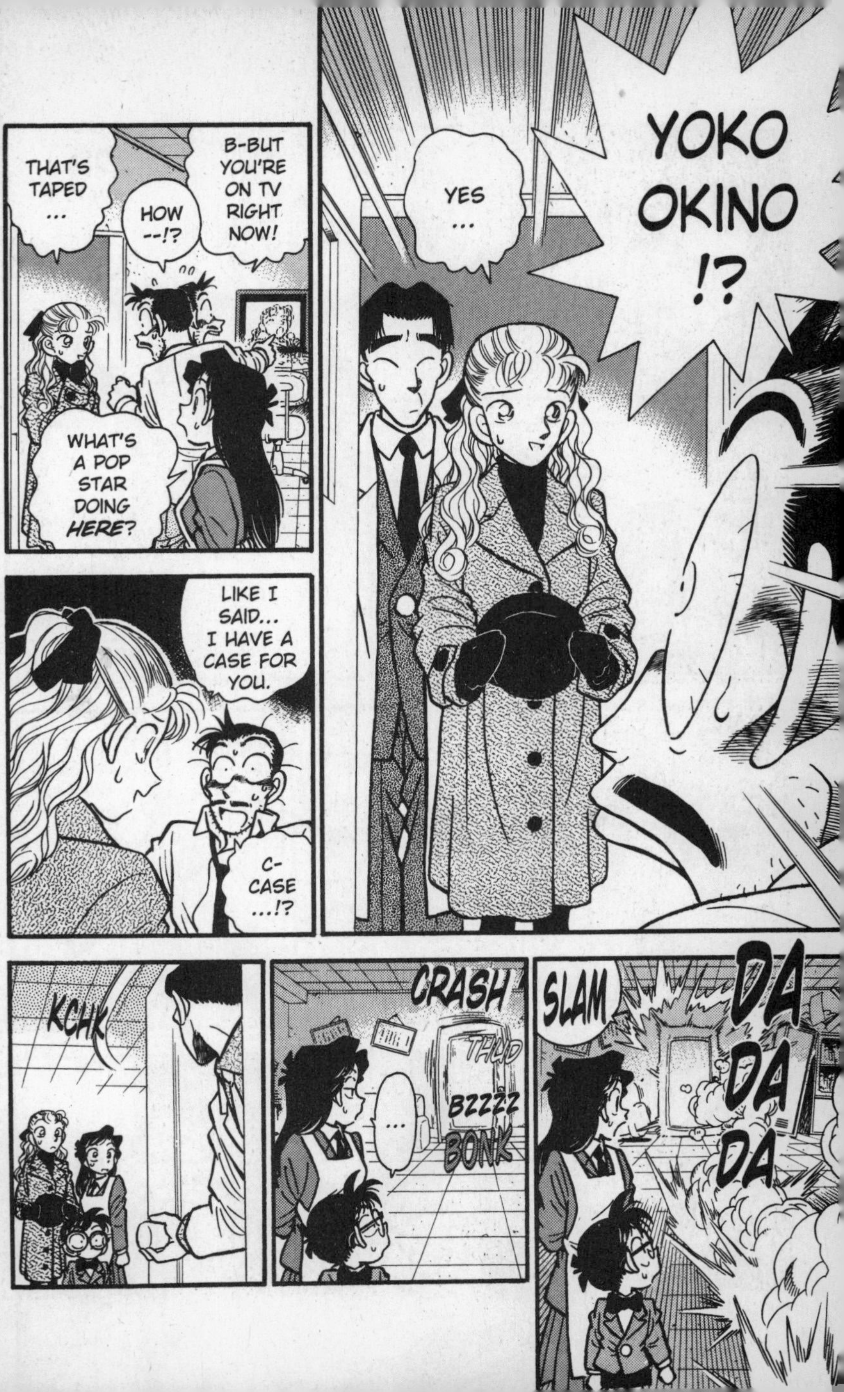
YOKO OKINO !?
YES ...
B-BUT YOU'RE ON TV RIGHT NOW!
HOW --!?
THAT'S TAPED ...
WHAT'S A POP STAR DOING *HERE*?
LIKE I SAID... I HAVE A CASE FOR YOU.
C- CASE ...!?
DA DA DA DA
SLAM
CRASH
THUD
BZZZZ
BONK
...
KCHK

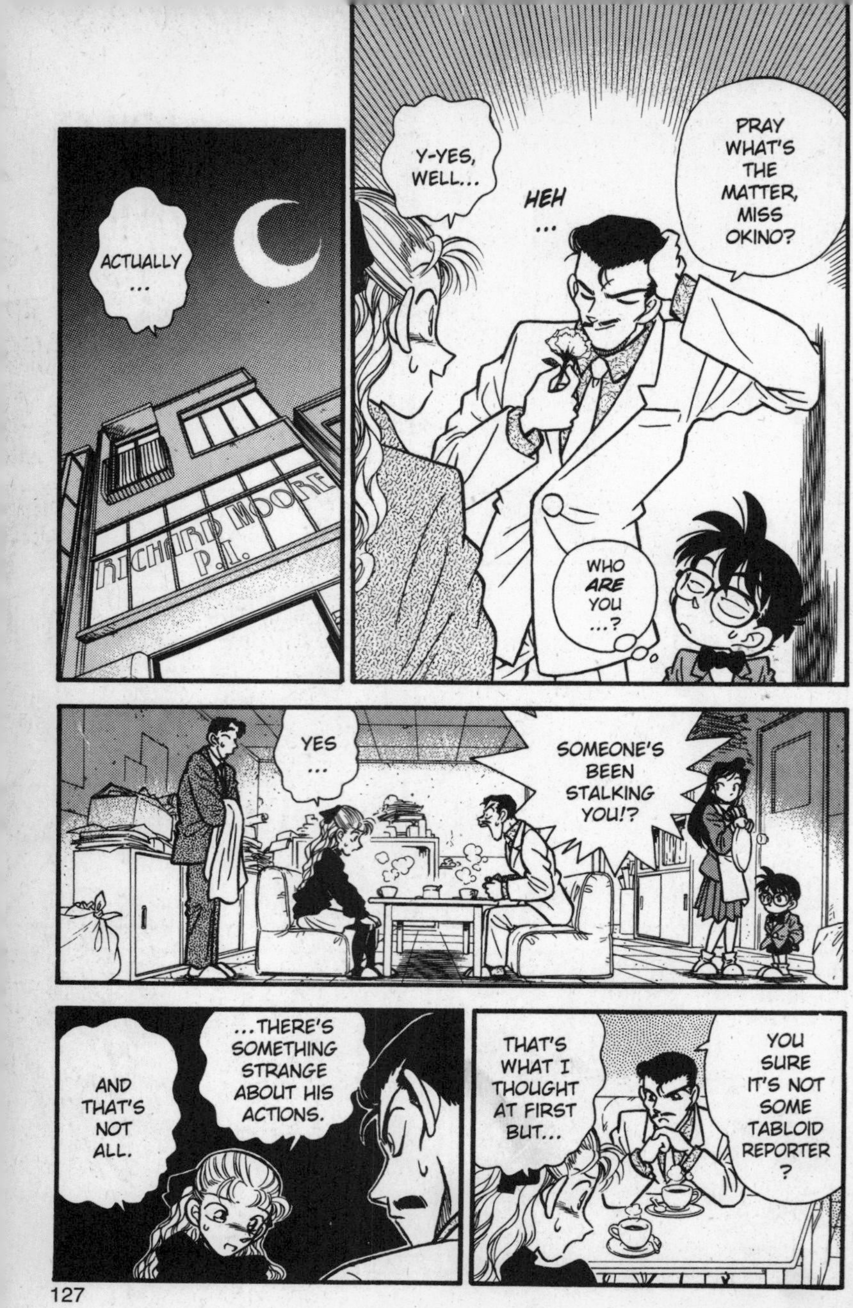
PRAY WHAT'S THE MATTER, MISS OKINO?
HEH ...
Y-YES, WELL...
WHO ARE YOU ...?
ACTUALLY ...
RICHARD MOORE P.I.
SOMEONE'S BEEN STALKING YOU!?
YES ...
YOU SURE IT'S NOT SOME TABLOID REPORTER ?
THAT'S WHAT I THOUGHT AT FIRST BUT...
...THERE'S SOMETHING STRANGE ABOUT HIS ACTIONS.
AND THAT'S NOT ALL.

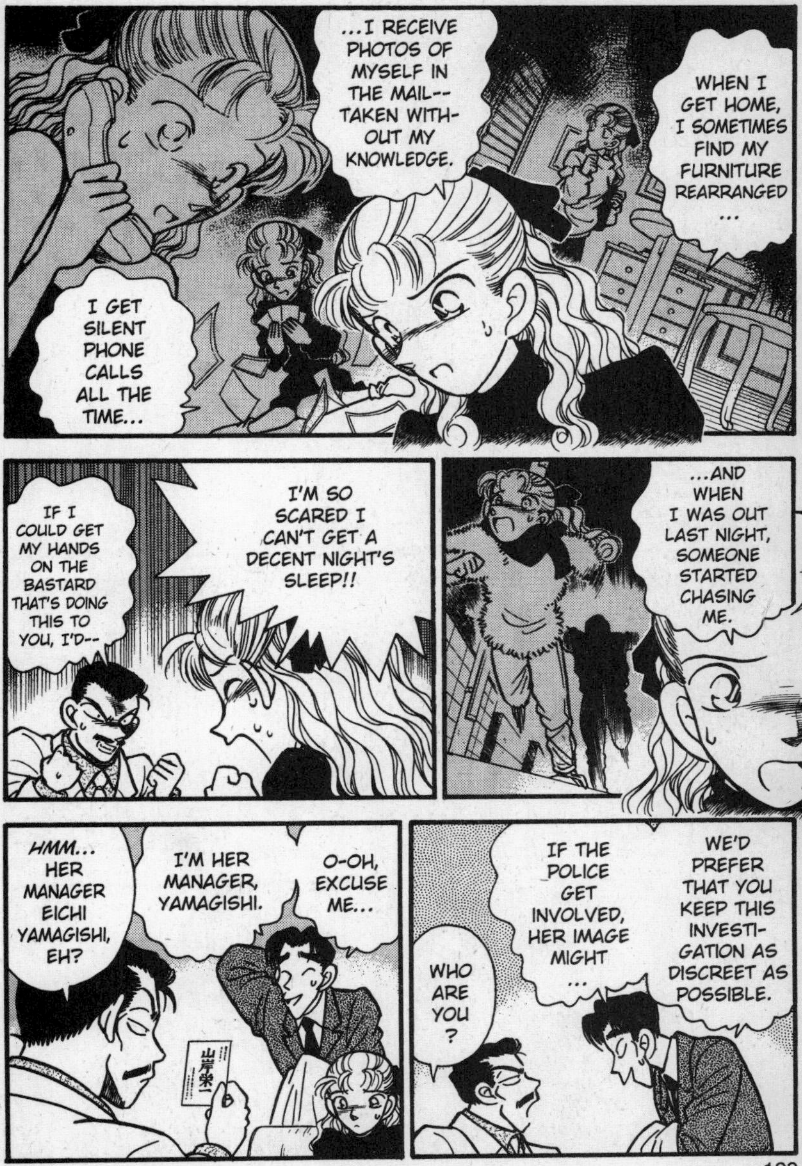
WHEN I GET HOME, I SOMETIMES FIND MY FURNITURE REARRANGED ...
...I RECEIVE PHOTOS OF MYSELF IN THE MAIL-- TAKEN WITH-OUT MY KNOWLEDGE.
I GET SILENT PHONE CALLS ALL THE TIME...
...AND WHEN I WAS OUT LAST NIGHT, SOMEONE STARTED CHASING ME.
I'M SO SCARED I CAN'T GET A DECENT NIGHT'S SLEEP!!
IF I COULD GET MY HANDS ON THE BASTARD THAT'S DOING THIS TO YOU, I'D--
WE'D PREFER THAT YOU KEEP THIS INVESTI-GATION AS DISCREET AS POSSIBLE.
IF THE POLICE GET INVOLVED, HER IMAGE MIGHT ...
WHO ARE YOU ?
O-OH, EXCUSE ME...
I'M HER MANAGER, YAMAGISHI.
HMM... HER MANAGER EICHI YAMAGISHI, EH?
山岸栄一

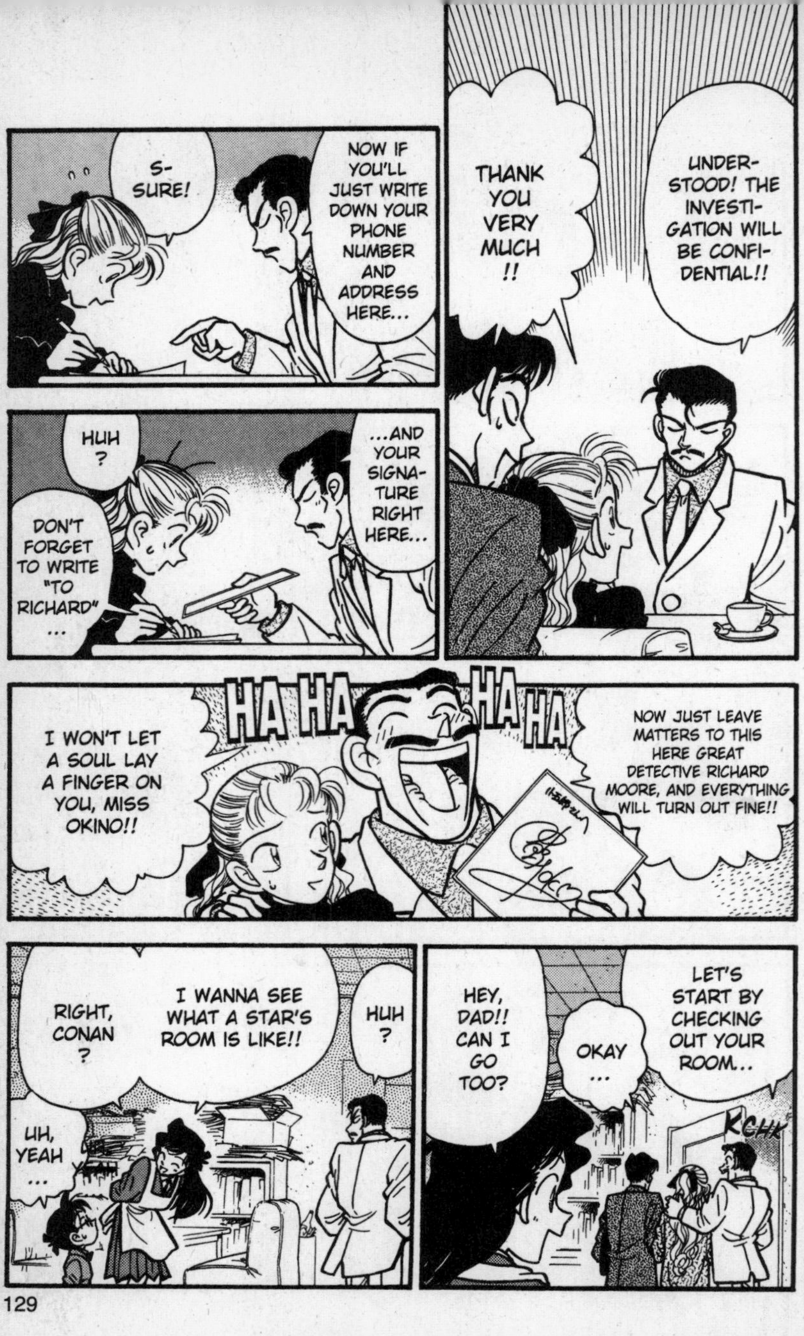
UNDER-STOOD! THE INVESTI-GATION WILL BE CONFI-DENTIAL!!
THANK YOU VERY MUCH !!
NOW IF YOU'LL JUST WRITE DOWN YOUR PHONE NUMBER AND ADDRESS HERE...
S-SURE!
...AND YOUR SIGNA-TURE RIGHT HERE...
HUH ?
DON'T FORGET TO WRITE "TO RICHARD" ...
NOW JUST LEAVE MATTERS TO THIS HERE GREAT DETECTIVE RICHARD MOORE, AND EVERYTHING WILL TURN OUT FINE!!
HA HA HA HA
I WON'T LET A SOUL LAY A FINGER ON YOU, MISS OKINO!!
LET'S START BY CHECKING OUT YOUR ROOM...
KCHK
OKAY ...
HEY, DAD!! CAN I GO TOO?
HUH ?
I WANNA SEE WHAT A STAR'S ROOM IS LIKE!!
RIGHT, CONAN ?
UH, YEAH ...

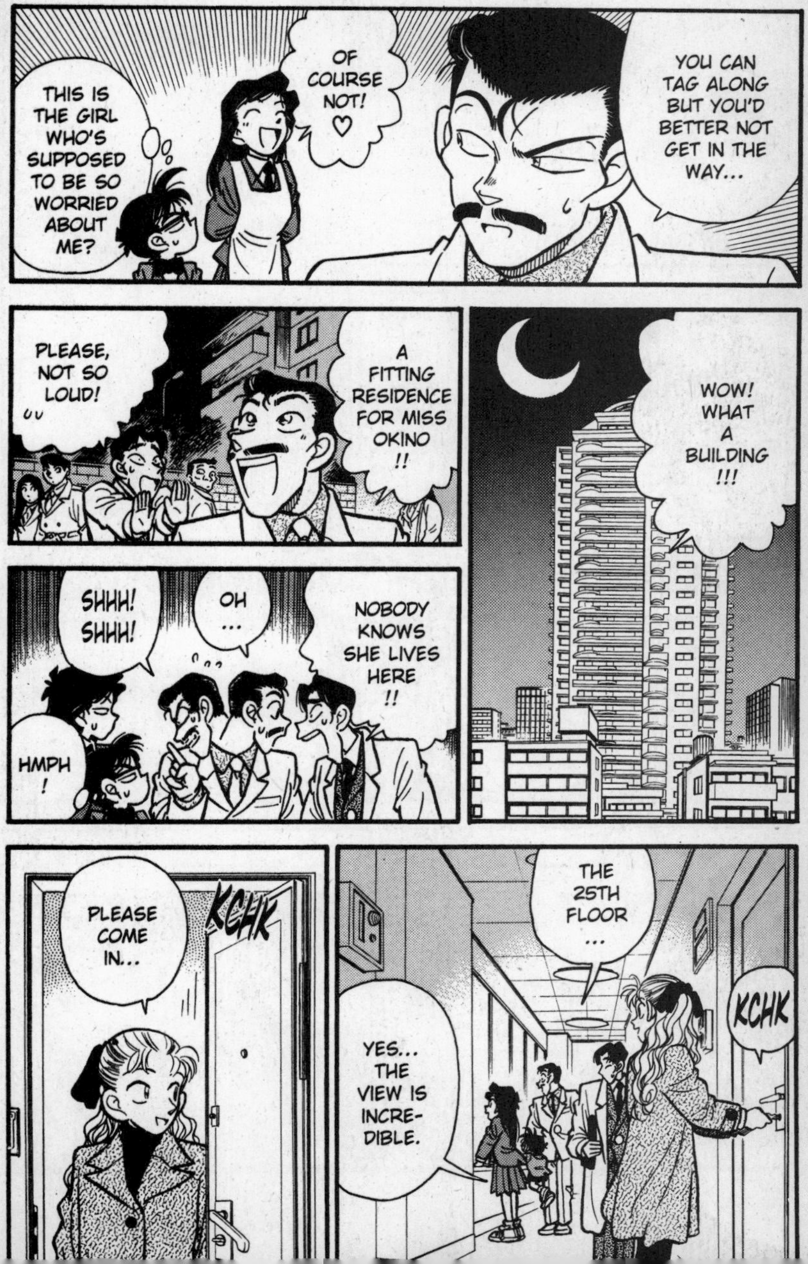
YOU CAN TAG ALONG BUT YOU'D BETTER NOT GET IN THE WAY...
OF COURSE NOT! ♡
THIS IS THE GIRL WHO'S SUPPOSED TO BE SO WORRIED ABOUT ME?
WOW! WHAT A BUILDING !!!
A FITTING RESIDENCE FOR MISS OKINO !!
PLEASE, NOT SO LOUD!
NOBODY KNOWS SHE LIVES HERE !!
OH ...
SHHH! SHHH!
HMPH !
THE 25TH FLOOR ...
KCHK
YES... THE VIEW IS INCRE-DIBLE.
KCHK
PLEASE COME IN...

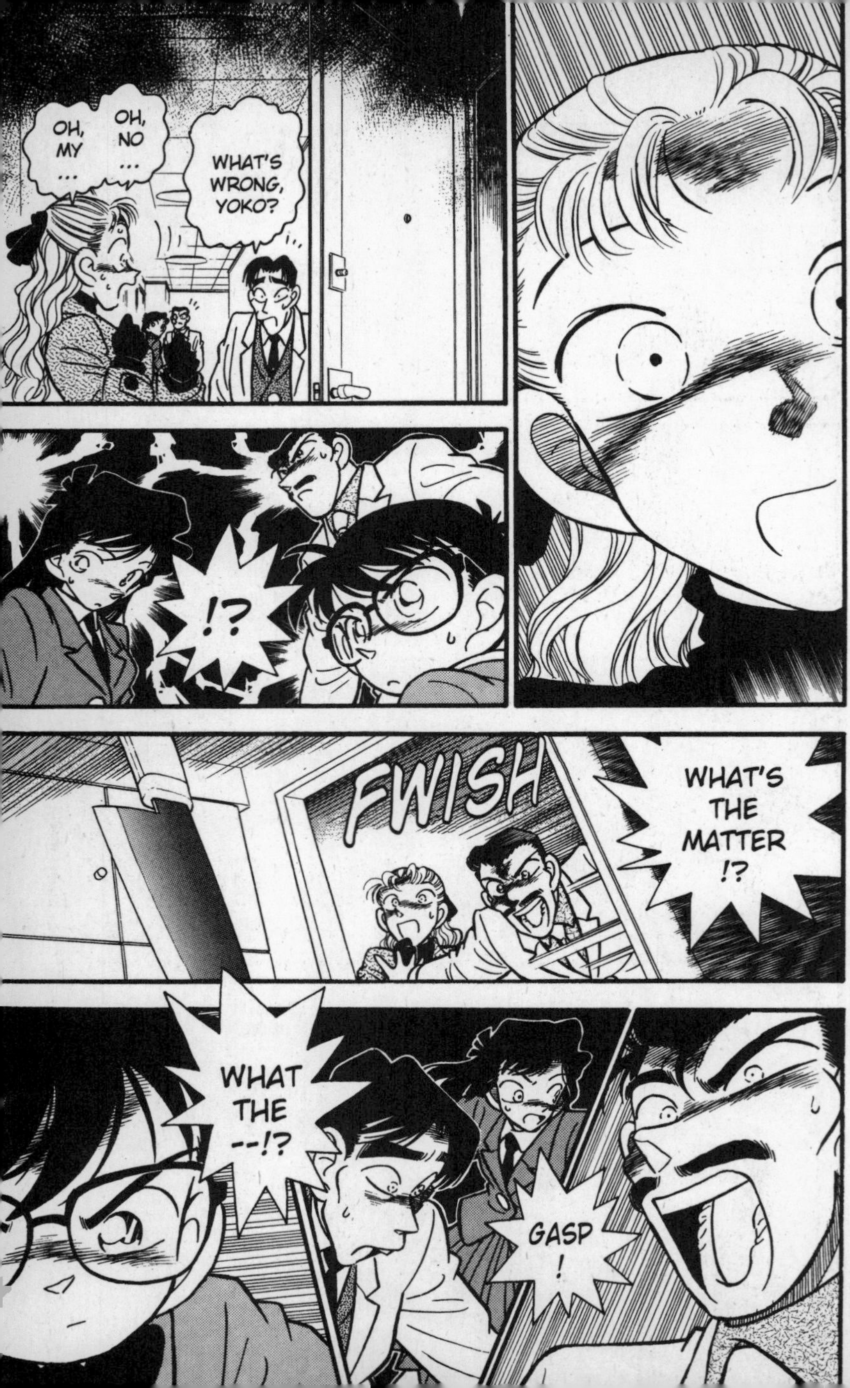
WHAT'S WRONG, YOKO?
OH, NO ...
OH, MY ...
!?
WHAT'S THE MATTER !?
FWISH
GASP !
WHAT THE --!?

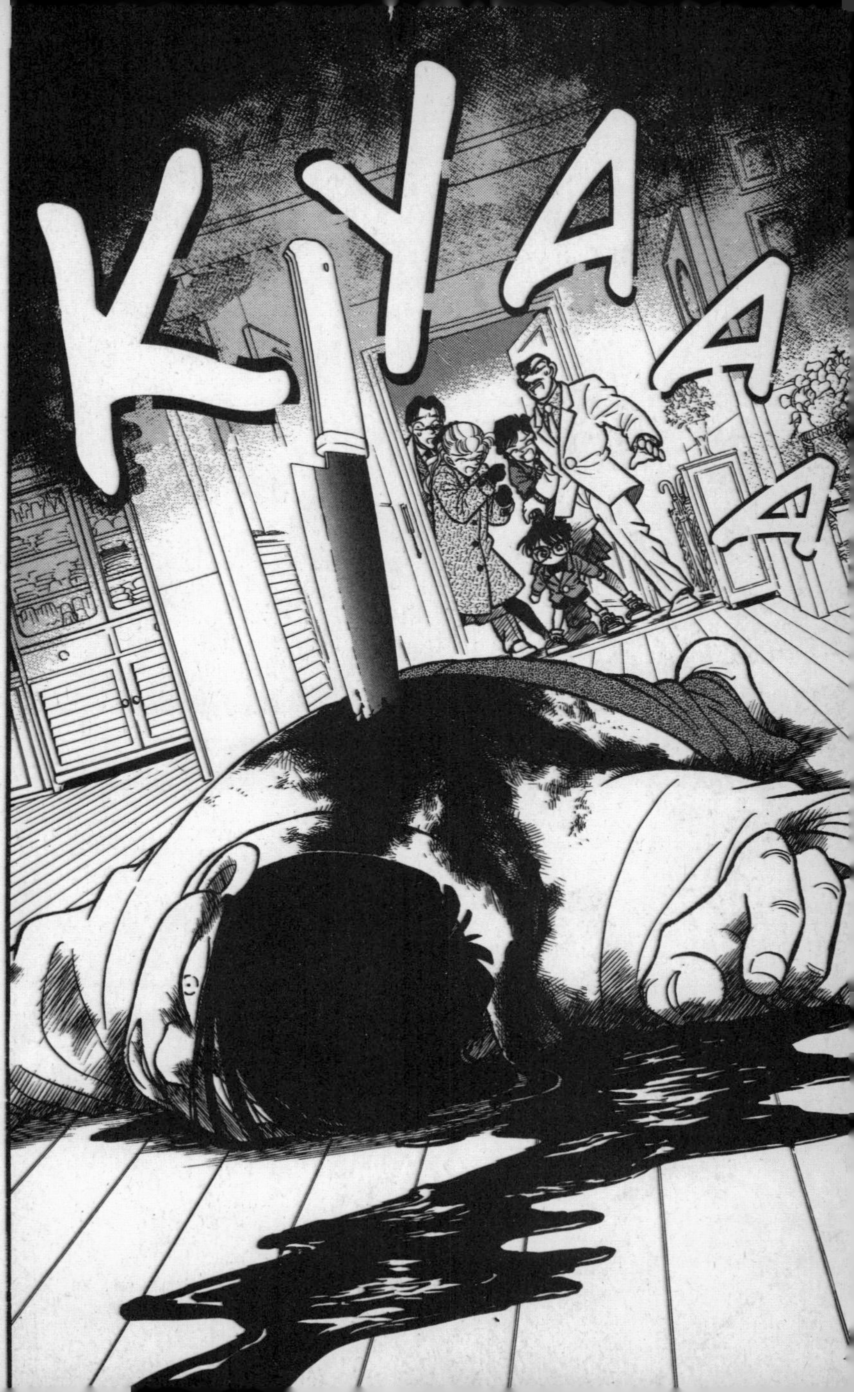
KYAAAA

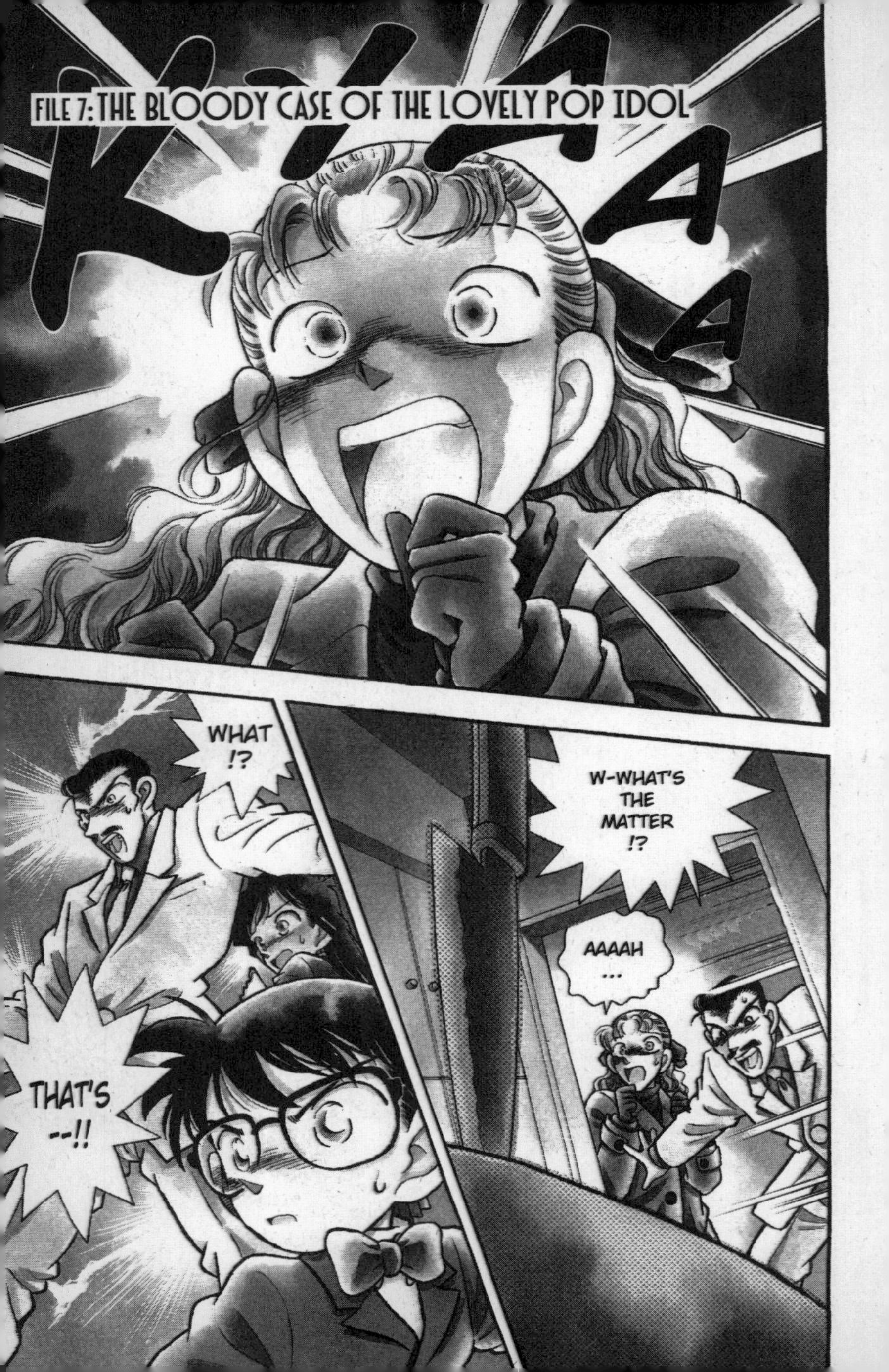
FILE 7: THE BLOODY CASE OF THE LOVELY POP IDOL
KYAAAA
W-WHAT'S THE MATTER !?
AAAAH ...
WHAT !?
THAT'S --!!

FILE 7: THE BLOODY CASE OF THE LOVELY POP IDOL

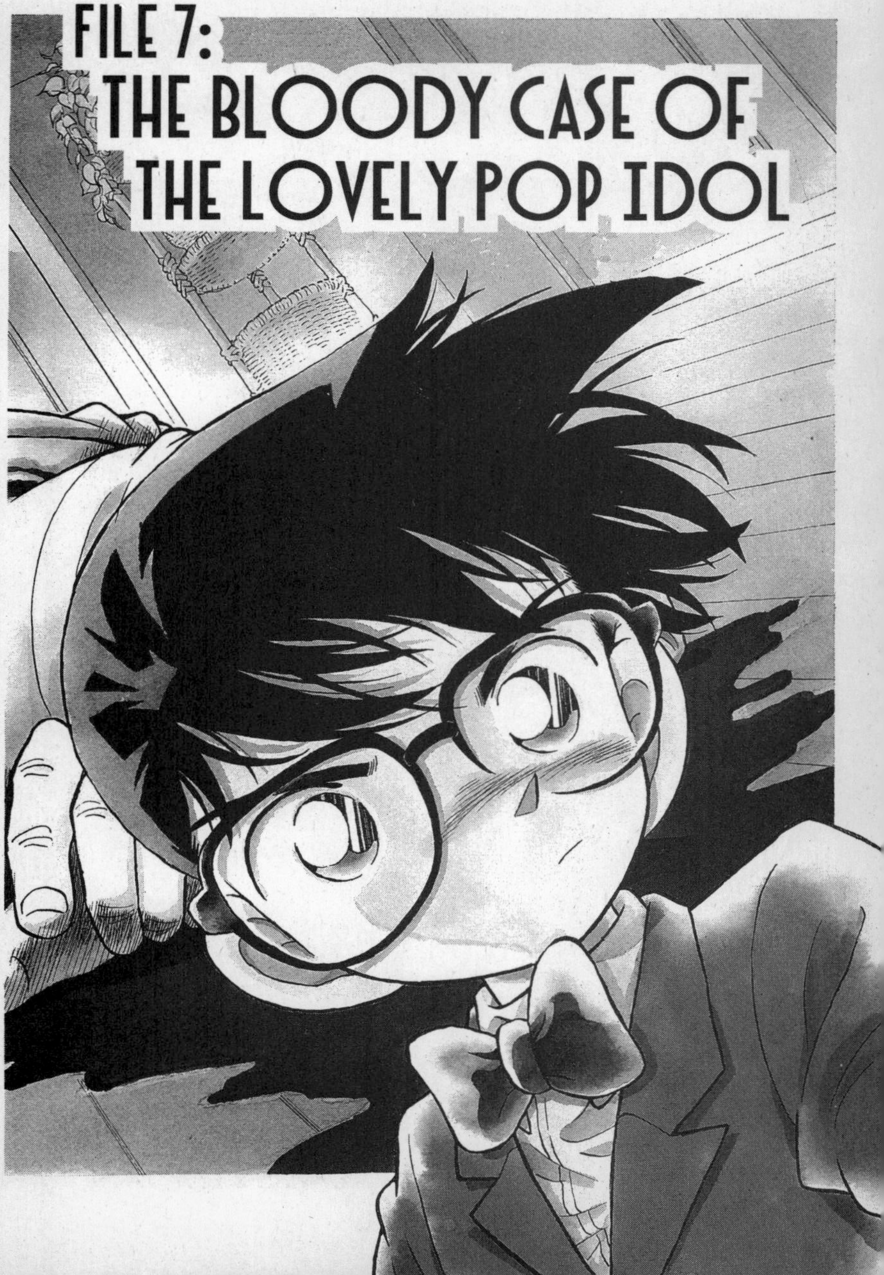

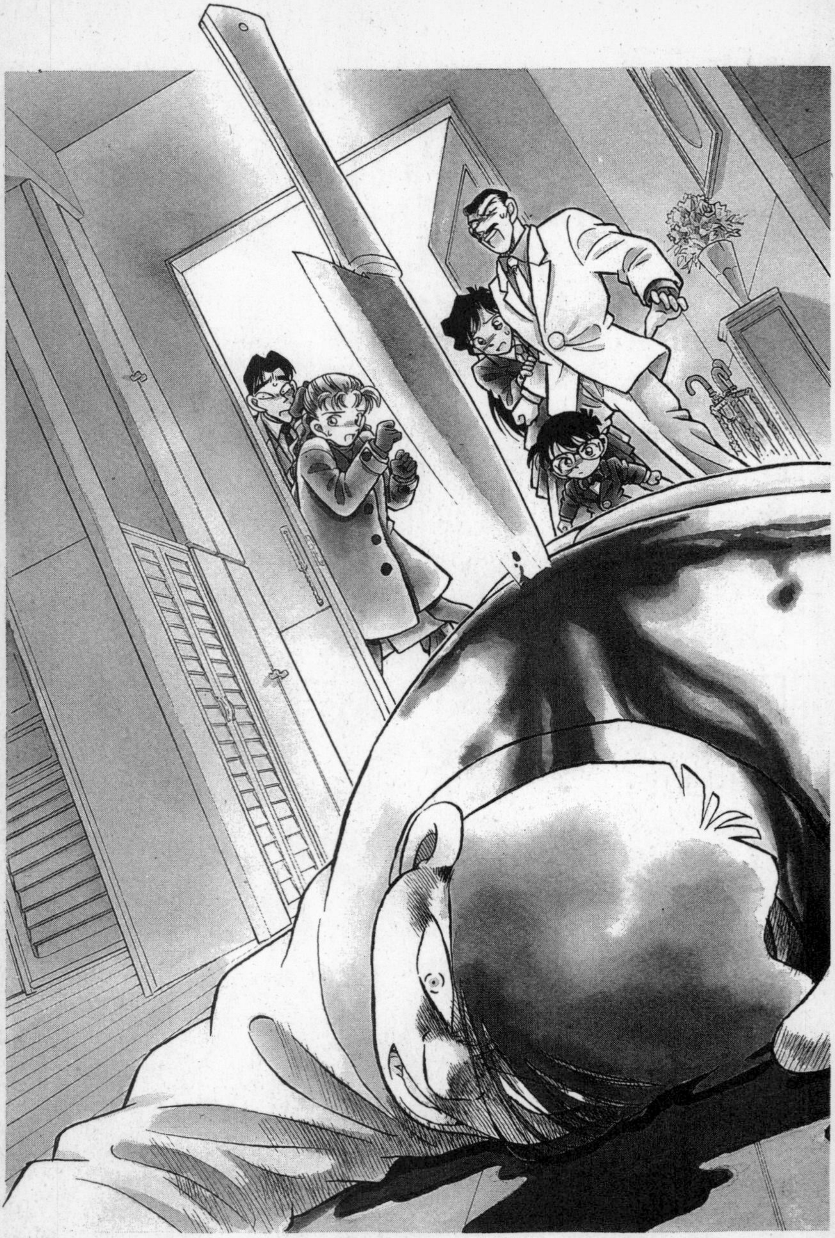

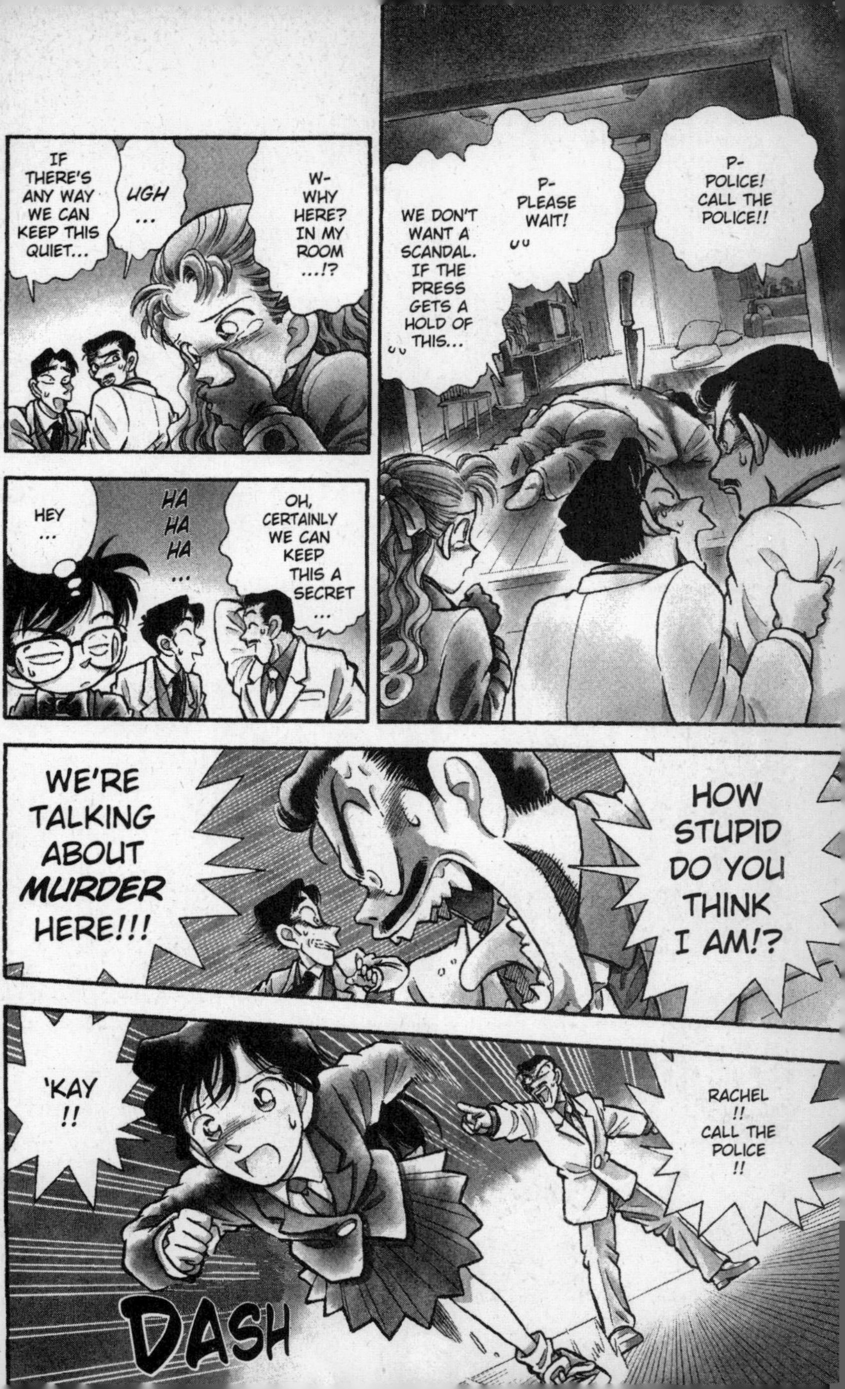

P-POLICE! CALL THE POLICE!!
P-PLEASE WAIT!
WE DON'T WANT A SCANDAL. IF THE PRESS GETS A HOLD OF THIS...
W-WHY HERE? IN MY ROOM ...!?
UGH ...
IF THERE'S ANY WAY WE CAN KEEP THIS QUIET...
OH, CERTAINLY WE CAN KEEP THIS A SECRET ...
HA HA HA ...
HEY ...
HOW STUPID DO YOU THINK I AM!?
WE'RE TALKING ABOUT MURDER HERE!!!
RACHEL !! CALL THE POLICE !!
'KAY !!
DASH

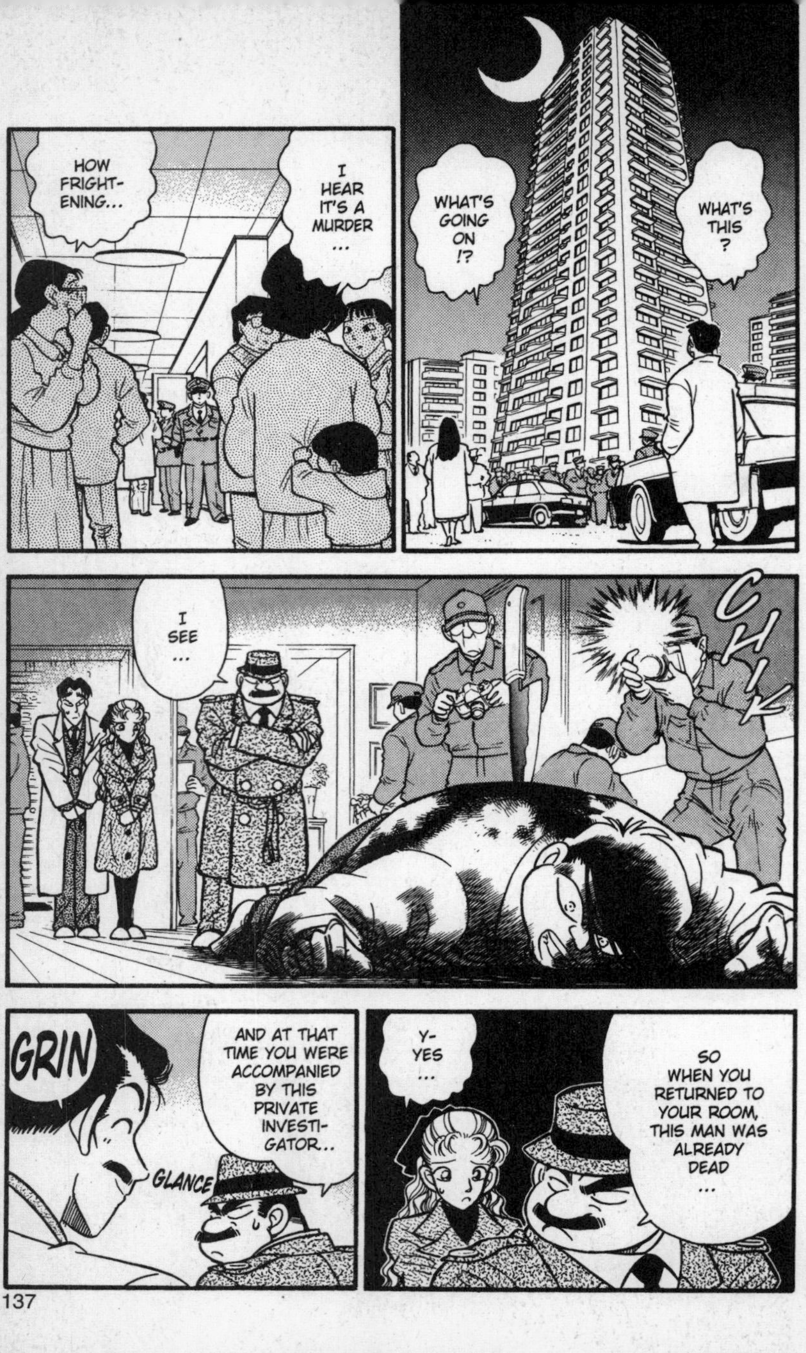

WHAT'S THIS ?
WHAT'S GOING ON !?
I HEAR IT'S A MURDER ...
HOW FRIGHT-ENING...
CHI
I SEE ...
SO WHEN YOU RETURNED TO YOUR ROOM, THIS MAN WAS ALREADY DEAD ...
Y-YES ...
AND AT THAT TIME YOU WERE ACCOMPANIED BY THIS PRIVATE INVESTI-GATOR...
GRIN
GLANCE

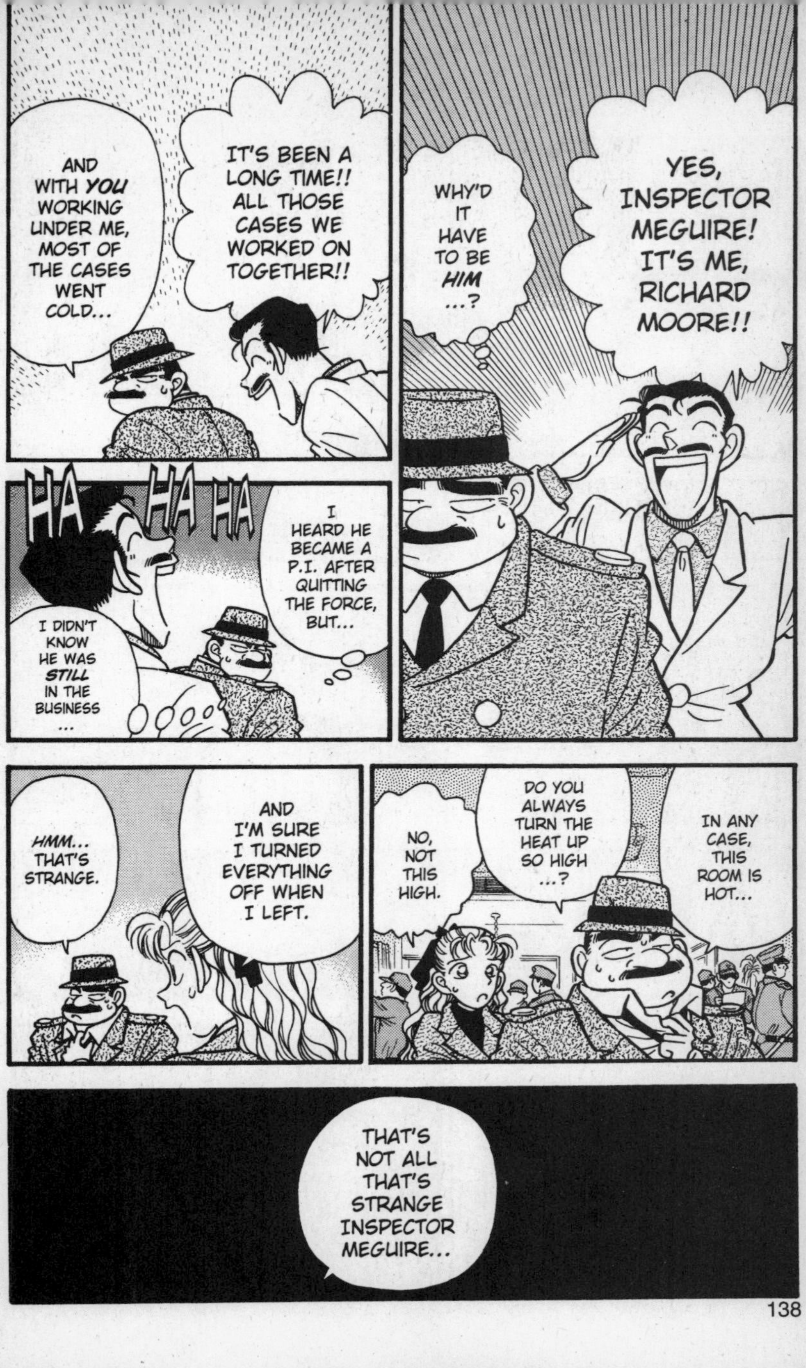
YES, INSPECTOR MEGUIRE! IT'S ME, RICHARD MOORE!!
WHY'D IT HAVE TO BE *HIM* ...?
IT'S BEEN A LONG TIME!! ALL THOSE CASES WE WORKED ON TOGETHER!!
AND WITH *YOU* WORKING UNDER ME, MOST OF THE CASES WENT COLD...
HA HA HA
I HEARD HE BECAME A P.I. AFTER QUITTING THE FORCE, BUT...
I DIDN'T KNOW HE WAS *STILL* IN THE BUSINESS ...
IN ANY CASE, THIS ROOM IS HOT...
DO YOU ALWAYS TURN THE HEAT UP SO HIGH ...?
NO, NOT THIS HIGH.
AND I'M SURE I TURNED EVERYTHING OFF WHEN I LEFT.
HMM... THAT'S STRANGE.
THAT'S NOT ALL THAT'S STRANGE INSPECTOR MEGUIRE...

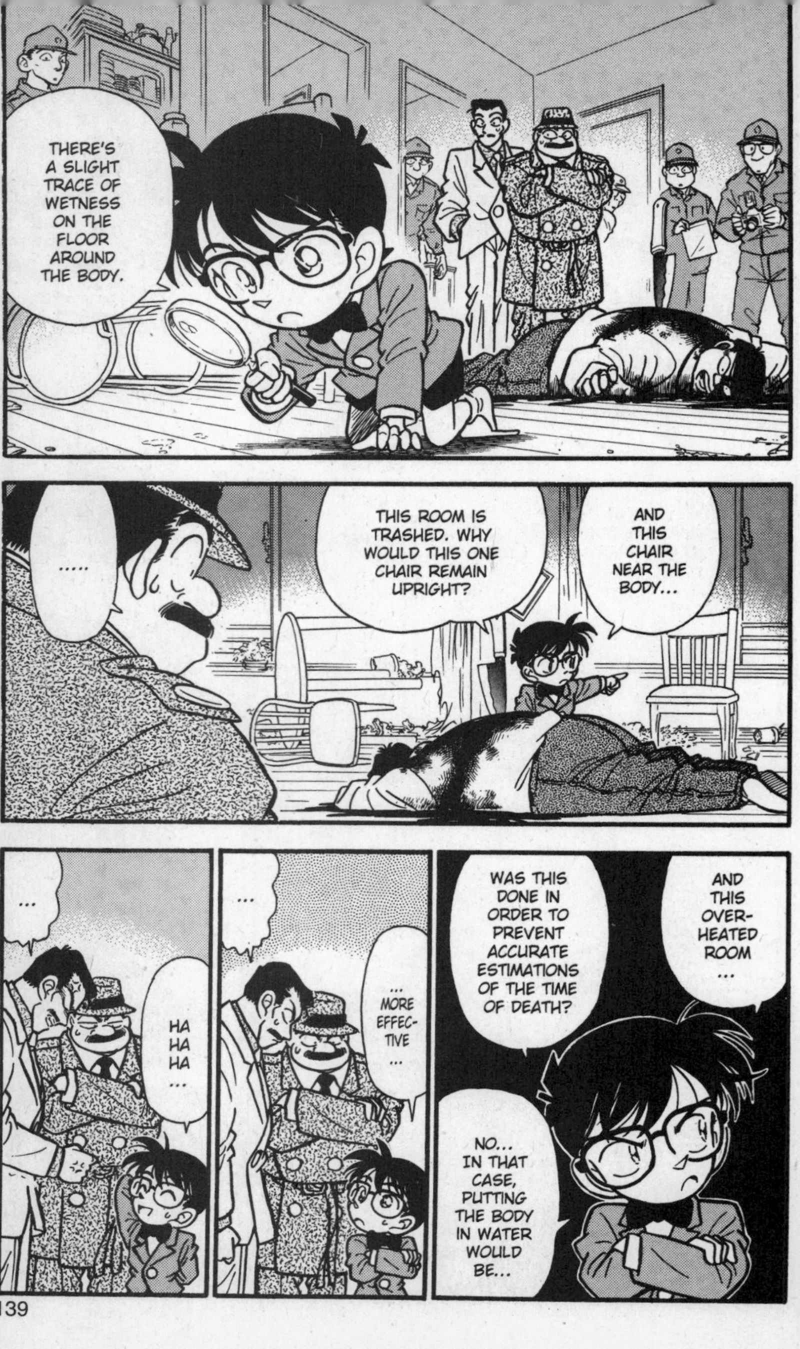
THERE'S A SLIGHT TRACE OF WETNESS ON THE FLOOR AROUND THE BODY.
AND THIS CHAIR NEAR THE BODY...
THIS ROOM IS TRASHED. WHY WOULD THIS ONE CHAIR REMAIN UPRIGHT?
.....
AND THIS OVER-HEATED ROOM ...
WAS THIS DONE IN ORDER TO PREVENT ACCURATE ESTIMATIONS OF THE TIME OF DEATH?
NO... IN THAT CASE, PUTTING THE BODY IN WATER WOULD BE...
... MORE EFFEC-TIVE ...
...
HA HA HA ...
...

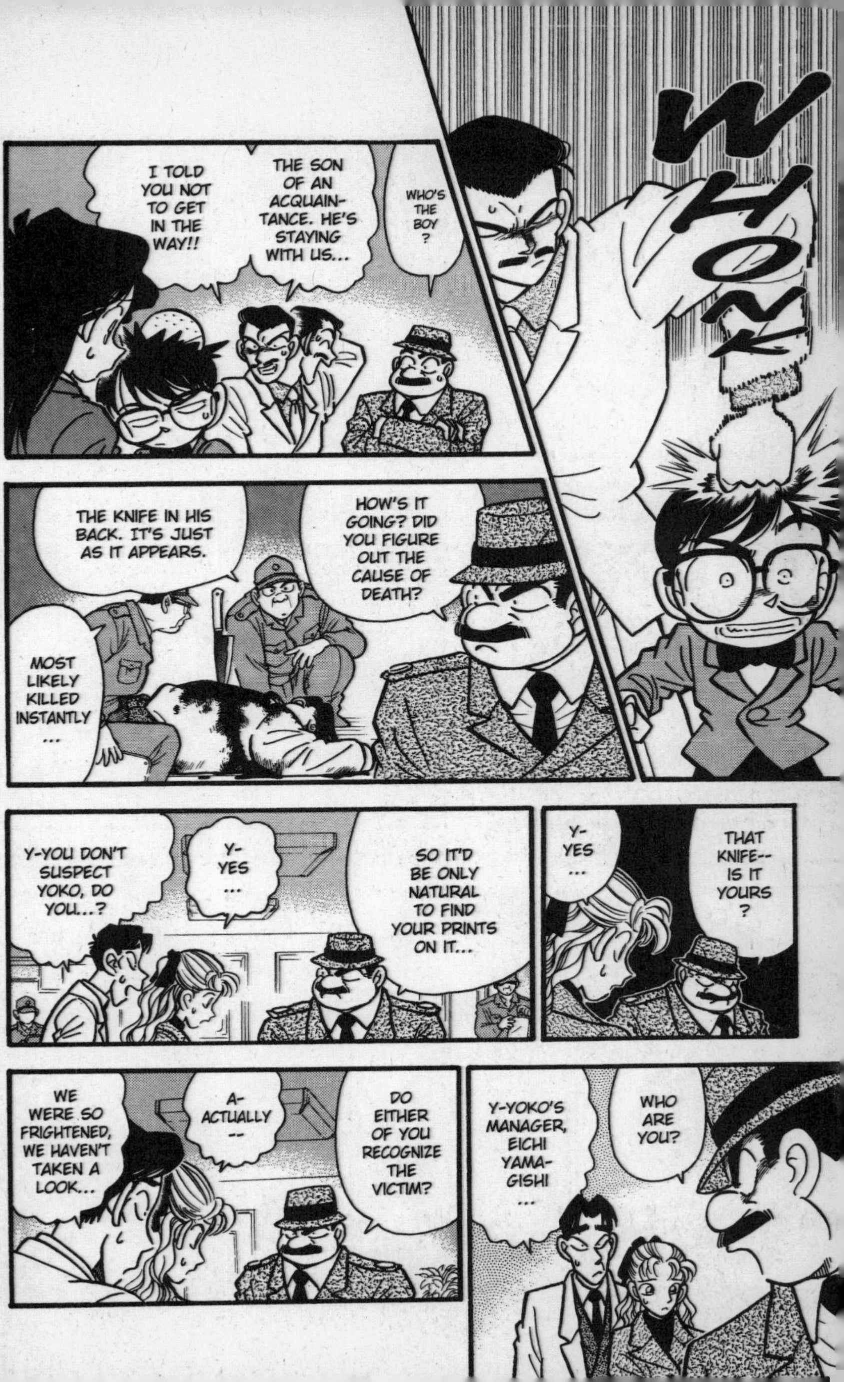
WHONK
WHO'S THE BOY?
THE SON OF AN ACQUAIN-TANCE. HE'S STAYING WITH US...
I TOLD YOU NOT TO GET IN THE WAY!!
HOW'S IT GOING? DID YOU FIGURE OUT THE CAUSE OF DEATH?
THE KNIFE IN HIS BACK. IT'S JUST AS IT APPEARS.
MOST LIKELY KILLED INSTANTLY ...
THAT KNIFE-- IS IT YOURS ?
Y- YES ...
SO IT'D BE ONLY NATURAL TO FIND YOUR PRINTS ON IT...
Y- YES ...
Y-YOU DON'T SUSPECT YOKO, DO YOU...?
WHO ARE YOU?
Y-YOKO'S MANAGER, EICHI YAMA-GISHI ...
DO EITHER OF YOU RECOGNIZE THE VICTIM?
A- ACTUALLY --
WE WERE SO FRIGHTENED, WE HAVEN'T TAKEN A LOOK...

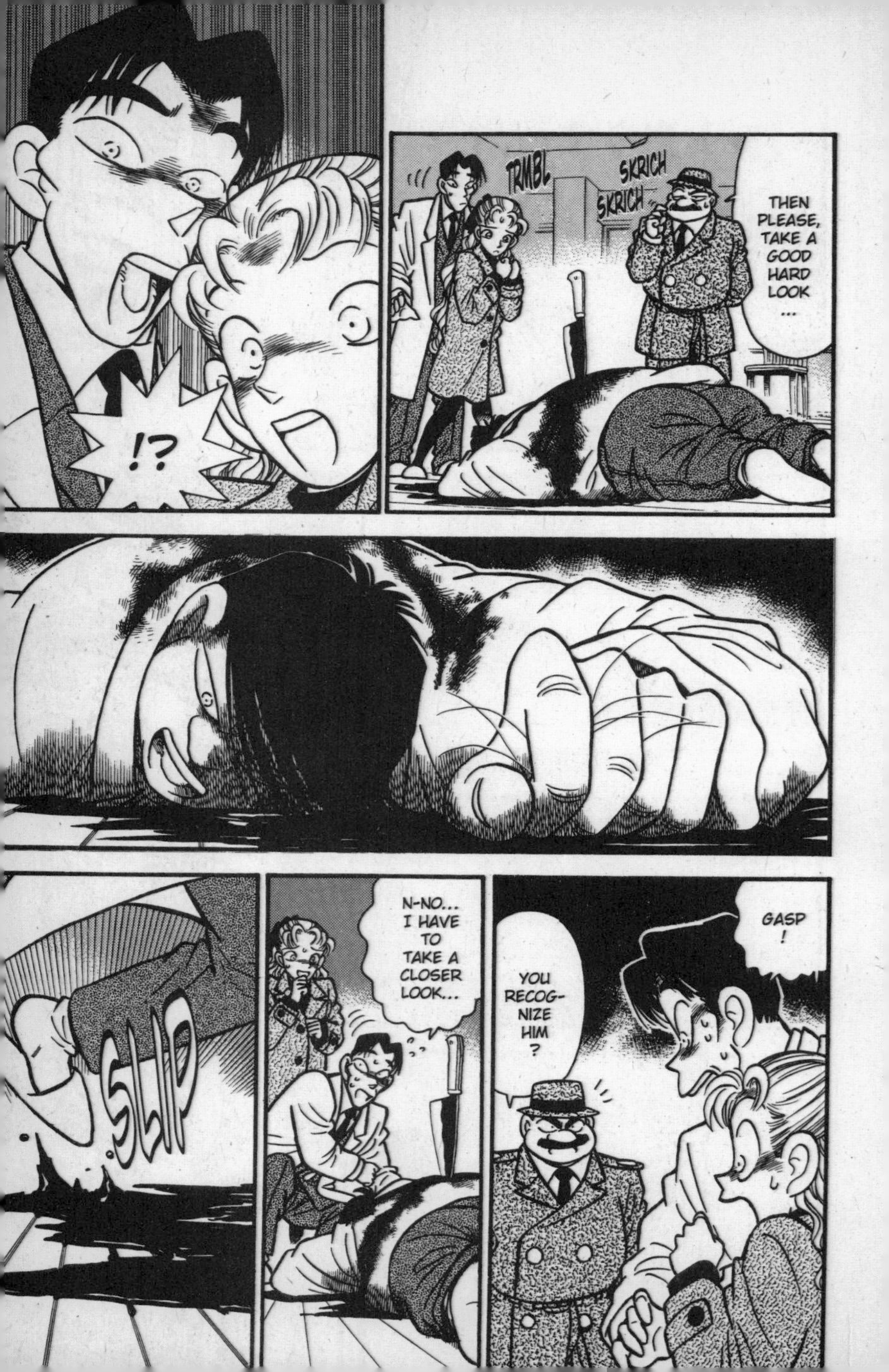
THEN PLEASE, TAKE A GOOD HARD LOOK ...
SKRICH
SKRICH
TRMBL
!?
GASP !
YOU RECOGNIZE HIM ?
N-NO... I HAVE TO TAKE A CLOSER LOOK...
SLIP

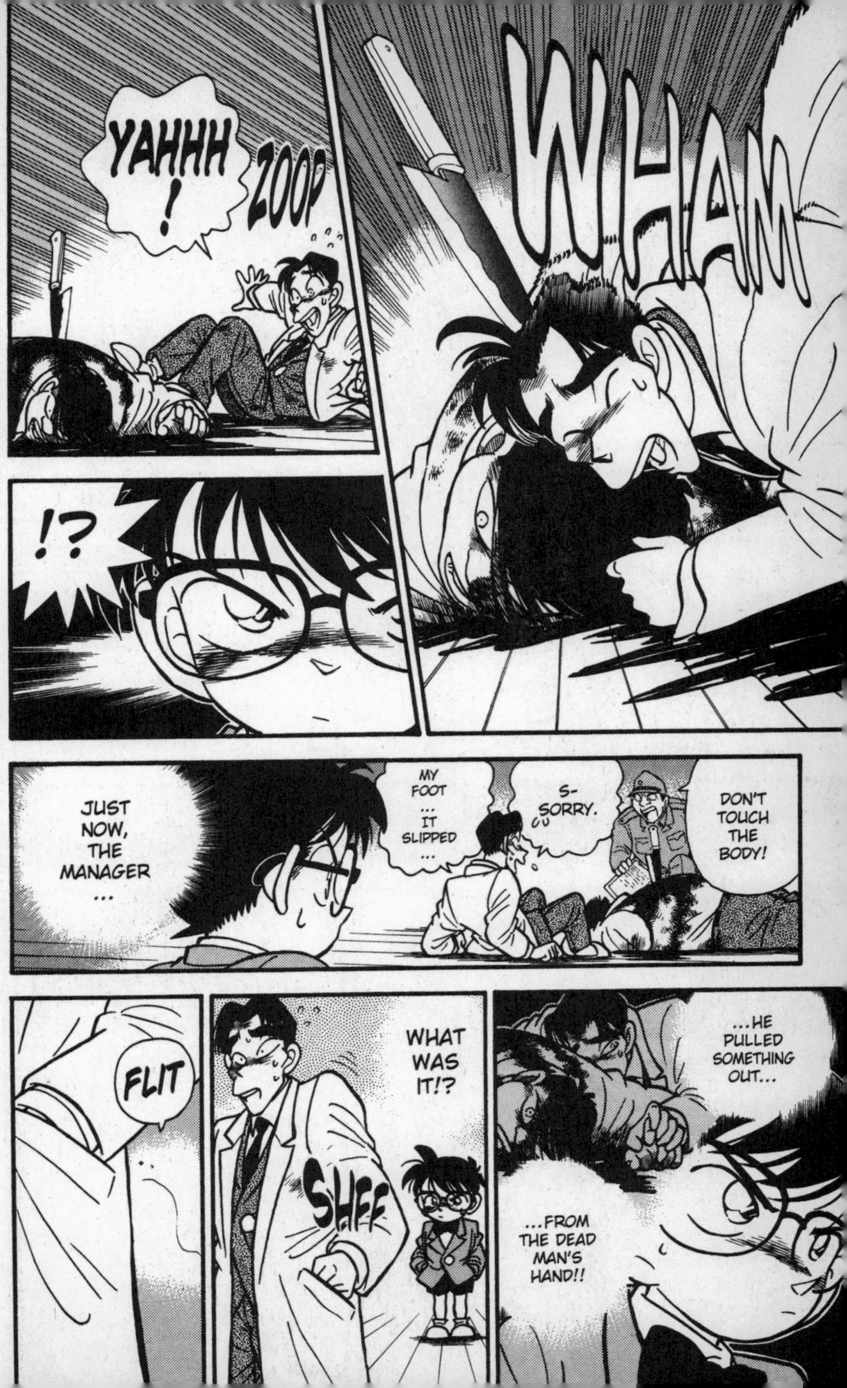
WHAM
YAHHH!
ZOOP
!?
DON'T TOUCH THE BODY!
S-SORRY.
MY FOOT ... IT SLIPPED ...
JUST NOW, THE MANAGER ...
...HE PULLED SOMETHING OUT...
...FROM THE DEAD MAN'S HAND!!
WHAT WAS IT!?
SHFF
FLIT

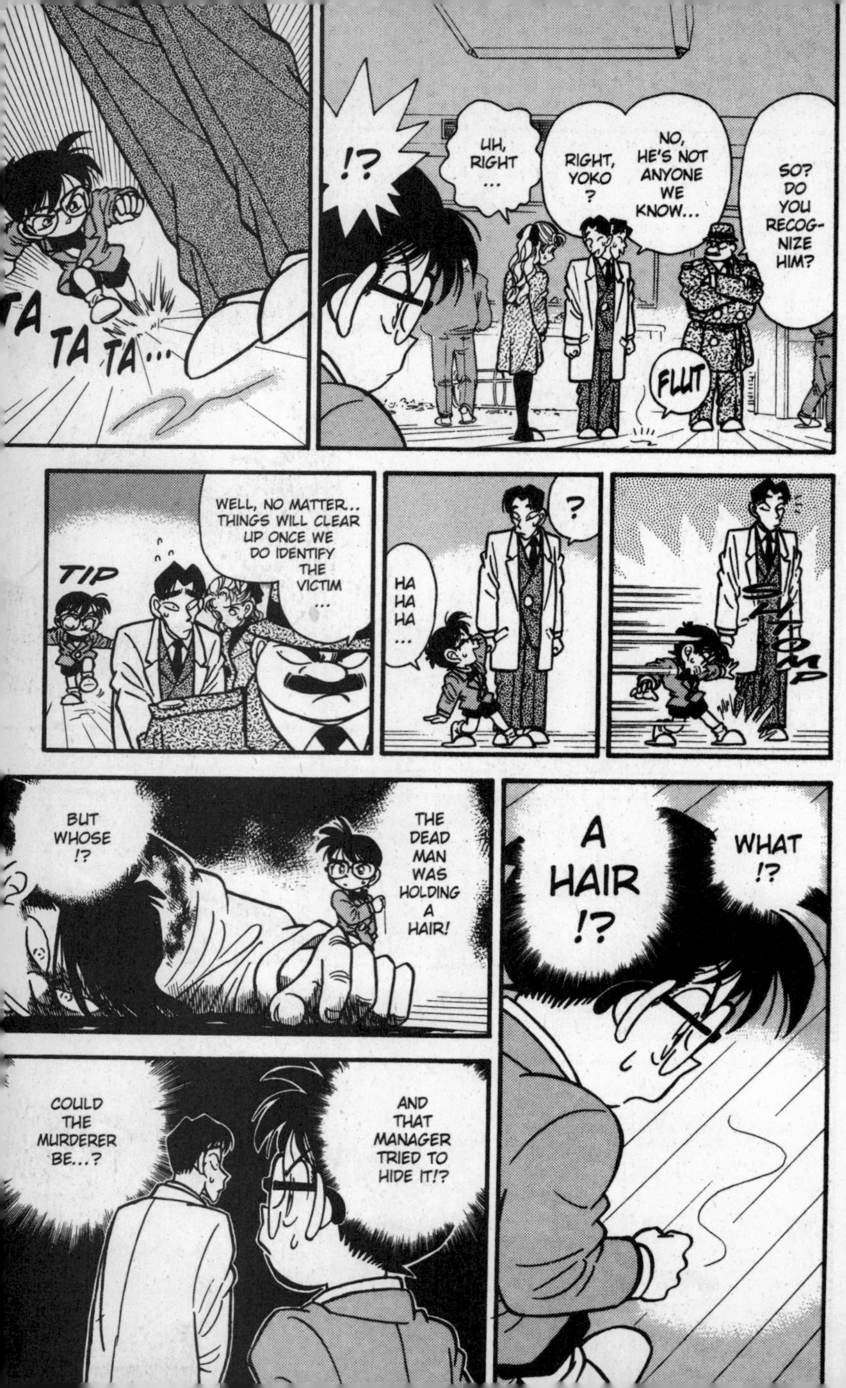

SO? DO YOU RECOGNIZE HIM?
NO, HE'S NOT ANYONE WE KNOW...
RIGHT, YOKO?
UH, RIGHT...
!?
FLUT
TA TA TA...
STOMP
?
HA HA HA...
WELL, NO MATTER... THINGS WILL CLEAR UP ONCE WE DO IDENTIFY THE VICTIM...
TIP
WHAT !?
A HAIR !?
THE DEAD MAN WAS HOLDING A HAIR!
BUT WHOSE !?
AND THAT MANAGER TRIED TO HIDE IT!?
COULD THE MURDERER BE...?

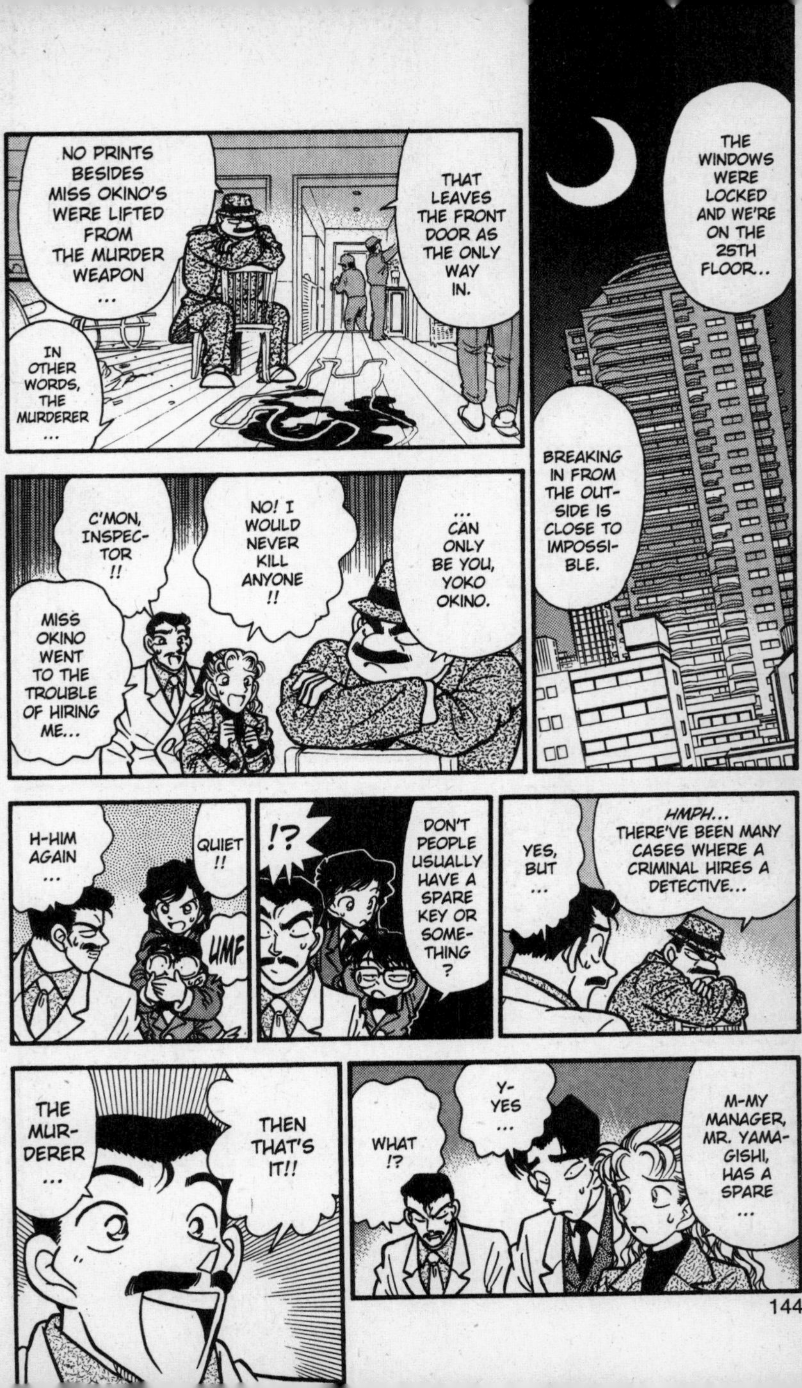
THE WINDOWS WERE LOCKED AND WE'RE ON THE 25TH FLOOR...
BREAKING IN FROM THE OUT-SIDE IS CLOSE TO IMPOSSI-BLE.
THAT LEAVES THE FRONT DOOR AS THE ONLY WAY IN.
NO PRINTS BESIDES MISS OKINO'S WERE LIFTED FROM THE MURDER WEAPON...
IN OTHER WORDS, THE MURDERER...
...CAN ONLY BE YOU, YOKO OKINO.
NO! I WOULD NEVER KILL ANYONE!!
C'MON, INSPEC-TOR!!
MISS OKINO WENT TO THE TROUBLE OF HIRING ME...
HMPH... THERE'VE BEEN MANY CASES WHERE A CRIMINAL HIRES A DETECTIVE...
YES, BUT...
DON'T PEOPLE USUALLY HAVE A SPARE KEY OR SOME-THING?
!?
QUIET!!
UMF
H-HIM AGAIN...
M-MY MANAGER, MR. YAMA-GISHI, HAS A SPARE...
Y-YES...
WHAT!?
THEN THAT'S IT!!
THE MUR-DERER...

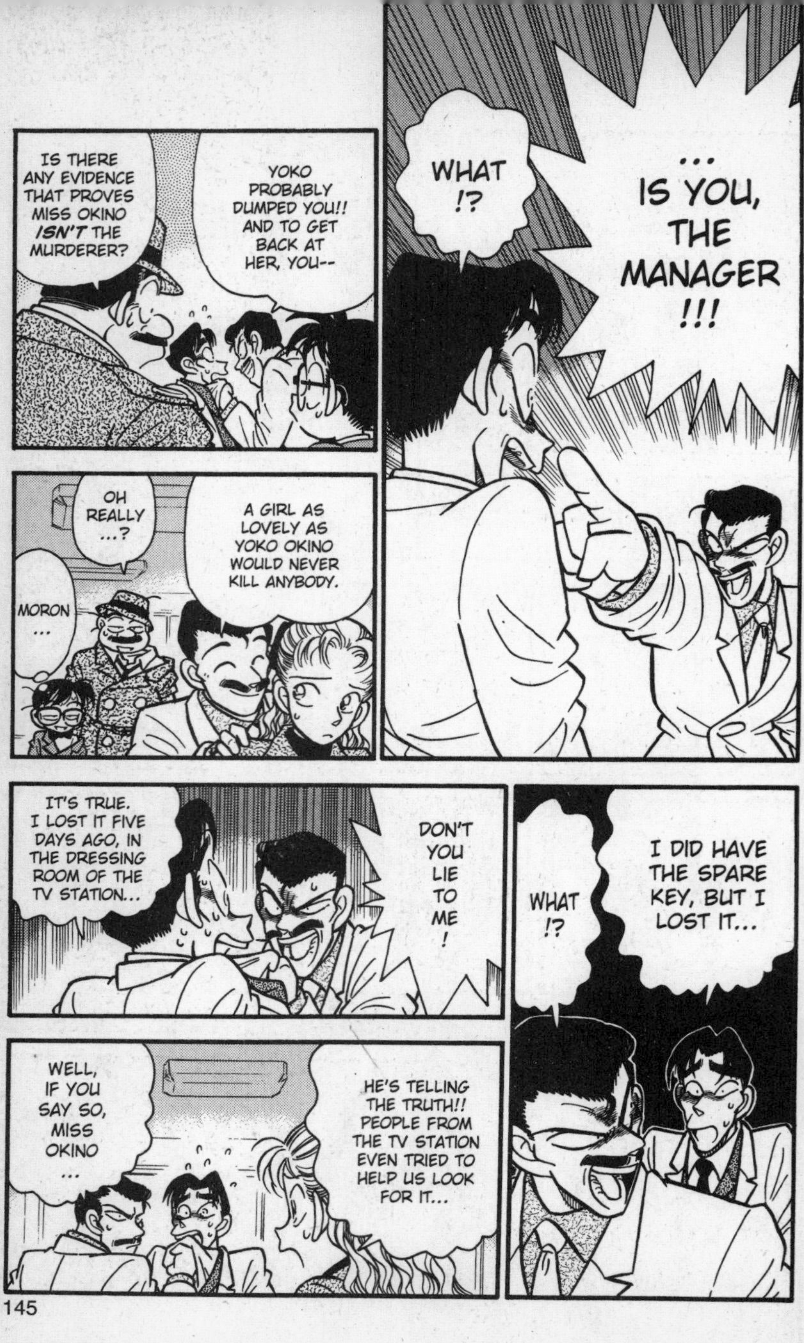
... IS YOU, THE MANAGER !!!
WHAT !?
YOKO PROBABLY DUMPED YOU!! AND TO GET BACK AT HER, YOU--
IS THERE ANY EVIDENCE THAT PROVES MISS OKINO *ISN'T* THE MURDERER?
A GIRL AS LOVELY AS YOKO OKINO WOULD NEVER KILL ANYBODY.
OH REALLY ...?
MORON ...
I DID HAVE THE SPARE KEY, BUT I LOST IT...
WHAT !?
DON'T YOU LIE TO ME !
IT'S TRUE. I LOST IT FIVE DAYS AGO, IN THE DRESSING ROOM OF THE TV STATION...
HE'S TELLING THE TRUTH!! PEOPLE FROM THE TV STATION EVEN TRIED TO HELP US LOOK FOR IT...
WELL, IF YOU SAY SO, MISS OKINO ...

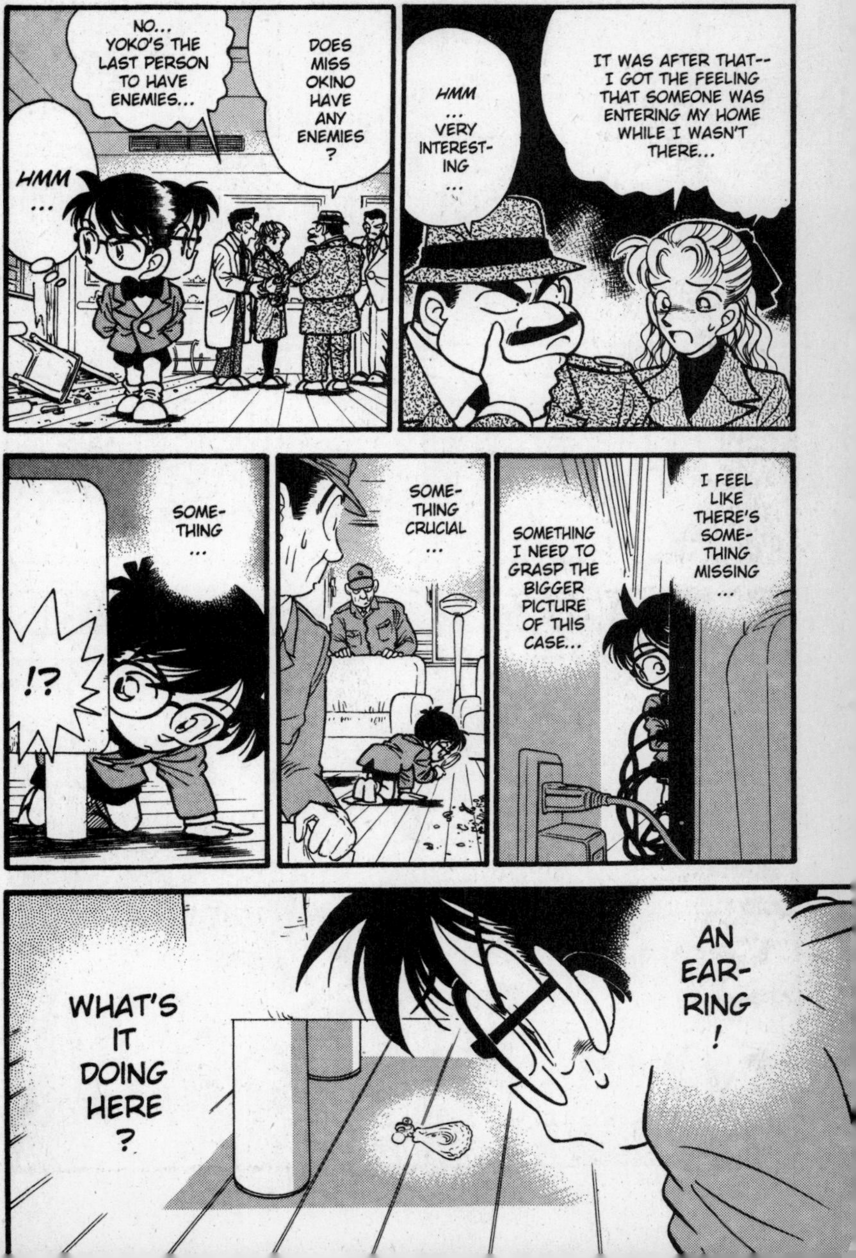
IT WAS AFTER THAT-- I GOT THE FEELING THAT SOMEONE WAS ENTERING MY HOME WHILE I WASN'T THERE...
HMM ... VERY INTEREST-ING ...
DOES MISS OKINO HAVE ANY ENEMIES ?
NO... YOKO'S THE LAST PERSON TO HAVE ENEMIES...
HMM ...
I FEEL LIKE THERE'S SOME-THING MISSING ...
SOMETHING I NEED TO GRASP THE BIGGER PICTURE OF THIS CASE...
SOME-THING CRUCIAL ...
SOME-THING ...
!?
AN EAR-RING !
WHAT'S IT DOING HERE ?

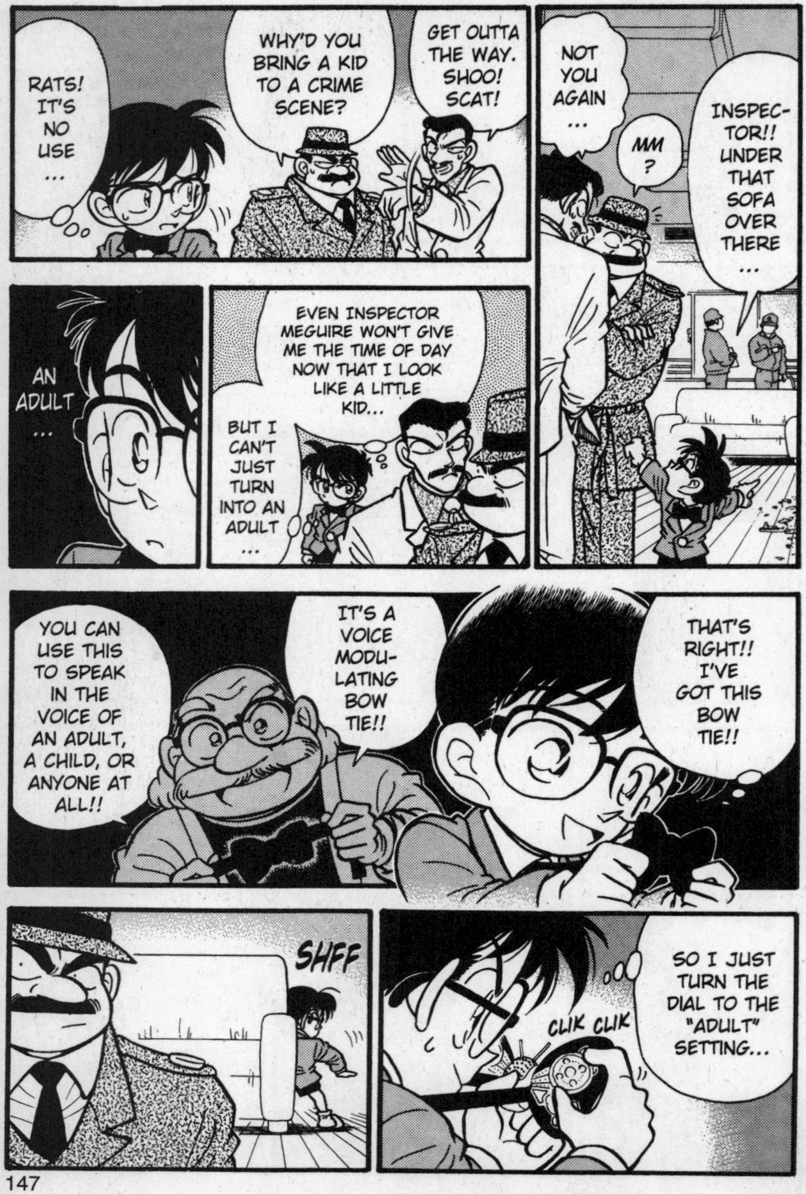
INSPECTOR!! UNDER THAT SOFA OVER THERE ...
MM ?
NOT YOU AGAIN ...
GET OUTTA THE WAY. SHOO! SCAT!
WHY'D YOU BRING A KID TO A CRIME SCENE?
RATS! IT'S NO USE ...
EVEN INSPECTOR MEGUIRE WON'T GIVE ME THE TIME OF DAY NOW THAT I LOOK LIKE A LITTLE KID...
BUT I CAN'T JUST TURN INTO AN ADULT ...
AN ADULT ...
THAT'S RIGHT!! I'VE GOT THIS BOW TIE!!
IT'S A VOICE MODU-LATING BOW TIE!!
YOU CAN USE THIS TO SPEAK IN THE VOICE OF AN ADULT, A CHILD, OR ANYONE AT ALL!!
SO I JUST TURN THE DIAL TO THE "ADULT" SETTING...
CLIK CLIK
SHFF

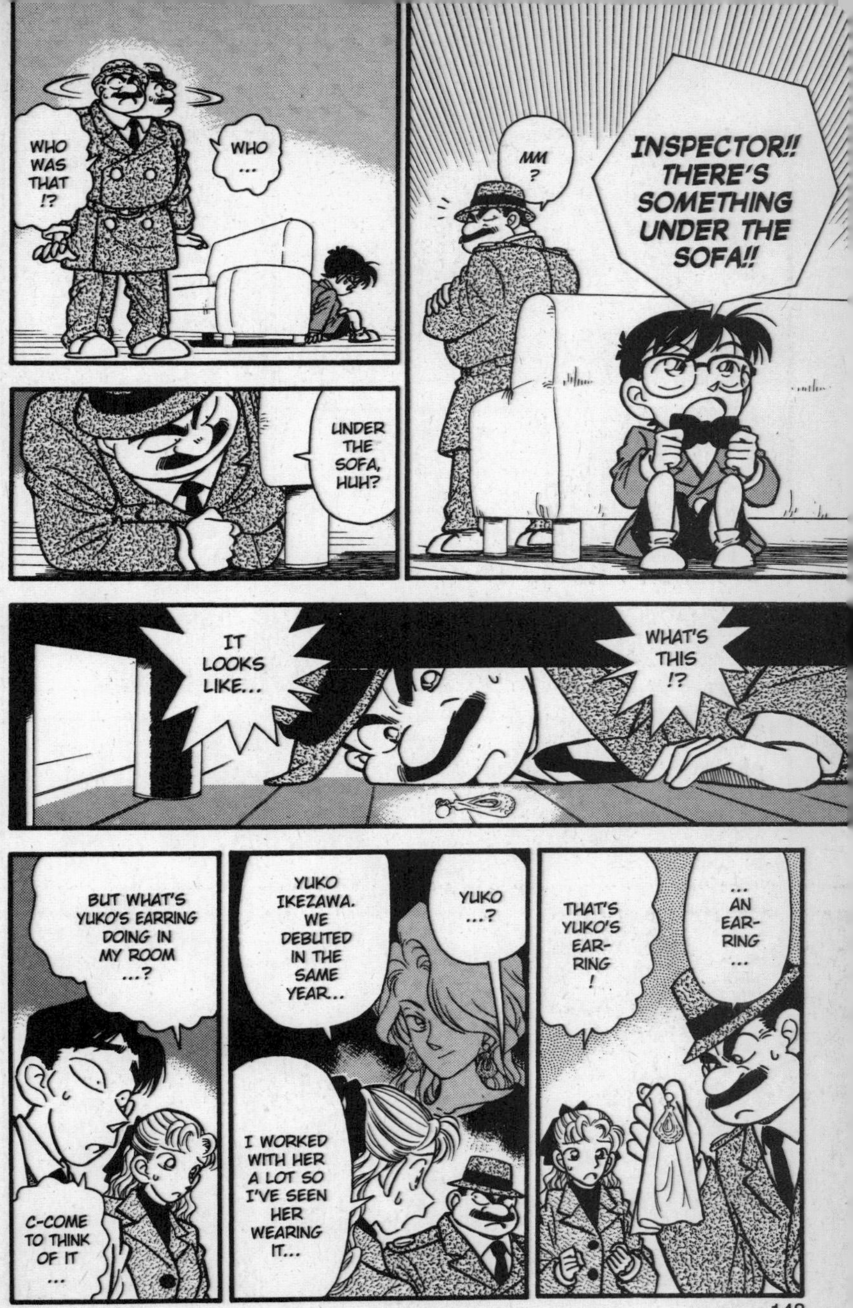

MM ?
INSPECTOR!! THERE'S SOMETHING UNDER THE SOFA!!
WHO ...
WHO WAS THAT !?
UNDER THE SOFA, HUH?
WHAT'S THIS !?
IT LOOKS LIKE...
... AN EAR-RING ...
THAT'S YUKO'S EAR-RING !
YUKO ...?
YUKO IKEZAWA. WE DEBUTED IN THE SAME YEAR...
I WORKED WITH HER A LOT SO I'VE SEEN HER WEARING IT...
BUT WHAT'S YUKO'S EARRING DOING IN MY ROOM ...?
C-COME TO THINK OF IT ...

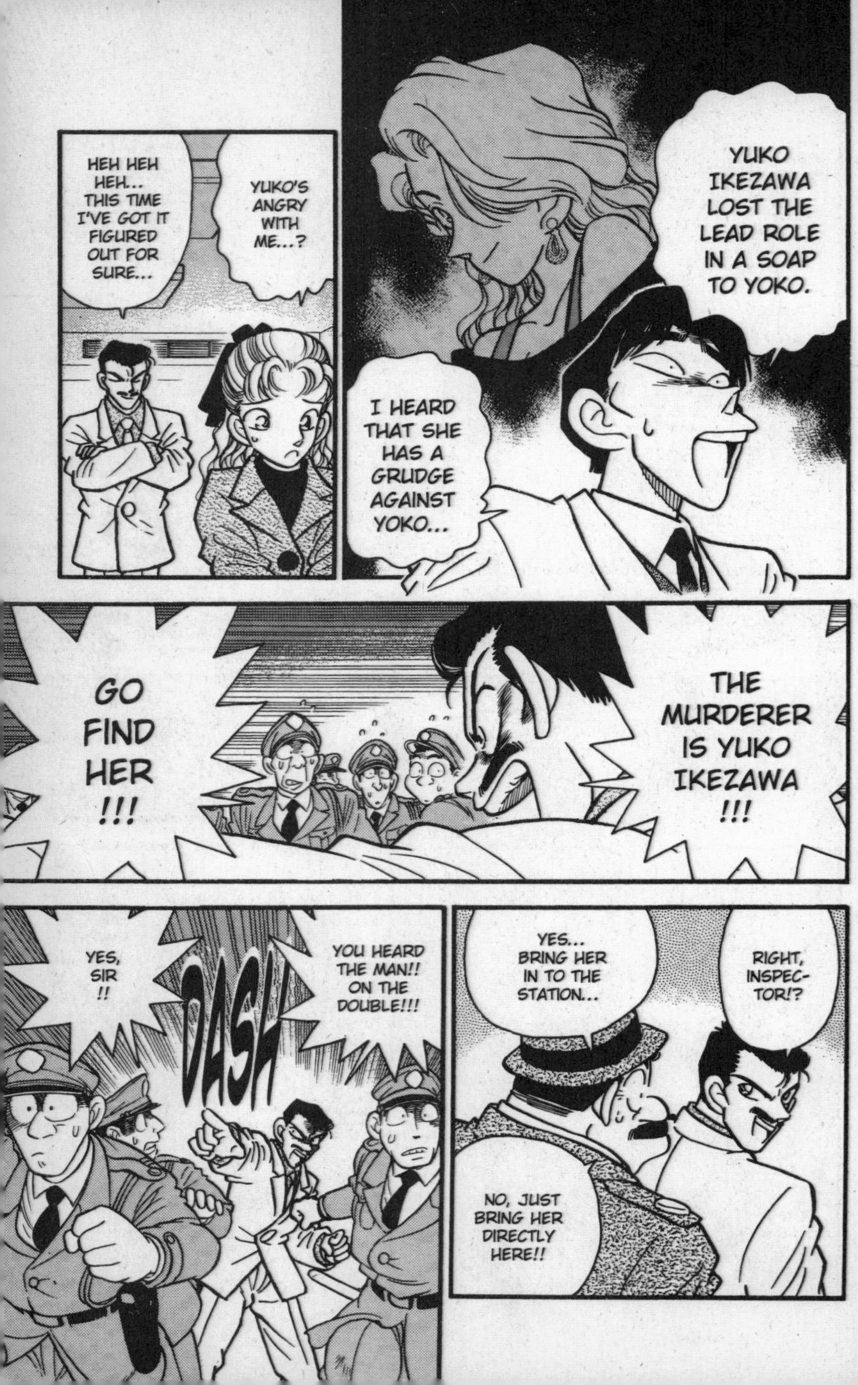
YUKO IKEZAWA LOST THE LEAD ROLE IN A SOAP TO YOKO.
I HEARD THAT SHE HAS A GRUDGE AGAINST YOKO...
YUKO'S ANGRY WITH ME...?
HEH HEH HEH... THIS TIME I'VE GOT IT FIGURED OUT FOR SURE...
THE MURDERER IS YUKO IKEZAWA !!!
GO FIND HER !!!
RIGHT, INSPECTOR!?
YES... BRING HER IN TO THE STATION...
NO, JUST BRING HER DIRECTLY HERE!!
YOU HEARD THE MAN!! ON THE DOUBLE!!!
DASH
YES, SIR !!

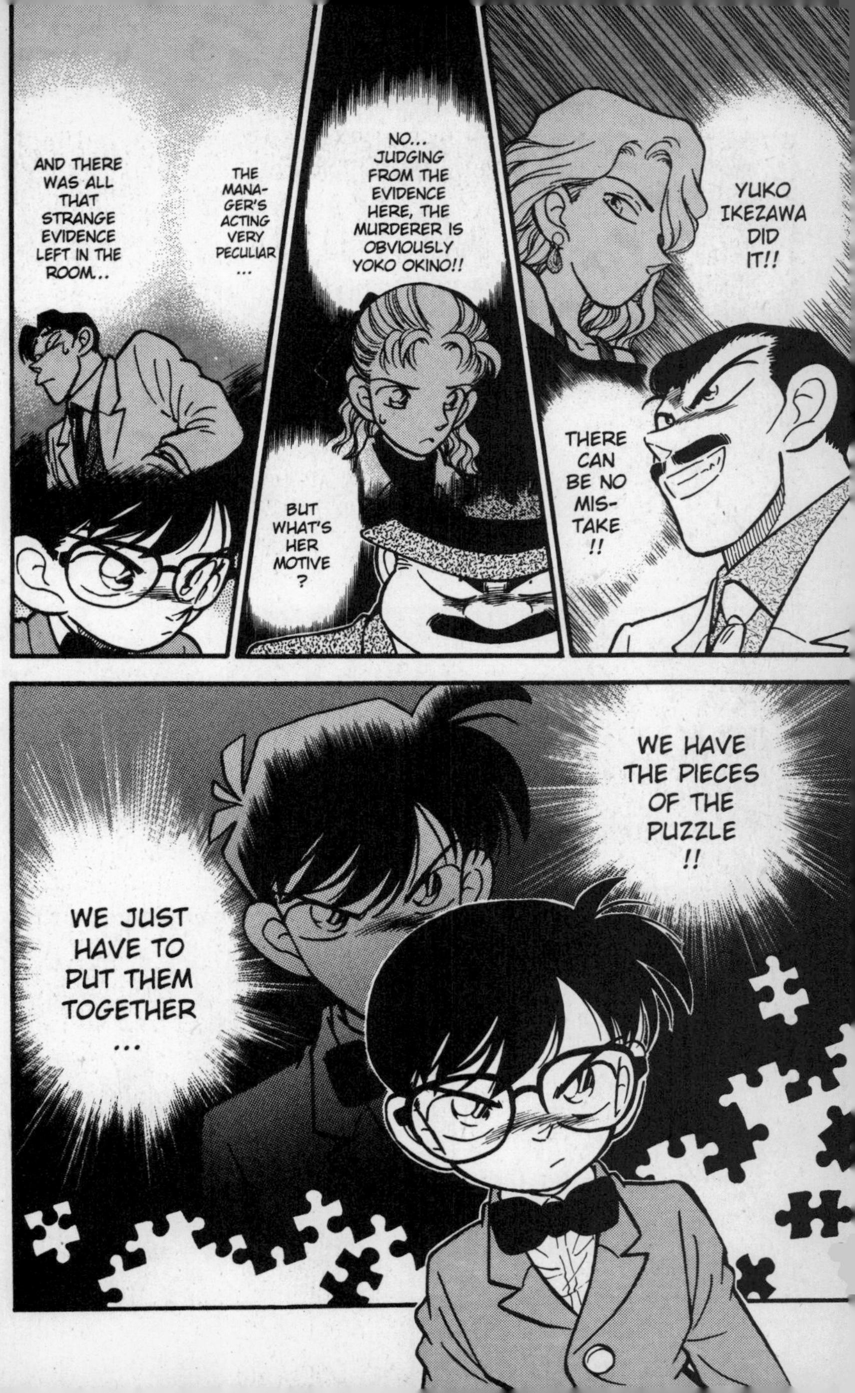
YUKO IKEZAWA DID IT!!
THERE CAN BE NO MIS-TAKE!!
NO... JUDGING FROM THE EVIDENCE HERE, THE MURDERER IS OBVIOUSLY YOKO OKINO!!
BUT WHAT'S HER MOTIVE?
THE MANA-GER'S ACTING VERY PECULIAR...
AND THERE WAS ALL THAT STRANGE EVIDENCE LEFT IN THE ROOM...
WE HAVE THE PIECES OF THE PUZZLE!!
WE JUST HAVE TO PUT THEM TOGETHER...

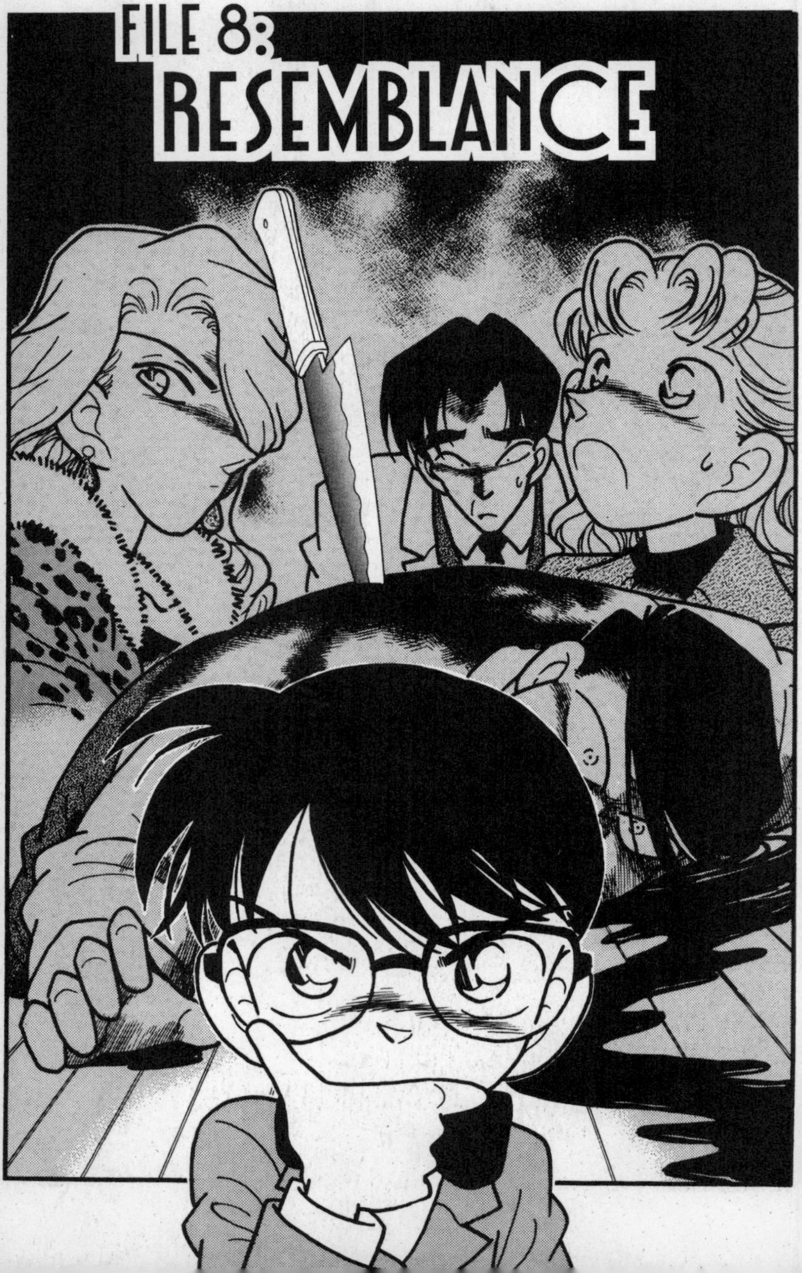
FILE 8:
RESEMBLANCE

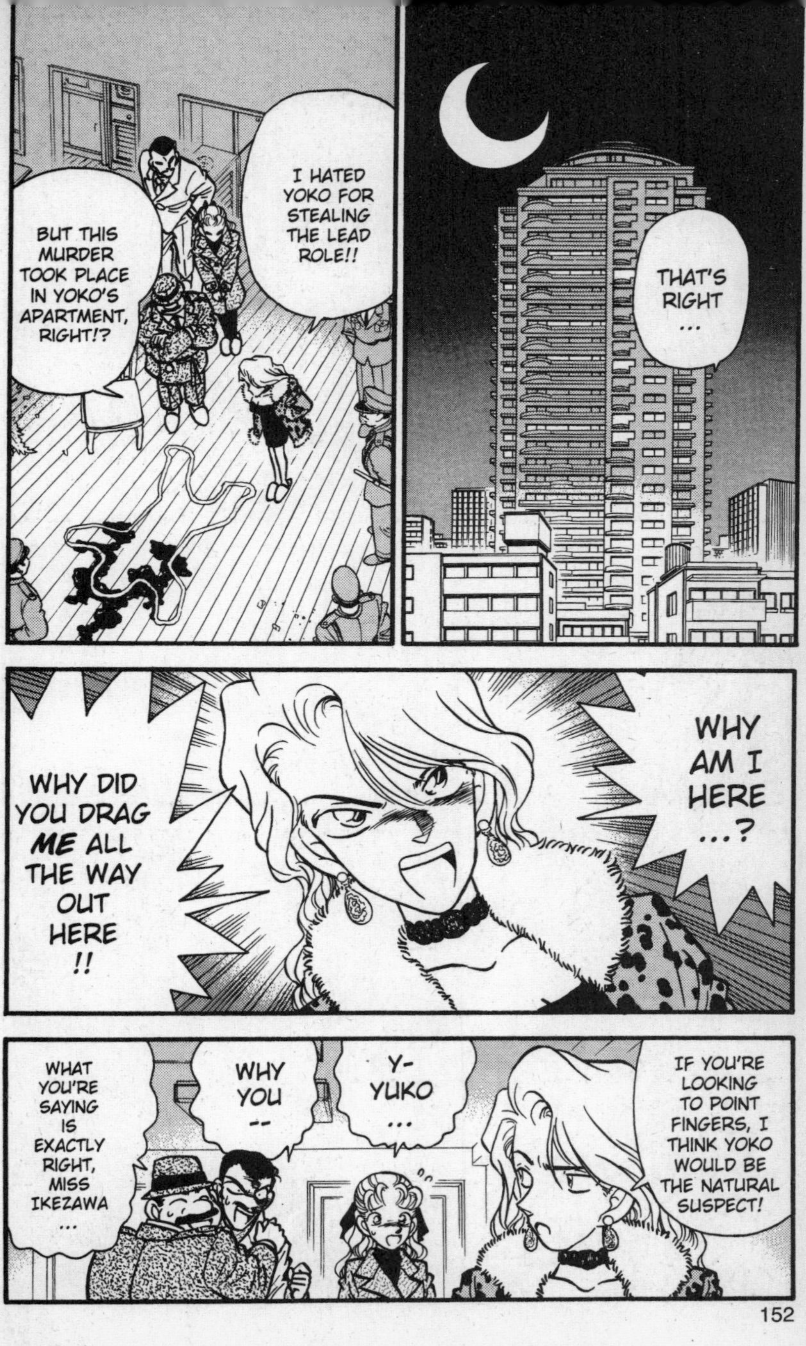
THAT'S RIGHT ...
I HATED YOKO FOR STEALING THE LEAD ROLE!!
BUT THIS MURDER TOOK PLACE IN YOKO'S APARTMENT, RIGHT!?
WHY AM I HERE ...?
WHY DID YOU DRAG *ME* ALL THE WAY OUT HERE !!
IF YOU'RE LOOKING TO POINT FINGERS, I THINK YOKO WOULD BE THE NATURAL SUSPECT!
Y- YUKO ...
WHY YOU --
WHAT YOU'RE SAYING IS EXACTLY RIGHT, MISS IKEZAWA ...

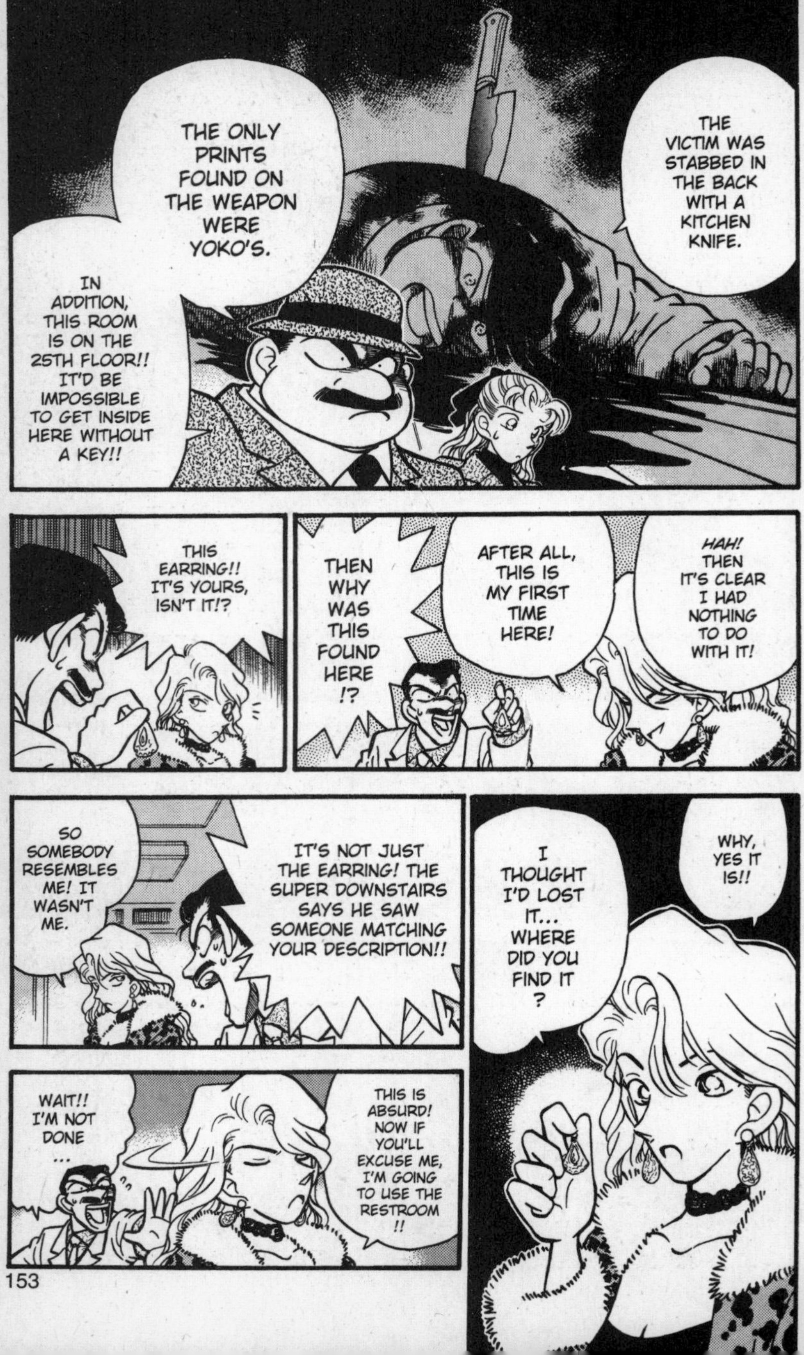
THE VICTIM WAS STABBED IN THE BACK WITH A KITCHEN KNIFE.
THE ONLY PRINTS FOUND ON THE WEAPON WERE YOKO'S.
IN ADDITION, THIS ROOM IS ON THE 25TH FLOOR!! IT'D BE IMPOSSIBLE TO GET INSIDE HERE WITHOUT A KEY!!
HAH! THEN IT'S CLEAR I HAD NOTHING TO DO WITH IT!
AFTER ALL, THIS IS MY FIRST TIME HERE!
THEN WHY WAS THIS FOUND HERE !?
THIS EARRING!! IT'S YOURS, ISN'T IT!?
WHY, YES IT IS!!
I THOUGHT I'D LOST IT... WHERE DID YOU FIND IT ?
IT'S NOT JUST THE EARRING! THE SUPER DOWNSTAIRS SAYS HE SAW SOMEONE MATCHING YOUR DESCRIPTION!!
SO SOMEBODY RESEMBLES ME! IT WASN'T ME.
THIS IS ABSURD! NOW IF YOU'LL EXCUSE ME, I'M GOING TO USE THE RESTROOM !!
WAIT!! I'M NOT DONE ...

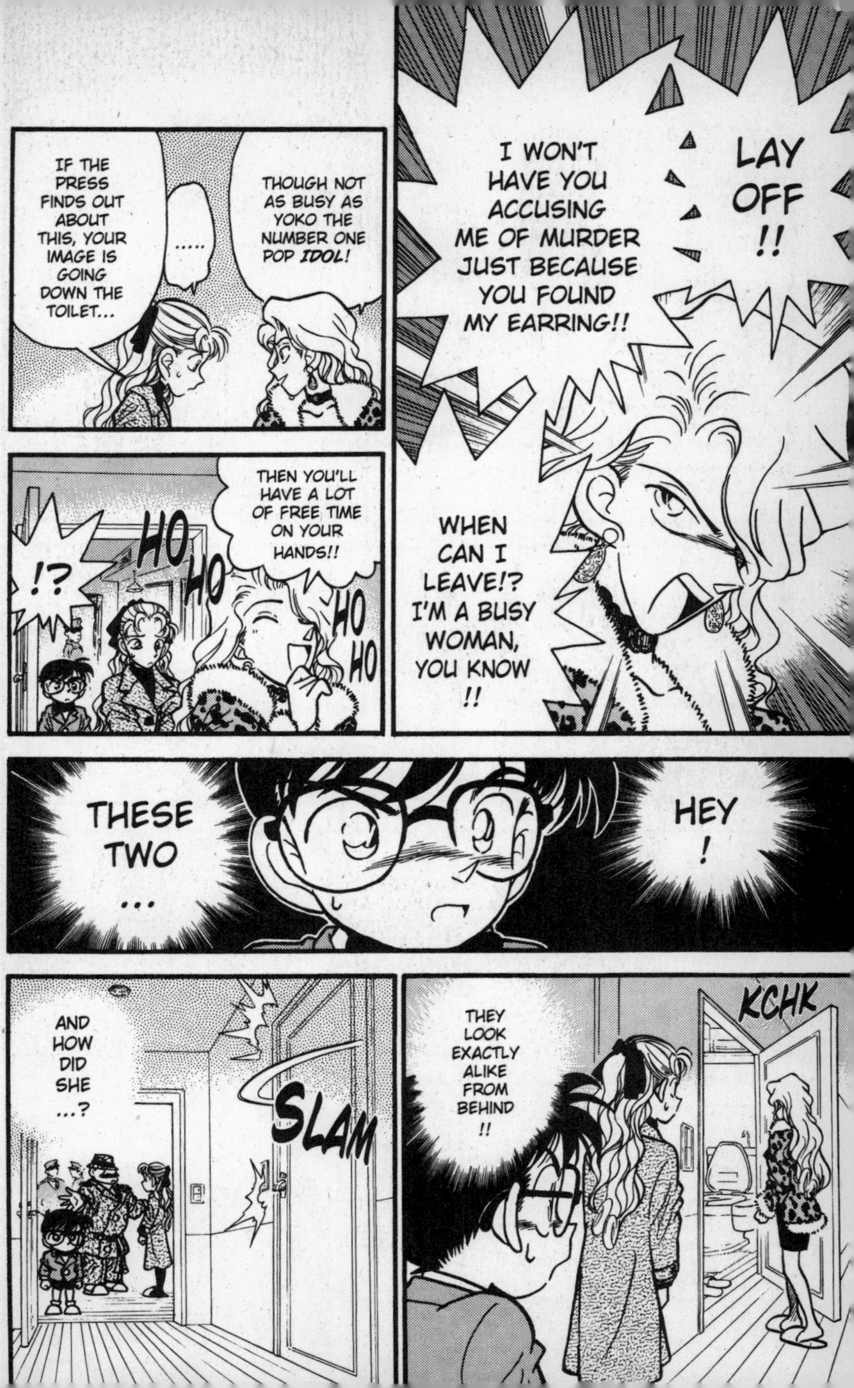

LAY OFF!!
I WON'T HAVE YOU ACCUSING ME OF MURDER JUST BECAUSE YOU FOUND MY EARRING!!
WHEN CAN I LEAVE!? I'M A BUSY WOMAN, YOU KNOW!!
THOUGH NOT AS BUSY AS YOKO THE NUMBER ONE POP *IDOL*!
.....
IF THE PRESS FINDS OUT ABOUT THIS, YOUR IMAGE IS GOING DOWN THE TOILET...
THEN YOU'LL HAVE A LOT OF FREE TIME ON YOUR HANDS!!
HO HO HO HO
!?
HEY!
THESE TWO...
KCHK
THEY LOOK EXACTLY ALIKE FROM BEHIND!!
SLAM
AND HOW DID SHE...?

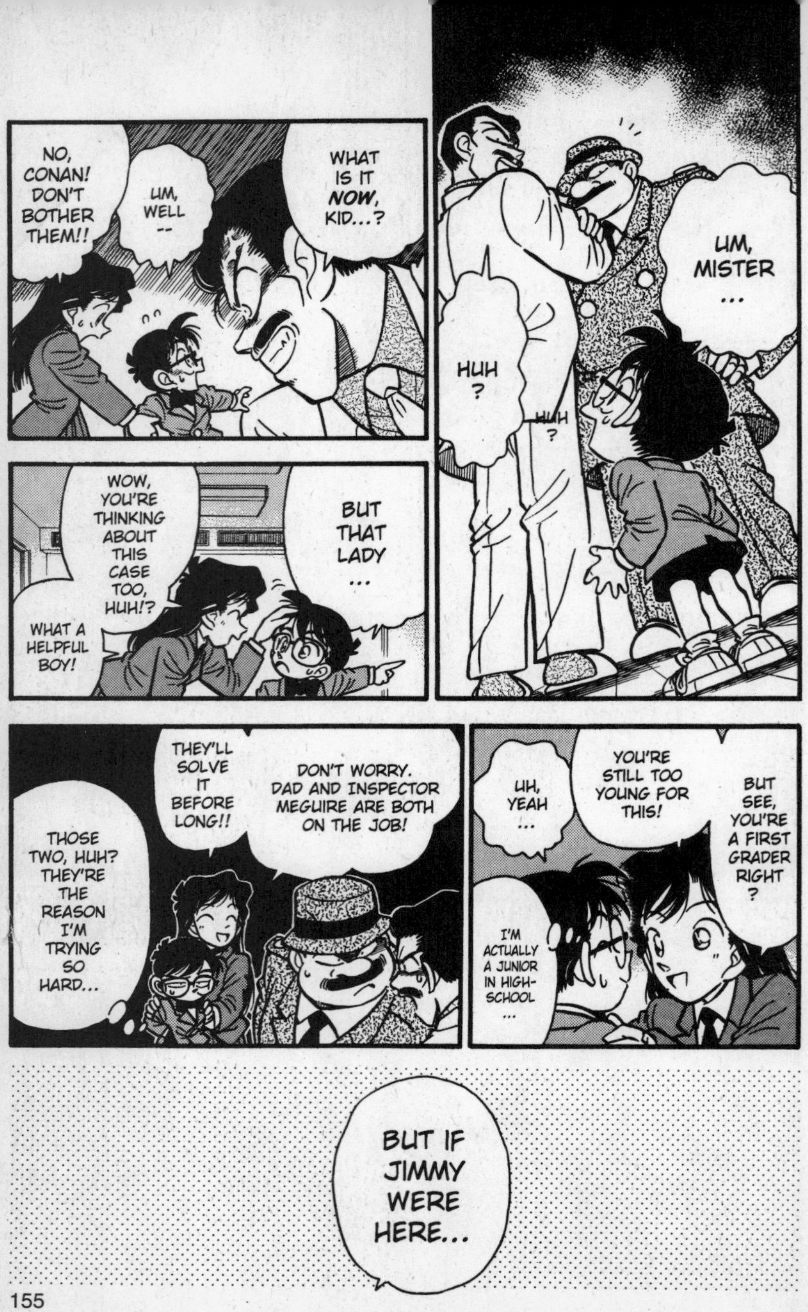
UM, MISTER ...
HUH ?
HUH ?
WHAT IS IT *NOW*, KID...?
UM, WELL --
NO, CONAN! DON'T BOTHER THEM!!
BUT THAT LADY ...
WOW, YOU'RE THINKING ABOUT THIS CASE TOO, HUH!?
WHAT A HELPFUL BOY!
BUT SEE, YOU'RE A FIRST GRADER RIGHT ?
YOU'RE STILL TOO YOUNG FOR THIS!
UH, YEAH ...
I'M ACTUALLY A JUNIOR IN HIGH-SCHOOL ...
DON'T WORRY. DAD AND INSPECTOR MEGUIRE ARE BOTH ON THE JOB!
THEY'LL SOLVE IT BEFORE LONG!!
THOSE TWO, HUH? THEY'RE THE REASON I'M TRYING SO HARD...
BUT IF JIMMY WERE HERE...

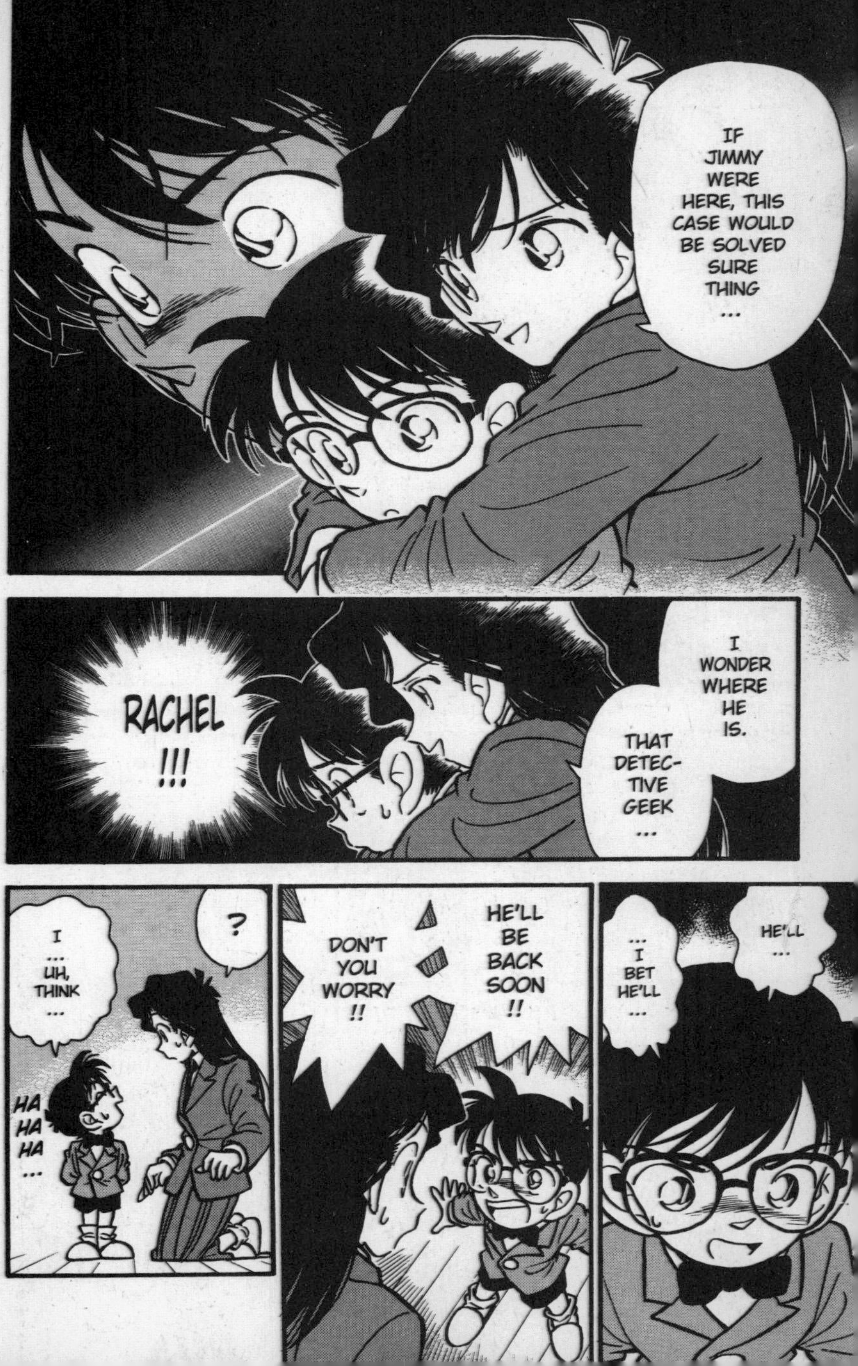
IF JIMMY WERE HERE, THIS CASE WOULD BE SOLVED SURE THING ...
I WONDER WHERE HE IS.
THAT DETEC-TIVE GEEK ...
RACHEL !!!
HE'LL ...
... I BET HE'LL ...
HE'LL BE BACK SOON !!
DON'T YOU WORRY !!
?
I ... UH, THINK ...
HA HA HA ...

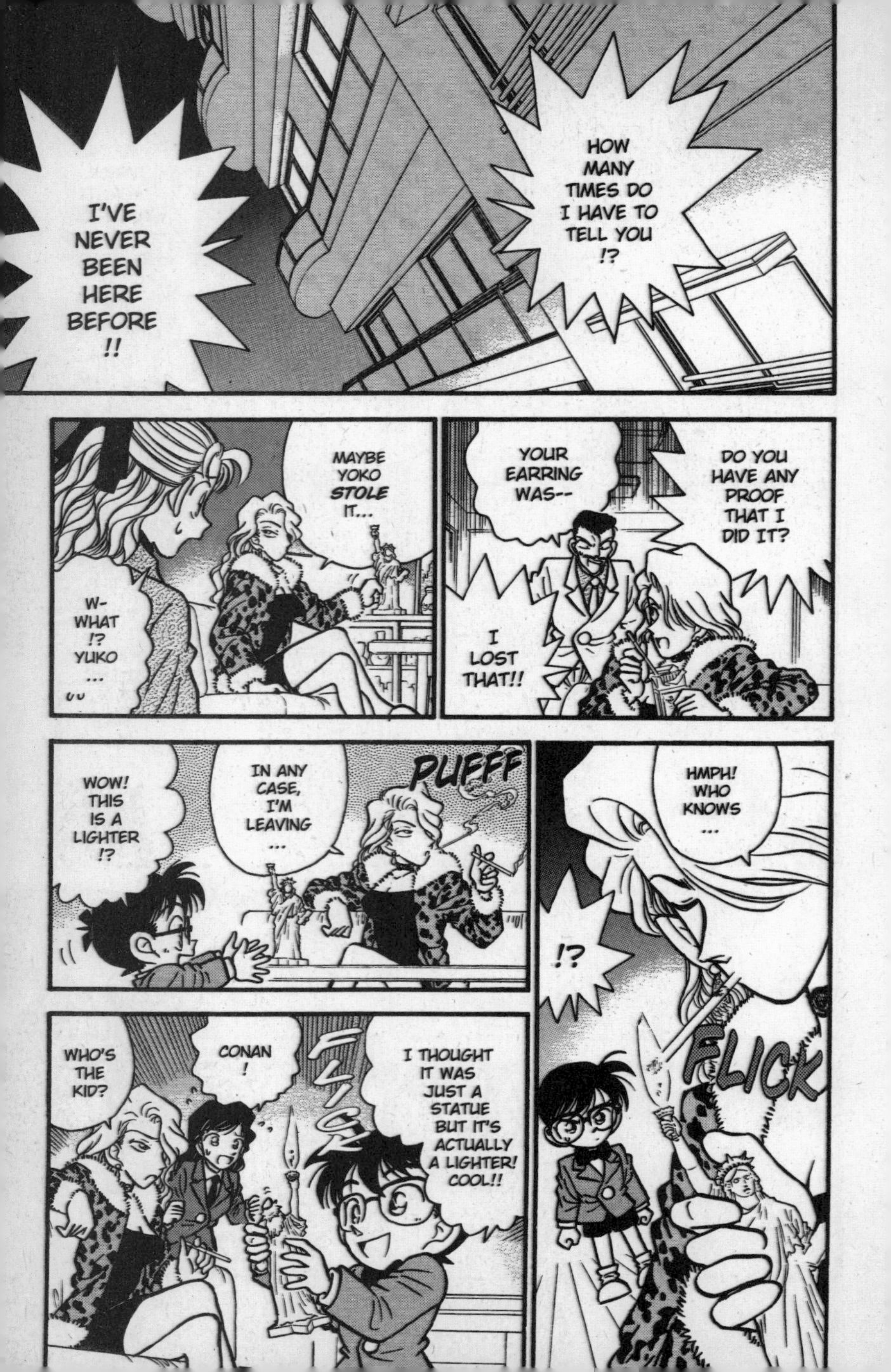
HOW MANY TIMES DO I HAVE TO TELL YOU !?
I'VE NEVER BEEN HERE BEFORE !!
DO YOU HAVE ANY PROOF THAT I DID IT?
YOUR EARRING WAS--
I LOST THAT!!
MAYBE YOKO STOLE IT...
W- WHAT !? YUKO ...
HMPH! WHO KNOWS ...
!?
FLICK
PUFFF
IN ANY CASE, I'M LEAVING ...
WOW! THIS IS A LIGHTER !?
I THOUGHT IT WAS JUST A STATUE BUT IT'S ACTUALLY A LIGHTER! COOL!!
FLICK
CONAN !
WHO'S THE KID?

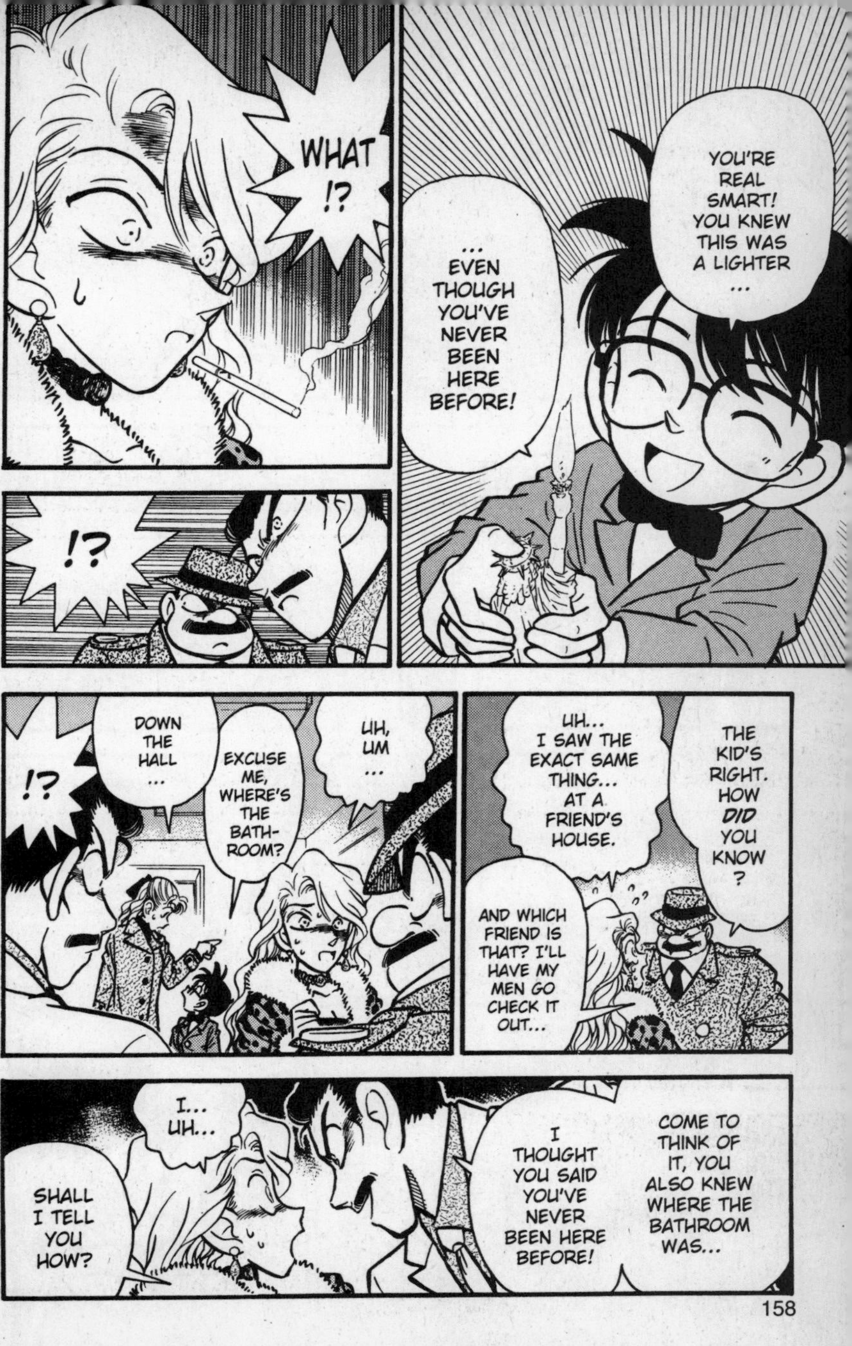
YOU'RE REAL SMART! YOU KNEW THIS WAS A LIGHTER ...
... EVEN THOUGH YOU'VE NEVER BEEN HERE BEFORE!
WHAT !?
!?
THE KID'S RIGHT. HOW *DID* YOU KNOW ?
UH... I SAW THE EXACT SAME THING... AT A FRIEND'S HOUSE.
AND WHICH FRIEND IS THAT? I'LL HAVE MY MEN GO CHECK IT OUT...
UH, UM ...
EXCUSE ME, WHERE'S THE BATH-ROOM?
DOWN THE HALL ...
!?
COME TO THINK OF IT, YOU ALSO KNEW WHERE THE BATHROOM WAS...
I THOUGHT YOU SAID YOU'VE NEVER BEEN HERE BEFORE!
I... UH...
SHALL I TELL YOU HOW?

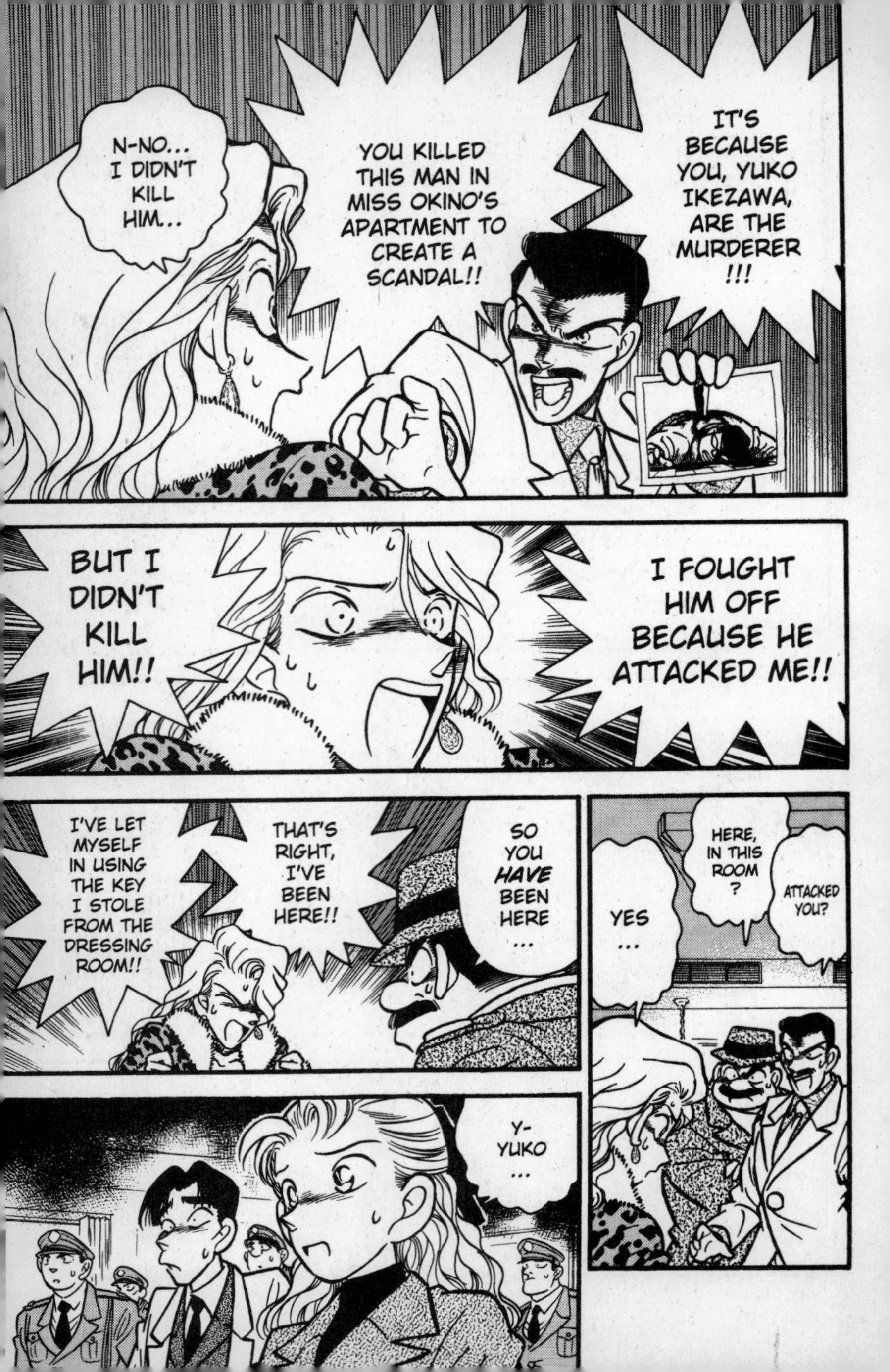
IT'S BECAUSE YOU, YUKO IKEZAWA, ARE THE MURDERER!!!
YOU KILLED THIS MAN IN MISS OKINO'S APARTMENT TO CREATE A SCANDAL!!
N-NO... I DIDN'T KILL HIM...
I FOUGHT HIM OFF BECAUSE HE ATTACKED ME!!
BUT I DIDN'T KILL HIM!!
ATTACKED YOU?
HERE, IN THIS ROOM?
YES...
SO YOU *HAVE* BEEN HERE...
THAT'S RIGHT, I'VE BEEN HERE!!
I'VE LET MYSELF IN USING THE KEY I STOLE FROM THE DRESSING ROOM!!
Y-YUKO...

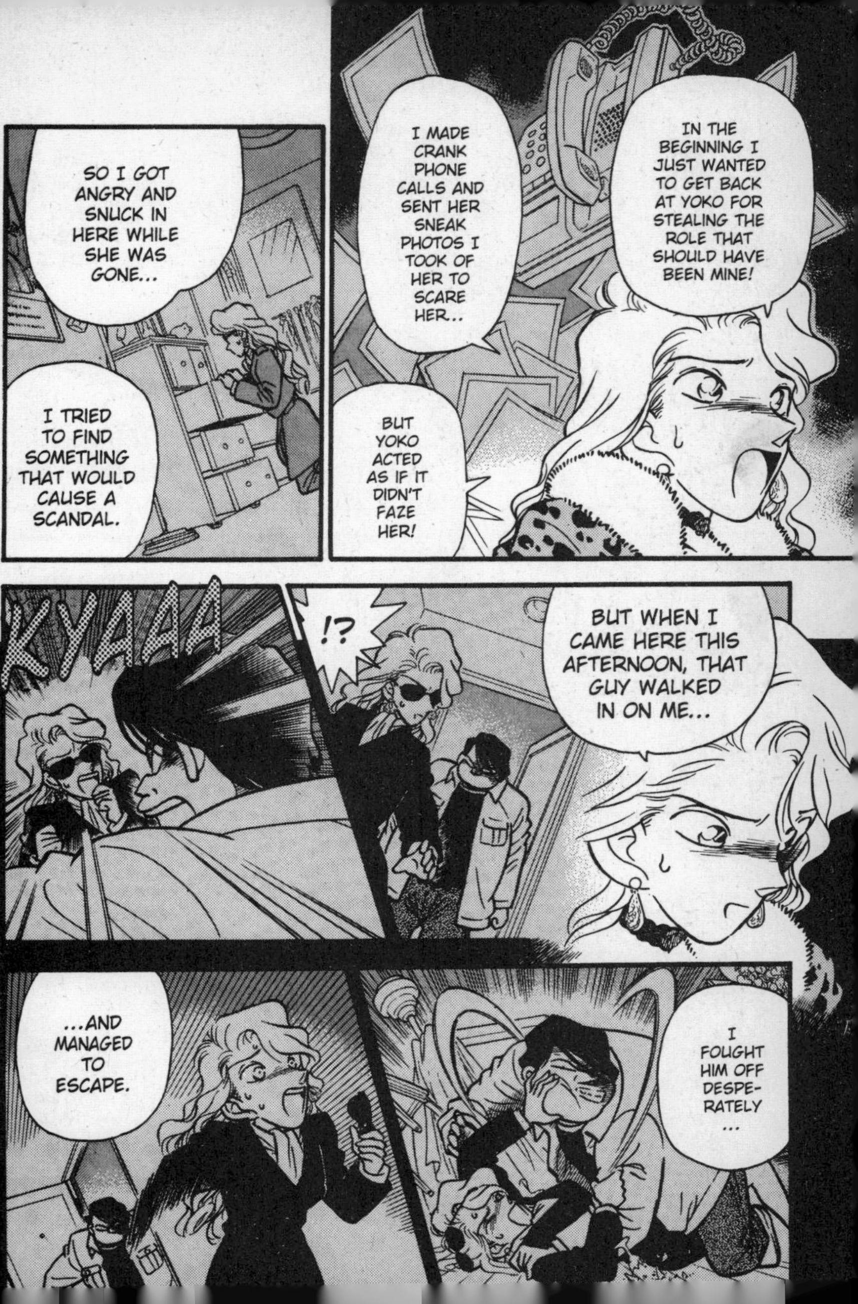
IN THE BEGINNING I JUST WANTED TO GET BACK AT YOKO FOR STEALING THE ROLE THAT SHOULD HAVE BEEN MINE!
I MADE CRANK PHONE CALLS AND SENT HER SNEAK PHOTOS I TOOK OF HER TO SCARE HER...
BUT YOKO ACTED AS IF IT DIDN'T FAZE HER!
SO I GOT ANGRY AND SNUCK IN HERE WHILE SHE WAS GONE...
I TRIED TO FIND SOMETHING THAT WOULD CAUSE A SCANDAL.
BUT WHEN I CAME HERE THIS AFTERNOON, THAT GUY WALKED IN ON ME...
!?
KYAAA
I FOUGHT HIM OFF DESPERATELY...
...AND MANAGED TO ESCAPE.

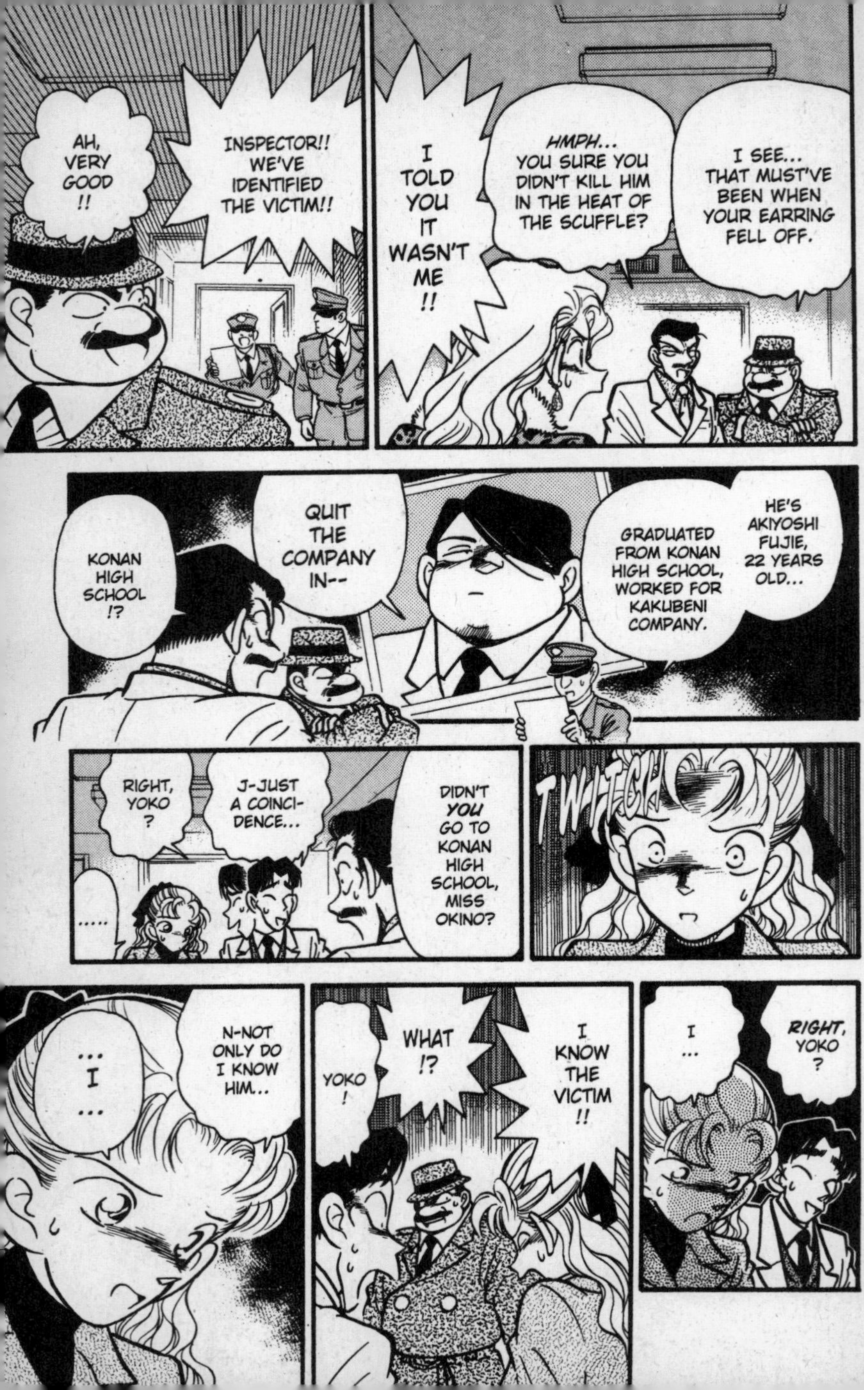
I SEE... THAT MUST'VE BEEN WHEN YOUR EARRING FELL OFF.
HMPH... YOU SURE YOU DIDN'T KILL HIM IN THE HEAT OF THE SCUFFLE?
I TOLD YOU IT WASN'T ME!!
INSPECTOR!! WE'VE IDENTIFIED THE VICTIM!!
AH, VERY GOOD!!
HE'S AKIYOSHI FUJIE, 22 YEARS OLD...
GRADUATED FROM KONAN HIGH SCHOOL, WORKED FOR KAKUBENI COMPANY.
QUIT THE COMPANY IN--
KONAN HIGH SCHOOL!?
TWITCH
DIDN'T *YOU* GO TO KONAN HIGH SCHOOL, MISS OKINO?
J-JUST A COINCIDENCE...
RIGHT, YOKO?
.....
RIGHT, YOKO?
I...
I KNOW THE VICTIM!!
WHAT!?
YOKO!
N-NOT ONLY DO I KNOW HIM...
...I...

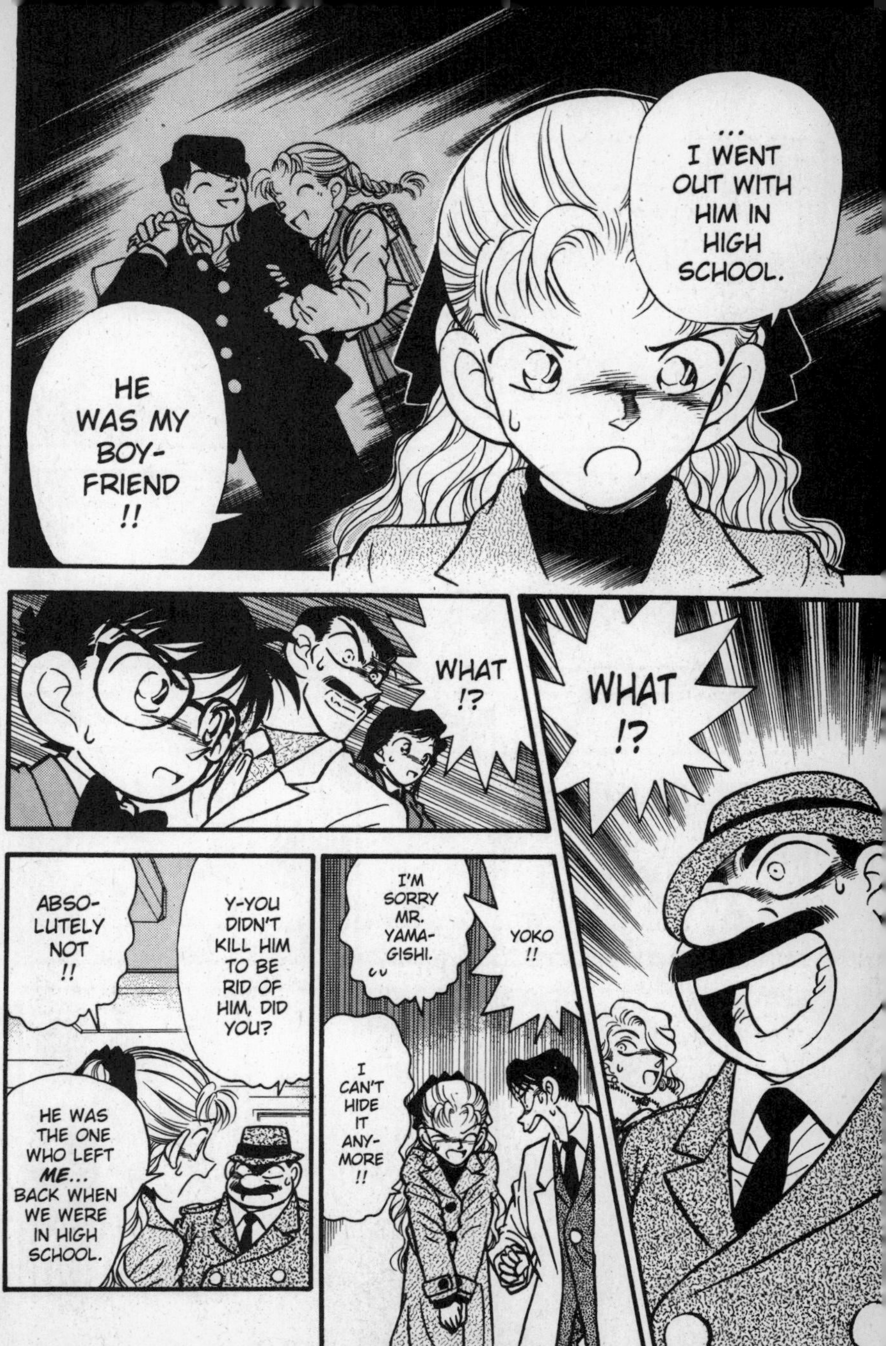
... I WENT OUT WITH HIM IN HIGH SCHOOL.
HE WAS MY BOY-FRIEND !!
WHAT !?
WHAT !?
I'M SORRY MR. YAMA-GISHI.
YOKO !!
I CAN'T HIDE IT ANY-MORE !!
Y-YOU DIDN'T KILL HIM TO BE RID OF HIM, DID YOU?
ABSO-LUTELY NOT !!
HE WAS THE ONE WHO LEFT *ME*... BACK WHEN WE WERE IN HIGH SCHOOL.

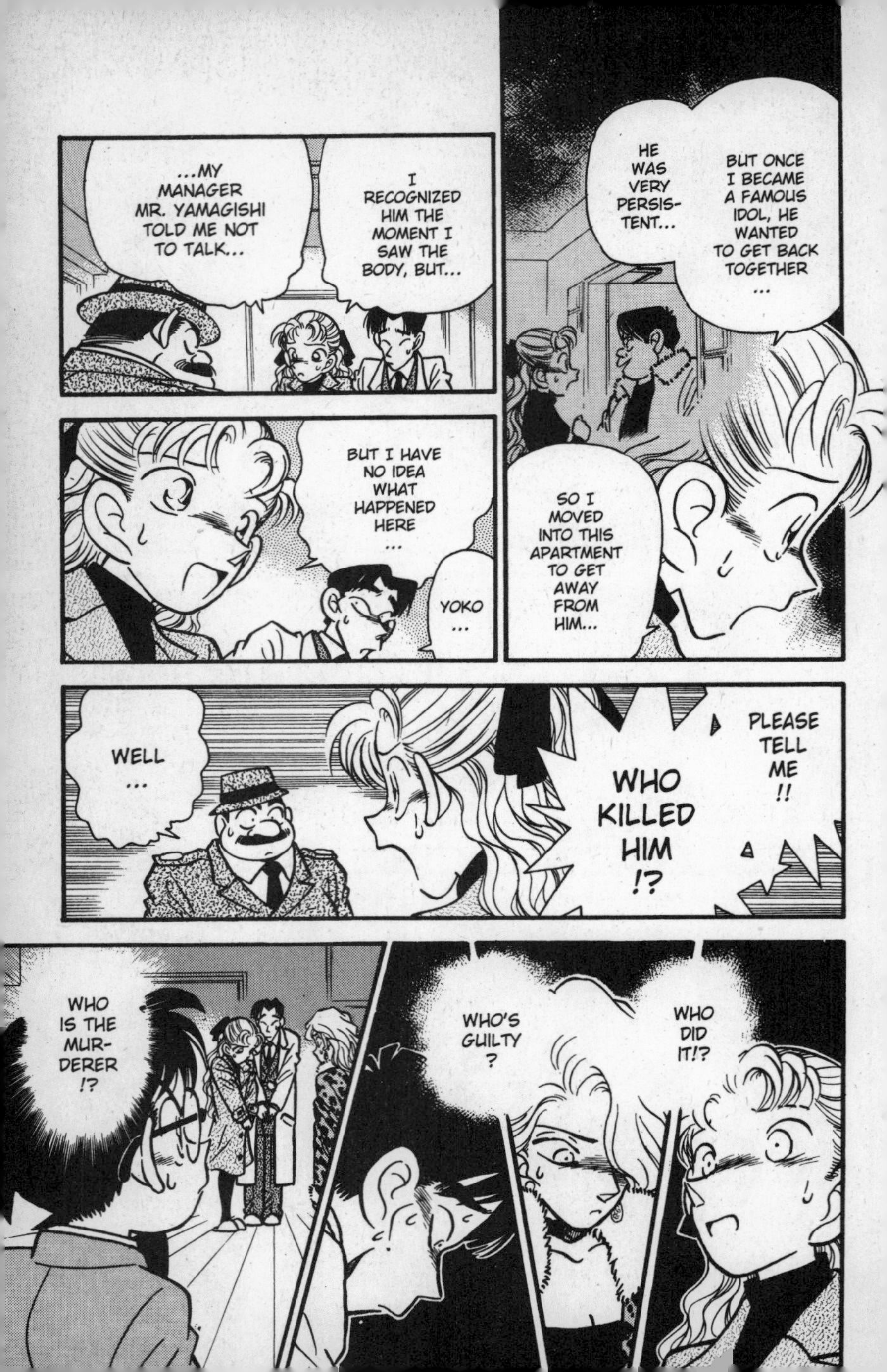
BUT ONCE I BECAME A FAMOUS IDOL, HE WANTED TO GET BACK TOGETHER ...
HE WAS VERY PERSIS- TENT...
SO I MOVED INTO THIS APARTMENT TO GET AWAY FROM HIM...
I RECOGNIZED HIM THE MOMENT I SAW THE BODY, BUT...
...MY MANAGER MR. YAMAGISHI TOLD ME NOT TO TALK...
BUT I HAVE NO IDEA WHAT HAPPENED HERE ...
YOKO ...
PLEASE TELL ME !!
WHO KILLED HIM !?
WELL ...
WHO DID IT!?
WHO'S GUILTY ?
WHO IS THE MUR- DERER !?

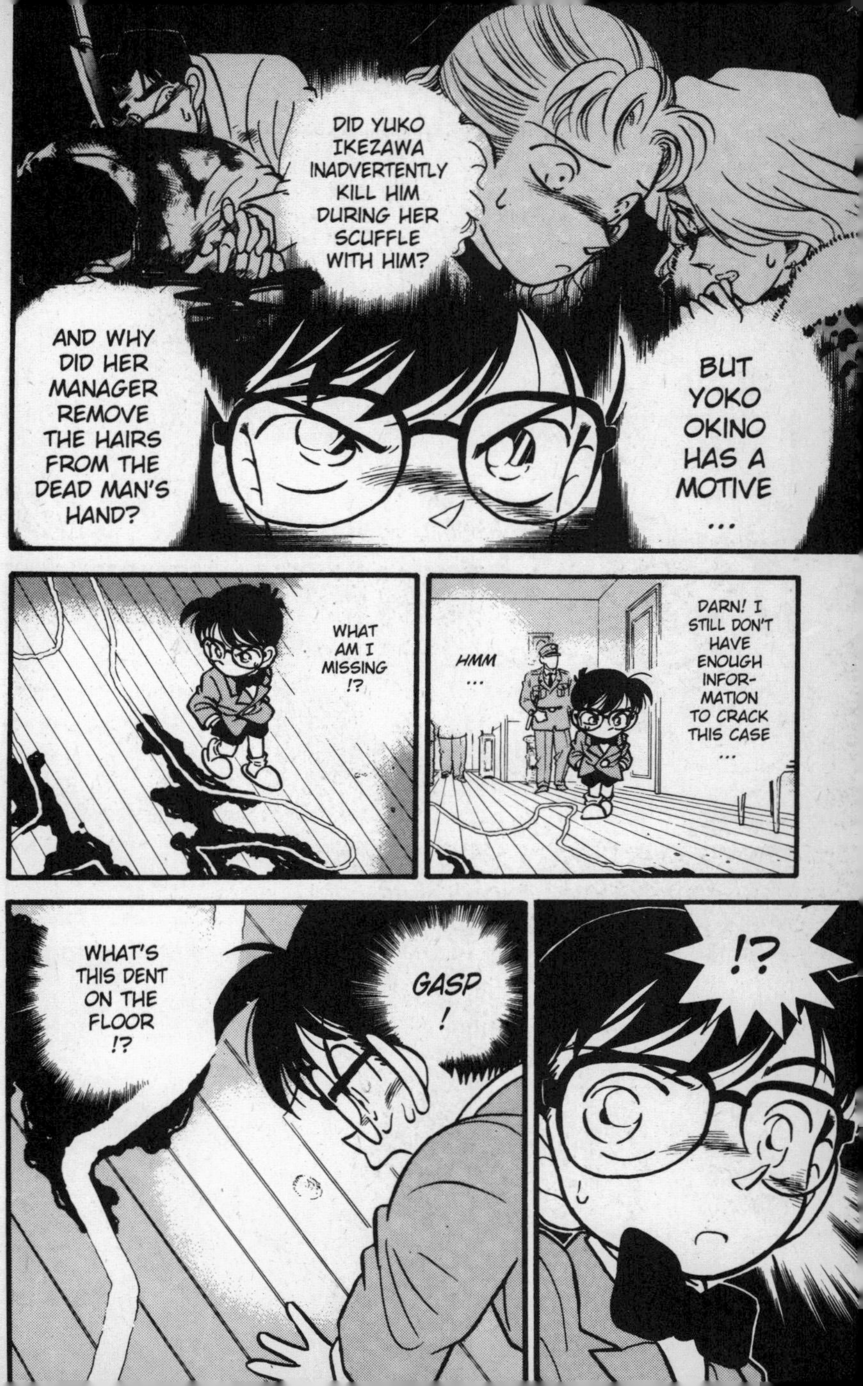
DID YUKO IKEZAWA INADVERTENTLY KILL HIM DURING HER SCUFFLE WITH HIM?
BUT YOKO OKINO HAS A MOTIVE ...
AND WHY DID HER MANAGER REMOVE THE HAIRS FROM THE DEAD MAN'S HAND?
DARN! I STILL DON'T HAVE ENOUGH INFOR-MATION TO CRACK THIS CASE ...
HMM ...
WHAT AM I MISSING !?
!?
GASP !
WHAT'S THIS DENT ON THE FLOOR !?

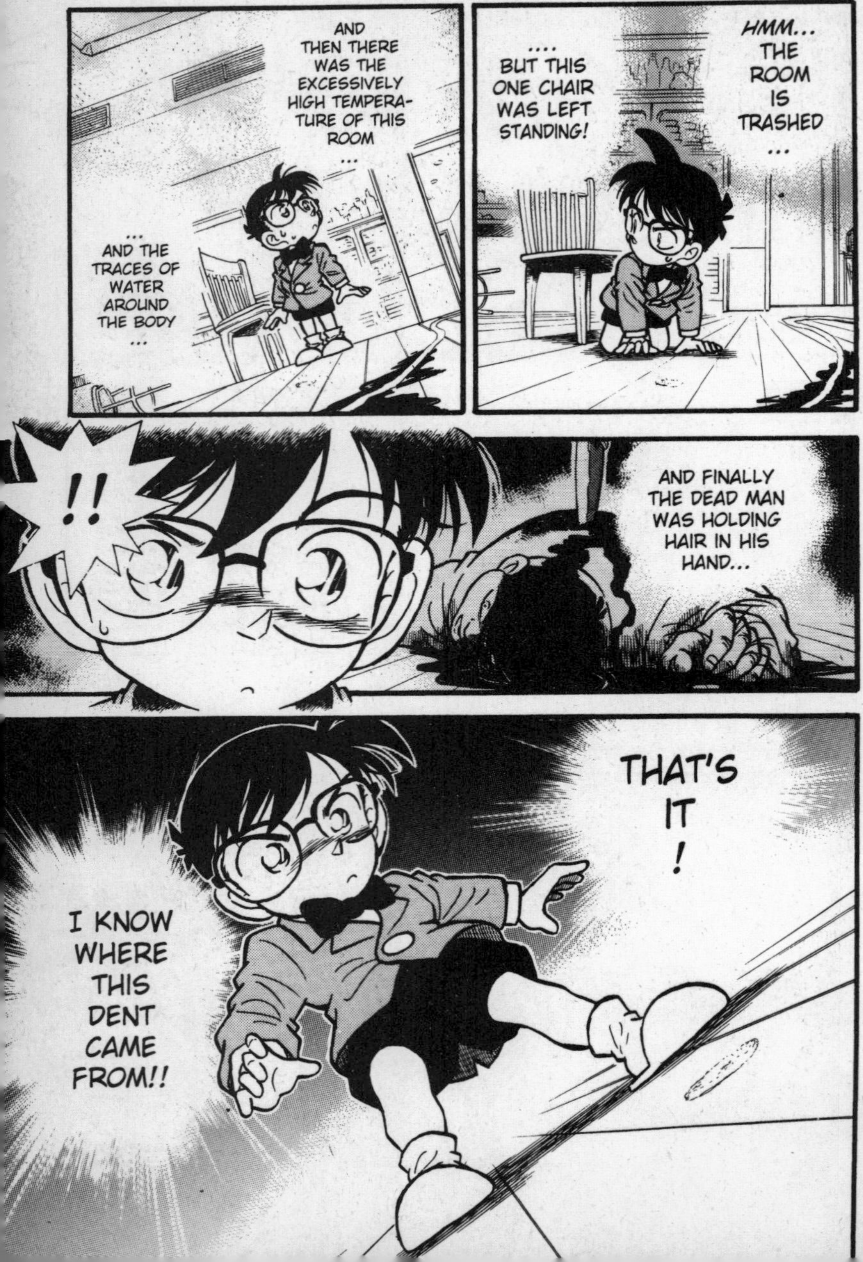
HMM... THE ROOM IS TRASHED ...
.... BUT THIS ONE CHAIR WAS LEFT STANDING!
AND THEN THERE WAS THE EXCESSIVELY HIGH TEMPERA-TURE OF THIS ROOM ...
... AND THE TRACES OF WATER AROUND THE BODY ...
AND FINALLY THE DEAD MAN WAS HOLDING HAIR IN HIS HAND...
!!
THAT'S IT !
I KNOW WHERE THIS DENT CAME FROM!!

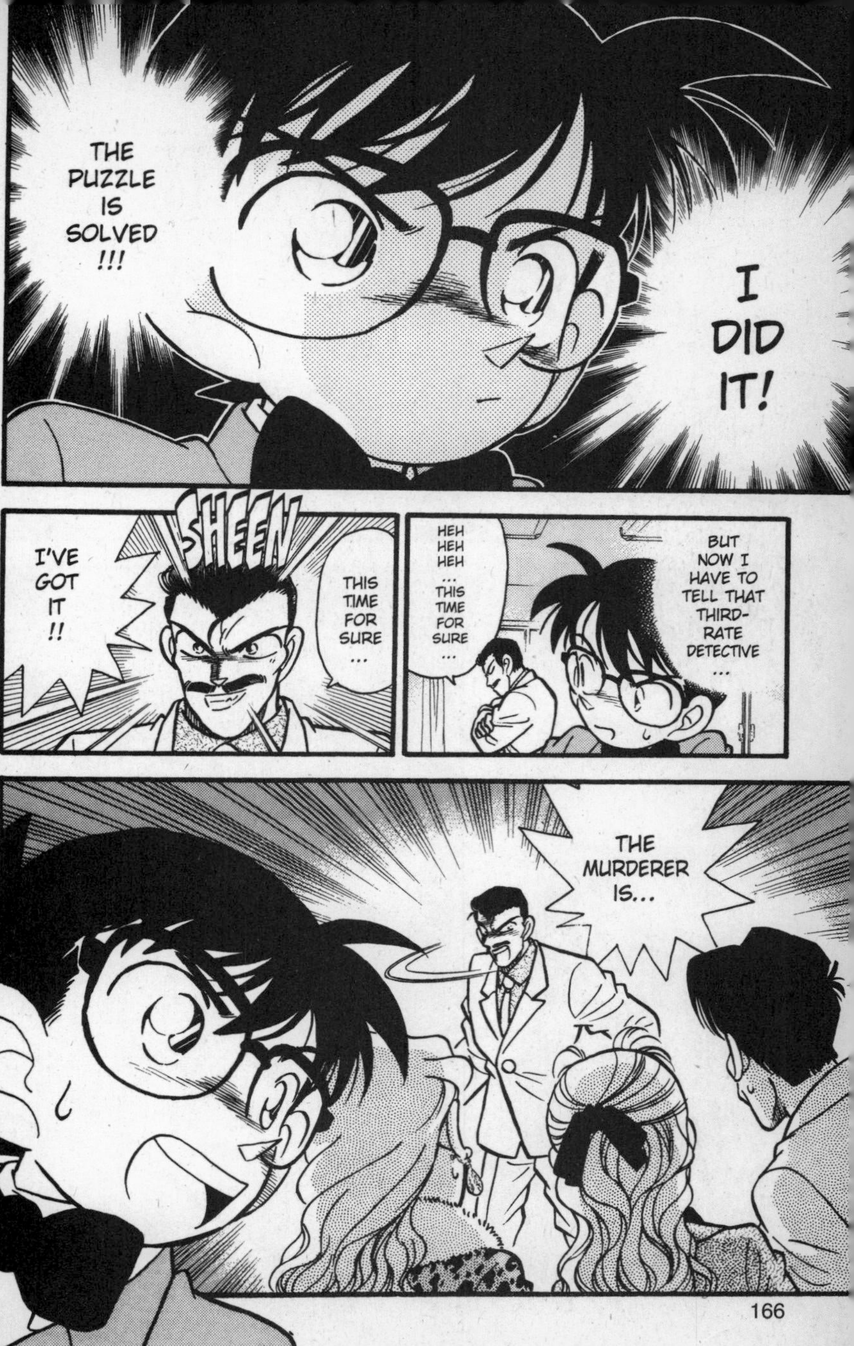
I DID IT!
THE PUZZLE IS SOLVED!!!
BUT NOW I HAVE TO TELL THAT THIRD-RATE DETECTIVE...
HEH HEH HEH... THIS TIME FOR SURE...
SHEEN
THIS TIME FOR SURE...
I'VE GOT IT!!
THE MURDERER IS...

FILE 9: AN UNFORTUNATE MISUNDERSTANDING

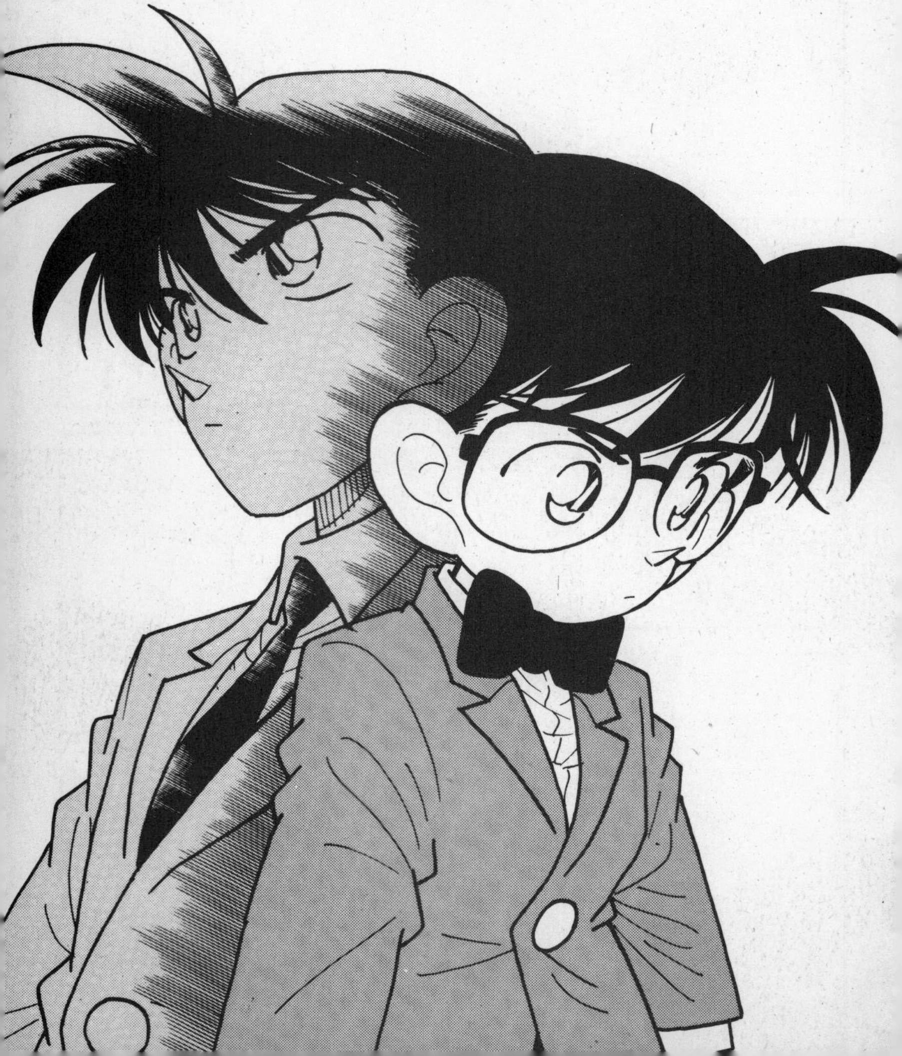

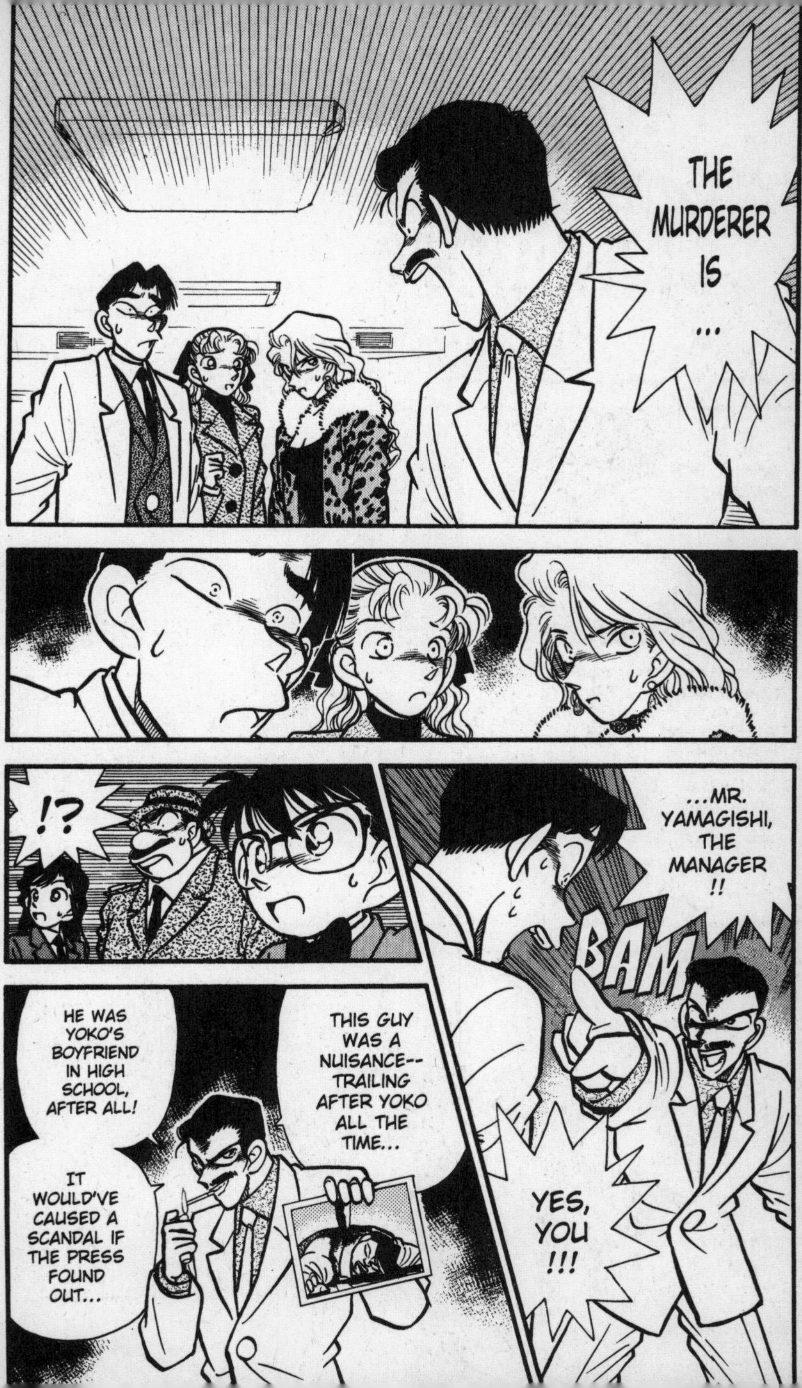
THE MURDERER IS ...
...MR. YAMAGISHI, THE MANAGER !!
BAM
YES, YOU !!!
!?
THIS GUY WAS A NUISANCE-- TRAILING AFTER YOKO ALL THE TIME...
HE WAS YOKO'S BOYFRIEND IN HIGH SCHOOL, AFTER ALL!
IT WOULD'VE CAUSED A SCANDAL IF THE PRESS FOUND OUT...

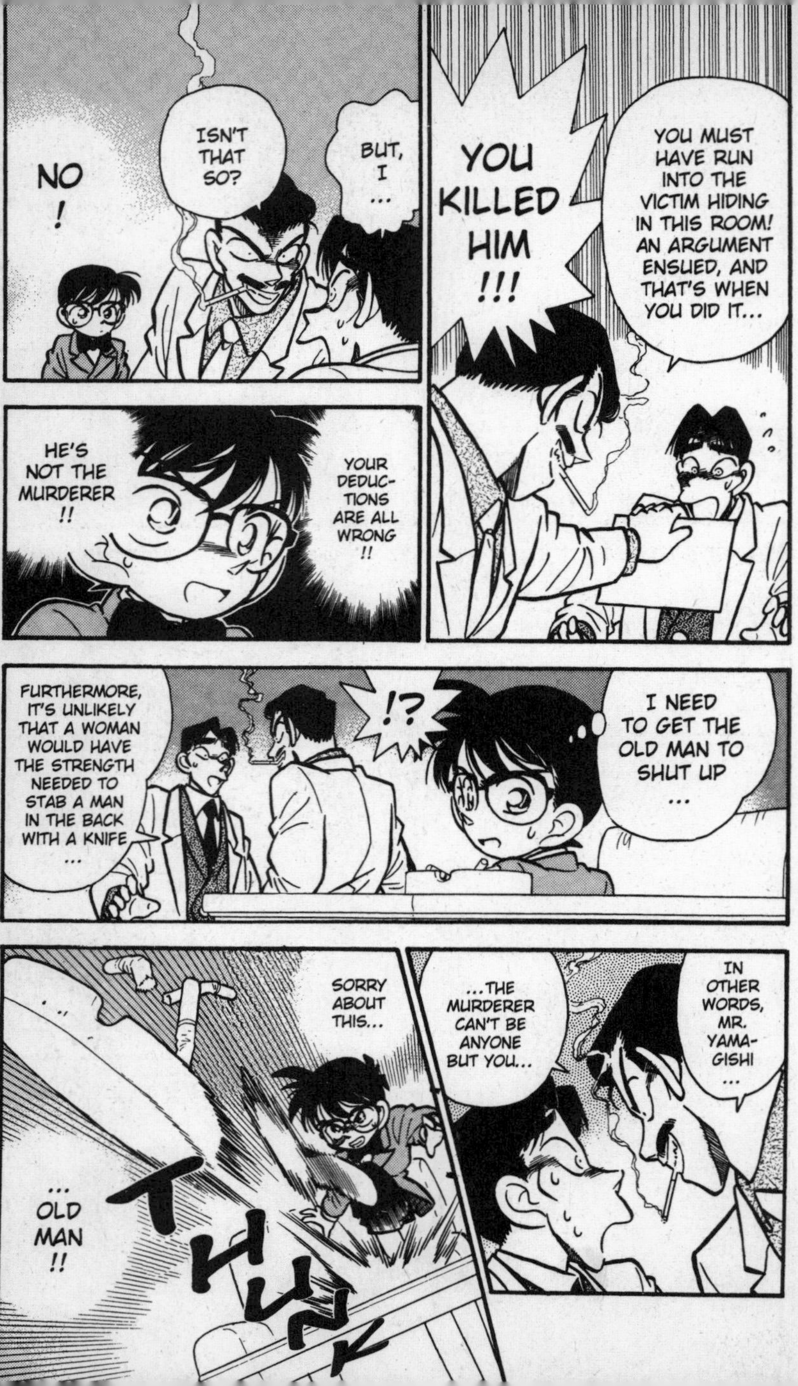
YOU KILLED HIM !!!
YOU MUST HAVE RUN INTO THE VICTIM HIDING IN THIS ROOM! AN ARGUMENT ENSUED, AND THAT'S WHEN YOU DID IT...
ISN'T THAT SO?
BUT, I ...
NO !
YOUR DEDUCTIONS ARE ALL WRONG !!
HE'S NOT THE MURDERER !!
I NEED TO GET THE OLD MAN TO SHUT UP ...
!?
FURTHERMORE, IT'S UNLIKELY THAT A WOMAN WOULD HAVE THE STRENGTH NEEDED TO STAB A MAN IN THE BACK WITH A KNIFE ...
IN OTHER WORDS, MR. YAMAGISHI ...
...THE MURDERER CAN'T BE ANYONE BUT YOU...
SORRY ABOUT THIS...
... OLD MAN !!
THUNK

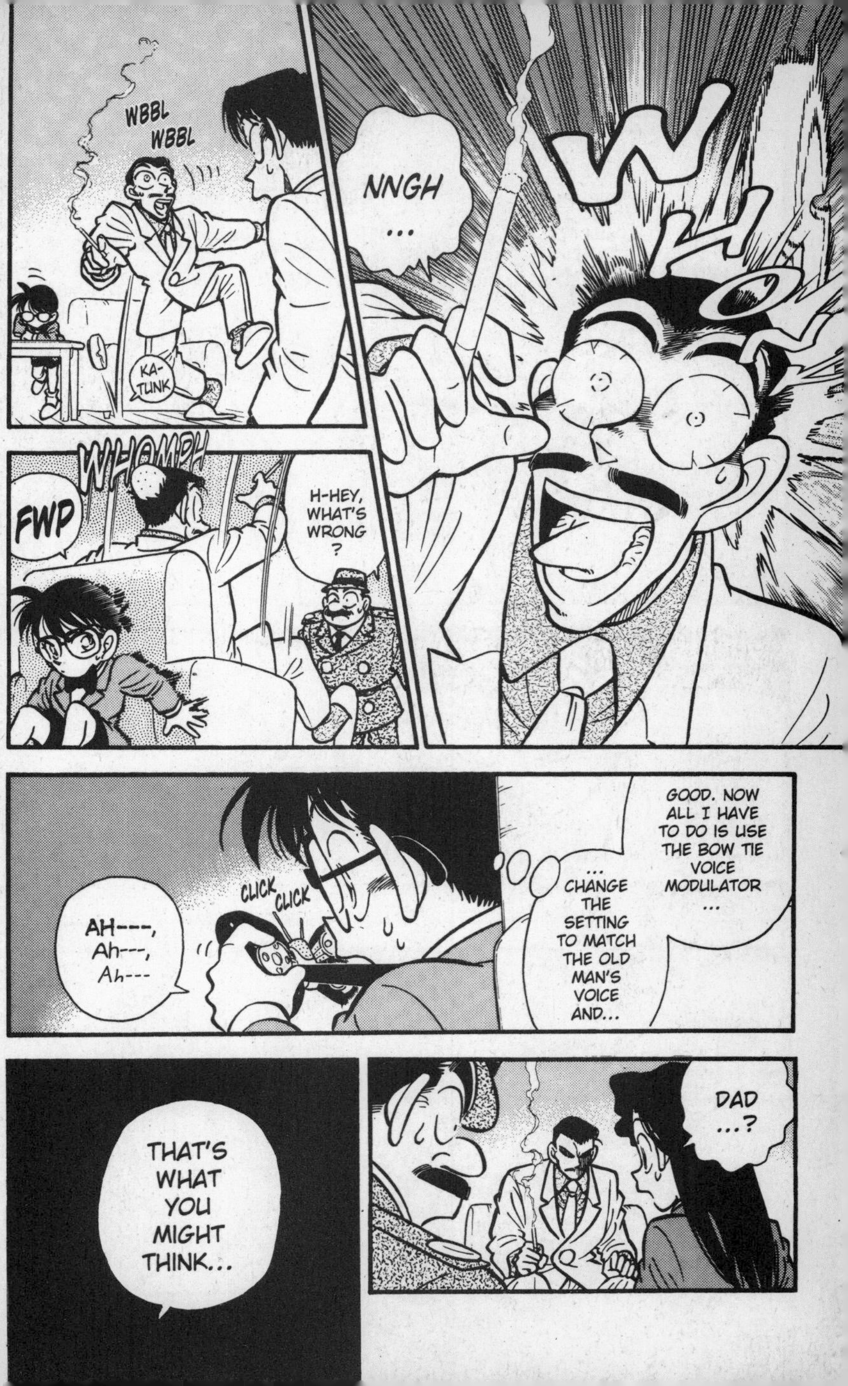
WHOA
NNGH ...
WBBL WBBL
KA-TUNK
H-HEY, WHAT'S WRONG ?
WHOMPH
FWP
GOOD. NOW ALL I HAVE TO DO IS USE THE BOW TIE VOICE MODULATOR ...
... CHANGE THE SETTING TO MATCH THE OLD MAN'S VOICE AND...
CLICK CLICK
AH---, Ah---, Ah---
DAD ...?
THAT'S WHAT YOU MIGHT THINK...

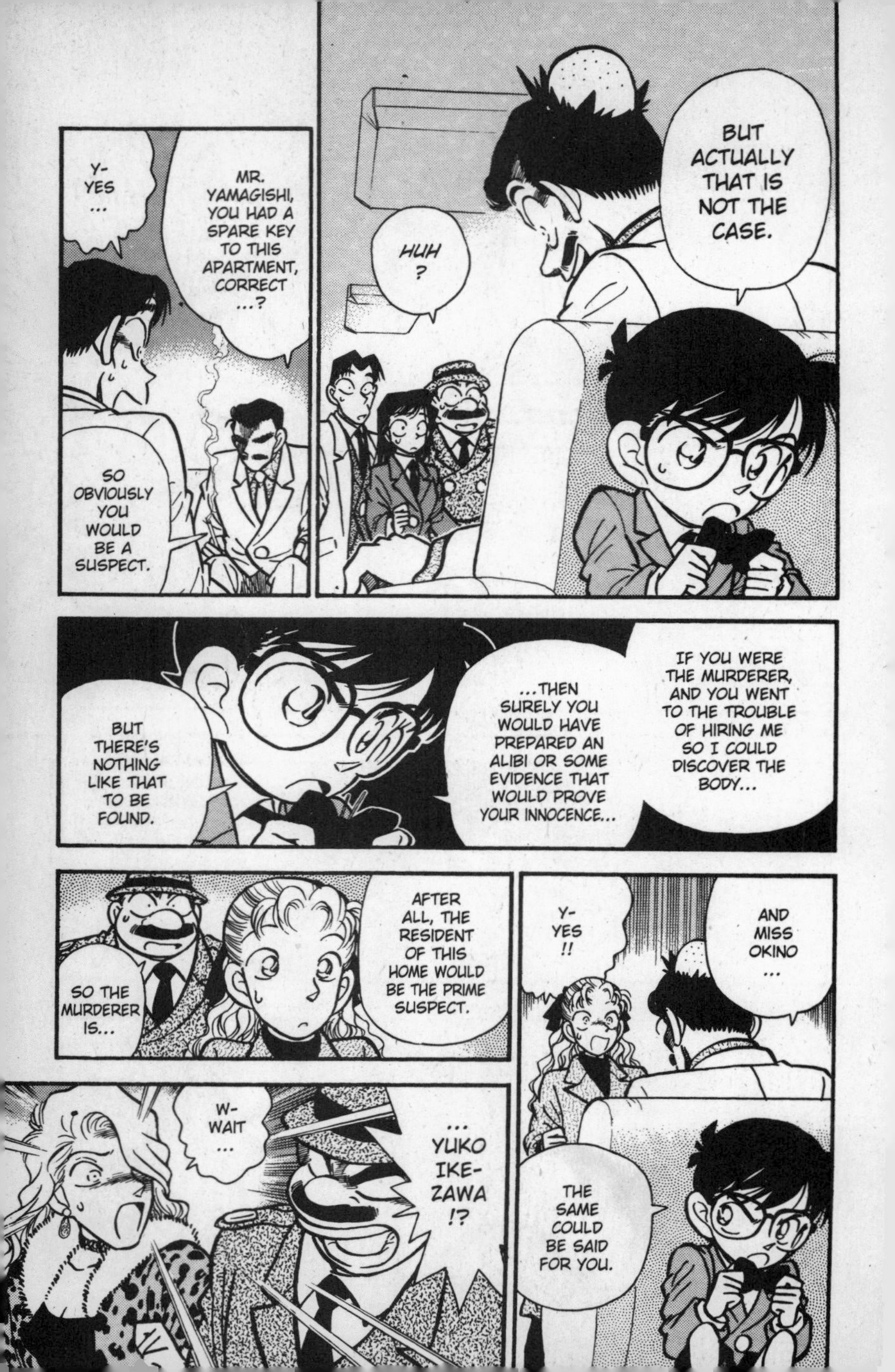
BUT ACTUALLY THAT IS NOT THE CASE.
HUH ?
MR. YAMAGISHI, YOU HAD A SPARE KEY TO THIS APARTMENT, CORRECT ...?
Y- YES ...
SO OBVIOUSLY YOU WOULD BE A SUSPECT.
IF YOU WERE THE MURDERER, AND YOU WENT TO THE TROUBLE OF HIRING ME SO I COULD DISCOVER THE BODY...
...THEN SURELY YOU WOULD HAVE PREPARED AN ALIBI OR SOME EVIDENCE THAT WOULD PROVE YOUR INNOCENCE...
BUT THERE'S NOTHING LIKE THAT TO BE FOUND.
AND MISS OKINO ...
Y- YES !!
THE SAME COULD BE SAID FOR YOU.
AFTER ALL, THE RESIDENT OF THIS HOME WOULD BE THE PRIME SUSPECT.
SO THE MURDERER IS...
... YUKO IKE- ZAWA !?
W- WAIT ...

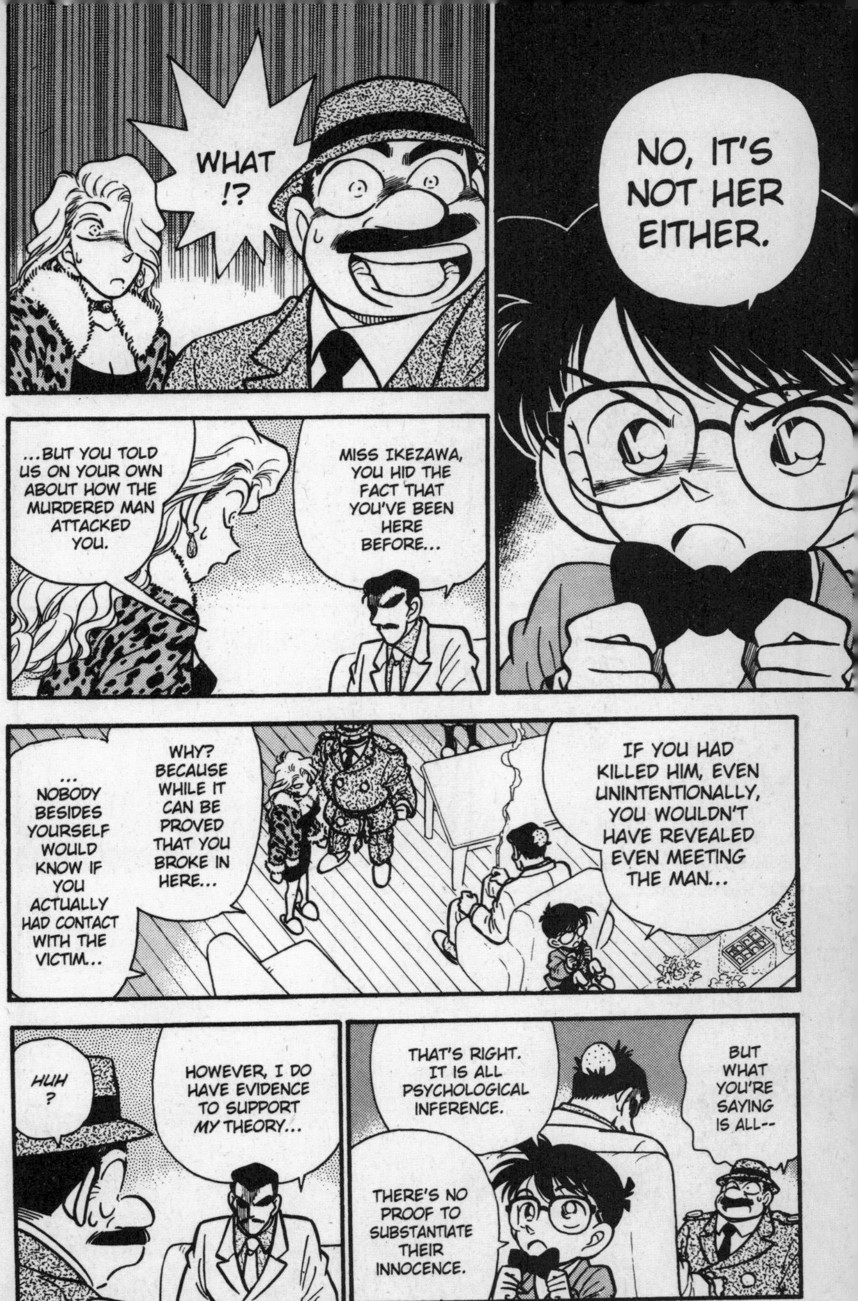
NO, IT'S NOT HER EITHER.
WHAT !?
MISS IKEZAWA, YOU HID THE FACT THAT YOU'VE BEEN HERE BEFORE...
...BUT YOU TOLD US ON YOUR OWN ABOUT HOW THE MURDERED MAN ATTACKED YOU.
IF YOU HAD KILLED HIM, EVEN UNINTENTIONALLY, YOU WOULDN'T HAVE REVEALED EVEN MEETING THE MAN...
WHY? BECAUSE WHILE IT CAN BE PROVED THAT YOU BROKE IN HERE...
... NOBODY BESIDES YOURSELF WOULD KNOW IF YOU ACTUALLY HAD CONTACT WITH THE VICTIM...
BUT WHAT YOU'RE SAYING IS ALL--
THAT'S RIGHT. IT IS ALL PSYCHOLOGICAL INFERENCE.
THERE'S NO PROOF TO SUBSTANTIATE THEIR INNOCENCE.
HOWEVER, I DO HAVE EVIDENCE TO SUPPORT *MY* THEORY...
HUH ?

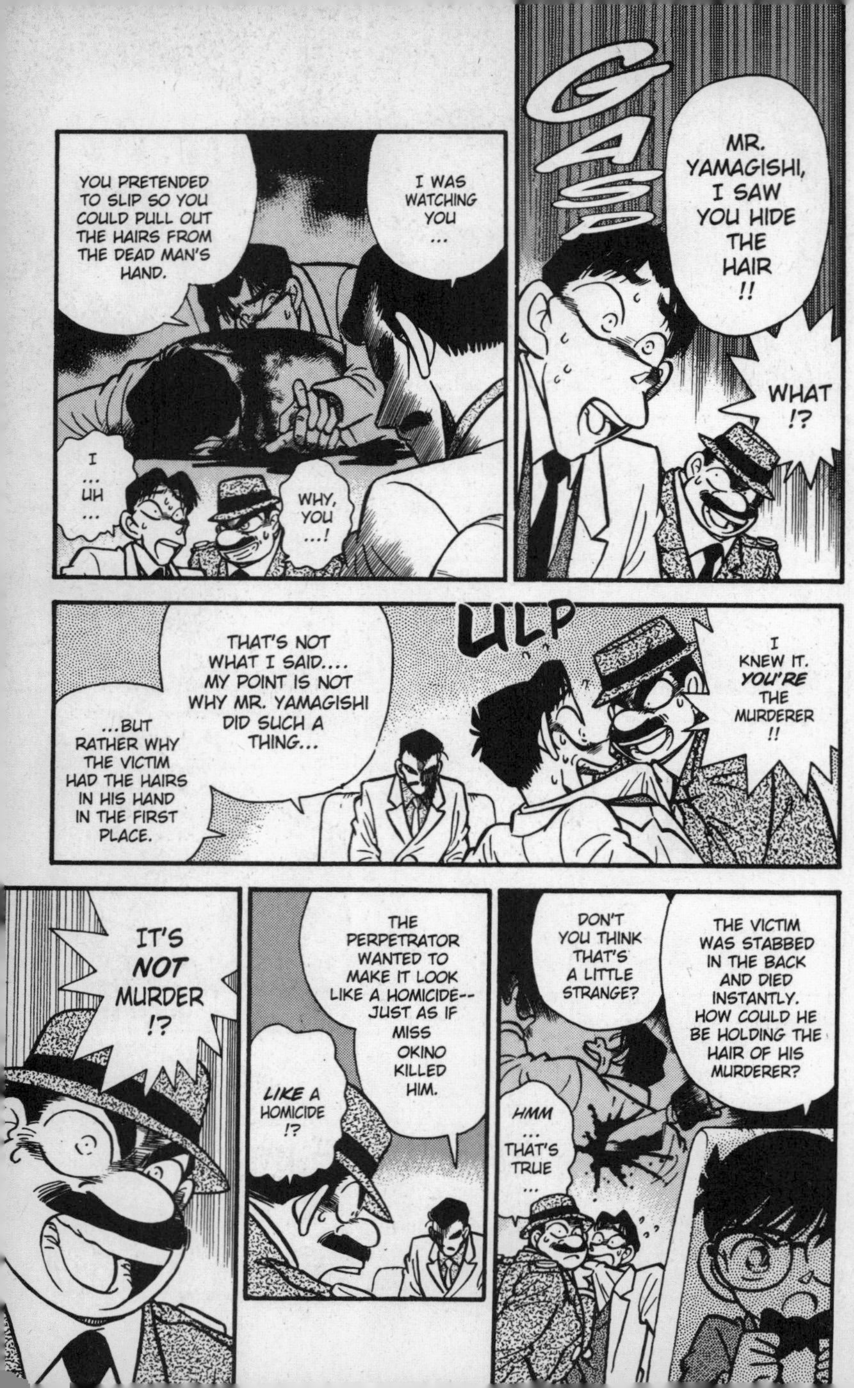
GASP
MR. YAMAGISHI, I SAW YOU HIDE THE HAIR!!
WHAT!?
I WAS WATCHING YOU...
YOU PRETENDED TO SLIP SO YOU COULD PULL OUT THE HAIRS FROM THE DEAD MAN'S HAND.
WHY, YOU...!
I... UH...
I KNEW IT. *YOU'RE* THE MURDERER!!
ULP
THAT'S NOT WHAT I SAID.... MY POINT IS NOT WHY MR. YAMAGISHI DID SUCH A THING...
...BUT RATHER WHY THE VICTIM HAD THE HAIRS IN HIS HAND IN THE FIRST PLACE.
THE VICTIM WAS STABBED IN THE BACK AND DIED INSTANTLY. HOW COULD HE BE HOLDING THE HAIR OF HIS MURDERER?
DON'T YOU THINK THAT'S A LITTLE STRANGE?
HMM... THAT'S TRUE...
THE PERPETRATOR WANTED TO MAKE IT LOOK LIKE A HOMICIDE--JUST AS IF MISS OKINO KILLED HIM.
LIKE A HOMICIDE!?
IT'S *NOT* MURDER!?

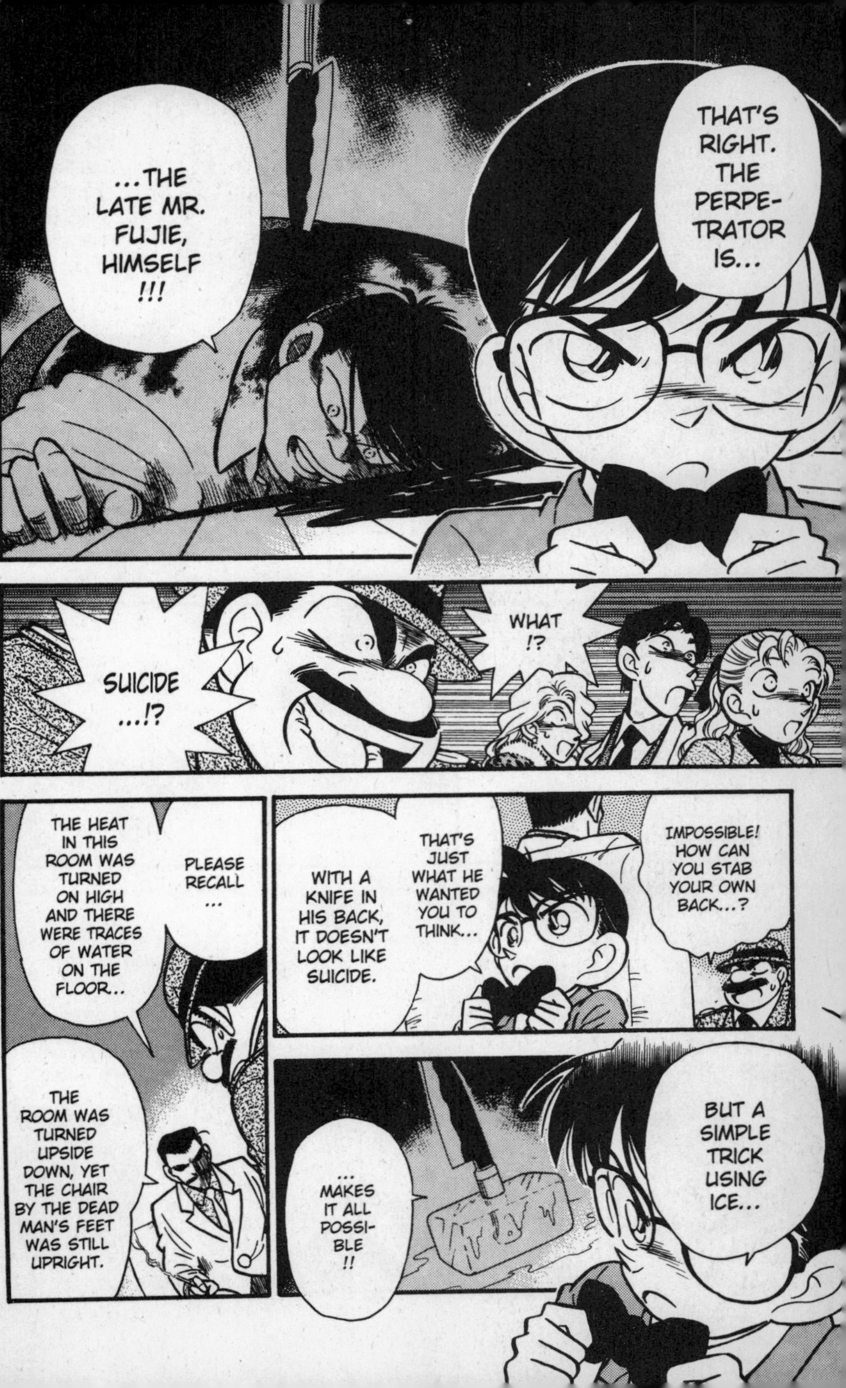
THAT'S RIGHT. THE PERPE-TRATOR IS...
...THE LATE MR. FUJIE, HIMSELF !!!
WHAT !?
SUICIDE ...!?
IMPOSSIBLE! HOW CAN YOU STAB YOUR OWN BACK...?
WITH A KNIFE IN HIS BACK, IT DOESN'T LOOK LIKE SUICIDE.
THAT'S JUST WHAT HE WANTED YOU TO THINK...
BUT A SIMPLE TRICK USING ICE...
...MAKES IT ALL POSSI-BLE !!
PLEASE RECALL ...
THE HEAT IN THIS ROOM WAS TURNED ON HIGH AND THERE WERE TRACES OF WATER ON THE FLOOR...
THE ROOM WAS TURNED UPSIDE DOWN, YET THE CHAIR BY THE DEAD MAN'S FEET WAS STILL UPRIGHT.

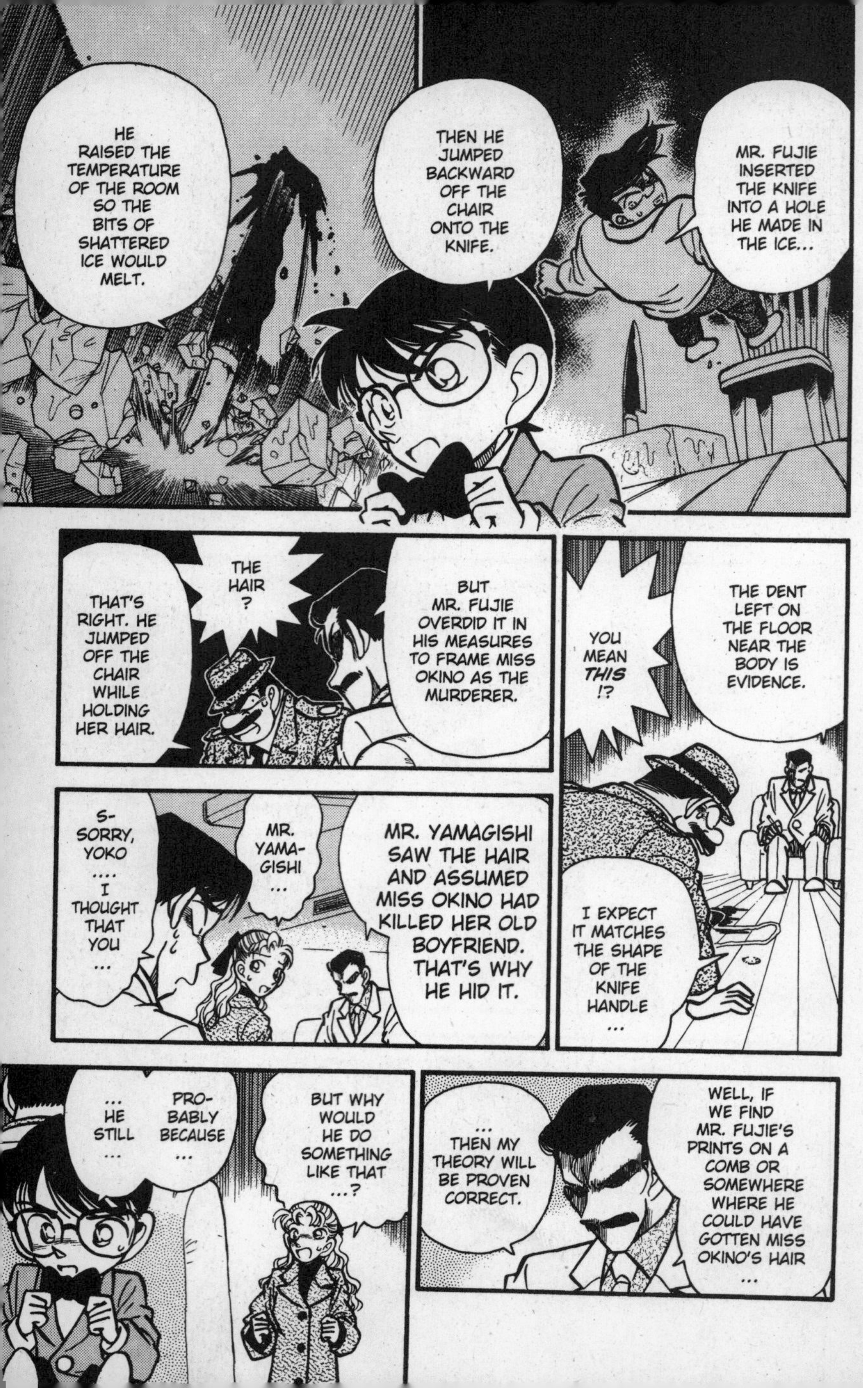
MR. FUJIE INSERTED THE KNIFE INTO A HOLE HE MADE IN THE ICE...
THEN HE JUMPED BACKWARD OFF THE CHAIR ONTO THE KNIFE.
HE RAISED THE TEMPERATURE OF THE ROOM SO THE BITS OF SHATTERED ICE WOULD MELT.
THE DENT LEFT ON THE FLOOR NEAR THE BODY IS EVIDENCE.
YOU MEAN *THIS* !?
I EXPECT IT MATCHES THE SHAPE OF THE KNIFE HANDLE ...
BUT MR. FUJIE OVERDID IT IN HIS MEASURES TO FRAME MISS OKINO AS THE MURDERER.
THE HAIR ?
THAT'S RIGHT. HE JUMPED OFF THE CHAIR WHILE HOLDING HER HAIR.
MR. YAMAGISHI SAW THE HAIR AND ASSUMED MISS OKINO HAD KILLED HER OLD BOYFRIEND. THAT'S WHY HE HID IT.
MR. YAMAGISHI ...
S-SORRY, YOKO .... I THOUGHT THAT YOU ...
WELL, IF WE FIND MR. FUJIE'S PRINTS ON A COMB OR SOMEWHERE WHERE HE COULD HAVE GOTTEN MISS OKINO'S HAIR ...
... THEN MY THEORY WILL BE PROVEN CORRECT.
BUT WHY WOULD HE DO SOMETHING LIKE THAT ...?
PROBABLY BECAUSE ...
... HE STILL ...

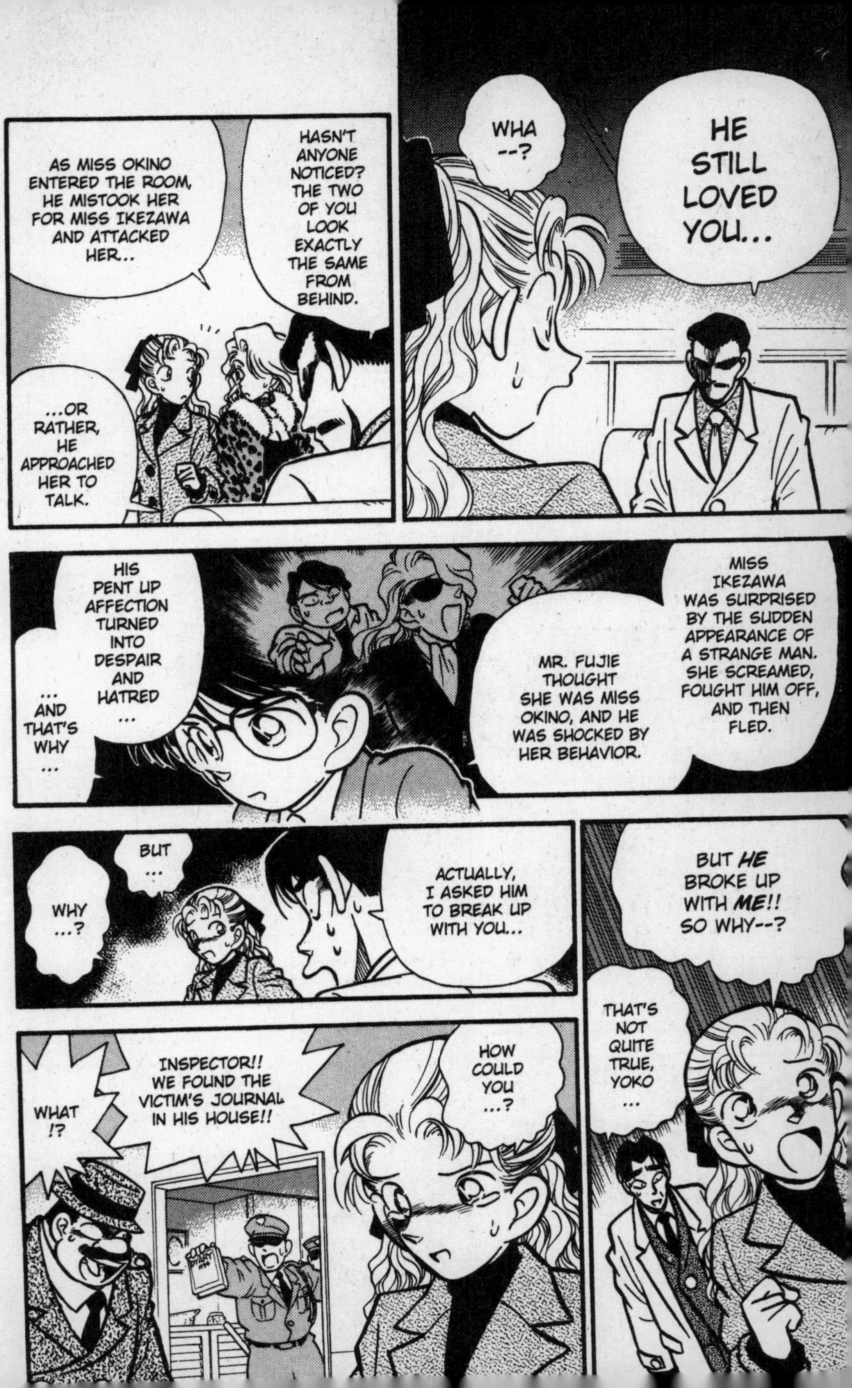

HE STILL LOVED YOU...
WHA--?
HASN'T ANYONE NOTICED? THE TWO OF YOU LOOK EXACTLY THE SAME FROM BEHIND.
AS MISS OKINO ENTERED THE ROOM, HE MISTOOK HER FOR MISS IKEZAWA AND ATTACKED HER...
...OR RATHER, HE APPROACHED HER TO TALK.
MISS IKEZAWA WAS SURPRISED BY THE SUDDEN APPEARANCE OF A STRANGE MAN. SHE SCREAMED, FOUGHT HIM OFF, AND THEN FLED.
MR. FUJIE THOUGHT SHE WAS MISS OKINO, AND HE WAS SHOCKED BY HER BEHAVIOR.
HIS PENT UP AFFECTION TURNED INTO DESPAIR AND HATRED...
...AND THAT'S WHY...
BUT *HE* BROKE UP WITH *ME*!! SO WHY--?
THAT'S NOT QUITE TRUE, YOKO...
ACTUALLY, I ASKED HIM TO BREAK UP WITH YOU...
BUT...
WHY...?
HOW COULD YOU...?
INSPECTOR!! WE FOUND THE VICTIM'S JOURNAL IN HIS HOUSE!!
WHAT!?

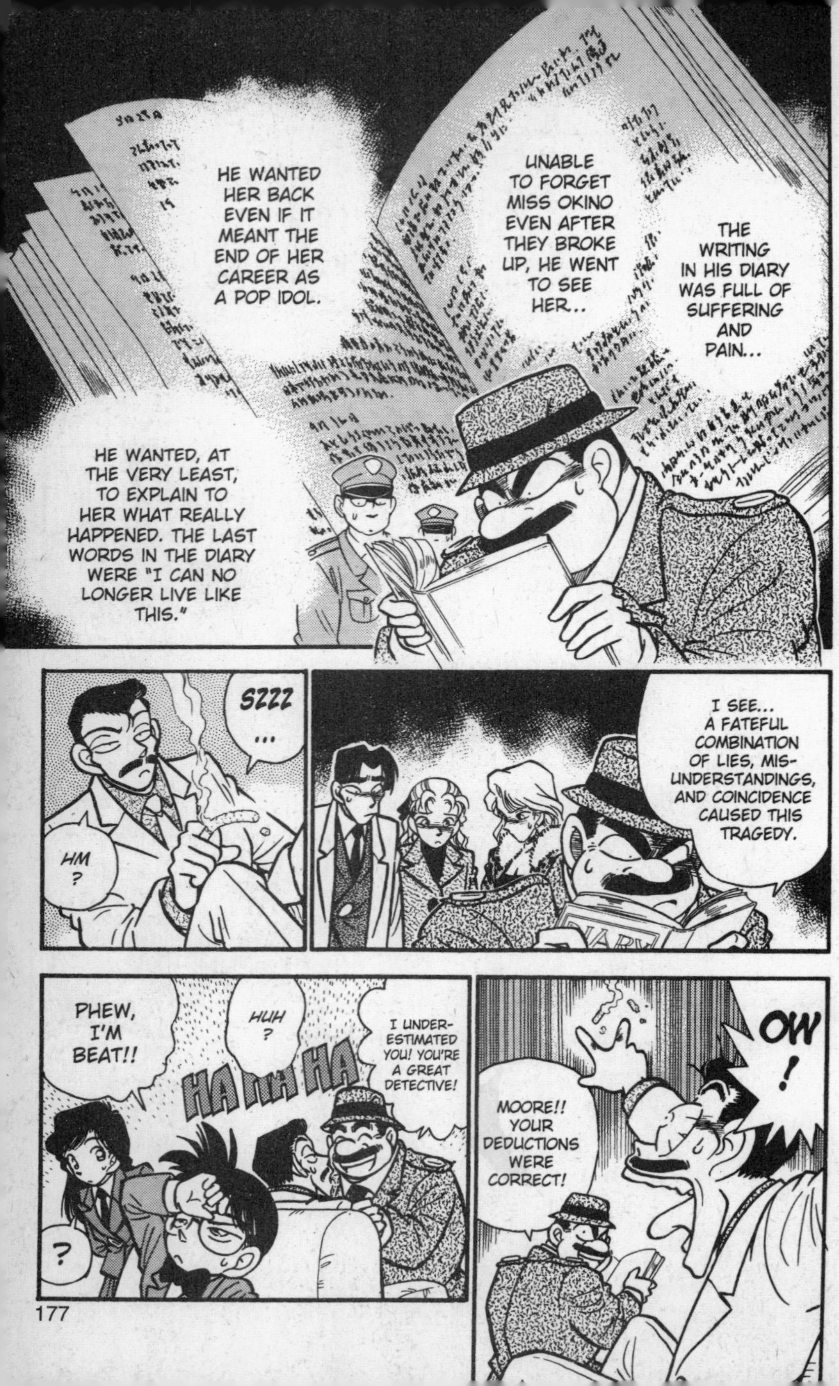
THE WRITING IN HIS DIARY WAS FULL OF SUFFERING AND PAIN...
UNABLE TO FORGET MISS OKINO EVEN AFTER THEY BROKE UP, HE WENT TO SEE HER...
HE WANTED HER BACK EVEN IF IT MEANT THE END OF HER CAREER AS A POP IDOL.
HE WANTED, AT THE VERY LEAST, TO EXPLAIN TO HER WHAT REALLY HAPPENED. THE LAST WORDS IN THE DIARY WERE "I CAN NO LONGER LIVE LIKE THIS."
I SEE... A FATEFUL COMBINATION OF LIES, MIS-UNDERSTANDINGS, AND COINCIDENCE CAUSED THIS TRAGEDY.
DIARY
SZZZ ...
HM ?
OW !
MOORE!! YOUR DEDUCTIONS WERE CORRECT!
I UNDER-ESTIMATED YOU! YOU'RE A GREAT DETECTIVE!
HUH ?
PHEW, I'M BEAT!!
HA HA HA
?

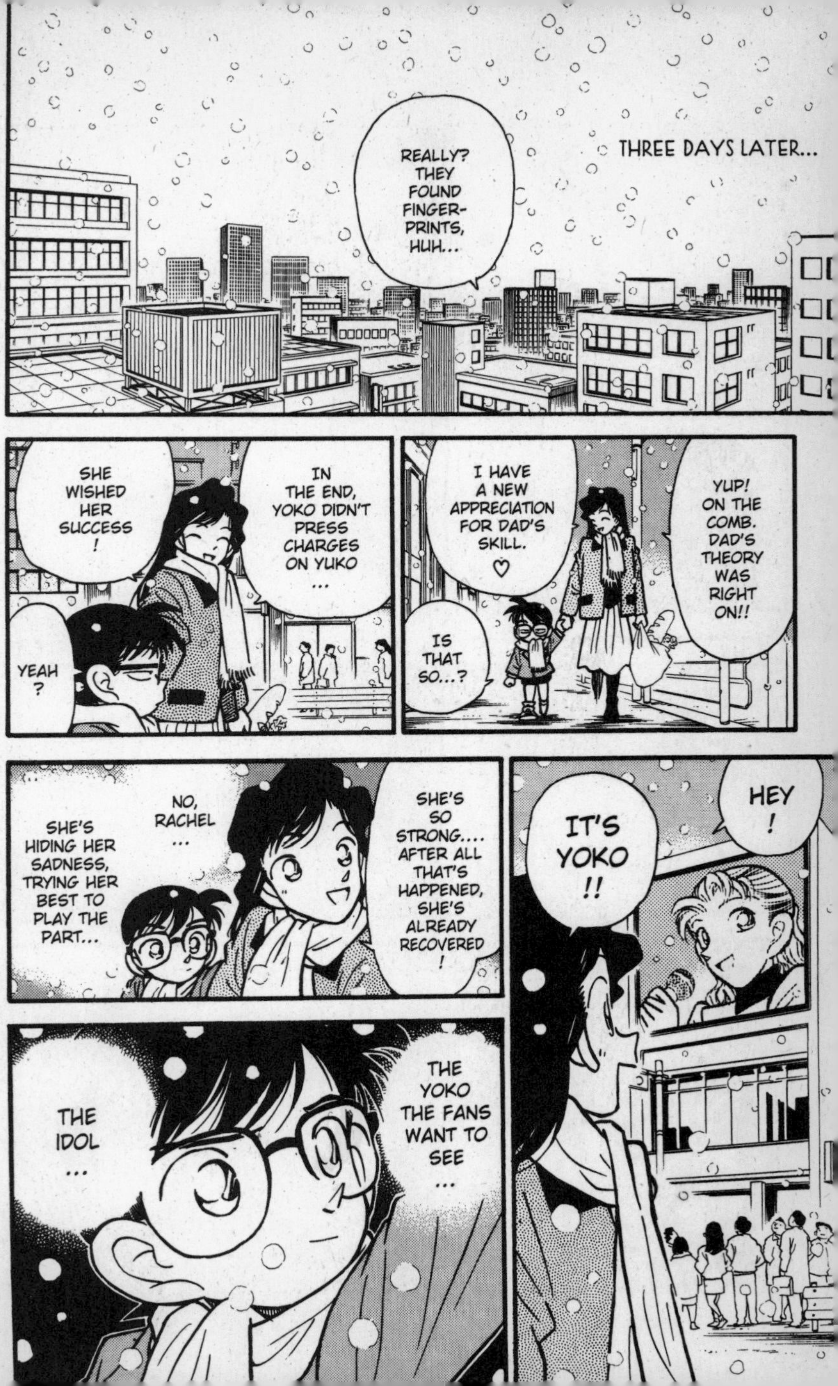
THREE DAYS LATER...
REALLY? THEY FOUND FINGER-PRINTS, HUH...
YUP! ON THE COMB. DAD'S THEORY WAS RIGHT ON!!
I HAVE A NEW APPRECIATION FOR DAD'S SKILL. ♡
IS THAT SO...?
IN THE END, YOKO DIDN'T PRESS CHARGES ON YUKO ...
SHE WISHED HER SUCCESS!
YEAH?
HEY!
IT'S YOKO!!
SHE'S SO STRONG.... AFTER ALL THAT'S HAPPENED, SHE'S ALREADY RECOVERED!
NO, RACHEL ...
SHE'S HIDING HER SADNESS, TRYING HER BEST TO PLAY THE PART...
THE YOKO THE FANS WANT TO SEE ...
THE IDOL ...

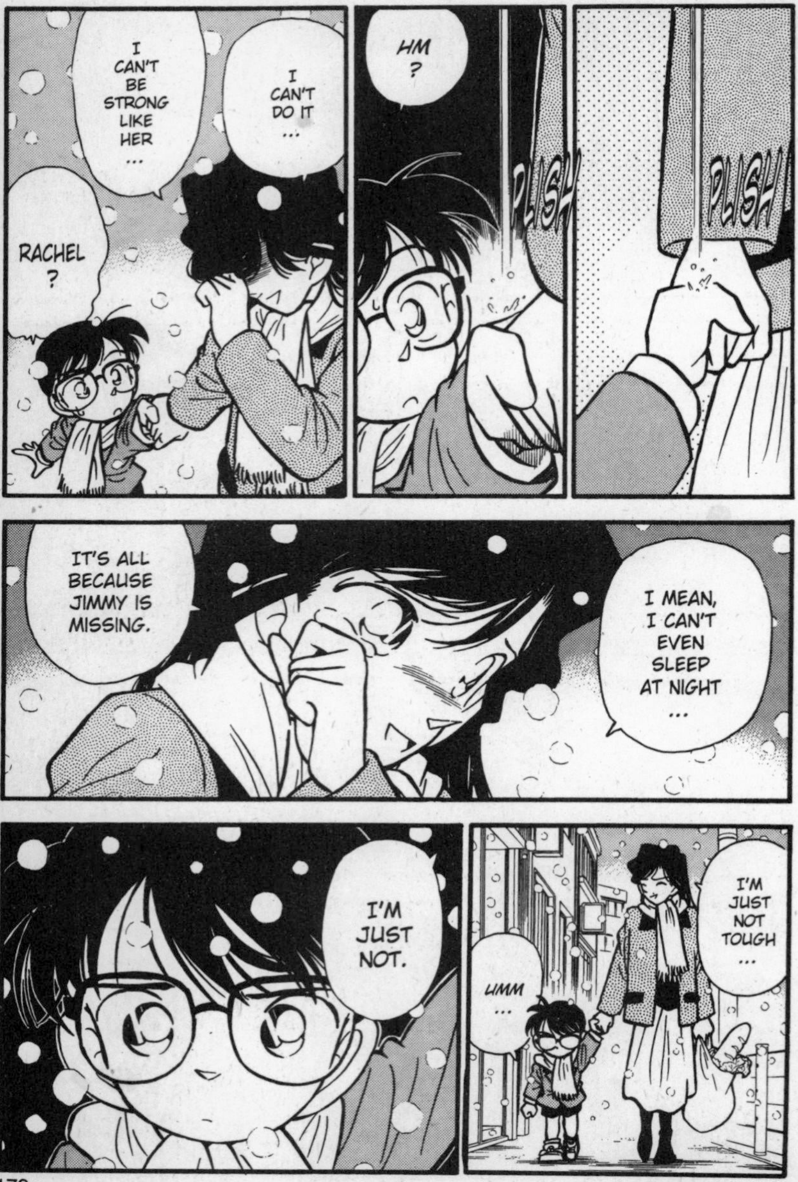
PLISH
HM ?
PLISH
I CAN'T DO IT ...
I CAN'T BE STRONG LIKE HER ...
RACHEL ?
I MEAN, I CAN'T EVEN SLEEP AT NIGHT ...
IT'S ALL BECAUSE JIMMY IS MISSING.
I'M JUST NOT TOUGH ...
UMM ...
I'M JUST NOT.

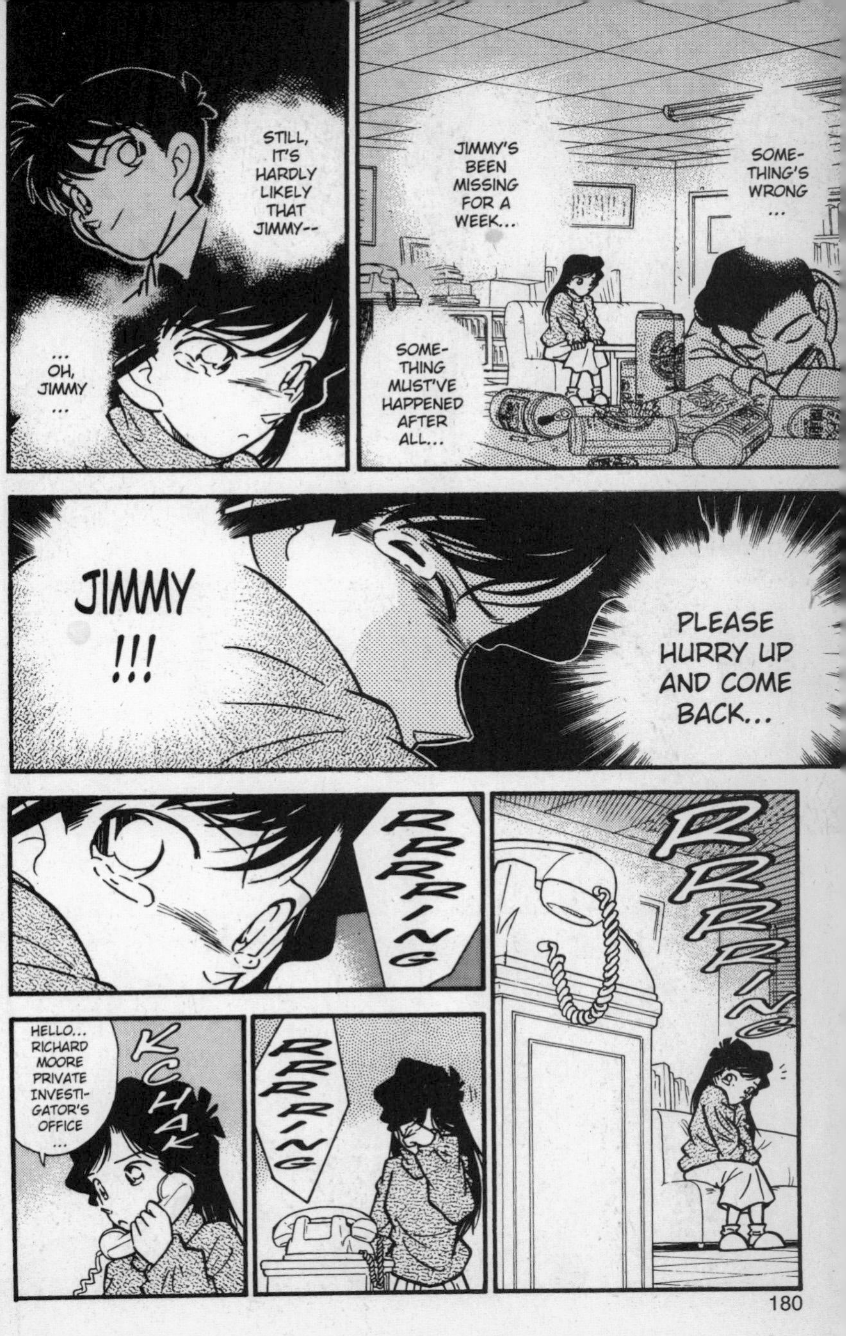
SOME-THING'S WRONG ...
JIMMY'S BEEN MISSING FOR A WEEK...
SOME-THING MUST'VE HAPPENED AFTER ALL...
STILL, IT'S HARDLY LIKELY THAT JIMMY--
... OH, JIMMY ...
PLEASE HURRY UP AND COME BACK...
JIMMY !!!
RRRRING
RRRRING
RRRRING
KCHAK
HELLO... RICHARD MOORE PRIVATE INVESTI-GATOR'S OFFICE ...

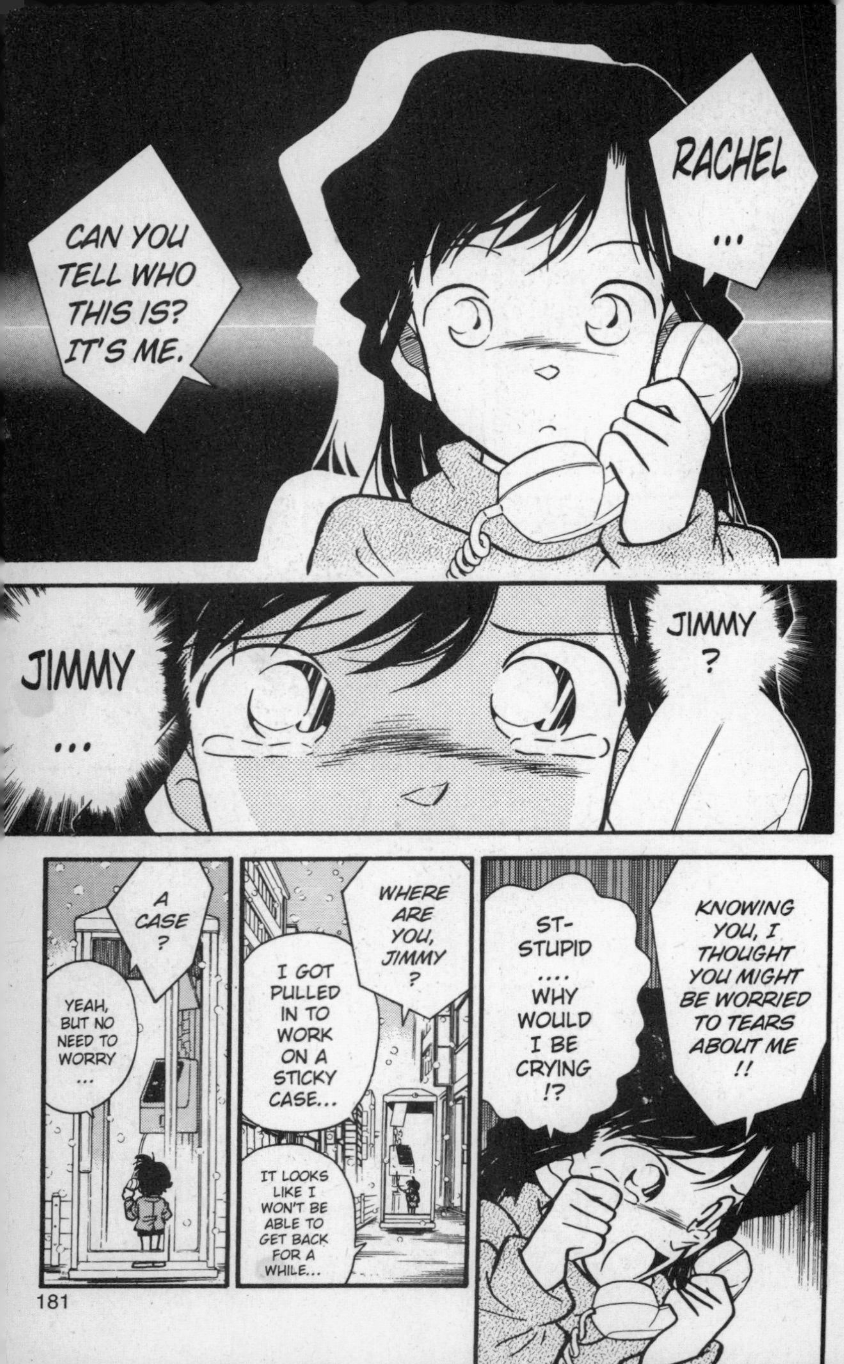
RACHEL ...
CAN YOU TELL WHO THIS IS? IT'S ME.
JIMMY ?
JIMMY ...
KNOWING YOU, I THOUGHT YOU MIGHT BE WORRIED TO TEARS ABOUT ME !!
ST- STUPID .... WHY WOULD I BE CRYING !?
WHERE ARE YOU, JIMMY ?
I GOT PULLED IN TO WORK ON A STICKY CASE...
IT LOOKS LIKE I WON'T BE ABLE TO GET BACK FOR A WHILE...
A CASE ?
YEAH, BUT NO NEED TO WORRY ...

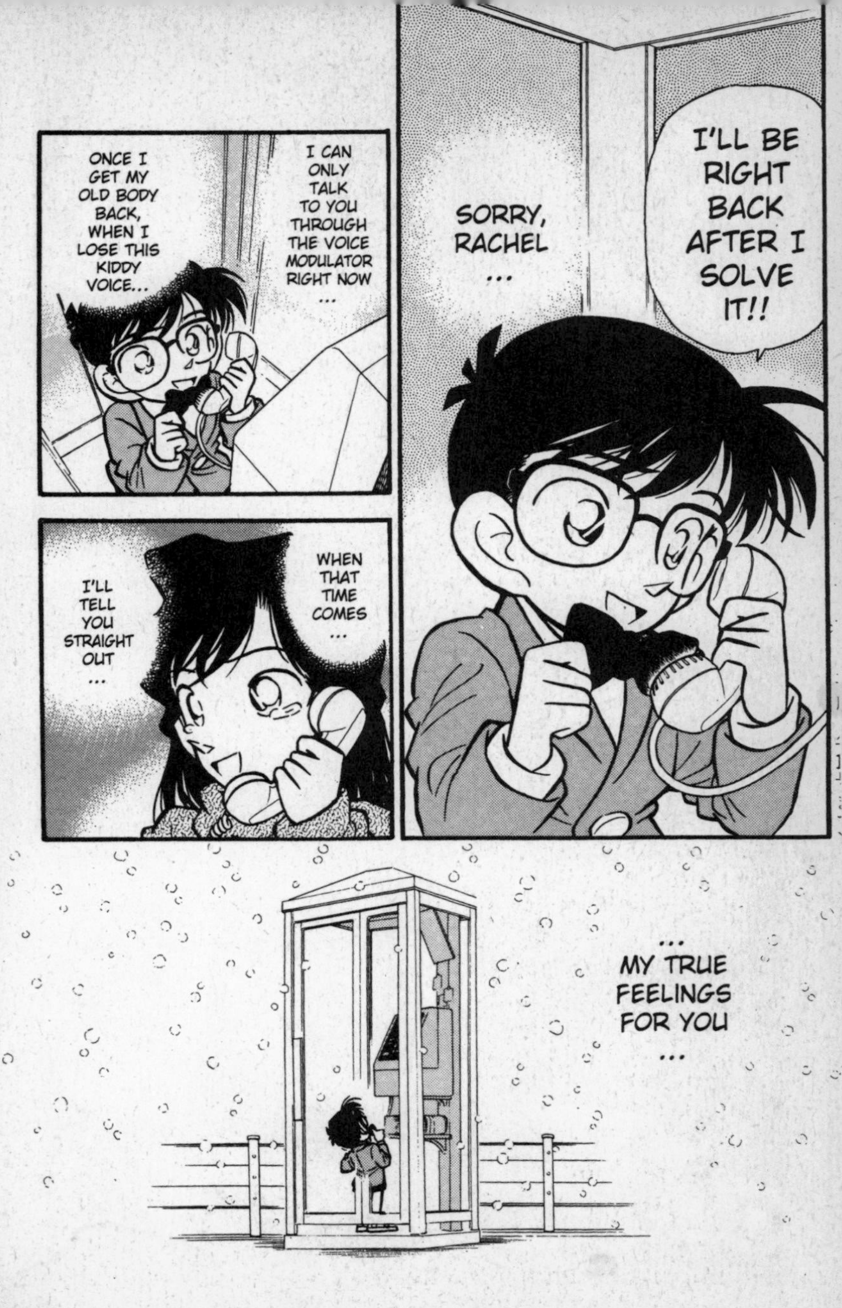
I'LL BE RIGHT BACK AFTER I SOLVE IT!!
SORRY, RACHEL ...
I CAN ONLY TALK TO YOU THROUGH THE VOICE MODULATOR RIGHT NOW ...
ONCE I GET MY OLD BODY BACK, WHEN I LOSE THIS KIDDY VOICE...
WHEN THAT TIME COMES ...
I'LL TELL YOU STRAIGHT OUT ...
... MY TRUE FEELINGS FOR YOU ...

CASE CLOSED™

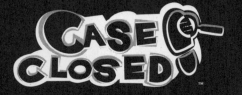

If you enjoy
CASE CLOSED
the editors recommend:

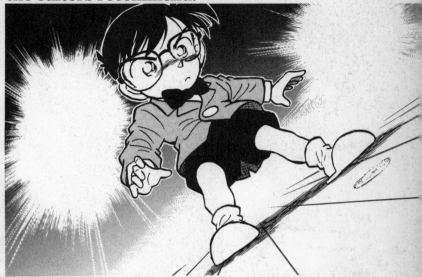

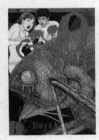

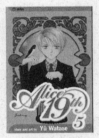

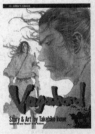

GYO

With hits like *UZUMAKI* and *TOMIE*, Junji Ito is Japan's manga master of horror. In *GYO*, something fishy is going down in Okinawa...something very fishy. With rich and detailed artwork and a creepy suspense filled storyline, this one is a real page-turner!

©2002 Junji Ito/Shogakukan, inc.

ALICE 19TH

Alice Seno is a shy girl who discovers that she has the potential to control a set of magically powerful words. But the price for this power might turn out to be Alice's very own sister. With a cute magical rabbit girl and a slew of hunky guys thrown into the mix, this is Yû Watase at her very best!

©2001 Yuu Watase/Shogakukan, inc.

VAGABOND

Even if "samurai manga" isn't your thing, Inoue Takehiko's incredibly realistic artwork and his fast-paced, incredibly well-researched story is good enough to satisfy any reader. And if "samurai manga" does happen to be your thing, well then, this manga is a must-read!

©1998-2004 I.T. Planning, Inc.

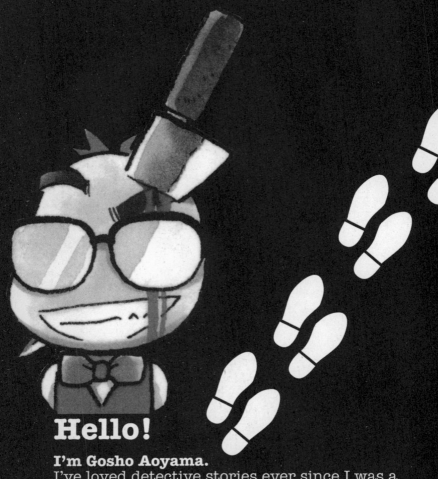

Hello!

I'm Gosho Aoyama.
I've loved detective stories ever since I was a
kid. Whenever I'm in a bookstore I can't help
but pick up anything that has "Holmes" or
"Great Detective" on the cover. For this series,
I try to squeeze out every bit of detective
story knowledge that I have.
Can you solve the crimes before Conan does?

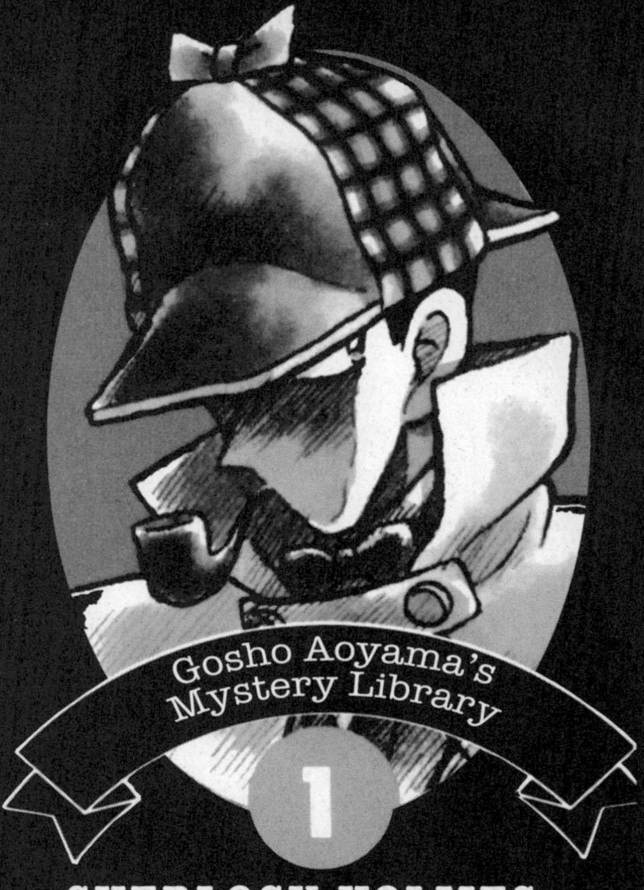
Gosho Aoyama's
Mystery Library
1

SHERLOCK HOLMES

Sherlock Holmes was the legendary great detective created by novelist Arthur Conan Doyle. Always cool and collected, Holmes has uncanny powers of observation and deduction. And he's even a master fencer. When he's not on a case he's at 221B Baker Street relaxing, smoking his pipe, and not doing much of anything. But when he gets hired for a case he goes all out like a wolf after its prey. The more complicated the case, the more excited Holmes gets. And apparently he doesn't have much interest in women. With the famous phrase "elementary, my dear..." he ribs his companion Dr. Watson for not keeping up with him. But as a reader, I'm in the same position as Watson. I highly recommend The Sign of Four.

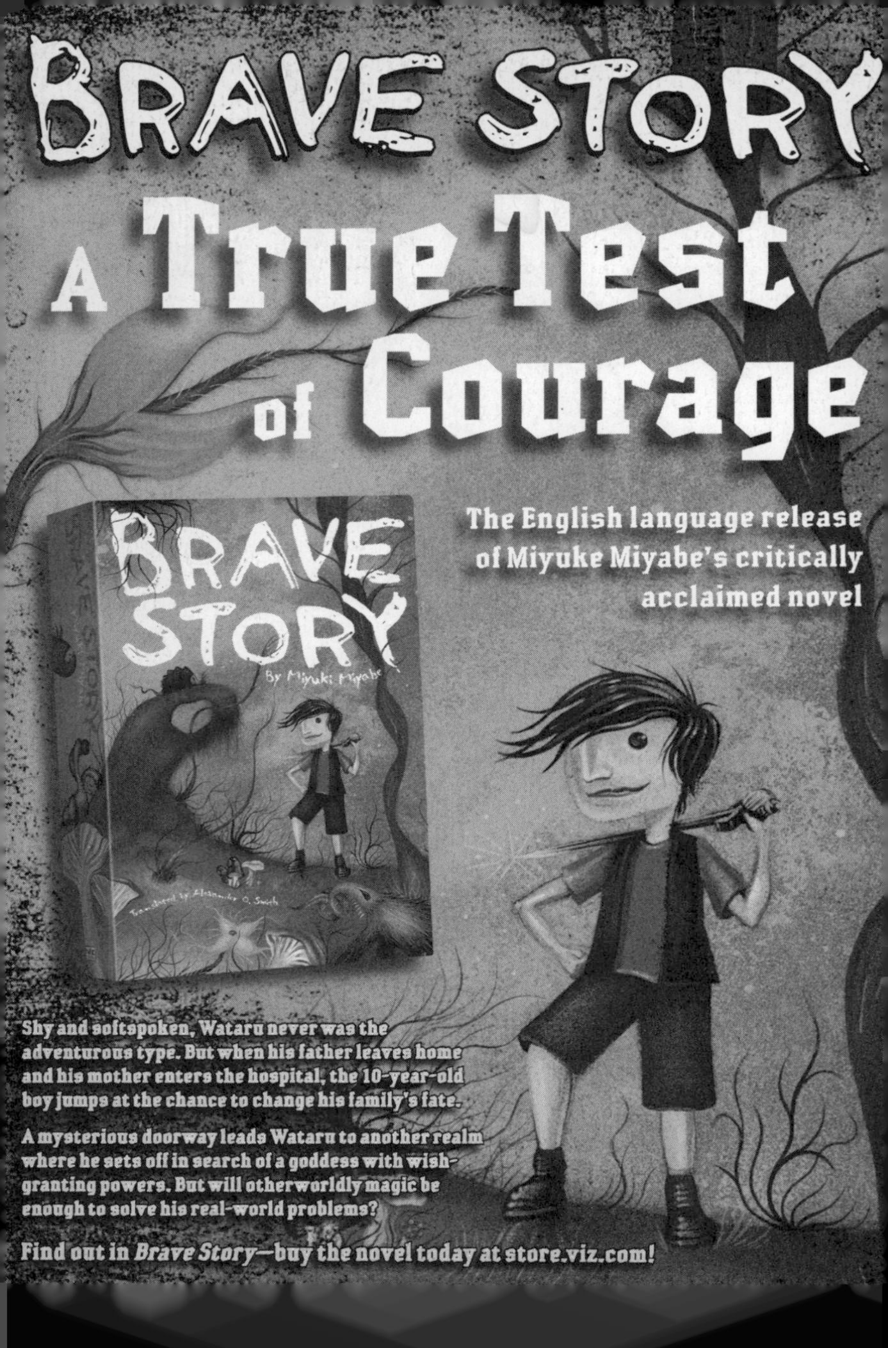
BRAVE STORY
A True Test of Courage
The English language release of Miyuke Miyabe's critically acclaimed novel
BRAVE STORY
By Miyuki Miyabe
Shy and softspoken, Wataru never was the adventurous type. But when his father leaves home and his mother enters the hospital, the 10-year-old boy jumps at the chance to change his family's fate.
A mysterious doorway leads Wataru to another realm where he sets off in search of a goddess with wish-granting powers. But will otherworldly magic be enough to solve his real-world problems?
Find out in Brave Story—buy the novel today at store.viz.com!

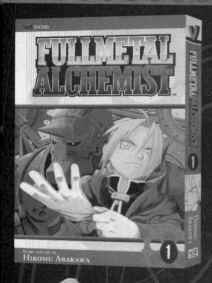
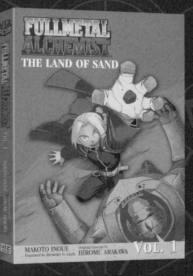
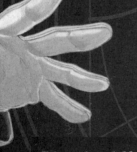

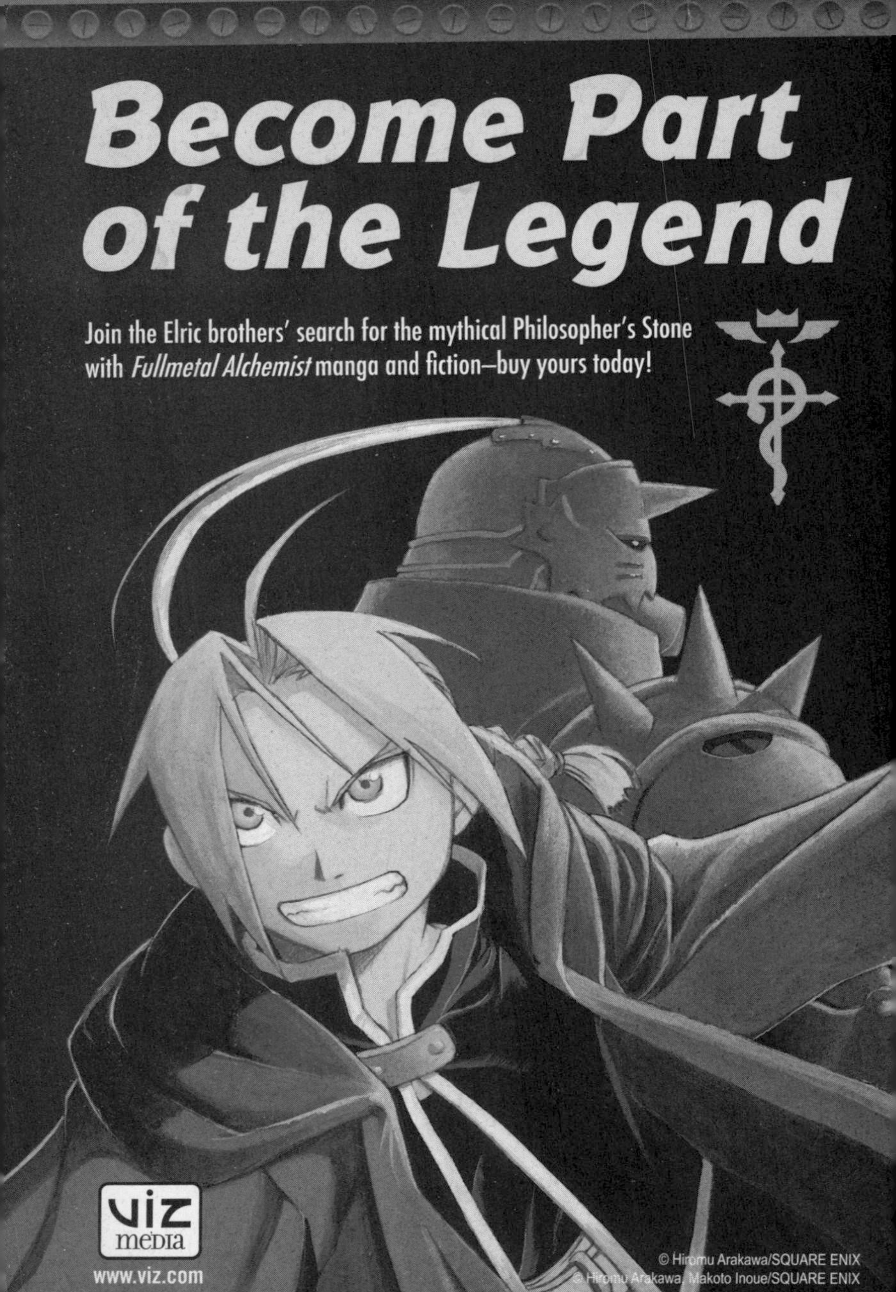
Become Part of the Legend
Join the Elric brothers' search for the mythical Philosopher's Stone with Fullmetal Alchemist manga and fiction–buy yours today!
VIZ media
www.viz.com
© Hiromu Arakawa/SQUARE ENIX
© Hiromu Arakawa, Makoto Inoue/SQUARE ENIX

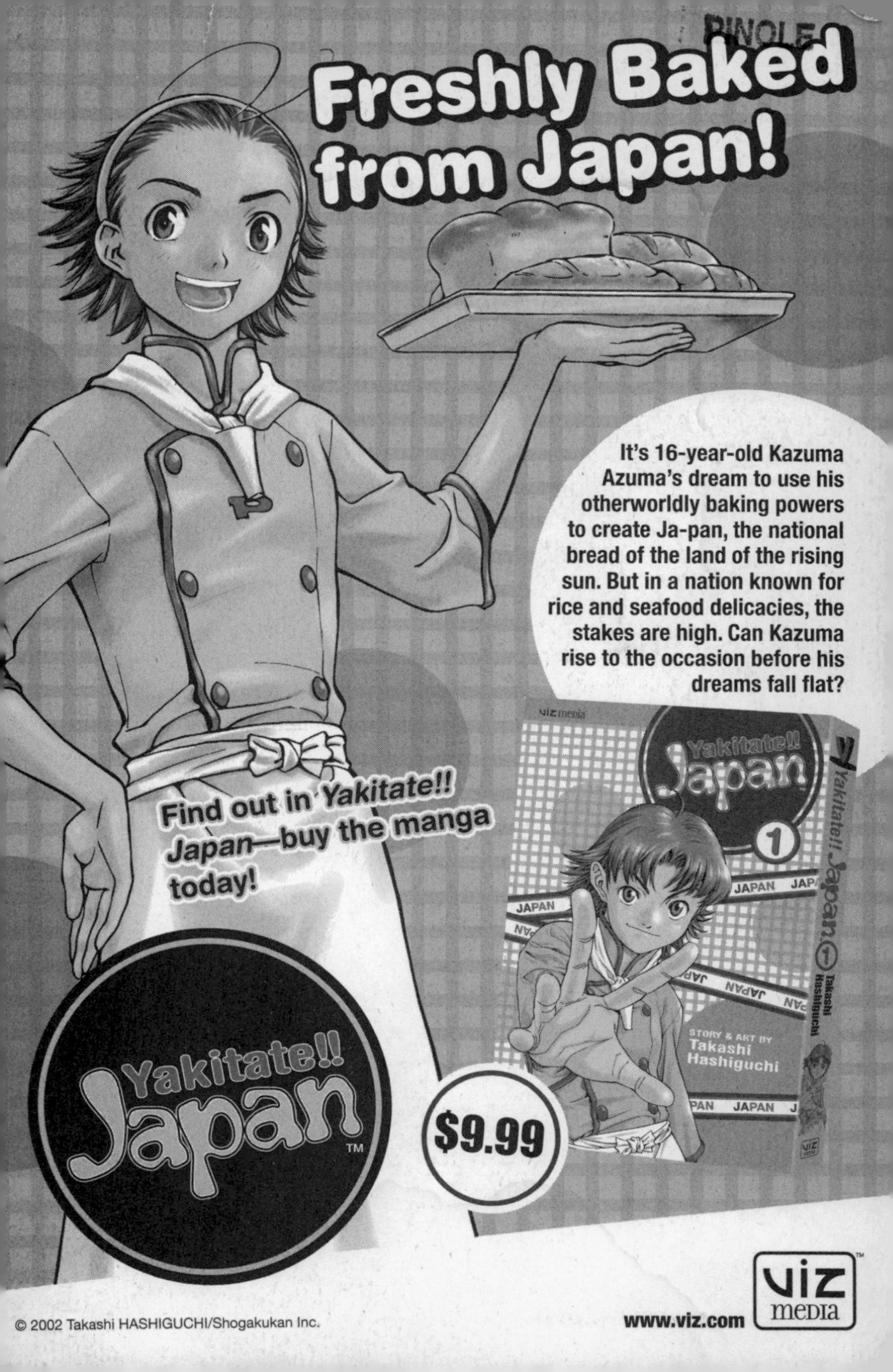
PINOLE
Freshly Baked from Japan!
It's 16-year-old Kazuma Azuma's dream to use his otherworldly baking powers to create Ja-pan, the national bread of the land of the rising sun. But in a nation known for rice and seafood delicacies, the stakes are high. Can Kazuma rise to the occasion before his dreams fall flat?
Find out in Yakitate!! Japan—buy the manga today!
viz media
Yakitate!! Japan
1
JAPAN
STORY & ART BY
Takashi Hashiguchi
Yakitate!! Japan 1
Takashi Hashiguchi
$9.99
Yakitate!! Japan™
© 2002 Takashi HASHIGUCHI/Shogakukan Inc.
www.viz.com
VIZ MEDIA™

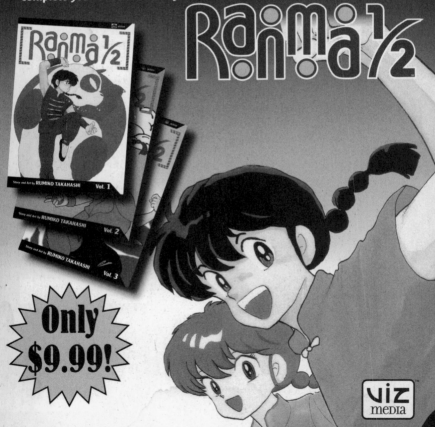

LOVE MANGA?
LET US KNOW WHAT YOU THINK!

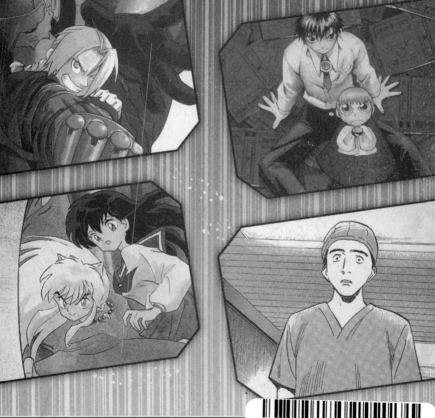

HELP US MAKE THE MA
YOU LOVE BETTER!

P9-AGT-309